'O' LEVEL *made simple* **MODULE - II**

INTRODUCTION TO MULTIMEDIA

(Based on NIELIT MAT-O2.R0 Syllabus for 'Multimedia & Animation Technology')

MAT-O2.R0

by

Prof. Satish Jain
B.Sc., B.E.(IISc), M.E.(IISc), M.Tech.(IIT Kanpur),
Wing Commander (Retd.)
Ex Professor of Information Technology,
Institute of Information Technology & Management
GGS Indraprastha University, Delhi.

and

Shashi Singh
MCA, M.Phil.

REPRINTED 2024

FIRST EDITION 2015

ISBN: 978-81-8333-535-5

Distributors:

BPB PUBLICATIONS
20, Ansari Road, Darya Ganj
New Delhi-110002
Ph: 23254990/23254991

DECCAN AGENCIES
4-3-329, Bank Street,
Hyderabad-500195
Ph: 24756967/24756400

MICRO MEDIA
Shop No. 5, Mahendra Chambers,
150 DN Rd. Next to Capital Cinema,
V.T. (C.S.T.) Station, MUMBAI-400 001
Ph: 22078296/22078297

BPB BOOK CENTRE
376 Old Lajpat Rai Market,
Delhi-110006
Ph: 23861747

Published by Manish Jain for BPB Publications, 20 Ansari Road, Darya Ganj, New Delhi-110002 and Printed by him at Manipal Technologies Limited, Manipal

www.bpbonline.com

Dedicated to

Mata Raja Rajeshwari, Sri Sharda Devi and *Sri Sai Baba*

whose blessings overcome all hurdles in life

ACKNOWLEDGEMENTS

We gratefully acknowledge the contribution made by the following persons in bringing out the book in this form:

- Ms. Geetha Iyer
- Mr. S. N. Singh
- Mr. Vivek Kumar Singh

PREFACE

This book is based on the MAT.O2.R0 syllabus for *Introduction to Multimedia* examination. Our objective in bringing out this book in this form is to explain to the students, technical concepts in an easy-to-understand language and in a simple manner. It is felt that most of the books available in the market do not cover the entire syllabus to meet the needs of the students. The syllabus set for this paper requires very thorough study of Multimedia and Animation Technology. Towards achieving this goal, we have pressed into service all our practical experience in Computer Science as well as in teaching field. This book should meet the requirement of students from any stream namely, commerce, science or arts.

The book covers various multiple media sources e.g. text, graphics, images, audio, animation and video fundamentals in simple English. The emphasis is laid on learning the representations, perceptions and applications of multimedia.

We have made this book user friendly by adding updated glossary of technical terms at the end of this book. These would be very handy as ready reference for key concepts of major topics discussed in this book. The glossary of technical terms will be specially helpful to students in answering objective questions asked in the examination.

A special feature throughout this book is that the important and crucial information has been shown with parallel and horizontal lines with a (☞) mark to draw attention of the reader, thus, providing a digest of concept(s) presented on those pages.

We shall feel obliged to the readers if they send us their critical opinion regarding the presentation, readability and coverage in this book and give us suggestions, if any, to improve the subject matter.

4th September, 2014

Authors

MAT.O2.R0 : Introduction to Multimedia

Outline of Course

S. No.	TOPIC		Minimum hours
1.	Introduction to Multimedia		08
2.	Representation of Multimedia Objects		20
3.	Concepts of Multimedia Editing		10
4.	Introduction to Compression Technology		06
5.	Multimedia Application Design		06
6.	Multimedia Authoring and Publishing		10
	Theory	=	**60**
	Practicals/tutorials	=	**60**
	Total	=	**120**

Detailed Syllabus

1. Introduction to Multimedia — 08 hrs

Definition of Multimedia, Multimedia objects: Text, Graphics, Animation, Audio, images, Video. Definition of HyperText and HyperMedia. Multimedia Applications in Education, Entertainment. Advertising world etc. Components of a Multimedia System, Desirable Features for a Multimedia System, requirements of Multimedia Communication

2. Representation of Multimedia Objects — 20 hrs

Representation of Analog Signals, A/D: Sampling and quantization

Text: Font and their representation (bitmap, true type)

Graphics: Raster & Vector representation, aliasing problems

Image: (bit depth, resolution, color (RGB, CMYK, HSB), introduction to BMP, GIF, TIFF, PNG and JPEG formats)

Audio (speech and wideband audio, sampling rate and aliasing, quantisation, introduction to MP3, WMA, WAV, MIDI, etc.)

Video (frame rate and resolution, interlaced and non interlaced video, colour planes (YCBCR, YUV), Video broadcast standards (PAL, NTSC, SECAM), HD Video, 3D TV, Video representation: AVI, MPEG, Quick Time, real video (.rm)

3. Concepts of Multimedia Editing — 10 hrs

Digital Audio, Music Sequencing and Notation, Image/Graphics Editing, Video Editing (Linear, Non-linear), Subtitling

4. Introduction to Compression Technology — 06 hrs

Concept of lossy and lossless compression. Concept of rate-distortion characteristics, Basics image compression (JPEG, JPEG 2000), Basics of Audio compression (MP3, MP4), Basics of Video Compression (MPEG, H.264)

5. Multimedia Application Design 06 hrs

Content design, technical design, visual design, design metaphors, example studies, interactivity

6. Multimedia Authoring and Publishing 10 hrs

Definition of an Authoring System, uses of an authoring system, Definition and function of Authoring Metaphor, Different Metaphors.

Offline Publishing: Flash, Power Point
Online Publishing: HTML5, Dreamweaver

In the second reading, go through the sample papers given at the end of the book. Solve these papers without consulting any book. After you have answered them, compare your response with the relevant matter available in the text of this book. Where you find your answers differ, re-study that part again.

Last, but not the least, you should simulate examination conditions by conducting a demo examination, taking any of the sample papers given at the end of the book and attempting to complete the answers within the stipulated time. After a day or two, evaluate your answers and if any doubts still persist, clarify them from a good text book or a computer specialist immediately. This way, you will be sure about the subject and will have confidence while answering the actual question paper.

WISH YOU A GRAND SUCCESS in the MAT.O2.R0 Examination, and a very bright future in the field of computer science.

Authors

Contents

Introduction to Multimedia

CHAPTER 1

Introduction to Multimedia

1.1 DEFINITION OF MULTIMEDIA

'Media' is something, which can be used for presentation of information. There are two basic ways to present information.
(a) Unimedia presentation
(b) Multimedia presentation

In unimedia presentation, a single media is used to present information. For example, a stereo system is a unimedia device because it presents information by using only sound media.
In multimedia presentation, more than one media is used to present information. For example, a TV system is a multimedia device because it presents information by sound and video media.

☞ *Multimedia presentations can be non-linear (interactive) or linear (passive)*

Multimedia, is a combination of media - used for creating audio, video, text, graphics and animation as shown in Figure 1.1.

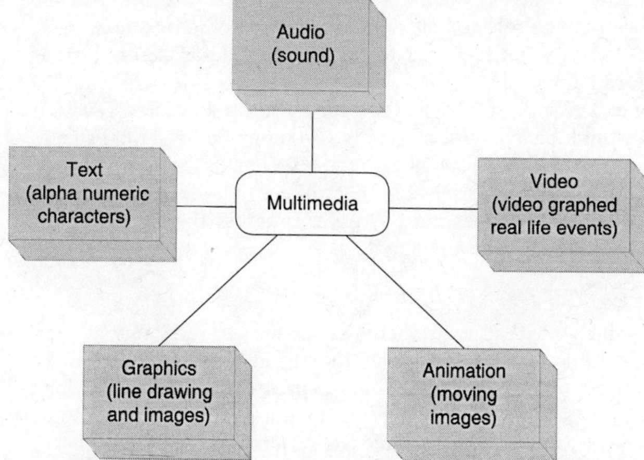

Figure 1.1 Multimedia is a combination of various media

Let us imagine a lion hunting its prey. A picture of a lion with a prey under its paws will reflect the mood a lot better than a hundred words. A 30-seconds sound clip of the same lion killing its prey will impact a lot better than many pictures. Again a 10-seconds full motion video of the lion chasing its prey before overpowering it will give much better perception than many minutes of pure sound of the spectacle. However when you put together all the above elements in one brust, it is a good example of multimedia.

Multimedia technology facilitates an integration of text, image, graphics, audio and video animation in digital form in computers. It provides new ways to enhance the delivery of information and its impact on the user.

☞ *Multimedia is a combination of text, graphics, audio, video and animation.*

Multimedia is a new trend in the field of computer science. Because it combines different media in one computer application, therefore, we call it multimedia. This enables the computer to be used as an entertainment tool, educational tool besides a business tool.
Multimedia information is displayed in picture/sound form and it does not include plain text exclusively. Thus, it includes pictures (graphics), sound (audio) and movies (video). Multimedia requires additional hardware which can handle sound, video, etc. The additional pieces of hardware are sound card, video capture card, etc. Apart from this, multimedia machines must have large size of main memory. Multimedia information, such as pictures, sounds and video are captured and digitized by input devices to get the information ready for manipulation by the computer. For example, to get a picture into the computer, we can scan it and then enter it in the computer.
Computer stores multimedia information in a variety of standard file formats. We can display or play multimedia information on output devices. For example, to play a sound file, we need speakers or headphones. In some cases, computer needs special hardware to connect to the output device. For example, to connect a speaker to a PC (Personal Computer), we need a sound card (which comes as a standard with most new computers).

1.1.1 Advantages of Multimedia

The use of multimedia offers many advantages which are as follows:
(a) *Enhancement of text only messages:* Multimedia enhances text only presentations by adding interesting sounds and compelling visuals.
(b) *Improves over Traditional Audio Video Presentations:* Audiences are more attentive to multimedia messages than traditional presentations done with slides or overhead transparencies.
(c) *Gains and Holds attention:* People are more interested in multimedia messages which combine the elements of text, audio, graphics and video because it offers greater understanding and retention of information.
(d) *Good for 'Computer–Phobics':* Those who are intimidated by computer keyboards and complex instructions are more comfortable with pressing buttons with a mouse or on a screen.
(e) Multimedia is entertaining as well as educational.

1.1.2 Multimedia Presentation and its Characteristics

Multimedia presentation is a digital show whose contents are expressed through various media type like text, image/graphic, audio, video and animation.

Some characteristics of multimedia presentation are:
(a) Use of multiple media
(b) Non-linear
(c) Interactive
(d) Integrity
(e) Digital representation

Use of Multiple Media

The first and the most important characteristic of multimedia presentation is the use of multiple or many types of media. The following media or combination of these are generally engaged in all multimedia projects:

Audio, text, graphics, animation and video.

Text is the first and simplest level in the multimedia hierarchy. Text has been main mode of communication for many years during the pre-multimedia era. With the recent explosion of the Internet and the World Wide Web.(WWW), text has become more important than ever. A picture is worth a thousand words. Pictures are of two types: the real world pictures captured by a camera, called *images*, and the hand-drawn pictures like sketches, diagrams and portraits, called *graphics*. *Sound* or *audio* in business multimedia applications enables a user to describe products, give instructions, enhance a presentation, or provide cues for some action by the viewer. Movies or videos are combination of image and sound. Those movies which depict real-world incidents are called *motion pictures* which are recorded on magnetic media, and those which depict artificial or imaginary scenarios are called *animation*.

Non-linear Presentation

When users can sit and watch it just as they watch movie, in such a case a project is linear. Starting at the beginning and running through to the end. TV shows and motion pictures are considered linear, because the user or viewer has to watch the information being displayed, in a pre-defined sequence of frames as determined by the producer or the creater of the show. The viewer cannot change the sequence of the frame or the timing between them if required.

When users are given navigational control and can go through the content at their own will, then multimedia becomes non-linear and user interactive. A hypertext system is meant to be read non linearly, by following links that point to other parts of the document or the other documents.

☞ *The World Wide Web (WWW) is the largest and most commonly used hypermedia application. Its popularity is due to the amount of information available from Web servers, the capacity to post such information, and the ease of navigating such information with a Web browser.*

Interactive Presentation

A multimedia application, which allows the user to interact with the ongoing proceedings in some way or other is called *interactive multimedia*. For example, in a slide show, interactivity generally consists of being able to control the pace (e.g. click to goto the next slide). The next level of interactivity is being able to control the sequence and choose where to go next. Next is media control: start/stop video, search text, scroll the view or zoom, etc. For example, click a button to start a video sequence within the presentation and pause the background music. Interactivity allows one to get involved with the presentation.

Digital Representation

Basically, there are methods of accessing information–sequential or serial access and direct or random access. A sequential access storage device is one in which the arrival at the location desired may be preceded by sequencing through other locations, so that access time varies according to location. In other words, information on a sequential–access device can only be retrieved in the same sequence in which it is stored. Moreover, working with a sequential access device, if an address required is out of order, it can only be reached by searching through all those addresses which are stored before it. For instance, data stored at the last few locations cannot be accessed until all preceding locations in the sequence have been traversed. This is analogous to a music tape casette. If 10 songs are recorded on a music tape and if you want to listen to (or access) the 8th song, you must listen to the 7 songs that comes before your favourite song before you can hear it. Although your player may "fast forward" the tape quickly past the first 7 songs, the first 7 songs are still accessed although not fully played.

Multimedia requires instant access to different portions of the presentation. This is best done inside a digital computer which stores data on random access device like hard disk, compact disks etc. Random access device is one in which any location in the device may be selected at random. Access to the information on stored device is direct, and approximately equal access time is required for each location. This is analogous to a music CD (Compact Disk). If 10 songs are recorded on a music CD and if you want to listen to (or access) the 6th song you need not listen to or fast forward the 5 songs that come before your favourite song. All you have to do is select track number 6 on the player and the player directly moves the pickup arm across the CD where 6th song begins and start playing it.

Integrity

This means that although there may be several media types present and playing simultaneously they need to be integrated or be part of a single entity which is in the presentation. We should not be able to separate out the various media and control them independently, rather they should be controlled from within the framework of the presentation.

1.1.3 Multimedia Project Design

A typical software project, using multimedia technology with specific aim of disseminating explicit information to a well-defined homogeneous or heterogeneous market segment, using various technologies and interactivity can be called as a *multimedia project*.

There are four basic stages in a multimedia project. Let us discuss each of them in brief.

Planning and Costing

The first task is to choose a topic on which we need to create the project. A project always begins with an idea or a need that you refine by outlining its messages and objectives. In general, one can select any topic, which can be explained and demonstrated using various media types. Before you begin developing, plan what writing skills, graphics, music, video and other multimedia expertise will be required. Estimate the time needed to do all elements, and prepare a budget to get the estimate of cost.

Designing and Producing

Typically, the design phase consists of storyboarding, flowcharting, prototyping, and user testing as well as a parallel production of media. Perform each of the planned tasks to create a finished product.

Once the subject matter has been chosen, the next step is to write a story. A story describe the overall content of the project. Once the overall subject matter has been finalized, the next step is to create a *script*. While story focuses on 'what' is communicated to his/her audience, a script emphasizes 'how' the content should be displayed to the user.

Once the script has been prepared, the next step is to prepare storyboard. The storyboard depicts what should be the layout of the project. The storyboard will decide which element has to come from the right side, which one from the left side, how they will combine and form the compound. A storyboard depicts the initial idea content of a multimedia concept in a series of sketches.

These are like "keyframes". A flowchart organizes the storyboard by inserting navigation information– the multimedia concept's structure and user interaction. The most reliable approach for planning navigation is to pick a traditional data structure. A hierarchical system is perhaps one of the simplest organizational strategies. Hierarchical structure provides a top down tree design. Typically, in this kind of mapping, the first main link branches out to different portions which, in turn-branch out further. Integrity is maintained by limiting the user movements within various branches. To move over from one branch to another, the user may have to come over to that portion where the branch starts, and make the move.

Next step of project design is implementation. Implementation means actually creating the physical presentation using required hardware and software.

Testing and Feedback

After implementation phase is completed; an important step of testing and feedback should be done for improving the quality of the project. This step involves distributing whole or part of the presentation to sections of the target audience or experts and getting feedback from them about the possible areas which will need improvement.

☞ *Always test your programs to make sure they meet the objectives of your project, they work properly on the intended delivery platforms, and they meet the needs of your client or end user.*

Delivery

The final phase in the production schedule is the delivery of the application to the intended client. Usually the run time version of the application files are copied onto a CD-ROM (Compact Disk Read Only Memory) and physically handed over to the customer.

1.2 MULTIMEDIA OBJECTS

Multimedia objects are files that contain e.g. images, scanned documents, audio recordings, video clips, etc., that relate to some fact within our common data.

An image is a two-dimensional picture, that has a similar appearance to some subject usually a physical object or a person. A digital image is a representation of a two-dimensional image using ones and zeros (binary). Depending on whether or not the image resolution is fixed, it may be of vector or raster type. Digital image" usually refers to raster images also called bitmap images.

Graphics are visual presentations on some surface, such as a wall, canvas, computer screen, paper, or stone to brand, inform, illustrate, or entertain. Examples are photographs, drawings, Line Art, graphs, diagrams, maps, engineering drawings, or other images. Graphics often combine text, illustration, and color.

A text, within literary theory, is a coherent set of symbols that transmits some kind of informative message. Text contains alphanumeric characters used to present information. Text delivers information that can have some meaning.

Audio is sound within the acoustic range available to humans. An Audio Frequency (AF) is an electrical alternating current within the 20 to 20,000 hertz (cycles per second) range that can be used to produce acoustic sound.

Animation is a simulation of movement created by displaying a series of pictures, or frames. Cartoons on television is one example of animation.

Movies or videos are combinations of image and sound. Video takes continuous motion and breaks it up into discrete frames, animation starts with independent pictures and puts them together to form the illusion of continuous motion.

1.3 WHAT IS HYPERTEXT?

Hypertext is a text based information, interlinked by means of relevant hyperlinks between various sub topics. Text that allows reader to jump spontaneously among onscreen documents and other resources by selecting highlighted keywords that appear on each screen. Hypertext appears most often on the World Wide Web. World Wide Web is the most popular and promising method of accessing the Internet. The main reason for its popularity is the use of a concept called *hypertext*.

An effectively designed hypertext document can help user rapidly locate the desired type of information from the vast mount of information on the Internet. Hypertext documents enables this by using a series of links. A link is a special type of item in a hypertext document that connects the document to another document that provides more information about the linked item.

You can use hypertext links by clicking on a section of text or an image in one Web page will open an entire Web page or an image of the linked Web page. The text or an image that gives such linkages are known as *hypertext*, or *hyperlink* or *hotspot*.

Hypertext feature is imperative to all titles which contain lots of reference material like the Microsoft Encarta. Windows help file system is also a good example of hypertext.

☞ *Links (also called anchors) mark text or images as elements that point to other HTML (Hyper Text Markup Language) documents, images, applets, multimedia effects or specific places within an HTML document.*

Hypertext improves accessibility of stored information by eliminating the need to follow rigorous set sequences. Advantages of this are easily understood when considering traditional methods. A word unknown to the reader of a book first leads to the index being searched. Failing this, the reader attempts to find reference to the word in another book. Many references required to research a subject can be is time consuming.

When information linked, indexed and stored on computer, hypertext helps this process and gives user the opportunity to take regular excursions to satisfy references.

1.4 WHAT IS HYPERMEDIA?

Hypermedia consists of hypertext combined with still or moving images and sound. Hypermedia authoring tool combines text, graphics, animated sequences and sound. Hypermedia applications developed using such tools can be thought of as interactive books that combine images, text and sound.

Hypermedia is a well-defined structural arrangement of information in the forms of audio, video, text, animation, graphics and other elements of multimedia pertaining to a particular topic or related to it, with relevant linkages in between them for example, the title 'Oceans' list out various forms of information, such as various facts about oceans, as texts, the oceans under water photographs, sounds of ocean, and under water video clips of the oceans. Now, when the user is reading some scientific facts about the sea shells - with a simple mouse click, he can view a photograph of the same. He may even try to listen to some actual underwater audio recordings and the video clips of the same. The linkages that exists between such different forms as well as different pieces of information, are called hyperlinks.

☞ *Hypertext is usually defined as non-linear access to text using links embedded in the text. This way going through material which is not of interest is avoided. Hypermedia is the extension of this non-linearity to other media types. Hypermedia is not constrained to be text-based. It can include other media, e.g. graphics, images and especially the continuous media-sound and video.*

Multimedia–the combination of text, graphics, and audio elements into a single collection or presentation becomes interactive multimedia when you give the user some control over what information is viewed and when it is viewed. Interactive multimedia becomes hypermedia when its designer provides a structure of linked elements through which a user can navigate and interact.

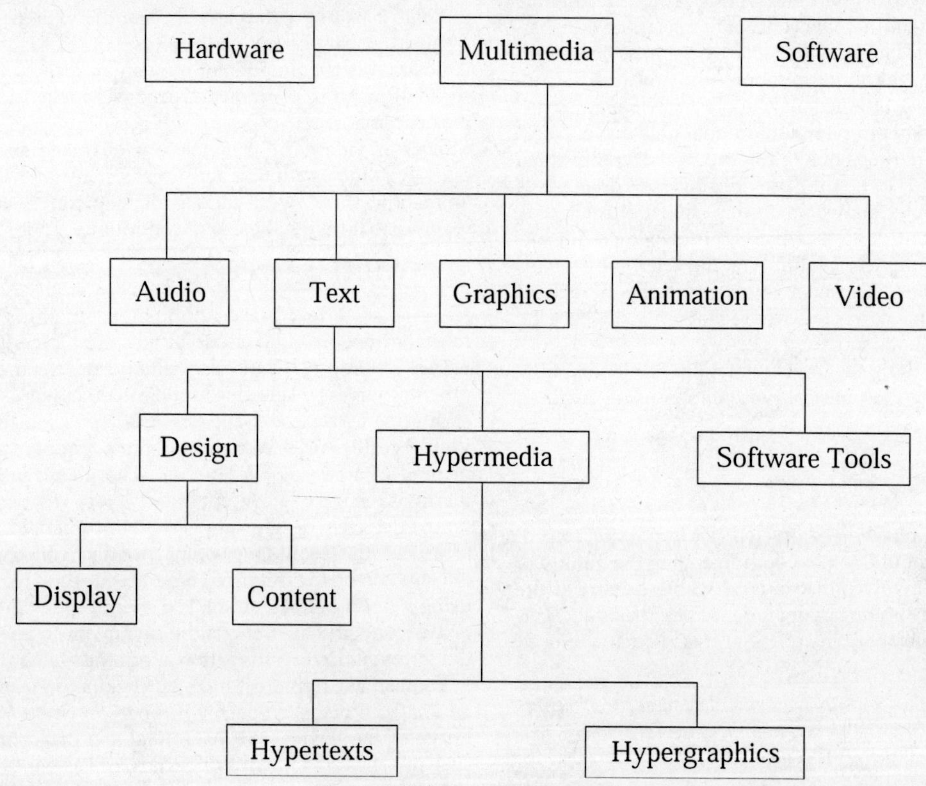

Figure 1.2 Hypermedia system

Here are a few thumb rules to adopt designing a hypermedia system:

1. Divide the contents into meaningful groupings. A better way to organize the contents, is to adopt a 'Top Down Tree' approach as shown in Figure 1.2. The top most level usually contains an index (or Titles) of all sub-topics, branching out to lower levels. As the levels comes down, the depth of information also descends to more intricate details.
   The greatest advantage of this methodology is that it allows only those who are interested in a particular topic to explore further, and others to bypass them. Thus, the interest the user develops as the title proceeds is kept alive throughout the proceedings.
2. For some titles, it is better to integrate hypertexts and hypergraphics and design the project just as an integrated hypermedia system. In such a system, the 'Hotwords' are usually linked to some graphic images, and photographs and vice versa. In fact, it is this methodology that is currently being adopted in most of the titles, as the producers felt that giving more and more text based information, tends to reduce the tempo of the multimedia experience. But enough care should be taken to design a proper mix between these two powerful indexing systems.
3. Enough care should be taken to provide an easy and unambiguous navigation system. Otherwise, the users may be caught at some point of the title and may not be able to return to the screen of their choice. This problem becomes compounded particularly with respect to hypertext systems with lot of hyperlinkages descending down to several levels of intricacy. To cope up, with this problem, all multimedia titles provide you the option of reaching the Main screen or Main menu from any sub-level so that the users feel confident, even if they are unable to track back their old navigation path.
4. Another useful feature will be provided a 'Back' option, at any point of time, so that the users can go back to previous levels of their navigation path, from the current screen.

1.5 HYPERTEXT, HYPERMEDIA AND MULTIMEDIA SYSTEMS

A book or an article on a paper has a given structure and is represented in a sequential form. Although it is possible to read individual paragraphs without reading previous paragraphs, authors mostly assume a sequential reading. Therefore, many paragraphs refer to previous learning in the document Novels, as well as movies a pure sequential reception. Scientific literature can consist of independent chapters, although mostly a sequential reading is assumed. Technical documents, such as manuals often consist of a collection of relatively information limits. A reference book for example, is generated by several authors and always only parts are read sequentially. There also exist many across references in such documentations which lead to multiple searches at different places for the reader. Here, an electronic help facility consisting of information on links, can be very significant. Hypertext and hypermedia have as a major property a non-linear information link. There exists not only a reading sequence but also reader decides on his/her reading path. In cases of hypertext and hypermedia, a graphical structure is possible in a document which may simplify the writing and reading processes.

A hypertext structure is a graph, consisting of nodes and edges (links). The nodes are the actual information units. The edges provides links to other information units. Links are connections between the conceptual elements, that is, the nodes that may consist of text, graphics, sounds, or related information in the knowledge base. Links are the navigation pathways and menus, nodes are accessible topics, documents, messages; and content elements. The forward movement in linear sorted documents is called a navigation, through the graph. At the user interface, the origin of pointers must be marked, so that the user can move to a further information unit. This origin of a pointer is called an *anchor*. The term anchor is used for the reference from one document to another document, images, sound, or file on the Web. A link anchor is where you come from, a link end is the destination node linked to the anchor. Some hypertext systems provide unidirectional navigation and offer no turn pathway, others are bidirectional.

A media-independent representation can happen through the selection of general graphical elements, such as buttons. The simplest way to navigate hypermedia structures is via buttons that let you access linked information (text, graphics, and sounds) that is contained at the nodes. When you have finished examining the information, you return to your starting location.

1.5.1 Hypertext System

A hypertext system is mainly determined through non-linear links of information. Pointers connect the nodes. The data of different nodes can be represented with one or several media types. In a pure text system, only text parts are connected. We understand hypertext as an information object which includes links to several media.

1.5.2 Multimedia System

A multimedia system contains information which is coded at least in a continuous and discrete medium. For example, if only links to text data are present, then this is not a multimedia system. It is a *hypertext.* A video conference, with simultaneous transmission of text and graphics, generated by a document processing program, is a multimedia application. Although it does not have any relation to hypertext and hypermedia.

1.5.3 Hypermedia System

A hypermedia system includes the non-linear information links of hypertext system and the continuous and discrete media of multimedia systems. For example, if a non-linear link consists of text and video data, then this is a hypermedia, multimedia and hypertext system. Figure 1.3 emphasizes the relation among multimedia, hypertext and hypermedia.

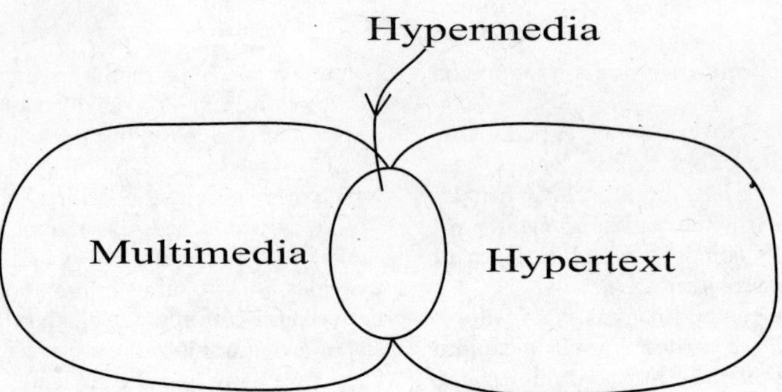

Figure 1.3 The hypertext, hypermedia and multimedia relationship

1.6 MULTIMEDIA APPLICATIONS

Multimedia can be used in any situation where computers are being used to deliver information. It may just be used to enhance areas that were previously text only, for example presentations or information kiosks. Multimedia e-mail and video conferencing allow information to be communicated better. Collaborative working tools are becoming cheaper and more widely available, and many video conferencing applications now allow application sharing. Multimedia is widely used in education, from preschool to post graduate courses. Interactive multimedia allows students to explore data and simulations allow the students to work on experiments. This can be particularly useful in a distributed environment with distance learning. Multimedia can also be used to enhance data presentation and data analysis, for example by converting the images from a satellite to sound, it becomes much easier to hear discrepancies in the data.

The WWW application computer system can be defined as equipment (hardware), processes (software), and people organized to perform a function. Using this definition, a business multimedia system can be defined as hardware, software and people organized to perform the functions of communication. Businesses use multimedia primarily for communication through presentations and for storage and retrieval of original documents and media files and distribute documents, movies, sound, and videotapes. Multimedia systems are also used to prepare presentations for marketing employee training, public relations and any other area in which mass communication is needed. Many companies commit resources (specialized personnel, photography and television studios, and other equipment) to mass produce these forms of communication.

Multimedia applications are used daily by growing number of people which are discussed in the following sub-sections:

1.6.1 Education

Multimedia has an enormous impact on education. Many schools in our country today using different types of computer-based teaching software based on multimedia to expose the knowledge in various fields. In the near future hand-held machines for the study of various subjects will emerge. This technology will enable students to learn at their own pace. In the present system of imparting education, it is necessary for students to cope up with the class. This situation will change the quality of education and can also be standardized and it will no more be function of the quality of teaching which varies from school to school. Similarly, students in engineering colleges use interactive multimedia presentations to learn the basics of electronics and implement, test and manipulate the circuit they design on a computer.

Multimedia is used to form digital library also. Digital library is a repository of large information in digital form. Such a library being virtual in nature because it stores reading material only in softcopy form, can remain open round the clock allowing users to access information from it at their own convenient time and location (from remote locations over the network).

1.6.2 Video Conferencing

Video conferencing is another application of multimedia with extremely great potential. Imagine that you are using a computer and you wish to communicate with a colleague. Video conferencing allows you to see your colleague in a window on your monitor screen and vice versa allowing you to talk face to face as if round a table.

In this system, each participating user has a PC (or a workstation) on his/her working desk, which has a video camera and mike attached to it. The PCs of all these users are interconnected together through a high speed network. The network is used to transmit audio, video and other data from one participant's PC to the PCs of other participants. A user willing to communicate with other users, talks in front of his/her PC. The audio visual equipment attached to his/her PC capture the information that is then transmitted to the PCs of other users. The coordination support software coordinates the precedes of the conference and resolves any conflicts when multiple users want to communicate simultaneously.

1.6.3 Training

The continual introduction of Information Technology (IT), and its pace of change, give rise to a thriving software training industry. For example, when a new program is introduced into an office environment the need for training or retraining is required. Now the cost of training drop off significantly for all those due to introduction of multimedia (CD-ROM disk). A manuals and training material both could be loaded from CD-ROM.

Ranging from simple introduction courses to sales techniques corporate and industry training has in recent years become ever more dependent upon technology. Computer-based Training

(CBT) now forms a substantial market using computers, multimedia represents a powerful solution to training, where employees can interact with video under computer control.

1.6.4 Entertainment

Media and Entertainment industry are a major benefactors of multimedia technology. Images, animation and sound are widely used for making animation movies. Capability of computer is widely used by musicians to record, edit and mix sounds. Entertainment CDs, games, comics and stories for children are used for education and training.

Video editing, mixing, 3D (Three Dimensional) animation and morphing are some of the techniques widely used for creating video films for various purpose.

1.6.5 Electronic Encyclopedia

Electronics books, dictionaries, encyclopedia and magazines extend the printed word into digital domain. They offer not only text illustrations, and photos but also add sound, video, and animation providing access and understanding not available with printed books. They offer greater storability, interactivity and retrievability.

They are typically delivered on a CD-ROM. Their contents vary depending upon topics and the group for which the content is been developed. Further enhancement is possible to make the matter rich by video clips and spoken texts.

In the area of advertising, multimedia will bring major change in the way it does business. It will allow freelance agencies to produce inexpensive rough cuts and prepare clips, thereby, significantly reducing the dominance of the larger advertisement agencies.

1.6.6 Commercial Application

Multimedia is also used in commercial applications. For example, some amusement arcades offer multimedia games that allow players to race cars. Architects use multimedia presentations to give clients tours of houses that are yet to built. Mail order business provides multimedia catalogues that allow prospective buyers to browse virtual showrooms.

Medical institutions use multimedia simulated surgery operations that enable prospective surgeons to perform operations on a computer generated virtual patient.

Now-a-days the telecommunications networks are global, and as information providers and content owners determine the worth of their products and how to change money for them, information elements will ultimately link up online as distributed resources on a data highway, which to acquire and use multimedia based information.

Full text content from books and magazines will be accessible by modern and electronic link, future movies will be played at home. Real time news reports from anywhere on earth will be available. Lectures from participating universities will be monitored for education credits, street maps of any will be viewable with recommendations for restaurants, in any language. Online travelogues will include testimonials and video tracks.

1.6.7 Business Application

Multimedia applications in business are used in a variety of ways, companies use multimedia computers in the following applications:

- Accounting, product catalogues and individualized presentation.
- Employees interactive training materials.
- Internet Web pages.
- New product development using Computer Aided Design (CAD) software.
- Sales and other types of group presentations.
- Self running presentations for trade show booth and kiosk applications.

1.6.8 Better Presentation

We can build presentation that includes sound effects, music, still pictures, animation, video and text. Hence multimedia presentation can be used to better explain subject matter to the students, which enhances comprehension capability of the students.

1.6.9 Foreign Language Learning

One can learn new language by interacting with the written and spoken words. Using a book for learning a foreign language is difficult because one is not sure how to pronounce the words written in text form. The book can have an accompanying audio tape to solve this problem, but it is inconvenient for the learner to keep rewinding the tape to find specific information. Moreover, the learner also does not have the flexibility to quickly hear the pronunciation for a specific word. Using a multimedia program incorporating both text and sound, the learner can see words and phrases on the screen as they are pronounced by the computer program. The learner also has the flexibility to request the computer to pronounce any word displayed on the screen by simply selecting that word or if user wants to understand the meaning of a word or phrase he/she may point to it to quickly display a translation for it in his/her native language.

1.6.10 Multimedia in Film Industry

Multimedia technology is used by the film industry for computer animated film and providing special effects in films. Several movies now contain many visual tricks that could never to be accomplished without the aid of computers. For example, in the Hindi movie, Chachi 420, the hero is shown being transformed from man to woman by the use of a computer graphics technique called *morphing*. In the English movie, Jurassic park, the dinosaurs were shown as living creatures by the use of multimedia technology only. In animation films of the past, animations were created by using hand-drawing technique, which was a very tedious and time consuming process. Because of hand-drawing, the quality of animations was also not very good. Using computer programs based on the precise mathematical laws of physics, animators can now create animations that are far more realistic than ever before.

1.6.11 Multimedia Kiosk

Multimedia kiosks are used in public places as information providers in place of help desks with an attendant. For example, a multimedia kiosk placed at an airport might provide the travellers with information on tourist attractions, restaurants, and hotels along with graphic images and maps showing how to get there. A multimedia kiosk generally has a touch screen monitor with a very user-friendly graphical user interface for ease of operation by general public.

1.6.12 Delivery of Multimedia

Multimedia requires a large amount of digital memory when stored in an end user's library, or large amounts of bandwidth when distributed over wires, glass fiber, or airwaves on a network. The greater the bandwidth the bigger the "pipeline", so more content will be delivered to end users quickly. There are two basic methods for delivering mutlimedia.

1. **CD-ROM/DVD-ROM** : CD-ROM/DVD-ROM (Digital Versatile/Video Disk - Read Only Memory) has become the most cost effective distribution medium for multimedia materials. These devices are used to store large amounts of some combination of text, graphics, sound and video. CD and DVD burners are used for reading disks and for making them too, in audio, video and data formats.
2. **Distributed networks** : Distributed networks allow computers to be connected to other computers which can provide an almost endless array of multimedia material. The Internet (and specifically the World Wide Web) is currently providing a distributed network approach to the delivery of multimedia material.

1.7 COMPONENTS OF MULTIMEDIA

Components of multimedia like text can be used for adding emphasis. Graphics can be used for giving visual impact, and animation can be used for attracting attention. Multimedia software is used for the creation, conversion, editing, and manipulation of either (digitized) analog data or pure digital data, which is ultimately used for conveying information.

1.7.1 Text

Text contains alphanumeric characters used to present information. Text delivers information that can have some meaning. Text is the simplest data type that requires the least amount of storage. Designing texts for multimedia involves the correct choice of font style, font color and font size. Content design involves both quantitative and qualitative aspects of multimedia text. Many text editing software tools are available for content development, title development and font design.

Hardware Requirement for Text

Text processing using computer requires the following hardware devices:

1. Keyboard is one of the most important input device for entering text data in a computer.
2. Optical Character Recognition (OCR) is another input device used to input a wide variety of document including pictures, graphics, typed text or handwritten text.
3. Monitor is an output device used to display information on the computer screen.
4. Printer is also an output device used to take out hard copy in the printed form.

Software Requirement for Text

Text processing capabilities are highly desirable in a multimedia computer system for better presentation and use of text information.

Text Editing

Text editors and word processing packages are used to generate, edit and layout a text document.

Text Style

The major attributes of text include paragraph styling, character styling (such as bold, italics, etc.), font families and sizes, and relative location in a document. For example, newspapers use a good combination of all these styles to better highlight more important news than less important ones.

Text Searching

Usage of text information can be greatly enhanced by text searching feature of a word processor. This feature allows the user to enter a word or phrase and quickly finds and displays that part of the text where the word or phrase appears in the text information with the word or phrase highlighted. Almost all word processing packages have this feature. Several software having this feature are also available on the Internet that help in searching the desired information.

Hypertext

Hypertext is an application of indexing text to provide a rapid search of specific text strings in one or more documents. This feature provides great flexibility of structuring and accessing computer-based text information. User can get the required information just by clicking on an anchor (a hotword). This means that if the user wants more information about a particular hotword, he/she can select that hotword just by clicking on it and it will open a window with additional text explaining the word or phrase.

☞ *Hypertext is a document that is prepared by using special linking facility for easier electronic access and manipulation.*

Text Importing and Exporting

The task of creating a text document can often be greatly simplified if the document preparation software has text importing feature. This is because some of the text you want to incorporate in your document may already exist as a file created by a word processor or a database file. The file can be simply imported into the new document at the desired location instead of retyping the entire text again. Similarly, text exporting feature is very useful in allowing other packages to use an existing document.

1.7.2 Pictures/Graphics

Computer graphics deal with the generation, representation, manipulation and display of pictures with the help of a computer. Graphics is an important component of multimedia by which we can illustrate information in video form. For example, to educate children with the help of multimedia, we can make illustration more descriptive with the help of pictures. Because for small children, it is difficult to explain new concepts with text. In a multimedia application meant for educating small children, displaying the photograph of a horse along with its text description makes the illustration much more effective. Without the photograph, it will be very difficult to explain using only text how a horse looks like.

☞ *Pictures, photographic image and other artwork are called graphics.*

Graphics Types

There are two types of computer graphics. These are:

(a) Line Drawing
(b) Images

Line Drawing These are drawings and illustrations in the form of 2D (Two dimensional) and 3D (Three dimensional) pictures from mathematical representation of simple objects like lines, circles, arcs, etc. Simple object types are used to create complex objects. For example, the picture of a chair can be drawn using lines and arcs.

The area of computer graphics that deals with this type of pictures is known as *generative graphics*. Generative graphics are extensively used in creating illustrative diagrams. Another very important application of generative graphics is CAD (Computer-Aided Design) and CAM (Computer-Aided Manufacturing). Now-a-days, CAD packages are extensively used in designing models for aircraft, ship and building structures. The greatest advantages of using CAD and CAM packages for such applications is that design changes may be quickly modified and also creating accurate assembly drawings and associated parts and subassembly list.

Images Images are defined as visual representation of the information. These are graphics and photographs composed of a collection of pixels, which are arranged in two-dimensional matrix. The area of computer graphics that deals with this type of pictures is called *cognitive graphics*. Cognitive graphics along with image processing techniques are extensively used in applications that deal with recognition and classification of pictures. For example, an image database containing images of people's fingerprints is commonly used now-a-days in criminal investigation and identification.

Hardware for Pictures/Graphics

Following are the hardware components needed for graphics:

(a) A locating device, such as mouse, joystick or a stylus to draw pictures on computer screen.
(b) A flatbed scanner or rectangular coordinate digitizer which is used as an input device for generative graphics applications for inputting existing line drawings to a computer.
(c) Scanners for capturing photographs and drawings as digital images.
(d) Computer screen for display graphics.
(e) Laser printers or plotters for output graphics in hard copy.

Software for Pictures/Graphics

In addition to the above listed devices, software packages given below will improve the presentation of graphics:

(a) **Software for painting or drawing:** Such packages allow the user to create graphics by using a mouse and modify and enhance graphic images produced using a scanner or screen capture software for better understanding. All these features make this software very useful in a multimedia application.
(b) **Screen capture software:** Screen capture software packages are used to capture the computer screen as a graphic image. These packages allow the users to save the graphic images in a variety of graphic formats and are also useful in converting a graphic image from one storage format to another because a multimedia software might have been designed to accept image only in a particular format.
(c) **Clip Art:** Clip art is a library of commonly used graphic images, such as personal computer, printer, telephone, building, etc. These images can be directly imported from the library and used in a multimedia application. This saves enormous amount of time and effort that might otherwise be required to create or search and capture a similar image object.
(d) **Software for high resolution:** In a multimedia application, we use very high quality images. Therefore, we need such software packages to enhance images for high resolution.

1.7.3 Audio

Computer audio deals with developing, recording and playback of audio with the help of a computer. Audio is very important component of multimedia because in many cases sound can be very useful for better understanding the information than in other ways. In some cases, sound may be the only way to provide the desired information. For example, the sound created by a dog called barking of a dog.

☞ *Speeches, music and other types of sounds are called audio. Audio element is generally used to enhance the usual multimedia environment.*

Computer Hardware for Audio

Audio needs the following computer hardware devices:

(a) A sound card.
(b) Input device, such as microphone, for audio input to record voice or music or any other type of sound in a computer. The A/D (Analog-to-Digital) converter of the sound board takes care of digitizing the input sound, which is in the analog form.
(c) Output device, such as speaker or headphones, for audio output to be recorded. The D/A (Digital-to-Analog) converter of the sound board takes care of converting the sound from its digital to analog form.
(d) Sound editors to cut and paste sound clipping and to add special effects.

Software for Audio

In addition to the above listed tools and devices, the following capabilities are highly desirable in a multimedia computer system with audio facility:

(a) **Audio clips:** With the help of audio clips (pre-made sound effects, music and narration) one can select and directly import and use audio in a multimedia applications. This saves time and effort that might otherwise be required to create a similar audio clip.

(b) **Software for high quality sound:** Multimedia application needs very high quality audio to reproduce the sound effectively. It is important to use not only the necessary hardware but also software support for both recording and playback of high quality audio.

(c) **Recording and playback capabilities:** A multimedia system with audio capability should allow the user to control the recording and playback of an audio sequence. For example, it should provide the user with options to "pause" and "replay" the sound sequence.

(d) **Voice recognition software:** This is used to identify the speaker of a given voice by matching the voice with a set of voices stored in a database along with details of the speaker of each voice.

1.7.4 Video

Computer video deals with the recording and display of sequence of images. Each individual image in sequence is called a frame. For a jerk-free full motion video, 25 to 30 frames have to be displayed per second. It is an important component of multimedia because it is very useful for illustrating concepts that involve movement.

Computer Hardware for Video

(a) Video camera for capturing video data.

(b) Video monitor for displaying video data.

(c) A video board, (video card) equipped with A/D and D/A converters. In addition to performing the basic function of A/D and D/A conversion of video signals, a video board also has connectors for video camera and video monitor.

(d) Video editors to cut and paste video sequences, to add special effects, and to create new video sequences from existing video sequences.

Software for Video

(a) **Video clips:** This is a library of video clips from which one can select and directly import a video clip and use it in a multimedia application. This saves time and effort that might otherwise be required to create a similar video clip.

(b) **Recording and playback capabilities:** A multimedia system with video capability should allow the user to control the recording and display the video sequence.

1.7.5 Animation

The term "*animation*" refers to any visual movement effect created automatically, i.e., without manual user interaction. Animation is one of the most dynamic form of multimedia. Unlike graphics, animations can provide dynamic movements to the objects. For example, to show a bird flying in the air, all that graphics can provide is a digital photograph of the same. However, with animations, we could actualy view the bird flying in the monitor of the PC. Computer animation deals with the generation, sequencing and display (at a specified rate) of a set of images (called frames) to create an effect of visual change or motion, similar to a movie film (video). Animation is an important component of multimedia because just as a picture is a powerful way to illustrate information, a small animation clip is even more powerful and is very useful for illustrating concepts that involve movement.

Hardware Requirements for Animation

1. Image generation tool and devices, such as scanners, digital camera, and video capture board interfaced to some standard video source like video camera or Video Cassette Recorder (VCR) are used to generate images to be used in animation.
2. Computer monitors with image displaying capability is the minimum requirement for displaying animation. In addition, multimedia computer systems capable of handling animation also require a graphics accelerator board that not only controls the resolution and number of colors of display, but also speeds up the refresh rate.

Software Requirements for Animation

1. **Animation creation software:** This software allows the user to create animation sequences from scratch by using a mouse and various simple objects, such as lines, circles and polygons with various supporting colors.
2. **Screen capture software:** Screen capture software packages are used to capture the displays of a computer screen as graphic images, which can be used in animation.
3. **Animation clips:** This is a library of animation clips from which one can select and directly import an animation clip and use it in a multimedia application. This saves enormous time and effort that might otherwise be required to create a similar animation clip.
4. **Software support for high resolution:** If the animation sequences of a multimedia application are made up of very high quality images, it is important to have not only the necessary hardware but also software support for displaying high resolution images having many colors to maintain high quality of animation display.
5. **Recording and playback capabilities:** A multimedia system with animation capability should allow the user to control the recording and display of an animation sequence. For example, it should provide the user with option to 'pause' or 'replay' the animation sequence.
6. **Transition effects:** Transition effect is used to describe the way that slide arrives on the screen. In cartoon film when one scene ends and another scene begins, there is a transitions between them. For example, the picture can fade out and then fade in to the new scene or the first scene slides off the screen as the second scene slides onto the screen. Animation can be more interesting if it is enhanced with transition effects, such as fade in, and fade out, layering, zooming and rotation of objects.

1.8 DESIRABLE FEATURES FOR A MULTIMEDIA SYSTEM

The following features are desirable for a multimedia system:

Very High Processing Power : needed to deal with large data processing and real time delivery of media.

Multimedia Capable File System : The file system is needed to deliver real-time media e.g. video/audio streaming. Streaming is a method of delivery of sound and video files over the Web, the computer begins playing the file as it continues to receive the rest of it, keeping ahead so playback does not pause or break up. A RAID (Redundant Array of Independent Disks) is a hard disk system that supports high speed data transfer rates.

Data Representations/File Formats supporting multimedia : It should be easy to handle yet allow for compression/decompression in real-time.

Efficient and High I/O : Input and output to the file subsystem needs to be efficient and fast. Needs to allow for real-time recordings as well as playback of data, e.g. direct to disk recording systems.

Special Operating System : To allow access to file system and process data efficiently and quickly. Needs to support direct transfers to disk, real-time scheduling, fast interrupt processing, I/O (Input/Output) streaming, etc.

Storage and Memory : Large storage units (of the order of 50–100 GB or more) and large memory (100 MB or more). Large caches also required and frequently of Level 2 and 3 hierarchy for efficient management.

Software Tools : User friendly tools needed to handle media, design and develop applications and deliver media.

1.9 REQUIREMENT OF MULTIMEDIA COMMUNICATION

A computer system capable of handling all multimedia information named text, voice, graphics, image, animation, audio and full motion video is called a *multimedia computer*. This computer is more powerful than any other ordinary personal computer.

Multimedia computers should support to capture, editing and viewing of video and audio data and provide facilities for the transfer of these data types between computers either through modems or through local and wide area networks.

Multimedia applications usually require more computer main memory and processing power than the same information represented by text alone. For instance, a computer running multimedia applications must have a fast CPU (Central Processing Unit) which is the electronic circuitry that provides the computational ability and control of the computer.

A multimedia computer also requires extra electronic memory to help the CPU in making calculations and to enable the video screen to draw complex images. The computer also needs a high capacity hard disk to store and retrieve multimedia information, and a compact disk drive to play CD or DVD-ROM applications. Finally, a multimedia computer must have a keyboard and a pointing device, such as mouse or a trackball, so that the user can direct the associations between multimedia elements.

1.9.1 Hardware Requirement for Multimedia

To develop the system of multimedia we use the various hardware/software components are:

CPU: The CPU, which is recommended for a multimedia computer should be Pentium 4 or other advanced chips (See Figure 1.4). It shows the block diagram of a computer system.

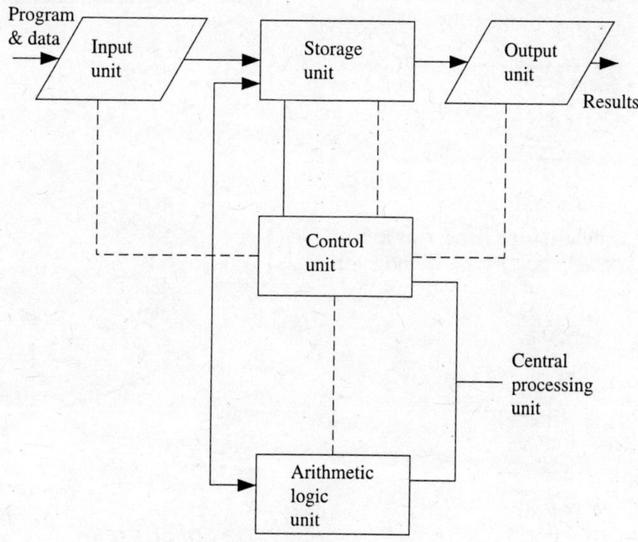

Figure 1.4 Block diagram representation of a computer system

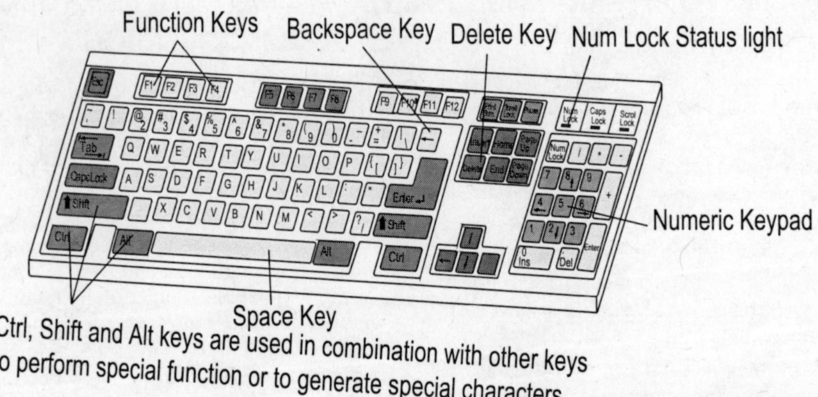

Figure 1.5 Keyboard depicting different keys' functions

Input Devices

Keyboard

Programs and data are entered into a computer through a keyboard which is attached to a computer. A keyboard is similar to the keyboard of a typewriter. It contains alphabets, digits, special characters, function keys and some control keys. When a key is pressed, an electronic signal is produced which is detected by an electronic circuit called *keyboard encoder* (See Figure 1.5).

A computer includes all the keys found on a typewriter plus some additional keys. These additional keys are cursor control (i.e., moving the cursor around on the screen), insert, delete, and scroll control keys. There are a total of 101 keys (some keyboards have more). At the right side of the keyboard is the numeric keypad with numbers and basic mathematical symbols.

Numeric keypad can also be used for cursor control. This double function of numeric keypad is controlled by Num Lock key.

☞ *At the top of the keyboard are function keys (F1 to F12). Their functions depend upon the program being run. F1 key is used to get help from the program.*

Mouse

A mouse is a pointing device. It is held in one hand and moved across a flat surface. Figure 1.6 shows a latest type of mouse or puck.

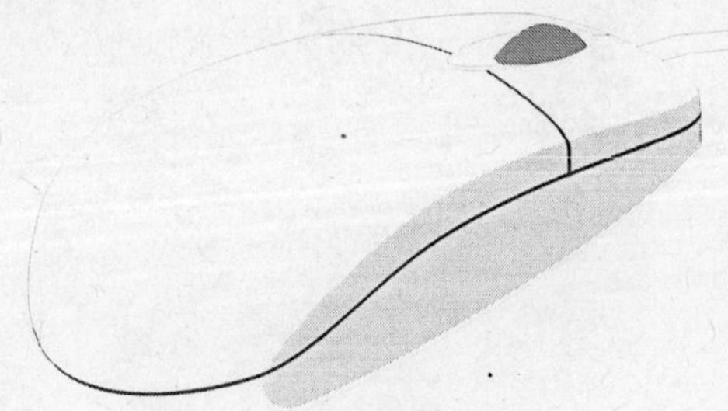

Figure 1.6 Mouse

Scanner

A scanner is a hardware device used to scan text or images into the computer (See Figure 1.7). Sometimes the information, picture or text that is available on paper is needed on the computer disk. The basic function of a scanner is to convert a document into a digital format. Scanners are basically desktop analog-to-digital converter. They take analog visual things, documents, magazine papers, photos, business cards, etc., and turn them into digitized bitmaps that a specialize software package can understand and translate into PC readable file.

Besides text scanning, scanners can also be used in image processing to capture pictures for printed publications, Internet Websites, and electronic presentations. A scanner can digitize a picture by converting dark and light areas of a graphic to dots, or pixels. A file is then saved in computer format for future use.

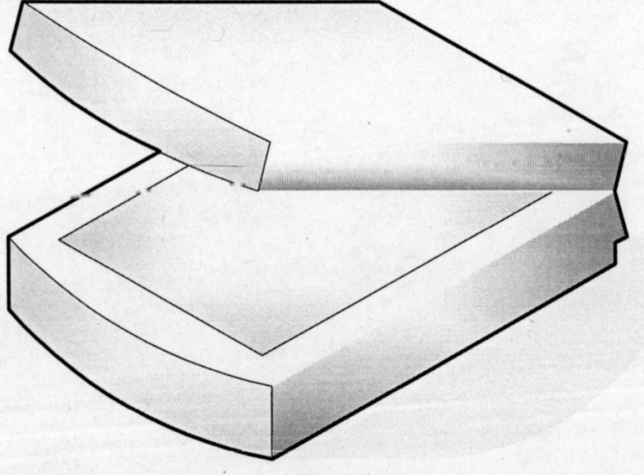

Figure 1.7 A Scanner

Types of Scanner

Different types of scanners are used for different applications. The capability and cost of scanners differ from type-to-type. The scanners required for industrial purpose are different from scanners meant for use at home or in small offices. Scanners are of three types. They are:

(a) Flatbed Scanner
(b) Sheetfed Scanner
(c) Handheld Scanner

Flatbed Scanner

A flatbed scanner is also known as desktop scanner and it works like a photocopier. This scanner allows the user to place a full piece of paper, book, magazine, photo or any other object onto the glass surface of the scanner. It has the capability to scan that object and convert it into digital form (See Figure 1.8).

Figure 1.8 Flatbed Scanner

Sheetfed Scanner

Sheetfed scanner is also known as rollerfed scanner. It works like a fax machine. The image is passed over a roller where it is captured. Sheetfed scanner is very versatile in scanning loose sheets of paper (See Figure 1.9).

☞ *Sheetfed scanner is a less expensive when compared to the flatbed scanner. Flatbed scanner can scan and store images from books without having to remove the page, which is not possible in the case of using the rollerfed scanner.*

Figure 1.9 Sheetfed Scanner

Handheld Scanner

A handheld or portable scanner is an optical scanner which is designed to be moved by hand across the object or document being scanned. Today, a hand scanner is extensively used with a PC or a word processor as an image inputting device. It is for optically reading image data out of a document by being operated by hand (See Figure 1.10).

Figure 1.10 Handheld scanner

☞ *Handheld scanners have been used for a number of applications, such as for barcode readers at points-of-sale of products or services, for recording data appearing on original documents for later reproduction or processing and for translating documents.*

Digital Camera

A digital camera records and stores photographic images in digital form that can be fed to a computer as the impressions are recorded or stored in the camera for later loading into a computer. It is a light-sensitive film that captures images and after development of the film, image prints are taken on photo paper. Digital photography uses a combination of advanced image sensor technology and memory storage, which allows images to be captured in a digital format. The captured images are instantly available to print with no need for a development process. Kodak, Canon and several other companies make digital cameras.

Microphone

A microphone, which was originally invented by Emile Berliner in 1877, is a device which allows you to record voice or sound and place them on to computers, generally as a *.wav* file. Microphones can also be used with other applications, such as a voice dictation program or a voice conference program (See Figure 1.11).

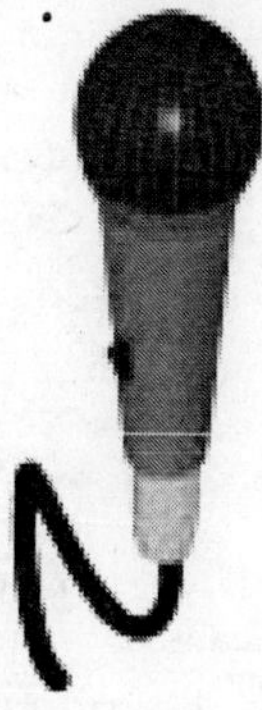

Figure 1.11 Microphone

When connecting the microphone to the back of the computer, the microphone will be placed in the hole which generally has Mic or Microphone written next to it.

Generally microphone is a separate computer component. Some manufacturers are integrating microphones into computers. Generally, integrated microphones can be found on laptops and some desktop monitors. Integrated Microphones are usually a small hole in front of the computer which when spoken into will record your voice.

Web Cameras

A Web camera allows a computer to accept input just by focussing on an object. The camera is focussed on the input object to take a picture of the object. Picture so taken can be transferred over computer network to a distant place.

The image of the object can be seen on the monitor of the distant computer connected through a network or through the Internet. Voice can also be transmitted over the network. Thus, two or more persons can talk and see one another in this way. This method is used in video conferencing.

Graphic Tablet

The digitizer or graphics tablet consists of a flat surface like a drawing pad. A pointing device is used along with this. A rough sketch can be converted to a fine drawing by transferring of point and line locations to the computer. This is done on an X-Y line coordinate system. The pointing devices used with the digitizer are many; a stylus or pen, a push-button cursor or puck, a power module or a console and a menu.

A grid pattern of horizontal and vertical lines is present below the flat surface of the digitizer. These lines detect electrical pulses at X-Y coordinate locations where a stylus or puck points. The digitiser is a popular input device generally used in CAD applications. It is available in many sizes.

Output Devices

Monitor: The Multimedia PC should be equipped with a monitor having Super Video Graphics Arrays (SVGA) card. The basic advantage of having SVGA is that it has a better resolution, thus its display will be of better quality for the graphics and pictures. Monitor comes in two types:

(a) CRT (Cathode Ray Tube)

(b) TFT-LCD (Thin Film Transistor-Liquid Crystal Display)

CRT Monitor

A VDU (Visual Display Unit) or CRT monitor is very similar to a television and its size (as in the case of TV) is measured in diagonal length of the screen. Monitors are available in 9", 12", 14", 15", 17", 19" and even in 21" size. It shows text or picture in color or black and white, depending on the type. Color monitors are more costly than black and white monitors. Whatever you type on the keyboard, you can see it on the monitor. Figure 1.12 shows typical CRT monitor.

TFT-LCD Monitor

LCD monitor is the flat panel type of monitor found on notebook PCs. TFT-LCD (Thin Film Transistor Liquid Crystal Display) is a variant of Liquid Crystal Display (LCD) which uses Thin Film Transistor (TFT) technology to improve image quality. TFT-LCD is one type of active matrix LCD. It is used in televisions, flat panel displays, projectors, etc. Figure 1.13 shows TFT LCD monitor.

TFT-LCD has a sandwich-like structure with liquid crystal filled between two glass plates. TFT Glass has as many TFTs as the number of pixels displayed, while a color Filter Glass has color filter which generates colors. Liquid crystals move according to the difference in voltage between the color Filter Glass and the TFT Glass. The amount of light supplied by Back Light is determined by the amount of movement of the liquid crystals in such a way as to generate color.

Figure 1.12 CRT Monitor

Figure 1.13 TFT-LCD Monitor

Printers

Printers provide information in a permanent readable form. They produce printed outputs of results, programs and data. The printers can be classified as:

(a) Impact printers

(b) Non-impact printers

Impact printers use an electro-mechanical mechanism that causes hammers or pins to strike against a ribbon and paper to print the text. Two types of impact character printers are available: dot-matrix printers and letter quality printers.

Non-impact printers use thermal, chemical, electrostatic, laser beam or inkjet technology for printing the text. Usually a non-impact type printer is faster than an impact type.

The disadvantage of non-impact type printers is that they produce only a single copy of the text whereas impact printers can produce multiple copies of the text.

Laser Printer

Laser printers are non-impact type printers. They print one page at a time. These printers use laser or some other light source to produce an image on a photosensitive drum. The computer controls the laser beam to turn it on and off when the laser beam is sent back and forth across the drum. An image is produced following the raster scan principle. The laser-exposed areas attract toner (an ink powder). Thereafter the drum transfers the toner to the paper. The paper then moves to a fusing station where the toner is permanently fused on the paper with heat or pressure. After this the drum is discharged and cleaned. Now the drum is ready for processing the next page. Laser printers are quiet and produce high-quality output. These printers are expensive and require periodic maintenance. Low-speed laser printers produce 10 pages or more per minute and are used with microcomputers. High-speed laser printers producing upto 30 pages per minute are used with mini and large computers. Laser printers have become popular for voluminous printing work. They are mainly used for desktop publishing work. Figure 1.14 illustrates a laser printer.

Figure 1.14 Laser Printer

Plotters

Plotters are output devices. They are used to produce precise and good quality graphics and drawings under control of the computer. They use ink pen or inkjet to draw graphics or drawings. Either single color or multicolored pens can be employed for drawings. Figure 1.15 shows a plotter.

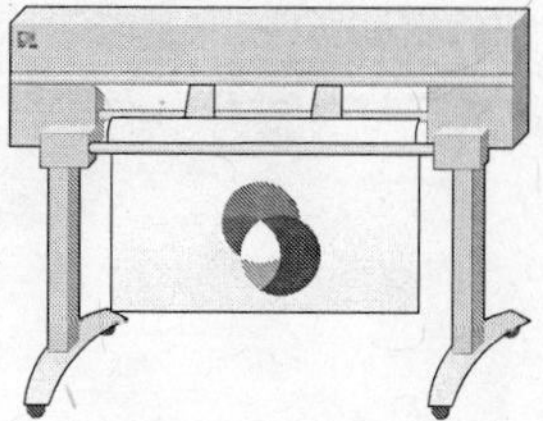

Figure 1.15 Plotter

Speakers

Speakers are hardware devices connected to a computer's sound card that outputs sounds generated by the card. A speaker makes sound by being fed on electrical signals which is changed or modulated, corresponding to the sound that is to be made. The speaker converts the changes or waves in the electrical signal to matching sound waves, which we hear. There is no volume control in the PC, since it was not intended to produce sophisticated sounds. Speakers are further attached to the system to enhance the sound quality. (See Figure 1.16).

Multimedia Projector

Multimedia projector is an output device connected to a PC and used to project information from a computer on to a large screen (a cloth screen or wall). The information is thus viewed by a large number of people. It is widely used for giving presentations. The presenter can directly point to, mark or edit the displayed information to make it more understandable. Audio, video, image and animation can be prepared on a PC and using a multimedia projector the presentation can be made more lively and interesting.

Figure 1.16 Speakers

Storage Devices

Hard Disk

Hard disk is a device used for mass storage of data. The data stored on a hard disk can be retrieved at a very fast speed. A hard disk is made up of a group of disks or disk platters, piled on top of one another in an airtight, dustproof case. Figure 1.17 shows a hard disk and its inside contents.

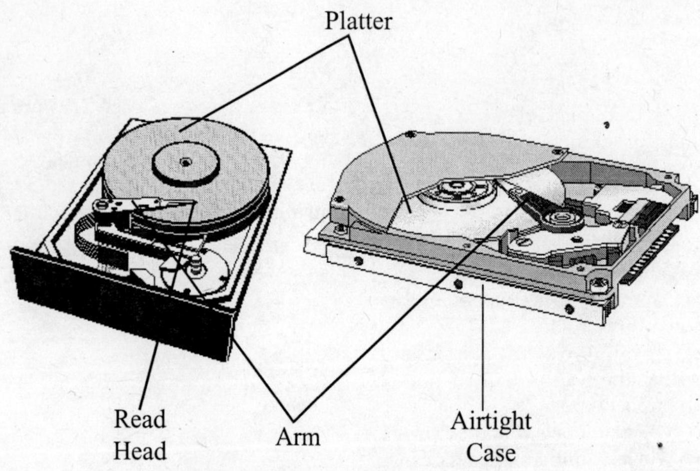

Figure 1.17 Structure of hard disk

Hard disks are available in the capacity of 80 GB or more. Depending on the type of programs you use, you can store very large sized database in these hard disks.

CD-ROM (Compact Disk Read Only Memory)

It is an optical Read Only Memory (ROM). The disk is made up of a resin, such as polycarbonate. It is coated with a material which will change its reflecting property when a high intensity laser beam is focussed on it. The coating material is highly reflective, usually aluminium. The high intensity laser beam forms a tiny pit along a trace to represent '1' and the surface without a pit known as 'land' represents '0'. Figure 1.18 shows a CD.

Figure 1.18 CD

Multimedia uses digitized audio and video, which not only take huge amount of storage space but also require high speed storage media, which can send large amount of data back and forth quickly to keep audio and video playing and recording smoothly.

For reading the data, a laser beam is employed. In some designs, separate laser beams are employed: one for writing and the other for reading. The reflected laser is sensed by a photodiode to read data. The intensity of the reflected light of laser changes as it encounters a pit. A pit spreads the light so that the photodiode receives less reflected light. But land reflects sufficient light to the photodiode. Thus, this change in reflected light is sensed and converted into electrical signals for data reading purposes.

CD-ROMs use long spiral tracks to store data. The track is divided into blocks of the same size. A CD-ROM disk rotates at a variable speed so that the pits are read by the laser at a constant linear speed. The speed of the disk is adjusted in such a manner that the track passes under the read/write head at a constant linear velocity.

CD-ROMs are an improvement over paper for large sized documents or databases since the information can be more easily searched and retrieved. But the cost of making the disk is still uneconomical especially for a limited number of copies.

Digital Video Disk (DVD)

Digital Video Disk (DVD) is introduced by Philips and Sony in 1995. It is an optical storage device that looks the same as a CD. A DVD has the same dimensions as a standard CD but cannot be read by a CD player, although a DVD player can read standard CDs. A DVD can store up to 4.7 to 17 GB of data.

Pen Drive

USB (universal Serial Bus) flash drives or pen drives are NAND-type flash memory data storage devices integrated with a USB interface. They are typically small, lightweight, removable and rewritable. It is a flash memory card that plugs into the computer's USB port. It is small enough to hook onto a key chain. It emulates a small disk drive and allows data to be easily transferred from one machine to another. It is also known as a flash drive, thumb drive, keychain drive, key drive, USB key drive and memory key drive (See Figure 1.19).

Figure 1.19 Pen Drive

Zip Drive

A *Zip drive* is a removable storage device that securely stores all your important computer data magnetically. Zip drives and Zip disks are durable, portable, easy-to-use, and extremely efficient. A zip disk of 250 MB capacity can store the same amount of data as 173 floppy disks.

Photo-CD: It is used to save photos in the compressed form. The compression allows for 100 photos to be recorded in one CD.

☞ *Sound output from a computer has been a feature of machines usually used for sending warning error messages or games. If better quality and capabilities for sound output or inputs are required, then there must be a device, which can be added to the basic machine. This device is known as sound card, which is added to the basic machine.*

1.9.2 Software for Multimedia

We can classify multimedia software or system software and authoring tools which are collectively used to develop multimedia applications. The former sets up the communications between the system resources and the application program. Examples are:

- Video for windows
- Quick time
- Indeo and digital video interactive
- Microsoft multimedia technologies

Video for Windows

This software has been developed by Microsoft to prepare video data to be use in multimedia applications. It is used to compress and decompress and play the video. Microsoft Video I, Intel Indeo, Cinepak or Microsoft Run Length Encoding (RLE) are examples of the codecs used for compressing the video data. The videos generated by VfW are stores in AVI (Audio Video Interleaved) format. In this approach the audio data is stored together with the image for each frame.

Videos can be captured, edited and played using the set of software included in the VfW. Editing involves various operations, such as cutting, inserting and merging video data to generate a new sequence of frames. VfW used VidCap to capture video, and VidEdit to edit it. It is a free software which comes with all the source codes.

QuickTime

This is a system software for Apple Macintosh. It enables the integration of video, audio, animation and graphics in a standard way in multimedia applications. It supports JPEG (Joint Photographic Experts Group), Apple Compact Video, Apple Animation Compressor, Real Time Video, MPEG (Moving Picture Expert Group) and motion JPEG.

QuickTime for Windows has been developed and the transfer of files between these two platforms has been made possible. In the Windows environment files with MOV (Moving Picture Experts Group) extensions are generated using QuickTime.

Indeo and Digital Video Interactive

Indeo is Intel Video (Indeo) technology and defines a file format for converting NTSC (National Television System Committee) and PAL (Phase Alternating Line) analog signals to digital video which can be stored and played back in a PC. The compression defined in Indeo is Real Time Video which uses a vector quantization scheme similar but less complicated than MPEG.

DVI (Digital Visual Interface) on the other hand defines a CD format based on Intel 80x86 processors. It is similar to CD_I (Compact Disk Interactive) and was developed for interactivity in games and generating special video effects.

Microsoft Multimedia Technologies DirectX by Microsoft is an example of new multimedia architecture designed to improve the application performance of Windows operating system. It is a low level API (Application Programming Interface) which includes:

- DirectDraw–composition engine for 2d and 3D video and animation.
- Direct3D rendering engine for real time 3D graphics.
- DirectSound–this provides device independent access to sound cards.
- DirectPlay–provides Internet connectivity for multiplayer games.
- DirectInput–provides connectivity to input devices, such as joysticks and virtual reality goggles.

The next set of software used in multimedia applications is the actual tools used to develop them. It is possible to divide these authoring tools into four categories.

- Programming languages
- Presentation software
- Simple interactive software
- Complex interactive software

Programming Languages

These are the 3rd and 4th generation programming languages, such as C/C++, Visual Basic and Delphi. If these are chosen to prepare the multimedia applications then one can achieve maximum control over the contents and developing interactive applications become easy. They require considerable programming experience. The other tools are developed using these languages are discussed below:

Presentation Tools

PowerPoint is an example of such presentation tools. We can also include graphics based word processing software where video and audio can be inserted. It ideals for applications which use text and simple graphics. Limited applications with audio and video can be developed.

These tools are fairly easy to learn and are suitable for developing simple multimedia applications in a short time.

Simple Interactive Software

These are suitable for developing multimedia applications where there is interactivity. Buttons or Hypertext can be used to navigate within the application. Most of such software is page based which means the contents and control elements are placed within pages and they are used to go to different parts of the application. Again limited use of digital video and audio is possible.

These programs are more difficult to learn compared to the previous class but they do not require much programming experience either. Adobe Acrobat, Astound are examples of this category.

Complex Interactive Software

These are the most powerful multimedia development tools. It is possible to incorporate programming languages into the applications and improve the control over the navigation and interaction. These are the following three types:

Page-Based : In these tools, the contents and controls are placed in pages. These pages can be accessed through linked items or controls. Since the educational software is based on page based tools therefore these are very useful in developing educational applications.

ToolBook is an example of page-based multimedia development software.

Time-Based These authoring software include a time-line where the pages or data components are inserted and display of different components can be controlled either by assigning a duration to each page or manually. This method can produce very successful animations and effects. The most common examples of these tools are *Director* and *Scala*.

Icon-Based These products use icons which make it possible to access to the contents or controls. They are useful for producing complex structural applications. Authorware is an example of such software.

Some of the recent software used in multimedia industry are:

Photoshop

Photoshop is most popular program for creating and image editing program. You can use Photoshop to alter image like photos, downloaded icons, or scanned artwork. Altering an image includes doing such things as changing the colors within an image, modifying the size and scale of an image, or putting one picture within another.

Photoshop is not a classic drawing or image creation program. Unlike a drawing program which stores information about images as mathematical expressions (called vectors), when Photoshop draws a line, the line is converted into little dots, called pixels.

Director

Director from Macromedia started out as a multimedia tool for sales presentations. Macromedia Director is the best solution for creating rich content and applications for CD/DVD-ROM, kiosks, Intranets, and the Web. Director allows users to build exceptionally rich content that delivers integrated interactive audio, video, vectors and bitmaps, text, fonts and much more. Director fully integrates with Macromedia Flash MX, so you can fully realize the potential of both applications by combining them together.

SoundEdit This software is Graphical User Interface or GUI-based audio editor which is primarily used for digitized audio. It is known for its outstanding simplicity of use. The main function of this software is to make audio manipulation especially accessible to those who are not audio professionals or even musicians. Other functions, such as sound capture and editing for multimedia are done through this software.

Premiere Adobe Premier is a powerful program for editing digital video. Premiere helps you create dynamic video or film, whether you are creating long video programs and motion picture films or short movies for CD-ROM or the Web. Like most editing software, Premiere works by importing video from a source, such as a video tape onto your hard drive, then allowing you to create new edited versions which you can export back to tape, disk or other medium. The major features of Adobe Premiere are:

- Capture high quality video from your DV (Digital Video) camcorder.
- Organize your audio and video clips, and edit them into a complete production.
- Enhance your work with transitions and effects, titles and animations.
- Save and share your productions as digital video files.
- Output streaming media formats to share on the Web.

Microsoft FrontPage FrontPage editor is introduced by Microsoft. It is a WYSIWYG (What You See Is What You Get) editor that is very easy to use and also allows you access to the HTML code in another window so you can make changes to your code if you want to. It also has a preview feature so you can see what your page looks like on Web browser with each new keystroke. To add text to your Web page all you have to do is choose your font, point and type. Adding graphics, links and other things are very simple.

Autodesk Maya It is 3D computer graphics software. This software is also known as Maya which runs generally on Windows and MAC OS X or Macintosh Operating System X (Ten) operating systems. This software is mainly used to create interactive 3D applications, such as video games, animated film, cartoons with special visual effects.

Alias/wave font Wavefront Technologies, a computer graphics company, was merged with Alias Research in 1995. This company is mainly used to produce computer graphics for movies and television commercials. This technique was useful to market their own software which uses computer animation and 3D tools to develop computer games.

Flash Macromedia Flash is a software that creates animations for a web designs. You can create a multimedia enriched content (Flash movies) containing images, sound, video and animation effects with this software. Adding more to this, the Flash software comes with a scripting language, called ActionScript, which provides interactivity to your Flash movies. Flash also comes with number of pre-built components including media components that load Flash video files or MP3 audio to enhance your Website.

Flash is basically a vector-based software that provides you with drawing tools to create vector objects. The drawing created in Flash can be saved as GIF files. Flash enables you to create animations on the objects of your movie. It creates animation using a process called *tweening*. Flash movies can be controlled by adding interaction to them. You can create or use an in-built button component as an interface element. For example, you can click a button to start or stop the movie. You can add digital sound and video as the contents of your Flash movie. Flash video refers to the Macromedia's FLV (Flash Live Video) format.

CoffeeCup CoffeeCup is GIF Animator software which is used to create animation. It allows first to browse images in a specified folder by previewing a thumbnail (icon image), and then drag-and-drop images in the form of animation. This software also allows users to convert Bitmap (BMP) and JPEG graphics into GIF (animated) files.

Ulead PhotoImpact Ulead PhotoImpact, also known as Iedit is a raster and vector graphics editing program which was developed by Ulead Systems. This software is featured with HTML tools, like rollover and imagemap assistant, background designer and button library, and also an HTML assistant. The latest version of this software is X3/13. This software is mainly used to create media-handling components including audio and video playback, recording, streaming and editing functions.

VideoLAN Client (VLC) Media Player VLC media player is portable and free-source streaming media server which supports many audio and video compression methods and file formats, including DVD-Video, video CD and streaming protocols. The main functions of this software are to stream (MoCN) Media over Computer Networks and also to transcode multimedia files. In 2012, a new VLC version has been developed for Android. Android is MOS (Mobile Operating System) which is mainly run on Linux kernel developed by Google. The process of transcoding multimedia files includes direct analog-to-analog or digital-to-digital digital conversion from one encoding to another, for example for video files, like NTSC, PAL (Phase Alternating Line), SECAM (SECAM or Sequentiel couleur a memoire; a French word which means 'Sequential Color with Memory'), and audio files, like WAV, MP3 (Moving Picture Experts Group Layer - 3).

REVIEW QUESTIONS WITH ANSWERS

1. Multiple Choice

1.1 Multimedia is combination of:
a. Text b. Audio and Video
c. Graphics d. All of the above

1.2 To make a good multimedia communication, you need:
a. Hardware and software b. Good ideas
c. Talent and skill d. All of the above

1.3 Multimedia hardware requires:
a. Sound card b. Video capture card
c. Large size of main memory d. All of the above

1.4 Which one of the following is not an input device?
a. Microphone b. Mouse
c. Scanner d. None of the above

1.5 Which one of the following is not an output device?
a. Monitor b. Printer
c. Plotter d. Digitizer

1.6 Which one is not a multimedia device?
a. TV System b. A book having only text (no diagram)
c. A modern personal computer d. None of the above

1.7 Which of the following is an example of hypermedia application?
a. World Wide Web b. PowerPoint
c. Adobe Acrobat d. All of the above

1.8 The elements of multimedia are:
a. Video, animation, interactivity
b. Sound, video, animation, interactivity
c. Graphics, sound, video, animation, interactivity
d. Text, graphics, sound, video, animation, interactivity

1.9 Historically, the term "hypertext" was used when textured information was linked in ____ ways.
a. Sequential b. Real time
c. Non-sequential d. Linear

1.10 Multimedia is used in which three main areas?
a. Television, Movies and Newspapers
b. Education, Television and Radio
c. Education, Information and Entertainment
d. All of the above

2. State whether the following statements are True or False

2.1 Pictures, photographic image and other artwork is called graphics or pictures.

2.2 Multimedia requires additional hardware which can handle sound, video, etc.

2.3 Images are defined as visual representation of the information.

2.4 Clip Art is a library of commonly used text.

2.5 Laser printers or plotters are used for output graphics in hardcopy.

2.6 Multimedia may include text-based elements.

2.7 If the sequence and timing of the multimedia elements can be controlled by the user, then one can name it as Non-Interactive Multimedia.

2.8 Touch screen is basically a monitor that allows user to interact with computer by touching the display screen.

2.9 A scanner's resolution is measured in megapixels.

2.10 Animation is used to create movements on the screen.

3. Match the following:

3.1	Multimedia	a.	Authoring tool for Internet and WWW
3.2	Animation	b.	Combination of media
3.3	Graphics	c.	Moving images
3.4	Unimedia	d.	Single media
3.5	Text	e.	Alphanumeric characters
3.6	OCR	f.	Input device
3.7	Transition effects	g.	The way that slide arrives on the screen

3.8	Multimedia kiosks	h.	Line drawing and images
3.9	Photoshop	i.	Public places as information provider
3.10	FrontPage	j.	Industry standard digital image software

4. Fill in the blanks

a.	Animation	b.	Microphone	c.	Multimedia
d.	Texts	e.	Optical character recognition	f.	Raster
g.	Resolution	h.	Microphone	i.	Bitmapped image
j.	Soundproof				

4.1 In ________ presentation, more than one media is used to present information.

4.2 __________ are alphanumeric characters used to present information.

4.3 _________ is used to codify printed text for direct input of printed text to computers.

4.4 _________ deals with displaying a sequence of images at a reasonable speed to create an impression of movement.

4.5 _________ is used for audio input to record a human voice or music or any type of sound in a computer.

4.6 The clarity of a monitor is known as ________.

4.7 Bitmapped graphics are called ________.

4.8 _________ is used for audio input to record a human voice or music or any type of sound in a computer.

4.9 A digital photograph is _____________.

4.10 If you do not want external voice to enter into the room where a voice over recording for a multimedia project takes place, then the room should be __________.

Answers

1.	1.1	d	1.2	d	1.3	d	1.4	d	1.5	d	1.6	b
	1.7	a	1.8	d	1.9	c	1.10	d				
2.	2.1	T	2.2	T	2.3	T	2.4	F	2.5	T	2.6	T
	2.7	F	2.8	T	2.9	F	2.10	T				
3.	3.1	b	3.2	c	3.3	h	3.4	d	3.5	e	3.6	f
	3.7	g	3.8	i	3.9	j	3.10	a				
4.	4.1	c	4.2	d	4.3	e	4.4	a	4.5	b	4.6	g
	4.7	f	4.8	h	4.9	i	4.10	j				

Questions with Answers

1. Explain the use of the following hardware components in multimedia.
   a. Scanner
   b. Sound card
2. a. Differentiate between Plain text, Formatted text and Hypertext text.
   b. What is *linear* and *nonlinear* media?
3. What is meant by the Multimedia and Hypermedia? Distinguish between these two concepts.
4. Give three examples of multimedia input devices.
5. Briefly explain applications of multimedia in our day to day life.

Answers to Short Questions

1. a. A scanner is a hardware device used to scan text or images into the computer. Sometimes, the information, picture or text that is available on paper is needed on the computer disk. For that we use scanner to convert a document into a digital format.

   Besides text scanning, scanners can also be used in image processing to capture pictures for printed publications, Internet Websites, and electronic presentations. A scanner can digitize a picture by converting dark and light areas of a graphic to dots, or pixels. A file is then saved in computer format for future use.

   b. Sound cards are essential part of all multimedia computers. Sound is usually used for sending warning error messages or games in machines. If better quality and capabilities for sound output or inputs are required, then there must be a device, which can be added to the basic machine. This device is known as sound card, which is added to the basic machine. Sound cards are basically meant for playback, digitization, recording and compressing the sound files.

2. a. Text can be of various types, such as *plaintext, formatted text* and *hypertext.*

   Plain text is also called unformatted text, consisting of fixed sized character from a limited character set, all having the same type of appearance.

   Formatted text are those text where appearance of text can be changed using font parameters, i.e., *bold, italic, underlined* varying shapes, sizes and colors, etc.

   Hypertext is a text based information, interlinked by means of relevant hyperlinks between various sub topics. Text that allows reader to jump spontaneously among onscreen documents and other resources by selecting highlighted keywords that appear on each screen. Hypertext appears most often on the World Wide Web. World Wide Web is the most popular and promising method of accessing the Internet. The main reason for its popularity is the use of a concept called *hypertext.*

   b. Multimedia is divided into linear and non-linear media. Media with linear content progresses without any control or change from user like a movie in a theatre. But, with non-linear multimedia systems, the media are interacting with the user and responds to the user inputs. Hypermedia is an application of multimedia with non-linear content.

3. *Multimedia:* Multimedia is a combination of media - used for creating audio, video, text, graphics and animation.

   Hypermedia: Hypermedia consists of hypertext combined with still or moving images and sound or we can say that Hypermedia is a well-defined structural arrangement of information in the form of audio, video, text, animation, graphics and other elements of multimedia pertaining to a particular topic or related to it, with relevant link in between them.

   Difference between Multimedia and Hypermedia:

   1. *Multimedia* is the presentation of media as text, images, graphics, video, and audio by the use of computers or the

information content processing devices whereas *Hypermedia* is the use of advanced form of hypertext like interconnected systems to store and present text, graphics and other media types where the content is linked to each other by hyperlinks.

2. Multimedia can be in linear or non-linear content format, but the hypermedia is only in non-linear content format.
3. Hypermedia is an application of multimedia, hence a subset of multimedia.

4. Examples of multimedia input devices are :

(a) ***Keyboard:*** Programs and data are entered into a computer through a keyboard which is attached to a computer. A keyboard is similar to the keyboard of a typewriter. It contains letters, digits, special characters, function keys and some control keys.

(b) ***Mouse:*** A mouse is a pointing device. It is held in one hand and moved across a flat surface. The mouse can also be used to draw sketches, diagrams, etc., on the monitor screen.

(c) ***Graphics Tablet:*** A *graphics tablet* is a graphic input device that functions like a drawing tablet. It can be used for sketching new images or tracing old ones, selecting from menus or simply moving the cursor on the screen, all of which can be provided within a single program. The user makes contact with the graphic tablet with a device called a cursor, which is a pen-like instrument that is connected to the tablet by a wire or without wires.

5. Multimedia can be used in any situation where computers are being used to deliver information. It may just be used to enhance areas that were previously text only, for example presentations or information kiosks. Multimedia e-mail and video conferencing allow information to be communicated better. Multimedia is widely used in education, from preschool to post graduate courses. Interactive multimedia allows students to explore data and simulations allow the students to work on experiments. Multimedia can also be used to enhance data presentation and data analysis. Multimedia applications are used daily by growing number of people which are discussed as under:

Entertainment: Media and Entertainment industries are a major benefactors of multimedia technology. Images, animation and sound are widely used for making animation movies. Capability of computer is widely used by musicians to record, edit and mix sounds. Entertainment CDs, games, comics and stories for children are used for education and training.

Video Conferencing: Video conferencing is another application of multimedia with extremely great potential. Imagine that you are using a computer and you wish to communicate with a colleague. Video conferencing allows you to see your colleague in a window on your monitor screen and vice versa allowing you to talk face to face as if round a table.

Training: The continual introduction of Information Technology, and its pace of change, give rise to a thriving software training industry. For example, when a new program is introduced into an office environment the need for training or retraining is required. Now the cost of training drop off significantly for all those due to introduction of multimedia (CD-ROM disk). A manuals and training material both could be loaded from CD-ROM.

DESCRIPTIVE TYPE QUESTIONS

1. Explain the components of multimedia.
2. Explain in detail the application of Multimedia in the field of education and entertainment.
3. What is the role of input and output devices in a computer system?
4. Name some of the input and output devices used with computers.
5. Hypertext and hypermedia are new ways of presenting and browsing information. What is the importance of them in multimedia application development? Give the difference between them.
6. What is multimedia? Explain.
7. What is hypermedia? Differentiate it from hypertext.
8. Explain the differences in the functions of DVD and a CD-ROM.
9. What are the characteristics of multimedia presentation?
10. What do you mean by multimedia objects? Discuss.

CHAPTER 2

Representation of Multimedia Objects

2.1 REPRESENTATION OF ANALOG SIGNALS

Various kinds of media we see in our daily life with the help of electronic equipments – say the music that's coming out of a Tape recorder or the movie clip that is being broadcasted in the television all these are basically analog signals in nature. The word analog means 'continuously varying' for example, the sound media, all sounds are produced by vibrations in a medium and this is usually the air surrounding the sound source. When a music is coming out of the speakers the surrounding atmospheric air is actually compressed or decompressed at various rates depending up on the source signal, and this process ultimately carries the sound through the media from the source to the destination.

When these variations are recorded electronically in some form of signals, over, say a magnetic media, then they become reproducible as the signals can be understood and played back later. This is the fundamental principle behind all electronic media handling devices and transmissions and the signals thus recorded are called *analog signals*. The path of a single analog wave is in the form of a curve. Mathematically, this curve is known as sine curve. The height of a signal wave at any point of time is its *amplitude* and the specific time intervals, at which it occurs is called its *frequency* (See Figure 2.1).

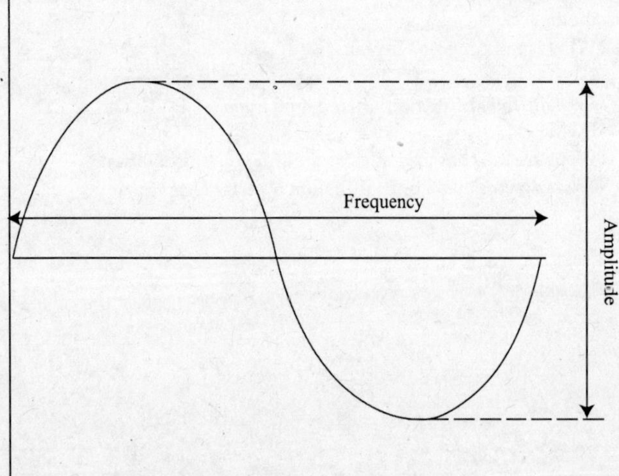

Figure 2.1 A typical analog signal representation in the form of a sine wave

At any point of time, only two states can be represented by computer viz low level (zeros) and high level (ones). These signals are called *digital signals*. When the original analog light waves of an image or sound waves of a sound are sampled and converted to binary digits is called *digitization*.

Traditional multimedia systems use specialized equipment that records sounds and graphics in an analog format, such as cassette tapes, records, or video cassette tapes. Analog equipment relies on waves to record information, such as sounds or video.

Technology has changed the hardware used to develop multimedia from the traditional analog equipment to computer-based or digital multimedia systems. Digital systems sample analog waves and convert them into a series of numbers, 0s and 1s (digital), for processing by a computer. Microcomputer-based multimedia systems provide hardware and software that allow a person to use a computer to combine text, still graphics or pictures, sound, video (motion graphics), and links to Websites and other software into a presentation. Multimedia presentations should allow users to interact with, navigate, and respond to the presentation.

2.2 ANALOG-TO-DIGITAL SAMPLING AND QUANTIZATION

Sound is stored in one of the two basic ways, called formats. The earlier format, stores sound in a form that resembles the original sound wave and is known as analog recording. This format is called analog because the form of the sound wave, called the waveform, in the recording is analogous to the original waveform. In other words, the recorded waveform is a copy of the original waveform.

The newer format for storing sound is digital recording, which represents a sound wave as a series of digital signals.

The process of converting analog signals to digital signals by way of taking discrete samples, is called *digitization of sound*. We can digitize sound from a microphone, a synthesizer, existing tape recordings, live radio and television broadcasts, and popular CDs (Compact Disks).

Digital, or digitized sound is easier to reproduce and manipulate without loss in quality than analog.

When voice or music is captured by a microphone, it generates an electrical signal. The signal consists of a fundamental sine wave of a certain amplitude and frequency. The amplitude of the signal represents the intensity of the sound, and the frequency represents the pitch of the sound. Sound is made up of continuous analog sine waves that tend to repeat for seconds at a time depending on the music or the voice. The analog sine waveforms are converted to digital format by feeding the analog signal to an analog-to-digital converter. Digital-to-analog conversion is the reverse process of analog to digital conversion. It transforms a sequence of discrete numbers back into continuous analog signal. Figure 2.2 shows the schematic representation of this process. Once the sound has been digitized, it can be processed like any other binary file.

During playback, the digital files are converted back to analog signals and are fed into the speakers.

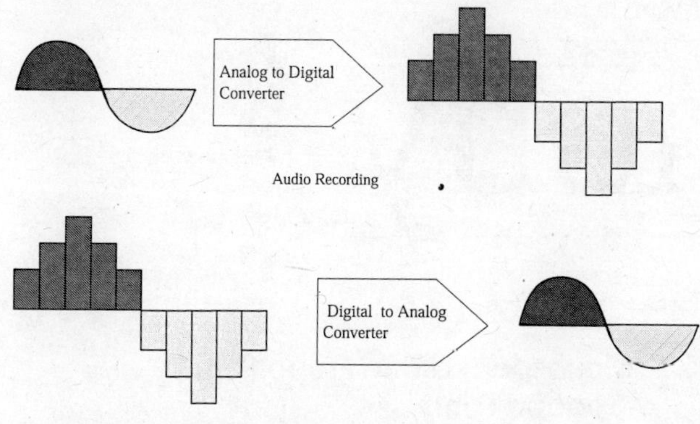

Figure 2.2 Schematic representation of A/D conversion and D/A conversion process circuitry

Analog-to-digital conversion transforms analog signal into a series of numeric representation by digitization. Digitization is composed of sampling and quantization.

Sampling is the process of turning the original analog sound waves into digital (binary) signals that the computer can save and later replay. The system samples the sound by taking snapshots of its frequency and amplitude at regular intervals. For example, at time X the sound might be measured with an amplitude of Y. The higher (or more frequent) the sample rate, the more accurately the digital sound replicates its real life source and larger the amount of disk space needed to store it.

☞ *The process where the analog signal is sampled over time at regular interval at which the sampling occurs is called the sampling rate.*

The sample (amplitude) obtained at the sampling time is represented by an 8-bit value (one byte) or 16-bit value (two bytes). Higher bit values up to 32-bits are used for very high fidelity sound. According to Nyquist theorem, the sampling rate must be at least twice the highest frequency component of the analog waveform to reproduce the signal properly. The higher the sampling rate, better the result. Sampling rate is measured in kilohertz (KHz) and its typical values are 8, 11, 22 and 44.1 KHz. For example, the sampling rate of CD-quality audio is 44.1 KHz, and that of telephone quality audio is 8 KHz.

☞ *The higher the sampling frequency, the better is the recorded signal, because, if more number of samples are taken during a given time intervals, the wave reform is relatively smooth and resembles the original signal.*

The value of each sound sample, during analog-to-digital converter process, is rounded off to the nearest integer value. This is called *quantization*. Quantization sometimes produces unwanted background noise. Quantization is measured in terms of number of bits and its typical values are 8, 12 and 16 bits.

☞ *The quality of audio is based on the quality of your recording and not the device on which your end user will play the audio, digital audio is said to be device independent.*

2.3 TEXT IN MULTIMEDIA

Text is the simplest form of data and requires the least amount of storage. Alphanumeric characters are used to present information in text form. Text is also the basic building block of a document. An electronic mail (e-mail) message almost invariably consists of some text fields. With the recent explosion of the Internet and World Wide Web (WWW), text has become more important than ever. Words and symbols in any form, spoken or written, are the most common system of communications. It is important to design labels for title screens, menus, and buttons using words that have the most precise and powerful meanings to express what you need to say. Text is used for names, addresses, descriptions, definitions and a variety of data attributes. The major attributes of text include paragraph styling, character styling (such as bold, italics and so on), font families and sizes, and relative location in a document.

Using text and symbols for communication is very recent human development that began about 6,000 years ago. When the first meaningful marks were scraped onto mud tablets and left to harden in the sun. Only members of the ruling classes and the priesthood were allowed to read and write the pictographic signs.

Today text and the ability to read it are doorways to power and knowledge. Reading and writing are expected as necessary skills within most modern cultures.

Text can be of various types such as *plaintext, formatted text* and *hypertext. Plain text* is also called unformatted text, consisting of fixed sized character from a limited character set, all having the same type of appearance. Formatted text are those text where appearance of text can be changed using font parameters, i.e., *bold, italic, underlined* varying shapes, sizes and colors etc. We may think of a book as a linear medium, basically meant to be read from beginning to end. Hypertext is meant to be read non-linearly, by following links that point to other parts of the same document, or other documents.

Text plays an important role in almost all multimedia projects. However the design and content of multimedia texts are so different from other types of text, such as newspaper or magazine texts and book texts.

The extent to which texts are used in a multimedia project mainly depends upon the subject or content it deals with. For example, a reference multimedia CD-ROM (Compact Disk Read Only Memory) like 'The Grollies multimedia Encyclopedia, may contain extensive text-based information whereas an education title like 'The Reading Blaster' which is meant for kids to learn words, may use text and pictures.

Texts are applied in multimedia projects in a variety of ways, to serve different purposes. In general following are included in a multimedia project:

1. Texts in titles
2. Texts in menu/navigation items
3. Texts in button bars or equivalents
4. Text that display:
   a. Volume of information (as in Encyclopedia)
   b. Something that may be ambiguous with speech (say, a recipe)
   c. Something that is very important (say scientific formula).

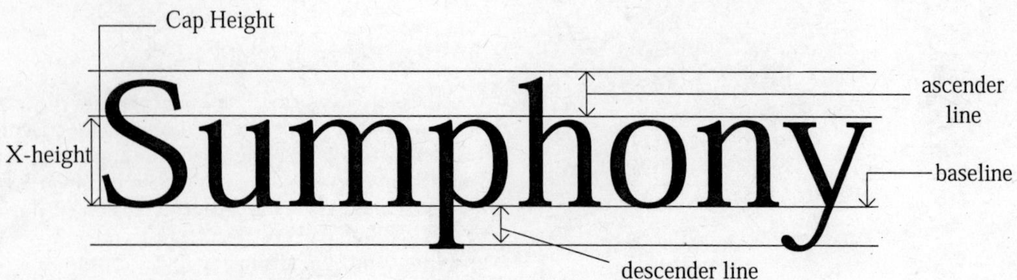

Figure 2.3 Various lines and dimensions related to a character

Text can be inserted into an application using various means. The simplest way is to type text using input device, such as keyboard. Another way of inserting text into an existing document by using copy and paste method. OCR (Optical Character Recognition) may be used to input a wide variety of documents including pictures, graphics, typed text or handwritten text.

2.4 FAMILIES AND FACES OF FONTS

A *typeface* is a family of graphic characters that usually includes many type sizes and styles.

Fonts refer to a specific typeface in a specific point size and style. A font is nothing but the set of all characters (including punctuation symbols, etc.) in a certain style. The term fonts and typefaces are not actually the same but are used interchangeably. A font or typeface is defined as a collection of characters and symbols with a common appearance, or design. *Courier* is an example of a font. Times is a different font (or typeface) used in printing newspaper and magazines.

A collection of all the variations of a font is called a *font family*. For example, the *Times Roman*, *Times Italic*, *Times Bold* and *Times Bold Italic* are called font families.

2.4.1 Font Styles

Different font styles are listed below:
Normal: This text is normal
Bold: **This text is bold**
Italic: *This text is Italic*
Underline: This text is underline
Strikethrough: ~~This text is strikethrough~~

2.4.2 Dimensions of Font

The size of typefaces and fonts is traditionally measured in points (1 inch = 72 points). Figure 2.3 shows the dimensions of font and lines are described below:

Baseline: An imaginary horizontal line on which characters rest.

X-height: The height of the main body of a letter. It is in the lowercase.

Cap height: The height of the main body of a letter when it is in the uppercase.

Ascender: The part of a letter that extends above the X-height when the letter is in the lowercase, as for certain letter, such as *h*.

Descender: The part of a letter that extends below the baseline when the letter is in the lowercase as for certain letters, such as *p* and *y*.

2.4.3 Monospaced and Proportionally Spaced Fonts

Fonts can be monospaced (fixed in width) and proportionally spaced (made variable in width). Let us discuss each of them in brief.

Monospaced fonts: Fonts like `Courier` use the same amount of horizontal space on a line for each character. With a monospaced font a letter i takes the same amount of horizontal space as the letter W. Monospaced fonts are used in legal documents. This is an inefficient use of space and causes uneven looking words.

Proportionally Spaced Fonts: Proportionally spaced fonts fit narrow letters in less space. Arial and Times New Roman are examples of proportionally spaced fonts used in MS Word. Figure 2.4 shows various type of fonts. Notice that white space on either side of the letter *i* in the Courier example.

2.4.4 Dingbats

Symbol, or Dingbat, typefaces consist of symbols (such as decorative bullets, clock faces, railroad timetable symbols, enclosed numbers) rather than normal text characters. Symbols can be used in a document for ornamental purpose or as bullets. They can also be combined to make logos. Some examples of dingbats are shown in Figure 2.4.

2.4.5 Ornamental Fonts

Ornamental typefaces are used exclusively for decorative purpose, and are not suitable for body text. These fonts are usually for the headings or cover designs of catalogues for the text in greeting cards, invitations, etc. Some examples of ornamental fonts are shown in Figure 2.4.

2.4.6 Serif and Sans Serif Fonts

Typefaces can be divided into two main categories *Serif* and *Sans Serif*.

Serif fonts

Serif fonts have five lines that finish off the main strokes, for example, at the bottom of a capital T or at the ends of the T's crossbar (See Figure 2.4). Times Roman and Garamond are common examples of Serif typefaces. Other examples of Serif fonts includes New Century, Schoolbook, Bookman, and Palatino. Serif fonts are probably the most used class in printed materials, including most books, newspapers and magazines.

☞ *Serifs fonts are used for body text.*

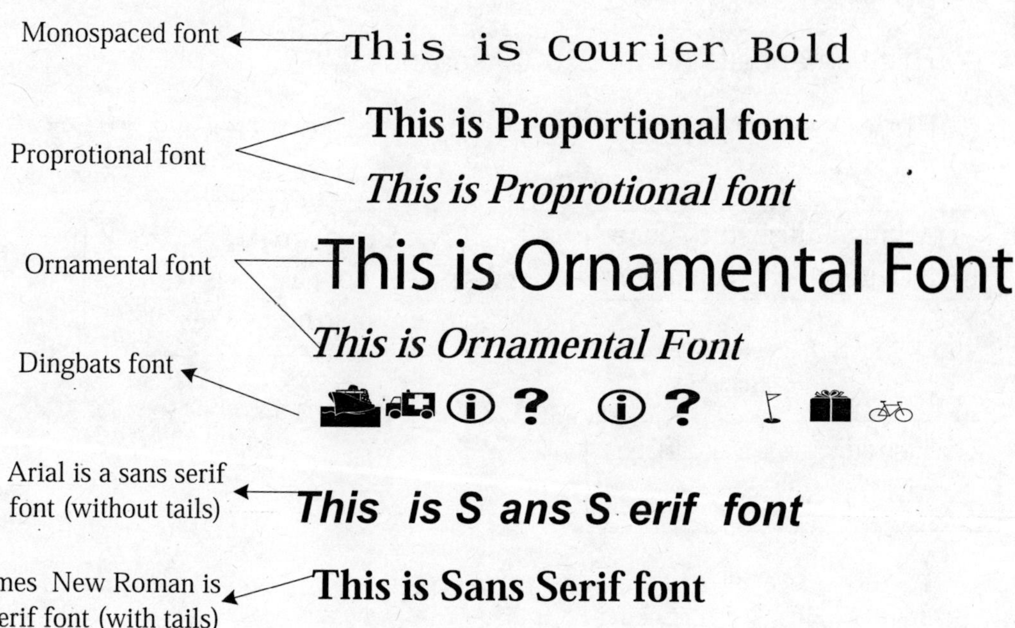

Figure 2.4 Various types of fonts

Sans Serif Fonts

The "finishing strokes" called Serifs, are absent in Sans Serif fonts (**T**) (See Figure 2.4). Helvetica, Verdana, Arial, Optima and Avant Grade are examples of Sans Serif fonts.

☞ *Sans Serif fonts are used for headlines and bold statements.*

Sans Serif fonts are far more legible and attractive when used in the small size of text field on a screen.

Text	Point
AaBbCcDd	8
AaBbCcDd	10
AaBbCcDd	16
AaBbCcDd	18
AaBbCcDd	20
AaBbCcDd	30
AaBbCcDd	36
AaBbCcDd	48

Figure 2.5 Different font sizes

2.4.7 Font Size

The size of the font is measured in points, and as the point size increases the size of the letter also increases. One point equals 1/72 th of an inch. Point size is the measure of a font's height but not its width. Different font sizes to be used for running text, headings, sub-headings, etc. Different font sizes are appear in the text given in Figure 2.5.

2.4.8 Scaling, Tracking, Leading and Kerning

Scaling means changing the size of a font. Horizontal scaling means changing the width of a font without changing the height. Vertical scaling means changing the height of a font without changing the width. Figure 2.5 shows a horizontal scaling of font.

Tracking adjusts the space to the right of each character. Increasing the tracking increases the amount of space between all texts. Decreasing the tracking reduces the space between all text and darkens a page. Figure 2.6 shows different tracking.

Leading means spacing between lines. In general, the amount of space added between each line of body type should be about 20% of the type size. Leading is defined as spacing between the above and below of consecutive lines of text. There are different types of spacing, single, double, 1/2 spacing, etc. Figure 2.7 shows different types of spacing between the lines.

Kerning is the space between individual characters.

This sentence is 90% horizontal scaling

This sentence is normal 100% scaling

This sentence is 150% horizontal scaling

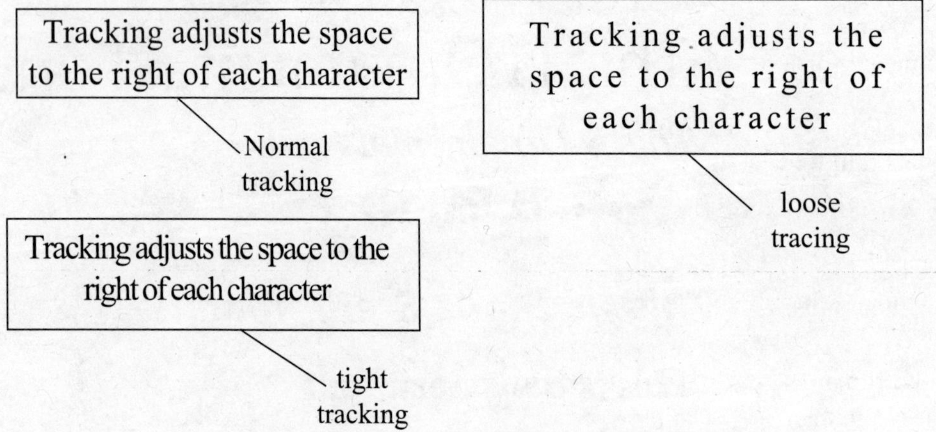

Figure 2.6 Showing different scaling and tracking

Leading means spacing between lines. In general, the amount of space added between each line of body type should be about 20% of the type size.

Leading means spacing between lines. In general, the amount of space added between each line of body type should be about 20% of the type size.

Leading means spacing between lines. In general, the amount of space added between each line of body type should be about 20% of the type size.

Figure 2.7 Different types of spacing between the lines

2.5 TYPES OF FONT FAMILIES

Two types of font families emerged as industrial standards amidst hundreds of other proprietary standards. These two families are called *Postscript* fonts and *TrueType* fonts. Let us discuss each of them in brief.

2.5.1 Postscript Fonts

Adobe introduced postscript in 1985. Postscript is a scaleable font system that is compatible with postscript printers. It allows user to see fonts on the screen the same way they would be printed. This was the first WYSIWYG (What You See Is What You Get). Up until these time fonts were in the form of bitmaps and were not screen scalable. Scalable fonts allow the user to adjust font size on the screen as well as at the printer. There are two kind of postscript fonts: Type 1 and Type 3.

Type 1 (also know as Postscript Type 1, or Adobe Type 1) is the font format for single byte Roman fonts for use with Adobe Type Manager (ATM) software and with Postscript printers. Type 1 fonts also contain hints, which are special instructions for grid fitting to help improve resolutions. Hints can apply to a font in general or to specific characters at a particular resolution. There are currently over 6,000 different Type 1 typefaces available.

Postscript Type 1 fonts are most widely used by graphic design and publishing professionals, because the raster image processors that process file on high resolution laser printer, image setters, are postscript based, and thus are more compatible with the postscript information contained in Type 1 fonts.

Type 3 (also known as postscript Type 3, or Adobe Type 3) consist of glyph defined using the full postscript language, rather than just a subset. Because of this, a Type 3 font can do somethings that Type 1 font cannot do, such as specify shading, color and fill patterns. Adobe Type Manager does not support Type 3 fonts.

2.5.2 True Type Fonts

True Type fonts format was originally developed by Apple computer and soon was used by Microsoft as well. True Type fonts are one piece–both the printer and the screen images are created from the same font file. In addition to printing smooth characters on printers, True Type would draw characters to a low resolution (72 dpi or 96 dpi) monitor.

True Type fonts are the easy choice for corporate and personal environments. As many businesses and home computers are Windows-based systems, and generally have a large selection of True Type fonts. These fonts are easy to add to your system, and you do not need any additional software to work with them.

Difference between Postscript and True Type Fonts

- Postscript fonts use an algebraic function of cubic polynomials whereas True Type uses a quadratic polynomial.
- True Type may be faster in the printing process.
- You can use True Type fonts on any PC. All versions of windows support True Type fonts as standard.

Except for Windows NT, 2000 and XP, you need an extra program called Adobe Type Manager (ATM) in Postscript fonts.

2.6 BITMAP FONTS

Bitmapped fonts are typefaces of a specific size and with specific attributes, or characteristics, such as boldface or italic. The bitmap is a record of the pattern of dots needed to create a specific character in a certain size and with a certain attribute. The bitmaps for a 36-point Times Roman medium capital A, for a 36-point Times Roman boldface capital A, and for a 30-point Times Roman medium capital A are all different and specific.

Bitmapped images are generally limited to text and are fast way to produce a printed page that uses only a few type fonts. If the hard copy is to include a graphic image in addition to bitmapped text, then to create the graphic, your software must be able to send the printer instructions that it will understand. Printers still come with a few bitmapped fonts stored on a chip, but the fonts of choice are increasingly outline fonts.

2.7 OUTLINE FONTS

Outline fonts, are not limited to specific sizes and attributes of a typeface. Instead, they consist of mathematical descriptions of each character and punctuation mark in a typeface. They are called outline fonts because the outline of a Times Roman 36-point capital A is proportionally the same as of 24-point Times Roman capital A.

☞ *Bitmapped fonts come in predefined sizes and weights. Outline fonts can be scaled and given special attributes, such as bold facing and underlining.*

Outline or vector fonts, are used with a Page Description Language (PDL), such as Adobe PostScript or Microsoft TrueType. A PDL treats everything on a page–even text – as a graphic. The text and graphics used by the software are converted to a series of commands that the printer's page description language uses to determine where each dot is to be placed on a page. Page description languages generally are slower at producing hard copy, but they are more versatile at producing different sizes of type with different attributes or special effects, and they create more attractive results. Outline fonts do not need to be a part of a printer. They can be stored on a PC's hard drive and used by the page description language as needed.

2.8 GRAPHICS IN MULTIMEDIA

Computer graphics are created using computers and, more generally, the representation and manipulation of pictorial data by a computer.

The development of computer graphics has made computers easier to interact with and better for understanding and interpreting many types of data. Developments in computer graphics have had a profound impact on many types of media and have revolutionized the animation and video game industry.

2D computer graphics is the computer based generation of digital images–mostly from two-dimensional models. 2D graphics models may combine geometric models (also called vector graphics), digital images (also called raster graphics), text to be typeset (defined by content, font style and size, color, position, and orientation), mathematical functions and equations, and more. These components can be modified and manipulated by two-dimensional geometric transformations, such as translation, rotation and scaling.

In 2D computer graphics, the computer screen may be considered as a canvas on which an image is drawn or composed. Several techniques exist for rendering 2D graphics on a computer screen; these may be broadly categorized into raster graphics, in which a rectangular array of pixels is drawn to the screen, and vector graphics, in which images are composed of mathematical representations of lines, curves, and other geometric shapes.

One of the major goals in computer graphics is to provide tools to the programmer for creating a pictorial description in form of graphs, drawings and pictures on the computer display from the mathematical description of images. The pictorial description necessary for generation by host computer will depend on the type of video display terminal used. A display file may contain several basic instructions. In case of raster scan display, a basic instruction will be 'Draw Vector' and the display file will be transferred to the display terminal by the host computer. A display file may contain several basic instructions. In case of raster scan display, the 'Draw Vector' instructions will not be a primitive instruction. A vector will be generated on the display by translating the vector into corresponding pixels and then by filling the refresh memory of the display. Therefore, the output of a hardware or a software vector generator can be used to set or reset bits in the refresh buffer of the display. This representation in the form of *bits*, where each bits corresponds to an individual pixel on the display screen, is also called a 'Bitmap'.

A bitmap is a rectangular array of points (i.e., pixels or picture elements), represented as zeros and ones, on the screen. The bitmap is stored in digital memory called *frame buffer*.

The display controller passes the contents of the frame buffer to the monitor. Each successive byte of data read from the frame buffer is converted into the corresponding video signal which is fed to the monitor producing a black and white pattern on the screen of the monitor.

Bitmaps are blocks of pixel data that can be output directly to a device, such as video display. Painting bitmap on the screen is faster as compared to use of functions like rectangle, line, etc. The drawback of bitmaps is that it takes a lot of memory.

☞ *The images can be stored either in bitmaps, that is in the form of bits (0's and 1's) or vector drawn maps, that is, in the form of features like lines, curves, etc., depending on the application.*

Unlike bitmap graphics, which use large collections of individual dots to create an image, vector graphics build images by using mathematical descriptions of objects like circles and lines. Figure 2.8 illustrates a good example of how a simple image like a circle can be created by using many individual pixels or a set of simple vector instructions.

Vector graphics uses combinations of computer commands and mathematical formulae to describe objects. They also let computer devices like monitors and printer figure out where to put all the actual dots to draw the objects.

☞ *Vector graphics are also called object-oriented graphics and draw type graphics.*

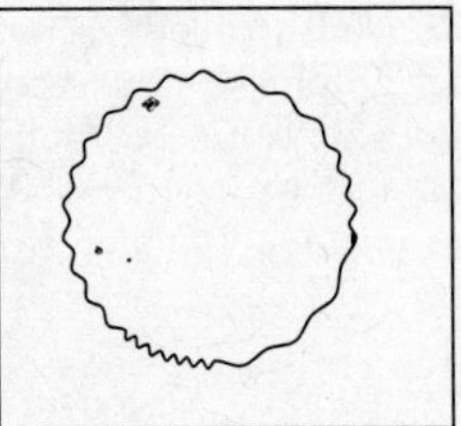

Circle created using bitmap pixels

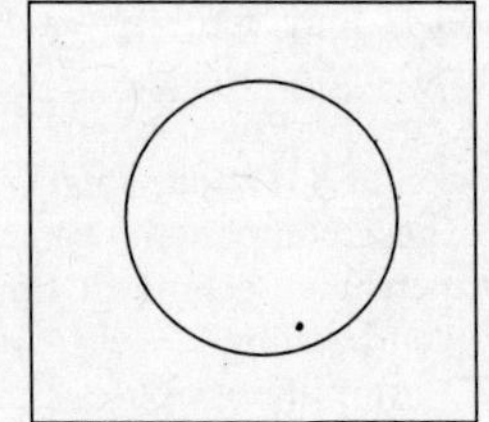

Circle created using Vector command

Figure 2.8 Circle created using bitmap and vector command

☞ *Defining images as a series of vectors is a more efficient way than defining images as bitmap. This is because, in bitmap method, even a simple image may have thousands of pixels and each pixel must be individually defined and stored in the memory of a computer. This occupies large space in the memory, whereas, the same image, in vector method, might be defined as a small number of curve segments.*

2.8.1 Capabilities and Limitations of Bitmap Images

Bitmap is one of many types of file formats for images stored in a computerized form. It carries the extension *.bmp*. Computers use bits of 1 and 0 to store data. Bitmap images are a map or a collection of individually colored, minute dots or pixels (picture elements) that are arrayed in a matrix or grid. Since each individual pixel is too small for the naked eye to perceive without the help of magnification, an array of these pixels forms a perceivably smooth graphic image.

To understand how a bitmap image is displayed, it is important to understand the computer display screen. The display is made up of rows and columns of tiny blocks, or pixels. In a bitmap image, each pixel is assigned at least 1-bit to indicate whether the pixel should reflect the background color, the foreground color, or some other color.

In the case of a page of black and white text, let us consider a single letter. The many pixels that make up that letter only requires 1-bit of data each. Either the pixel will be black or white: 1 or 0.

When a bitmap displays a colored image, such as a lake scene, there are several shades of gradation in colors and lighting. In this case, each pixel in the bitmap might have 16, 24, or 48 bits of information associated with it. The more bits, the greater the resolution of the bitmap and the larger the file.

- Compression techniques are used to shrink the file size of the bitmap while maintaining as much data as is necessary to render a good picture. One such format is the 8-bit *.gif* format, which uses a pallette of 256 colors. The advantage of the compressed *.gif* is that it is a smaller file that can be resized with satisfactory results, as it uses lossless compression. The disadvantage is that it cannot faithfully reproduce images containing more than 256 colors.
- Bitmaps are an image type most appropriate for photo-realistic images and complex drawings requiring fine detail.
- Limitation of bitmapped image includes large file sizes and the inability to scale or resize the image easily while maintaining quality. A bitmap image when magnified to larger sizes leads to increase in distance between pixels. At a certain stage individual pixel become visible as single – colored squares and the image takes on a boxy appearance with degradation in quality. This phenomenon is called *pixelation*.

☞ *Because bitmaps store so much information in the highest resolutions, they make very beautiful images. However, a bitmap images does not rescale well. If blown up using graphics program, the bitmap image becomes blocky and blurred. If reduced, it loses clarity.*

- You can grab a bitmap image from a screen, scan it with a scanner, download it from a Website, or capture it from a video capture device.
- You can then manipulate and adjust many of its properties, and cut and paste among many bitmaps using specialized image editing programs.
- You can import a color or gray scale bitmap from the Macintosh to Windows, the colors will seem darker and richer.
- Because bitmap images are built pixel-by-pixel, they can be easily edited. Zooming in on a bitmap image in any graphics program allows the user to add, delete, or change the color of individual pixels.

2.8.2 Capabilities and Limitations of Vector Images

Vector images are a collection of individual objects rather than picture elements. A vector image can be composed of points connected by lines, or nodes (control points) connected by Bezier curves.

- Vector images are most appropriate for lines, boxes, circles, polygons and other graphic shapes that can be mathematically expressed in angles, coordinates and distances.
- Each individual object contained in a vector image is defined by a mathematical equation. This means that vector images are not resolution dependent. Thus, each vector object is scalable and can generally be resized without any loss of image quality. As such, vector images are ideal for graphics, such as maps and company logos that often require scaling.
- A vector object can be filled with color and patterns, and you can select it as a single object.

- Each individual object may be edited to contain attributes such as outline, color and fill. Modifying the object's attributes will not change the basic object. The size of the object can also be transformed or shaped by using and adjusting its control points.
- Vector drawn objects use a fraction of the memory space required to describe and store the same object form.
- Vector images have no white pixel backgrounds. This means that you can put a vector object above another without blocking out the object underneath.
- Vector images typically have small file size because one such file contains only the mathematical equations that determine the Bezier curves to define the image. A vector image file does not contain the image itself.
- For the Web pages, that use vector graphics in plug-ins such as Flash, download faster and when used for animation, draw faster than bitmaps.
- Converting bitmaps to vector drawn objects is difficult, however, autotracing programs can compute the bounds of shapes and colors in bitmapped images require a plug in (such as a Flash player) for display on a Web page.
- Vector images cannot be used for photo realistic images and photos.
- There have been improvements to vector drawing software which enables users to approximate photorealistic vector objects. Attributes, such as transparency can now be adjusted using vector imaging tools. Bitmap textures can now also be applied to vector objects. Shading and blending are also some of the new vector imaging tools functionalities. Still, most vector images look like sharply drawn cartoon images.

2.8.3 Capabilities and Limitations of Vector Images

Vector images are a collection of individual objects rather than picture elements. A vector image can be composed of points connected by lines, or nodes (control points) connected by Bezier curves.

- Vector images are most appropriate for lines, boxes, circles, polygons and other graphic shapes that can be mathematically expressed in angles, coordinates and distances.
- Each individual object contained in a vector image is defined by a mathematical equation. This means that vector images are not resolution dependent. Thus, each vector object is scalable and can generally be resized without any loss of image quality. As such, vector images are ideal for graphics, such as maps and company logos that often require scaling.
- A vector object can be filled with color and patterns, and you can select it as a single object.
- Each individual object may be edited to contain attributes such as outline, color and fill. Modifying the object's attributes will not change the basic object. The size of the object can also be transformed or shaped by using and adjusting its control points.
- Vector drawn objects use a fraction of the memory space required to describe and store the same object form.
- Vector images have no white pixel backgrounds. This means that you can put a vector object above another without blocking out the object underneath.
- Vector images typically have small file size because one such file contains only the mathematical equations that determine the Bezier curves that define the image. A vector image file does not contain the image itself.
- For the Web pages, that use vector graphics in plug-ins, such as Flash, download faster and when used for animation, draw faster than bitmaps.
- Converting bitmaps to vector drawn objects is difficult, however, autotracing programs can compute the bounds of shapes and colors in bitmapped images require a plug-in (such as a Flash player) to display on a Web page.
- Vector images cannot be used for photo realistic images and photos.
- There have been improvements to vector drawing software which enables users to approximate photorealistic vector objects. Attributes, such as transparency can now be adjusted using vector imaging tools. Bitmap textures can now also be applied to vector objects. Shading and blending are also some of the new vector imaging tools functionalities. Still, most vector images look like sharply drawn cartoon images.

2.9 ALIASING PROBLEMS

Aliasing is a Web design term used to describe the undesirable distortion of visual elements on a computer screen. These peculiarities take many forms, such as the appearance of jagged or stair-stepped edges along what is supposed to be a smooth, curvy surface or diagonal lines on the screen (also known as "the jaggies"). Anti-aliasing is a software technique used in imaging systems (such as Photoshop) to make these curved edges or diagonal lines look smooth and continuous. It is often referred in games and on graphics. In games, it is normally used in those images that are used for creating a realistic 3D image on the screen. Anti-aliasing does not actually smooth any edges of images it merely fools the eye. It brings a much more pleasing image to the eye. Something like what comes out of a high class printer rather than what you can be used to seeing when on a computer screen.

☞ *Anti-aliasing is a kind of correction that smoothens the rough edges of a selection by softening the color transition between edge pixels and background pixels.*

Jagged edges in images are caused by the limitations of a computer screen, whether it is CRT (Cathode Ray Tube) or TFT/LCD (Thin Film Transistor/Liquid Crystal Display) screen. Monitors are capable of producing nearly perfect straight lines either horizontally or vertically, but, when you draw a diagonal line on a computer screen, it creates blocks of color diagonal lines displace these blocks slightly causing jagged edges.

Without anti-aliasing, an image would look stair-stepped, without smooth transitions between colors. In anti-aliasing, there is no loss of details because only the edge pixels change.

2.9.1 Advantages of Applying Anti-aliasing to Graphics

(a) It can smooth out screen fonts.
(b) It can round the edges look to have smooth curves.
(c) It can significantly improve the clarity of even the poorest quality images and scanned documents.
(d) Type can be easier to read due to better quality fonts.
(e) Games look a lot prettier and more realistic.

2.10 IMAGES IN MULTIMEDIA

Images are defined as visual representation of the information. Images are pictures and photographs composed of a collection of pixels (picture elements). A pixel is the smallest unit that makes up an image on your computer monitor.

Images are generated by the computer in two ways: as bitmaps (or paint graphics) and as vector drawn (or just plain drawn) graphics. Bitmaps are used for photo realistic images and for complex drawings requiring fine detail. Vector drawn objects are used for lines, boxes, circles and other graphic shapes that can be mathematically expressed in angles, co-ordinates and distances. The appearance of both types of objects depends on the display resolution (i.e., two dimensional representation) and capabilities of computer's graphics hardware and monitor. Both types of images are stored in various file formats and can be translated from one application to another and from one computer platform to another.

2.10.1 Color Science

Color is a vital component of multimedia. Color adds depth to images, enhances images and helps set objects apart from the background. Color or gray scale are a part of life. We include color description in phrases like the girl is wearing red saree, the color of the sky is blue, the grass is green and so on.

Light comes from an atom when electron passes from a higher to lower energy level, each atom produces uniquely specific colors. This is known as the *quantum theory*. This theory was developed by Physicist Max Planck in the late 19th century. Niels Bohr, another physicist, later showed that an excited atom that has observed energy and whose electrons have moved into higher orbits will throw off that energy in the form of quanta, or photons, when it reverts to a stable state. This is where light comes from.

Color science is an important discipline in industries, such as digital printing and printer manufacturing, photo finishing, pharmaceutical, biomedical, medical imaging, remote sensing, surveying, astronomy, oceanography, and in many other areas of science.

Color science allows one to measure color and manipulate color with reference to the human visual system, which begins with a device (input or output) characterization step. Device characterization allows us to understand how a given device responds to colors (input) or creates colors from a known signal (output). Once the device has been characterized using as much of its signal range as possible, a model can be constructed to manipulate input signals and transform them into new signals that give the desired result. The organization or management of color reproduction among input, output, and intermediate display devices is known as "*color management*".

The measurement of color, which is termed as colorimetry, creates the foundation from which color can be manipulated. Mathematical models pertaining to the human visual system allow us to compute approximations to perceive color from raw spectral measurements and to define the color numerically.

As industries respond to consumer demand for increasing color quality in most products, the importance of color science to the development of these products correspondingly increases.

2.10.2 Color

Color is the frequency of a light wave within the narrow band of the electromagnetic spectrum to which human eye responds.

In other words, color is a sensation that light of different frequencies generates on our eyes. The higher frequencies producing the blue end and the lower frequencies producing the red end of the visible spectrum. White light is a combination of all the colors of the spectrum.

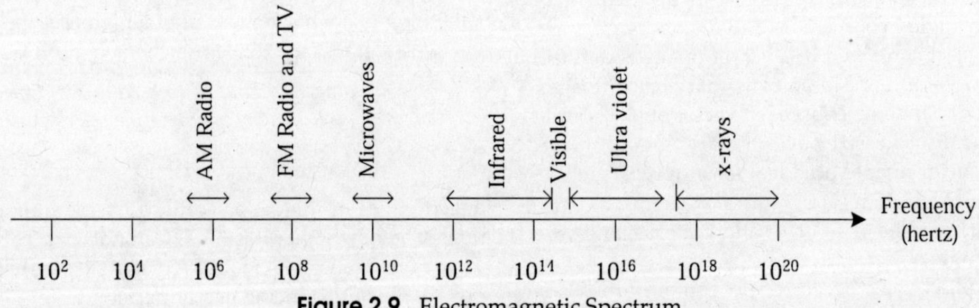

Figure 2.9 Electromagnetic Spectrum

Visible light is a form of electromagnetic radiation or radiant energy, as are radio frequencies or x-rays. The radiant energy spectrum contains audio frequencies, radio frequencies or x-rays. The radiant energy spectrum contains audio and radio frequencies, infrared, visible light, ultraviolet rays, x-rays, and gamma rays. Radiant energy is measured in terms of frequency or wavelength. The relationship between two is:

$$\lambda = \frac{c}{f} \text{ meters}$$

where λ is the wavelength in meters, c is the velocity of light in meters per second, and f is the frequency of the radiation in hertz. The position of radiant energy in the spectrum is normally expressed in terms of frequency. The wavelength can also be used as a unit of measurement.

When we perceive as "light", or different colors, is a narrow frequency band within the electromagnetic spectrum. A few of the other frequency bands within this spectrum are called *radio waves*, microwaves, infrared waves, and x-rays. Figure 2.9 shows the approximate frequency ranges for some of the electromagnetic bands.

Each frequency value within the visible band corresponds to a distinct color. At the low frequency end is a red color (4.3×10^{14} hertz), and the highest frequency we can see is violet color (7.5×10^{14} hertz). Spectral colors range from the reds through orange and yellow at the low frequency end to greens, blues, indigo and violet at the high end.

When a narrow beam of white light is passed through a prism, the light is dispersed, generating a spectrum of colors due to reflection. The color spectrum generated consists of violet, indigo, blue, green, yellow, orange and red. A white object appears white when viewed under white light because it reflects almost all the visible radiation and absorbs none. A black surface on the other hand, absorbs all visible radiation, and practically none is reflected.

Different colors are generated by mixing the primary colors: red, green and blue.

Because the eye's receptors are sensitive to red, green and blue lights, by adjusting combinations of these three colors, the eye and brain will interpolate the combination of colors in between. Although the eye perceives colors based upon red, green and blue, there are actually two basic methods of making color. These are additive color and subtractive color. Let us discuss each of them in brief.

Additive Color

In the Additive color method, a color is created by combining colored light sources in three primary colors: Red, Green, And Blue (RGB). This is the process used for a TV or Computer monitor.

☞ *Additive mixing generates the required color by adding two primary colors. For example, mixing red with green gives yellow color.*

Subtractive Color

In the subtractive color method, color is created by combining colored media, such as paints or ink that absorb (or subtract) some parts of the color spectrum of light and reflect the others back to the eye. Subtractive color is the process used to create color in printing.

☞ *Subtractive mixing generates a color by mixing secondary colors that selectively absorb unwanted colors and reflect the required color. For example, mixing yellow and magenta gives red color.*

2.10.3 Color Characteristics

A more intuitive way of describing color is presented in the Hue, Saturation and Brightness (HSB).

Hue: Hue is a particular tone of color, distinct from all others; red, green, and blue are all hues. For example, the eye can discriminate between red and blue color of equal intensity because of the difference in hue.

Saturation: The saturation of a color is the relative intensity, or purity, of that color. Lowering the saturation of red hue will make the color look more patel or faded.

Brightness: The brightness or lightness of a color refers to the amount of black added to the color, making the color appear darker. For example, to create "midnight blue" or "brick red" would require adding black to a particular hue.

☞ *The HSB color is closely related to the way we actually perceive color. Hue is equivalent to color wavelength, saturation is the intensity of the wavelength, and brightness is the overall amount of light.*

2.11 COLOR MODELS

A color model is an orderly system for creating a whole range of colors from a small set of primary colors. There are two types of color models, those that are subtractive and those that are additive. Additive color models use light to display color while subtractive models use printing inks. Colors perceived in additive models are the result using transmitted light. Colors perceived in subtractive models are the result of reflected light.

Since additive color models display color as a result of light being transmitted (added) the total absence of light would be perceived as black. Subtractive color models display color as a result of light being absorbed (subtracted) by the printing inks. As more ink is added, less and less light is reflected. Where there is a total absence of ink the resulting light being reflected (from a white surface) would be perceived as white.

Every color display system is capable of handling only a limited number of colors, at any given point of time. Systems with bare minimum configuration can mange to show up to 16 different colors, for any given image, whereas those with higher configuration can throw up to 16 million colors in a single screen or even more.

☞ *It is difficult for the human eye to recognize more than 256 different combinations of colors at any fraction of time.*

This total number of colors that could be handled by the monitor depends upon the memory capacity of the *Video Controller Card* (The card which serves as the interface between the computer and the display device) popularly known as the VRAM (Video Random Access Memory).

Let us imagine that the entire screen of the color display system is made up of small dots, called *pixels*. The colors that are to be displayed by each pixel, at any fraction of time, are stored as color data inside the VRAM. Thus, the total number of colors that could be displayed by the system at any point of time, depends upon the amount of color data that could be stored inside the VRAM.

The number of colors that could be stored by each bit in VRAM is obviously the total number of Zero-One combinations possible. Ultimately, the total number of memory bits in VRAM, dedicated for storing the color data, decide the total number of colors that would be available for the display, at any point of time.

As the entire screen is made up of small dots called pixels. Many such pixels are there on the screen, at any given point of time is known as the resolution of the monitor.

The color of a pixel on your computer monitor is typically expressed as an amount of red, green and blue. It takes more computer memory and processing speed to digitally manage and display the greater combination of red, green, and blue values that make more shades of color visible to the eye.

Models or methodologies used to specify colors in computer terms are RGB (Red, Green, Blue), HSB (Hue, Saturation, Brightness), HSL (Hue, Saturation, Lightness), CMYK (Cyan, Magenta, Yellow, Black) CIE (Chromacity) and others.

One method for defining a color model is to specify a set of two or more primary colors that are combined to produce various other colors. Common color models defined with three primary colors are RGB and CMYK models. Video monitor displays use the RGB model, while hard copy devices produce color output using the CMYK model. Using the 24-bit RGB (Red, Green, Blue) model, you specify a color by setting each amount of red, green, and blue to a value in a range of 256 choices, from zero to 255.

Several color models have been developed over the years to represent color mathematically. The following briefly describes the models:

CMYK Model: The **Cyan**, **Magenta**, **Yellow**, and **Black** (CMYK) color model is less applicable to multimedia production. This model is used in Desktop Publishing printing devices. It is a color subtractive model and is best used in color printing only.

Chromacity Model: The Chromacity (CIE) model describes color value in terms of frequency, saturation, and illuminance. It is a three-dimensional model with two-dimensions, x and y, defining the color, and the third dimension defining the illuminance. It is an additive model since x and y are added to generate different colors. CIE model is more closely resembles how human being perceive color, but certain devices, such as scanners are unable to replicate the process.

HSB (Hue, Saturation, Brightness) and HSL (Hue, Saturation and Lightness) Models: Light sources are described in terms of their dominant frequency (or hue), luminance (or brightness), and purity (or saturation). Complementary color sources are those that combine to produce white light. Saturation is the intensity of color. Lightness or brightness is the percentage of black or white mixed with a color. A lightness of 100 percent will yield a white color. 0 percent is black, the pure color has a 50 percent lightness.

In the HSB (Hue, Saturation, Brightness) and HSL (Hue, Saturation, Lightness) models, you specify hue or color as an angle from 0 to 360 degree on color wheel, and saturation, brightness, and lightness as percentages.

RGB Model: The television, monitor, and camera hardware manufactures developed the RGB model to be used in the design of image capture devices, televisions, and color monitors. The model is additive, in that different intensities of Red, Green, And Blue (RGB) are added to generate various colors. This model is not suitable for image processing.

YIQ, YUV and YCC Models: YIQ and YUV were developed for broadcast TV. Y component represents the luma information, and I and Q represent the chrominance information. They are based on luminance and chromiance expressed as the amplitude of a wave and the phase of the wave relative to some reference. YUV model is subtractive model. YUV model is used in full motion video.

The photo YCC (YCbCr is sometimes abbreviated to YCC) model has been developed by Kodak to provide a definition that enables consistent representation of digital color images from negatives, slides, and other high quality input. YCC is used for photo CD images.

2.12 COLOR PALETTES

Color palettes are mathematical tables that define the color of a pixel displayed on screen. On the Macintosh these tables are called color lookup tables. In Windows, the term palette is used for tables.

Basically, the image stores not color but instead just a set of bytes. A color lookup table is used to store and index the color values of the image. Within the image file, instead of storing the actual RGB values, the Index number of row containing that specific color value is stored.

The color palette provides us various colors that we can use to modify color of objects. We can either use colors already available in the palette or create color of our own choice in the color window.

Thus, we have the following set of standard number of colors that could be deployed for multi-color display purposes:

Color depth	**Colors available**
1-bit per pixel	2 Colors
4-bits per pixel	16 Colors
8-bits per pixel	256 Colors (known as 8-bit color)
16-bits per pixel	65,536 Colors (known as 16-bit color)
24-bits per pixel	16.7 Million Colors (known as 24-bit color or 'True Color' as it almost resembles the actual world, also with millions of colors)

Color depth defines the number of bits required to store the information of each pixel in the image, and in turn determines the total number of possible colors that can be displayed in the image. For example, an 8-bit image requires each pixel to be represented by an 8-bit number and can display a total of 2^8 or 256 colors.

☞ *Color depth is the maximum number of colors that are used in screen to display the image.*

In bitmap images, the chosen color depth will affect the final file size. Color depth is sometimes referred to as *bit depth* because it is directly related to the number of bits used to represent the color of a single pixel in a bitmapped image or video frame buffer. This concept is known as bit per pixel (bpp). High color depth gives a broader range of distinct colors. For example, a 24-bit video adapter has a color depth of 2 to the 24th power about 16.7 million colors.

☞ *The higher the number of colors then the more realistic the image will appear on the screen.*

The total number of colors that could be displayed on the screen, decide the quality of the pictures that will be displayed, to a significant extent. Monitors equipped with a minimum of 8-bit displays (i.e., with 256 colors), give a decent performance and are recommended for all users level multimedia applications. However, professionals start with 16-bit display systems and usually end up with 24-bit colors.

2.13 FILE FORMATS

There are many standards for image or graphic files. But they are all incompatible with each other. Most of the multimedia programs can, however, load or save a wide variety of graphic formats. In this section, we will introduce you to some of the more popular image formats.

2.13.1 BMP

A bitmap is a type of image file format used to store digital images. The BMP format is a commonly use raster graphic format for saving image files. The BMP format stores color data for each pixel in the image without any compression. For example, a 10x10 pixel BMP image will include color data for 100 pixels. This method of storing image information allows for high-quality graphics, but also produces large file sizes.

2.13.2 GIF

GIF stands for *Graphics Interchange Format*. It is another format that is widely used for picture displayed on the World Wide Web. GIF file format is commonly used to display indexed color graphics and images in Hypertext Markup Language (HTML) documents over the World Wide Web. GIF files have **.gif** extension.

GIF image format was created by CompuServe in 1987 to make it possible for images to be viewed while online (i.e. while on the Internet). GIF files format supports only a maximum of 256 colors. Thus, if color depth is not important, one can opt for GIF files. Color depth is the number of bits required to store the information of each pixel in the image, and in turn determines the total number of possible colors that can be displayed in the image. If you want to maintain quality and color of the images, then choose the JPEG format.

2.13.3 JPEG

JPEG (Joint Photographic Experts Group) format is one of the most common graphic file format for Web applications. JPEG format is also used to display photographs and other continuous tone images in Hypertext Markup Language (HTML) documents over the World Wide Web and other online services.

The JPEG format was created by a group of photographic experts to store full-color spectrum, continuous-tone images that is, for images not restricted to dual-tone (black and white) only. This standard allows generation of compressed files for gray-scale images, photographic images, and still video which can be utilized by various multimedia storage and communication applications. JPEG images are of much higher fidelity as well as in higher compressed form than images of GIF format. However, download speed, over the Internet, is much lower with JPEG files. That is, it takes longer time to download graphic files that use JPEG format than those that use GIF format.

☞ *When you create a JPEG image or convert an image into JPEG, you are asked to specify the quality of the image you want. Since the higher quality requires larger memory space, one can make a compromise between image quality and file-size.*

2.13.5 PNG

PNG stands for *Portable Network Graphics* (pronounced as "ping"). It was created as a free-of-cost replacement for GIF. GIF cannot be included in commercial software without paying license fees to the owners. PNG handles 1-to 48-bit images, and is a lossless, well-compressed format like GIF. However, it is still not very popular format.

PNG supports a large set of technical features; including superior lossless compression feature. Compression in PNG is called the ZIP (Zone Information Protocol) method. PNG comes in two formats, PNG-8 and PNG-24.

PNG-8: is similar to the GIF format. The difference is that in the PNG format, images can be stored with a maximum of 256 colors and brilliantly supports 1-bit transparency. It is because of efficient color data saving of PNG format.

PNG-24: comes with 24-bit color support and is much efficient to JPEG because, PNG-24 is a lossless compression format and is more suitable for the creations of larger files in comparison to JPEG. The files of PNG format have *.png* extension.

2.13.6 TIFF

TIFF (Tagged Image File Format) is an industry standard file format designed to represent raster image data generated by scanners, frame grabbers, and paint/photo retouching applications. It is designed to describe raster images in several color spaces (or color models) with different data compression schemes.

The TIFF design is flexible enough to take advantage of the functionality offered by image capture devices. TIFF is extensible, allowing new functionality of imaging devices to be added by enhancing the specification without sacrificing downward compatibility.

TIFF is widely used for transferring bitmap images between application programs. TIFF images have **.tiff** or **.tif** extension. It is used in desktop publishing, faxing, 3-D applications and medical imaging applications. It is a file format designed by Microsoft Corporation of USA.

2.13.7 EXIF

EXIF stands for *Exchangeable Image File Format*, and is a standard for storing interchange information in image files, especially those using JPEG compression. Most digital cameras now use the

EXIF format. The format is part of the DCF (Design Rule for Camera File System) standard created by JEITA (Japan Electronic Information Technology Association) to encourage interoperability between imaging devices.

2.13.8 PS

PS (PostScript) is Adobe Systems' PostScript format. PostScript is not an image format, but it is a page description language, originally conceived so that computers could send very accurate page descriptions to *laser* printers.

PostScript page description language developed by Adobe Systems, is one of the most common formats for exchanging graphics images. EPS (Encapsulated PostScript) files can contain highly detailed, extremely complex graphic in both vector and bitmap form which can be incorporated into many desktop publishing and vector editing packages.

If you are using desktop publishing or page layout software, such as PageMaker, you can import EPS (Encapsulated PostScript) graphics onto your page, position and scale them whatever you like, and print them as part of your page. If you are using vector editing software such as Adobe Illustrator or CorelDRAW, you may be able to open EPS documents and edit the contents as you would do in any other vector format.

You can save black and white or even color pictures as Postscript file. However, postscript file-size is very large and therefore it is not a very efficient format. Moreover, it retains the exact shape of the page when printed on a printer containing Postscript driver.

EPS graphics have a drawback. In most cases, they must be printed to the Postscript printer. When EPS graphics are printed to a non-postscript printer, they usually appear as outlined boxes; because the printer cannot interpret the postscript printing codes, it just prints a box to indicate where the graphic would appear.

2.13.9 PDF

PDF stands for *Portable Document Format*. This format is designed by Adobe. It is a file format that captures all the elements of a printed document as an electronic image. This can then be viewed, navigated, printed or forwarded to someone else. To view and use these files, you need Acrobat Reader software.

PDF files are useful for documents, such as magazine articles, product brochures, etc., in which you want to preserve the appearance of the document. This is because, PDF files are read only and cannot be modified easily by the viewer.

2.14 AUDIO IN MULTIMEDIA

Multimedia technology is multidimensional where audio is one of the dimensions that adds voice, music, and sound capability to applications to enliven and enrich applications with a natural user interface. Early in 1990's, PC applications were only visual, without any audio output capability and an application would utilize speaker output with different tones to alert a user to error conditions or task completion. Today different applications take audio input from musical keyboards, microphones, cassette tape, live music, wave file input, or audio CDs. This is a rich set of inputs and brings professional audio recording to the PC.

Product or business presentations, product catalogs, product brochures, product manuals, installation instructions, maintenance manuals, training manuals, on-line help, and voice mail are some of the many applications that can utilize different audio technologies for voice narration and sound effects with music. In a movie, we can feel the intensity of an actor from voice inflections. Music adds tempo to the scene, and sound effects generate thrills and excitement. All these audio effects in a movie tie us to scenes by captivating us emotionally and logically. Similarly, audio brings excitement thrills and entertainment to multimedia applications, thereby increasing the attention span and achieving better comprehension of the message.

Sound is defined as the auditory sensation produced by the mechanical vibrations of objects. Sound is usually represented as waves, periodic waves corresponding to musical sound and a periodic waves corresponds to noise. *Acoustics* is the branch of science dealing with the study of sound and is concerned with the generation, transmission and reception of sound waves. There are different methods to produce mechanical vibrations, such as beating a drum, ringing a bell and breaking a glass on floor.

During the vibration, pressure variations are created in the air surrounding it. Mechanical vibrations produced by different objects are called *sound waves*. The pattern of the oscillation is called *waveform* (See Figure 2.10).

☞ *Sound waves can travel through various mediums, such as air, water and metals. The speed of sound depends on the medium in which it is travelling.*

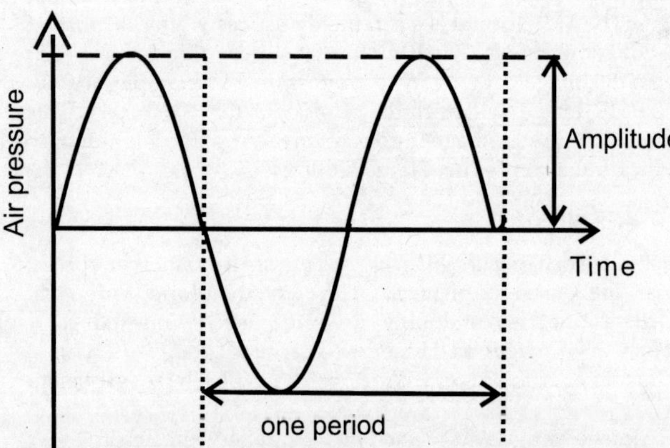

Figure 2.10 Air pressure wave oscillation

The waveform repeats the same shape at regular intervals and this portion is called a *period*. The frequency of a sound is the reciprocal value of the period. It represents the number of periods in a second and is measure in Hertz (Hz) or cycles per second (cps). Multimedia systems typically make use of sound only within the frequency range of human hearing (from 20 Hz to 20 kHz). The sound with in the human hearing range is called *audio* and the waves in this frequency range is called *acoustic* signals. For example, speech is an acoustic signal produced by humans. A sound also has an amplitude. The amplitude of a sound wave is the measure of the displacement of the air pressure wave from its mean, or quiescent state.

2.14.1 Basic Properties of Sound

Two of the basic properties of any sound are its pitch and intensity.

Pitch is the rate at which vibration are produced. It is measured in the number of Hertz (Hz), or cycle per second. One cycle is a complete vibration back and forth. The number of Hz is the frequency of the tone; the higher the frequency, the higher the pitch. In fact, the lowest note on a piano has a frequency of 27 Hz, and the highest note has a frequency a little higher than 4 KHz. Frequency Modulation (FM) radio stations can broadcast notes with frequencies as high as 15 KHz.

The intensity of sound is called its *amplitude*. This intensity determines the sound's volume and depends on the strength of the vibrations producing the sound. A piano string, for example, vibrates gently when the key is struck softly. The string swings back and forth in a narrow arc, and the tone it sends out is soft. If the key is struck more forcefully, however, the string swings back and forth in a wider arc, producing a greater amplitude and a greater volume. The loudness of sounds is measured in decibels (db).

☞ *The amplitude of sound waves corresponds to its loudness, the frequency corresponds to its pitch, and waveform to the quality.*

2.15 CATEGORIES OF SOUND

There are various uses of sound, such as it is used for, communicating, making sound alarms, sound signals and also for creating music. To use similar sound signals at different places, you need to reproduce it. To reproduce sound you need to record it so that the recorded sound can be played back when required. The two categories of sound are:

- Analog sound
- Digital sound

2.15.1 Analog Sound

Any recorded sound is known as *analog sound* and it is represented by the fluctuations in the amplitude. Amplitude of a wave is the maximum displacement of a particle in the path of a wave and is a measure of the peak-to-peak height of the wave. In analog sound recording, the fluctuations in the amplitude are recorded continuously on a recording media. The continuous recording of the amplitude fluctuations on a recording media provides the information necessary for the reproduction of the sound wave. Analog sound systems make use of the recorded sound wave signals to read and reproduce sound wave signals. Figure 2.11 shows the representation of analog sound.

Analog sound is recorded on magnetic tapes, disks and magnetic drums. Analog sound signals need more storage space for recording and storing the sound signals.

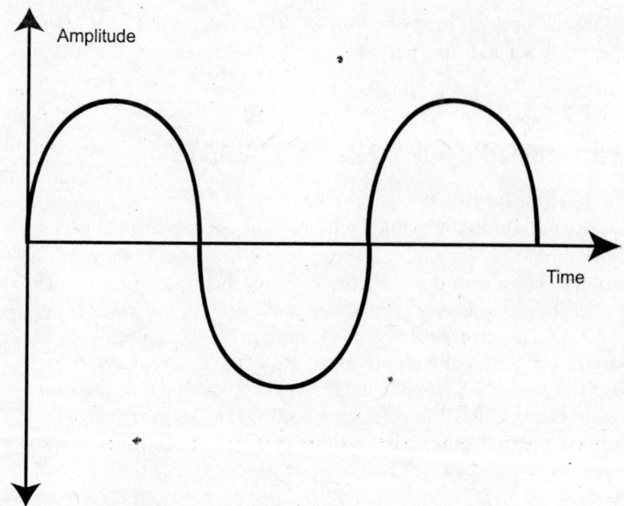

Figure 2.11 Analog representation of sound

2.15.2 Digital Sound

Digital sound is a term applied to sound that has been digitized into binary code. The representation of sound waves in the binary format, which means representation using only zeros and ones, enables the computers to use digital sound. Sound waves are converted to digital form by means of a circuit that assigns a value or binary set of numbers that correspond to the shape of the incoming electrical wave or current. As computer cannot understand analog data. It must first be converted into digital data. When analog sound is converted to digital, it is generally saved as a wave file.

Digital sound files can be processed like any other binary file in the computer. Computers can playback sound files using audio playback software.

Figure 2.12 shows the digital representation of sound.

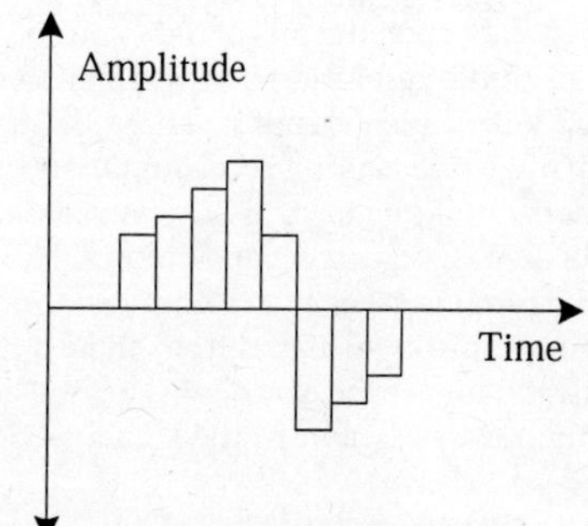

Figure 2.12 Digital representation of sound

☞ *Digital sound or audio is the technology, by which sound signals are represented as a series of binary digital data, i.e., zero and ones, which the computers can understand and comprehend.*

Digital audio is incorporated in to the computer because of its advantages over the analog system. The advantages of the digital sound system over the analog sound system are:

- Protects the sound files from degradation or distortion.
- Enables easy editing as compared to analog audio.
- Produces clear and audible sound after recording the playback.
- Requires less storage space than analog audio.

2.16 FREQUENCY AND BANDWIDTH

Time interval taken between two samples of the original analog data, during digitizing is known as *frequency* or *sampling rate.*

Sound is the varying pressure wave travelling through a medium. When sound travels through air, the atmospheric pressure varies periodically. The number of pressure variation per second is called frequency of sound. The sampling rate is measured in terms of Hertz (Hz), which is the term for cycles per second. A sampling rate of 6000 Hz (6 kHz) implies that the samples are taken better than one with a 4000 Hz sampling rate. The sampling rate determines the frequency at which samples will be drawn for the recording. Sampling at higher rates (such as 44.1 kHz or 22.05 kHz) more accurately captures the high-frequency content of the sound. In other words, the higher sampling rate implies that more samples are taken during the given time interval and the quality of reconstruction is better.

> ☞ *The higher the frequency, the more high pitched a sound is perceived. The sounds produced by drums have much lower frequencies than those produced by a whistle.*

The number of zeroes and ones (bits) required to represent a given signal in digital form is called *bandwidth* or *sampling size.*

Bandwidth is how much data, expressed in bits per second (bps), you can send from one computer to another in a given amount of time. The greater the bandwidth of your connection, the less time you will spend waiting for text, images, sounds and animated illustrations to upload and download from computer-to-computer.

> ☞ *Bandwidth is how much data, expressed in bits per second (bps) you can send from one computer to another in a given amount of time.*

Sampling size depends upon the bits of data your digital sound systems can handle. Audio resolution (such as 8 or 16 bits) determines the accuracy with which a sound can be digitized. Using more bits for the sample size yields a recording that sounds more like its original. For example, by using 8-bits, we have 256 discrete levels which can be used to construct an analog signal. Digitized signal with 16-bit sampling size, which implies 65,536 discrete levels, is much more indistinguishable from the original signal, than its 8 bit. Thus, the higher the sampling size, the better is the reproduction, as the reconstruction of the signal is closer to the original.

- A sampling rate of 4 kHz at 8 bits is considered the minimal acceptable for (mono) voice grade sound. A sampling rate of 8 kHz at 16 bits is required for music quality. For CD-quality stereo sound, the sampling rate is 44.1 kHz at 16 bits. Multi-channel stereophonic sound requires even higher quality.

Aliasing can occur in signals sampled in time, for instance digital audio, and is referred to as temporal aliasing. In digital sound, aliasing is a static distortion resulting from a low sampling rate-below 40 kilohertz (kHz).

An alias occurs when a signal above half the sample rate is allowed into, or created within, a digital system. It's the anti-aliasing filter's job to limit the frequency range of the analog signal prior to (Analog-to-Digital) A-D conversion, so that the maximum frequency does not exceed half the sampling rate.

2.17 AUDIO FILE FORMAT

A sound file's format is simply a recognized methodology for organizing the digitized sound's data bits and bytes into a data file. The structure of the file must be known before data can be saved or later loaded into a computer to be edited or played as sound.

Digital audio files, that have been recorded, are mostly saved in the Windows audio format .wav files. Creative's .voc file for format is also popular in Windows. In Apple Machintoshs, the usual sound format is *.aif.*

There are various types of sound files to support different types of playback requirements. Different types of software are used to playback different kinds of sound files. Types of sound files are discussed in following sections.

2.17.1 AIFF

AIFF (Audio Interchange File Format) is a proprietary Audio Format developed by Apple. This format can store monaural or multichannel sampled sounds in a range of sample rates and sample resolutions. The extension for this file type is *.aif* and *.ief* when it is used on a PC. An AIFF file contains the raw audio data, channel information (monophoic or stereophonic), bit depth, sample rate and application-specific data areas. The application-specific data areas let different applications add information to the file header that remains there even if the file is opened and processed by another application. For example, a file could retain information about selected regions of the audio data used for recalling zoom level not used by other applications.

> ☞ *The AIFF format does not support data compression so AIFF files tend to be large. However, there is another format called AIFF-Compressed file format.*

2.17.2 MIDI

MIDI refers to Musical Instrument Digital Interface. In computer science, it is a serial interface standard that allows for the connection of music synthesizers, musical instruments and computers.

Synthesizers are electronic instruments which allow us to generate digital samples of sound of various instruments synthetically, i.e., without the actual instrument being present. The sound samples can be modulated through appropriate hardware to change their loudness, pitch, etc.

MIDI sound file stores a list of events that describe a specific step, which is used by a play back device or sound card to generate the sound specified by the events in the MIDI file. The playback device or the sound cards have predefined tasks of generating sound for each step in the events of the MIDI sound file. MIDI sound files are smaller than digital audio files.

The MIDI is partly based on hardware and partly on a description of the way in which music and sound are encoded and communicated between MIDI devices. The hardware portion of the standard defines different types of input/output channels, called MIDI ports. It also specifies a particular type of cable (MIDI cable) that plugs into the ports. The three types of ports defined by the MIDI specification are as follows:

(a) **MIDI In**: It is used for receiving a MIDI message. Synthesizer or other MIDI device receives MIDI messages via its MIDI In port.

(b) **MIDI Out**: It is used to sending a message to other devices. MIDI devices send their own messages to other devices via the MIDI Out port.

(c) **MIDI Thru**: Message is sent and received through the MIDI Thru port. It also echoes the message back out through the MIDI Thru port so that other devices can receive them.

The information transmitted between MIDI devices is in a form called a MIDI message, which encodes aspects of sound such as pitch and volume as 8-bit bytes of digital information. MIDI devices can be used for creating, recording and playing back music. Using MIDI, synthesizers and sequences one can communicate with each other, either keeping time or acutely controlling the music created by other connected equipment.

☞ *MIDI files do not store the actual sound, but rather instructions that enable devices called synthesizers to reproduce the sounds or music. MIDI files are much smaller than WAV files, but the quality of the sound reproduction is not nearly as good.*

2.17.3 WAV

A Wav (Wave Form) file is an audio file format, developed jointly by Microsoft and IBM (International Business Machines). WAV sound files end with a *.wav* extension. It has became a standard PC audio file format that can be played by nearly all Windows applications that support sound. WAV files store actual sounds, much as music CDs and tapes do. WAV files can be large and may require compression. In addition, to the uncompressed raw audio data, the WAV file format stores information about the file's number of traces (mono or stereo), sample rate and bit depth.

We can digitize sound from a microphone, a synthesizer, existing tape recordings, live radio and television broadcasts, popular CDs and from favorite long playing recordings and for that matter we can digitize sounds from any source. Digitized sound is sampled sound. The sound is sampled at regular intervals and each sample of the sound is stored as digital information in bit and bytes. The frequency at which the sound is sampled is called sampling rate, and is usually in the range 11 kHz-44 kHz. The amount of information stored at each sample point is the sample size, which is called *resolution*. Each discrete sample is stored either as 8 or 16 bits of data. The larger the sample size, the better the data describes the recorded sound.

☞ *WAV file format is the standard file format to store digital audio data on Windows platform. This sound file format is supported by most of the audio playback software.*

2.17.4 MP3

MP3 (Moving Pictures Expert Group Layer–3) is a file format for storing compressed digital audio on computers. By using compression, MP3 files take up only one-tenth of the space of uncompressed high-quality audio.

MP3 format gets its name from having crated under the auspices of MPEG (Moving Picture Experts Group). It is a working group of the International Internet Standards Organization (ISO) and the International Engineering Consortium (IEC) who developed International standards for compression, decompression, processing and codded representation of moving pictures, audio and their combination. MP3 files generally end with extension *.mp3*. These files can be download from a number of Websites. Winamp (PC) MacAmp (Mac) and mpg123 (UNIX) are popular MP3 players.

To create a MP3 file, use a program called a *ripper* to get a selection from a CD onto hard disk and another program called an *encoder* to convert the selection to an MP3 file.

☞ *MP3 sound files are compressed audio files that maintains their original sound quality and require less storage space. MP3 is a popular format for storing and listening music on the World Wide Web.*

2.17.5 WMA

WMA stands for Windows Media Audio. WMA, an audio format owned by Microsoft, is a part of Microsoft's Windows Media technology, which includes Microsoft's Digital Rights Management tools, Windows Media Video encoding technology and Windows Media Audio encoding technology.

2.17.6 ASF

Microsoft's ASF (Advanced Streaming Format) is an extensible file format designed to store synchronized multimedia data. It supports data delivery over a wide variety of networks and protocols while still proving suitable for local playback. The explicit goal of ASF is to provide a basis for industry-wise multimedia interoperability. Each ASF file is composed of one or more media streams. The file header specifies the properties of the entire file, along with stream-specific properties. Multimedia data, stored after the file header, references a particular media stream number to indicate its type and purpose. The delivery and presentation of all media stream data is synchronized to a common time-line. ASF's functionality is similar to the one provided by Apple's QuickTime.

2.17.7 RM

RM (Real Media) audio files are streaming audio files that can be played at the same time as they are being downloaded. Streaming audio files can start the playback of the audio when sufficient data for playback has been downloaded. The file extensions used by these files is *.ram*.

2.17.8 AVI

AVI (Audio Video Interleaved) is a multimedia file format that can be used for storing sound and moving pictures in Resource Interchange File Format (RIFF) developed by Microsoft. As AVI combines audio and video into a single frame or track, it saves valuable disk space and keeps audio in synchronization with the corresponding video. AVI files are widely supported by media player and video production programs.

2.18 VIDEO IN MULTIMEDIA

Video is the technology for electronically capturing, recording, processing, storing, transmitting, and reconstructing a sequence of still images representing scenes in motion. Full motion video consists of photographic detailed recording of motion. Like audio, video can also be analog or digital. Digital video is a term which refers to moving pictures that are stored on a computer hard disk for editing or playback. Video deals with the recording of a real life event produced by a device, such as digital video recorder. Video data also requires large storage space and needs to meet the real time constraints on retrieval, delivery, and display. Video is an important component of multimedia because it is very useful for illustrating concepts that involve movement.

Today, video places the highest performance demand on any computer system and the digital has replaced analog as the method of choice for making video for multimedia. Video is incorporated into multimedia projects, for many reasons.

- The project has certain relevant sequences/material that can be videographed.
- The project has certain sequences/material that cannot be produced with the help of animation.
- The project has to be made more attractive with video.
- The project has live lectures or demonstration or other pre recorded material to be incorporated.

☞ *Computer video deals with the recording and display of sequence of images.*

2.18.1 Frame Rate

Video is a combination of image and audio. It consists of a set of still images called *frames* displayed to the user one after another at a specific speed known as *frame rate*. Frame rate is the number of frames displayed each second. A television, however, does not deal with video in terms of frames. Instead, it displays a video using half-frames, called *fields*. Each frame contains exactly two fields. One field is made up of the odd horizontal lines in a frame. This is called the *odd field* or the top field since it contains the top line of the image. The other field is made up of the even horizontal lines in a frame. This is called the even field or bottom field. Since there are two fields in every frame, a television actually updates the display at 60 fields per second. Each field is displayed $1/60^{th}$ of a second after the preceding field.

2.18.2 Resolution

The visual resolution of a video signal or display is the amount of detail that can be seen. This is different from the resolution format of a signal or display. For example, in a computer application, a XGA (extended Graphics Array) signal has a format resolution of 1024 horizontal pixels and 768 vertical pixels (lines), and is the implied visual resolution. However, if the signal or display has any limitations that can degrade the performance, it may not be possible to actually view all of this detail.

2.18.3 Visual Resolution in Television Systems

Visual resolution in television systems is accurately specified in terms of a parameter called "TV lines." This parameter is typically used to indicate horizontal resolution, but the same technique can be used for vertical resolution. TV lines are determined by viewing a test pattern consisting of alternating black and white lines that are placed closer and closer together. The pair of lines with the closest spacing that can be distinguished as separate lines determines the resolution. The lines that can be extrapolated across the screen to a width equal to one picture height are the TV lines extrapolated across the screen to a width equal to one picture height are the TV lines of resolution.

2.18.4 Visual Resolution in Computer Systems

Computer resolution formats are typically specified by the visible number of pixels in the horizontal and vertical dimensions. For example, a VGA (Video Graphics Adapter) format signal has 640 visible pixels in the horizontal direction and 480 visible pixels in the vertical direction. An XGA format signal has 1024 visible pixels in the horizontal direction and 768 visible pixels in the vertical direction. In a well-designed computer system that is specified to reach a given maximum format resolution, all of the signal processing would be designed such that the visual resolution would be at least as good as the format resolution. If any circuit in the chain does not have the required performance, the visual resolution will be less than the format resolution.

2.18.5 Measuring Frame Size and Resolution

The individual video images that make up a moving sequence is called *frames*. Video formats and individual clips are typically described in term of the resolution of individual frames and the frame rate at which they are played.

Several attributes of frame size are important when editing video digitally: pixel (picture element) and frame aspect ratio, clip resolution, project frame size, and bit depth. A pixel is the smallest unit that can be used to create a picture. You cannot accurately display anything smaller than a pixel. Resolution is the dimension of an image, in pixels, typically expressed as the number of horizontal pixels across and the number of vertical pixel down.

2.18.6 Aspect ratio

The rectangle shape of an image or frame, expressed as the width-to-height ratio is called aspect ratio. For example, the frame aspect ratio of NTSC (National Television System Committee) video is 4:3, whereas some motion picture frame sizes use the more elongated aspect ratio of 16:9 (See Figure 2.13).

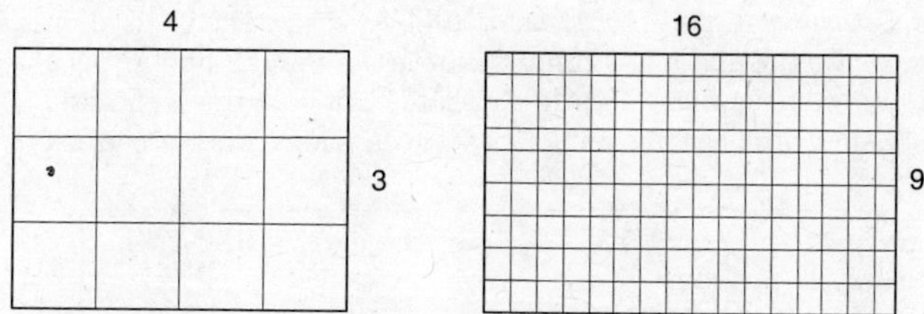

Figure 2.13 A frame using a 4:3 aspect ratio and a frame using the wider 16:9 aspect ratio

2.18.7 Frame Size

In Adobe Premiere, you can specify a frame size for playing back video from the Timeline, and if necessary, for exporting video to a file. Frame size is expressed by the horizontal and vertical dimensions of a frame. For example, 640 by 480 pixels. In digital video editing, frame size is also referred to as resolution. In general, higher resolution preserves more image detail and requires more memory to edit. As you increase frame dimensions, you increase the number of pixels Premiere must process and store for each frame, so it is important to know how much resolution your final video format requires. For example, a 640 by 480 pixel NTSC frame contains 307,200 pixels, while a 720 by 576 PAL (Phase Alternating Line) image contains 349,920 pixels. If you specify too low a resolution, the picture will look coarse. Specifying very high resolution will use more memory than necessary.

2.18.8 Interlaced

Computer monitors and television screens do not display video in the same fashion. A computer monitor updates the image only once for each frame of video. Because of this, both fields that make up a video frame are shown simultaneously. Thus, a computer monitor displays video at 30 fps. This is called a *progressive scan display*.

A television, on other hand, updates each field of a video frame separately. Because of this, the television must update its display twice to show a complete frame. It first updates the odd field, and $1/60^{th}$ of a second later it updates the even field. It continues to alternate between the odd and lines 60 times each second. Thus, a television displays video at 60 fields per second. This is called an *interlaced display*.

The field-based nature of video also allows a video to be recorded in one of the two ways. In the first method, called progressive video, the two fields that make up a frame represent the same instant in time. This means that each entire frame also represents a single instant in time. This is the preferred format for watching video on a computer screen because unlike a television, a computer monitor displays both fields of a frame at the same time.

Interlaced and progressive types of scanning systems differ in the technique used to "paint" the picture on the screen. Television signals and compatible displays are typically interlaced, and computer signals and compatible displays are typically progressive (non-interlaced). These two formats are incompatible with each other; one would need to be converted to the other before any common processing could be done.

2.18.9 Interlaced and non-interlaced Video

A picture on a television or computer monitor consists of horizontal lines (See Figure 2.14). There is more than one way to display those lines. Most personal computers display using *progressive scan* (or non-interlaced) display, in which all lines in a frame are displayed in one pass from top to bottom before the next frame appears. Television standards such as NTSC, PAL, and SECAM standards are interlaced, where each frame is divided into two fields. Each field contains every other horizontal line in the frame. A TV displays the first field of alternating lines over the entire screen, and then displays the second field to fill in the alternating gaps left by the first field. One NTSC video frame, displayed approximately every $1/30^{th}$ of a second, contains two interlaced fields, displayed approximately every $1/60^{th}$ of a second each. PAL and SECAM video frames display at 1/25 of a second and contain two interlaced fields displayed every $1/50^{th}$ of a second each. The field that contains the top-most scan line in the frame is called the *upper field*, and the one field is called the *lower field*.

2.19 COLOR PLANES

A color space has a number of planes that define the colors. The most obvious color space is RGB, whereby the luminance (brightness) of the red, green and blue color components are stored separately in each plane. Each industry that uses color employs the most suitable color model. For example, the RGB color model is used in computer graphics, YUV or YCbCr (Luminance; Chroma:Blue; Chroma:Red) is used in video systems.

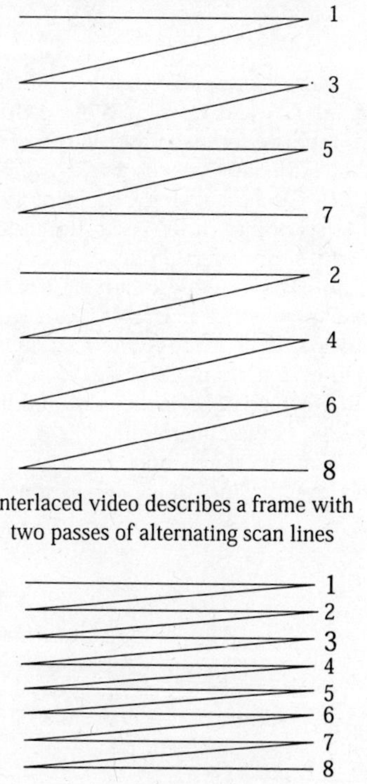

Figure 2.14 Interlaced and progressive scan

2.19.1 YCBCR

The YCbCr color space is widely used for digital video. YCbCr is a scaled and offset version of the YUV color space. In this format, luminance information is stored as a single component (Y), and chrominance information is stored as two color-difference components (Cb and Cr). Cb represents the difference between the blue component and a reference value. Cr represents the difference between the red component and a reference value.

2.19.2 YUV

The YUV color model is the basic color model used in analog color TV broadcasting. Initially YUV is the re-coding of RGB for transmission efficiency (minimizing bandwidth) and for downward compatibility with black-and white television. The YUV color space is "derived" from the RGB space. YUV is actually the name of the color space that is common to all "YUV" pixel formats. Contrary to RGB formats (Red-Green-Blue), YUV colors are represented with one "luminance" component called Y (equivalent to grey scale) and two "chrominance" components, called U (blue projection) and V (red projection), respectively. The luminance can be computed as a weighted sum of red, green and blue components; the color difference, or chrominance, components are formed by subtracting luminance from blue and from red.

2.20 VIDEO BROADCAST STANDARD

There are three broadcast, video standards and recording formats in use, namely, NTSC, PAL and SECAM.

2.20.1 NTSC

National Television Standard Systems Committee (NTSC) is a broadcast standard used in USA and in some other countries. These standards define a method for encoding information into the electronic signal that ultimately creates a television picture. As specified by the NTSC standard, a single frame of video is made up of 525 horizontal scan lines drawn onto the inside face of a phosphor-coated picture tube every $1/30^{th}$ of a second by a fast-moving electron beam. The drawing occurs so fast that our eye perceives the image as stable. The electronic beam actually makes two passes as it draws a single video frame, first laying down all the odd-numbered lines. Each of these passes (which happen at a rate of 60 Hz) paints a field. The process of building a single frame from two fields is called *interlacing*. It is a technique that helps to prevent flicker on television screens. Remember that computer monitors draw the lines of an entire frame in one scan, without interlacing.

2.20.2 PAL

The *Phase Alternate Line* (PAL) is broadcast video standard used in India and some other countries. PAL is an integrated method of adding color to a black and white television signal that paints 625 lines at a frame rate of 25 frames per second. Like NTSC, the even and odd lines are interlaced, each field taking $1/50^{th}$ of a second to draw (50 Hz).

2.20.3 SECAM

The *Sequential Color and Memory* (SECAM) system is used in France, Russia, and a few other countries. Although SECAM is a 625-line, 50 Hz system. It differs greatly from both the NTSC and the PAL color systems in its basic technology and broadcast method.

Standards → Features ↓	**NTSC**	**PAL**	**SECAM**
Scanlines/frames	525	625	625
Scanning technique	interlaced	interlaced	interlaced
Refresh rate (frames/second)	29:97	25	25
Aspect ratio	4:3	4:3	4:3
Transmission	Analog	Analog	Analog
Modulation	AM	AM	FM
Used in	US, Japan, and some Asian countries	India and Western Europe (except France)	France, Eastern, Europe, Russia and Middle East

Figure 2.15 Features of the three broadcast TV Standards

In SECAM, the chrominance signal is transmitted using a frequency modulated color sub-carrier, transmitting one of the color difference signals on every other scanline, and the other color difference signals on alternate scanlines. It also has better color resolution than NTSC. A summary of the characteristic features of the three analog TV signal standards is given in Figure 2.15. Two major broadcasting systems that have evolved for commercial use out of this effort are as follows:

(a) MUSE (Multiple SubNyquist Sampling Encoding)
(b) HD-MAC (High Definition Multiple Analog Components)

The main features of these two systems are given in Figure 2.16. As shown in Figure, the (scanning/frame and refresh rate) are different for the two systems.

Standards → Features ↓	**MUSE**	**HD-MAC**
Scanlines/frame	1125	1250
Refresh rate (frame/second)	60	50
Transmission	Analog	Analog
Modulation	FM	FM
Media	Broadcasting Satellite	Broadcasting Satellite
Used in	Japan	Europe

Figure 2.16 Features of the Two HDTV Standards

2.20.4 HD (*High Definition*) Video

High Definition (HD) video is video of higher resolution than as defined in is standard definition. While there is no specific meaning for high-definition, generally any video image with more than 480 horizontal lines. HDTV provides a significant higher resolution than traditional format in a 16:9 aspect ratio. This aspect ratio allows the viewing of Cinemascope and Panavision movies.

2.20.5 3D TV

3D TV (Three Dimensional Television) is an emerging technology that allows consumers to enjoy three-dimensional movies, television programs and video games in their homes.
There are actually three different types of 3D TV technology: passive, active, and autostereoscopic (more commonly known as glasses-free 3D TV).

2.21 VIDEO REPRESENTATION

File Format, in computer science, is the structure of a file that defines the way through which it is stored on the hard disk and laid out on the screen or taken as printout print. The format can be fairly simple and common (files stored as plain ASCII (American Standard Code for Information Interchange) text or it can be quite complex and may include various types of control instructions and codes used by programs and by printers and other devices. Examples include RTF (Rich Text Format), DCA (Document Content Architecture), PICT, DIF (Data Interchange Format), DXF (Drawing Exchange Format), TIFF (Tagged Image File Format), and EPSF (Encapsulated PostScript Format).

As with audio, in the early days of the Web, adding movie/video to a Web page meant using one of the currently available movie/video formats (such as QuickTime or AVI) and linking it to a page for download.

The evolution of streaming media has changed that, and now adding movie/video content like movie trailers, news broadcasts, even live programming to a Website is much more practical and widespread.

While downloading files from the Web, you will undoubtedly encounter many different types of file formats. The way to identify the file type is by looking at its extension, typically expressed as a dot followed by 2 to 4 letters (.xxx). You will need to identify the file type to know whether it will work on your computer, and whether you will need a particular type of software to decompress, play, or view it. Some of the movie/video file formats are as follows:

(a) `.avi`: The standard movie/video format for Windows.
(b) `.mpg/mpeg`: A standard movie format for saving movies on the Internet, using the MPEG (Motion Picture Expert Group) compression scheme.
(c) `.mov`: The common format for QuickTime movies, the Macintosh native movie platform.

2.21.1 AVI File Format

Audio Video Interleave (AVI) format is the standard Windows format for audio/video data. This format exports a movie as a Windows video, but discards any interactivity. Because, AVI is a bitmap-based format, movies that contains long or high-resolution animations can quickly become very large in a file size.

☞ *AVI is a good format for opening a Flash animation in a video-editing application.*

An AVI file is a sound and motion picture file that requires a special player software that may be included with your Web browser, such as Internet Explorer version 5.0 and above. However, some other browsers may require downloading of facilities for reading AVI files.

☞ *AVI is a raster-based video format that will transfer nicely into a video editing application.*

2.21.2 MPEG File Format

MPEG is the acronym for Moving Pictures Experts Group, a committee that developed the MPEG standard. It is a set of specifications for compressing and playing back full-motion video, including movies and video clips. MPEG rules cover both encoding, for storage on disk and decoding, for digital playback. Viewing a MPEG video on a microcomputer requires a MPEG decoder, which can be hardware, software, or a combination of the two.

MPEG achieves high compression rate by storing only the changes from one frame to another, instead of each entire frame. Although MPEG is a lossy compression method, the loss of video data is generally imperceptible to human eye. For this reason, MPEG generally produces better-quality video than competing formats, such as AVI and QuickTime.

For example MPEG-1, MPEG-2, MPEG-4 and MPEG-7 and MPEG-21. MPEG is a family of popular multimedia file formats and associated compression schemes defined by the Moving Pictures Expert Group. MPEG-1 video was designed for use on CD-ROMs and provides picture quality somewhat comparable to VHS. MPEG-2 video was designed for use on DVD (Digital Versatile/Video Disk), and can provide high quality full screen video with smaller file sizes.

☞ *MP3 is an audio file format, especially popular for downloading songs over the Web. It uses lossy compression to significantly reduce file size, but often with little perceptible loss in sound quality.*

2.21.3 SWF File Format

Macromedia Flash (SWF or Shock Wave File) is a file format of the Macromedia Flash Player for creating and displaying Interactive vector-based images and animated Web graphics. Macromedia Flash files are very compact and of high quality, making them ideal for use on the Web. The SWF file format was designed as a very efficient delivery format and not as a format for exchanging graphics between graphics editors. It was designed to meet the following goals:

(a) **On-screen Display:** The format is primarily intended for on-screen display. Therefore, it supports anti-aliasing, fast rendering to a bitmap of any color format, animation and interactive buttons.

(c) **Network Delivery:** The files can be delivered over a network with limited and unpredictable bandwidth. The files are compressed to be small and support incremental rendering through streaming.

(d) **Simplicity:** The format is so simple that the user has to depend upon only a very limited set of operating system functionalities.

(e) **File Independence:** Files can be displayed without any dependence on external resources, such as fonts.

(f) **Scalability:** Different computers have different monitor resolutions and bit depths. Files work well on limited hardware, while taking advantage of more expensive hardware when it is available.

(g) **Speed:** The files are designed to be rendered very quickly with high quality of graphics.

☞ *Flash (SWF) files cannot be imported into CorelDRAW. You can, however, link, embed, export, and publish Macromedia Flash files to the Web.*

The SWF format for images on the Internet has several valuable advantages over other format types. Some of these advantages include:

(a) Since it has good compression, the Web pages can be loaded extremely fast.

(b) It can also support embedded forms, script, user interface components and XML (eXtensible Markup Language) feeds.

(c) It allows vibrant animations and sounds in its presentation.

2.21.4 MOV File Format

The QuickTime (MOV or Movie) file format is used for video and animation. QuickTime files run on all Macintosh computers and on Windows based computers that have a QuickTime driver installed.

QuickTime is a file format for storing and playing back movies with sound. QuickTime files usually appear with the `.MOV` extension in Windows. With its high compression, Quick Time 4.0 was the first version to fully support streaming audio and video. The QuickTime 5 also plays MP3s, MIDIs and WAV files. Because it can handle multiple audio, video and graphic file formats, QuickTime is popular for multimedia development.

☞ *MOV files are animation files that support 24-bit and 8-bit color. Multiple tracks are not supported in MOV files.*

2.21.5 DAT File Format

DAT file format is not a video file format, rather video data given an alternative extension. DAT Files containing generic input or output. For example, if you open up a VCD (Video Compact Disk) and take a look at its contents, you will notice there are several folders is there and not one single `.mpg` file. The files have either a VCD or DAT extension. The actual videos you burned are not the VCD files but the DAT files. With a VCD, the video files are converted to DAT files named sequentially in the following format - AVSEQ01.DAT, AVSEQ02.DAT, AVSEQ03.DAT, etc. You will find these DAT files in the folder MPEGAV on the CD. Thus, DAT file can be played from your hard drive, just like regular video files, except that you will have to choose **Open With** to associate the DAT file with Windows Media Player 7 and up, which will recognize it as a valid video file.

2.21.6 MPEG

MPEG standards have been developed by the moving picture experts group convened by the International Standard Organization (ISO) and the International Electro technical commission to create standards for digital representation of moving pictures and associated audio and other data.

MPEG–1

MPEG–1 specification was released in 1992. In this you can deliver 1.2 Mbps of video and 250 kbps of two channel stereo audio using CD-ROM technology.

The MPEG-1 standard was developed in response to industry needs for an efficient way of storing and retrieving video information on digital storage media. One such inexpensive medium is the CD-ROM (Compact Disk Read Only Memory), other storage and transmission media can include DAT, Winchester disk, optical disk, ISDN (Integrated Services Digital Network) and LAN (Local Area Network). In fact, the data rate is variable and all decoders must be able to decode at rates up to 1.856 mb/s. The video is strictly progressive (i.e., non interlaced) and picture quality is equivalent to VHS (Video Home System).

MPEG–2

MPEG–2 specifications was released in 1994. It is completely different system from MPEG–1, requires higher data rates (3 to 15 mbps) but delivers higher image resolution, picture quality, interlaced video formats and interlaced video formats and interlaced video formats. MPEG-2 is the video compression standard required for Digital Television (DTV) and making DVDs.

The MPEG-2 standard was developed to provide the capability of compressing, coding, and transmitting high quality, multichannel, multimedia signals over broad-band networks. Since MPEG-2 was designed mainly as a transmission standard, it supports a variety of packet format and provide error correction capability that is suitable for transmission over cable and satellite links.

MPEG–4

MPEG–4 specification was released in 1998 and 1999. It provides a content based method for assimilating multimedia element. It offers not only indexing, hyperlinking, querying, browsing uploading, downloading, and deleting functions but also "hybrid natural and synthetic data coding". With MPEG–4, multiple views, layers, and multiple sound tracks of a scene, as well as stereoscopic and 3D views are available, making virtual reality workable.

Recently, the focus of video coding has shifted to object based coding at bit rates of 8 Kb/s or lower and 1 Mb/s or higher. Key aspects of this newly proposed MPEG-4 standard include independent coding of objects in a picture frame, the ability to interactively composite these objects into a scene at the display; the ability to combine graphics, animated objects in the scene, and the ability to transmit scenes in higher dimensionality formats (e.g. 3D). Also, inherent in the MPEG-4 standard is the concept of video scalability, both in the temporal and spatial domains, in order to effectively control the video bit rate at the transmitter, in the network, and at the receiver so as to match the available transmission and processing resources.

> ☞ *MPEG-4 builds on the combines elements from three fields– digital television interactive graphics, and the World Wide Web. It aims to provide a merging of the production, distribution, and display elements of these three fields.*

MPEG–21

MPEG–21 is an audio/video specification providing an Intellectual Property Management and Production (IPMP) system. The idea here is that when you get what is called a digital item, e.g. an image on the Web appears where you right-click to download that the file will let you know where to go to find who holds the rights to it.

2.21.7 RealVideo (.rm)

RealVideo is usually paired with RealAudio and packaged in a RealMedia (.rm) container. RealMedia is suitable for use as a streaming media format, that is one which is viewed while it is being sent over the network. Streaming video can be used to watch live television, since it does not require downloading the entire video in advance. Player for RealVideo is RealNetworks RealPlayer SP and is available for various platforms including Windows, Macintosh, and Linux.

2.22 ANALOG AND DIGITAL VIDEO

Analog Video: Video in which all the information representing images is in a continuous scale electrical signal for both amplitude and time is called *analog video*. Analog video exists on videotape (i.e., VHS, 3/4" S-VHS, Beta-SP formats) because the signal bears an exact, continuous relationship to the original information (it is analogous to the original).

Analog signals suffer because of their need to be amplified. Each time a video tape is copied, the analog signal must be amplified. This amplification process injects a certain amount of noise or graininess into the image (with audio tape it is called "hiss") and this noise occurs every time a copy is made. So, a copy of a copy suffers greatly because of the need to amplify the signal each time a copy is made. This is referred to as *generational loss*.

Analog video records 30 individual still images on tape each second. Playing these images back in succession helps create the illusion of movement.

Analog signals are continuous in nature and the size of video image is measured in horizontal scan lines and vertical lines of resolution for analog video.

Digital Video: Video where all the information representing images is in some kind of computer data form, which can be manipulated and displayed by a computer is called *digital video*. Digital video uses binary numbers (strings of zeros and ones) to represent each pixel of each frame. Since zeros and ones are the equivalent to "on" and "off" electrical states.

Setting up a production environment for making digital video, requires hardware that meets minimum specifications for processing speed, data transfer, and storage. A digital video architecture is made up of a format for encoding and playing back video files by a computer and includes a player that can recognize and play files created for that format. The major digital video architecture are Apple's Quick Time, Microsoft's windows media format and real network's real media.

Digital signals are discontinuous by nature and the size of video image is measured in pixels for digital video.

Advantages of digital representation of a video are given as under:

(a) Digital representation of video permits storing video on digital devices or in memory, so that it is easily processed and integrated into various multimedia applications.

(b) Direct access of digital video makes non-linear video editing simple.

(c) Repeated recording of digital video is possible without degradation of image quality.

(d) Compression helps to reduce the size of digital video files to great extent which required a lower bit-rate to transfer them over communication channels.

2.23 TYPES OF VIDEO SIGNALS

Video signals can be organized in three different ways:

(a) ***Component Video:*** Higher end video systems, such as studios make use of three separate video signals for the red, green and blue image planes. This is referred to as *component video*. This kind of system has three wires (and connectors) connecting the camera or other devices to TV or monitor. For any color separation scheme, component video gives the best color reproduction since there is no 'cross-talk' between the three different channels.

(b) ***Composite Video:*** Composite video is also called CVBS (Color Video Baseband Signal or Color, Video, Blanking and Sync), contains luminance (intensity), chrominance (color), sync information in one signal. This is the type of signal used by broadcast color TV's and it is downward compatible with black and white TV.

(c) ***S-Video:*** S-Video is also called Separated Video or Super Video. S-Video uses two wires: one for luminance (intensity) and another for chrominance (color) signal. Thus, luminance and chrominance signals are transferred separately, resulting in the greater image quality. The special S-Video connector also carries left and right signals for stereo.

2.24 ANIMATION IN MULTIMEDIA

Animation is one of the most dynamic form of multimedia. Unlike graphics, animations can provide dynamic movements to the objects. For example, to show a bird flying in the air, all that graphics can provide is a digital photograph of the same. However, with animations, we could actually view the bird flying in the monitor of the PC.

> ☞ *Animation is a special effect that creates the illusion of movement with successive images.*

An animation is created by recording a series of still images of drawings, objects, people, etc., in various positions of incremental movement. It may not be necessary to move the objects to create the illusion of movement – colors and the background can be changed from frame-to-frame so that there is a perception of a moving object. There are many ways to achieve varying levels of animation. The animation when played does not appear as static images but combine to produce the illusion of unbroken motion.

Animation consists of a series of drawings or photographs on paper that are viewed with a mechanical device or by flipping through a hand-held sequence of images. For example, a pad of paper containing drawings of a boy raising his hands as shown in Figure 2.17), can be used to create an animated drawing.

Figure 2.17 Still images which when flipped through in front of our eyes, at a fast rate, create a motion picture

2.24.1 Keyframes and Tweening

Each still image in a motion picture is known as a *frame*. The number of frames that must be flipped through per second must be such that the human eye does not recognize that the movie is actually a series of individual images. On an average, a film animator must make twenty-four images for each second of animation.

Keyframes are the first and the last frame of an action. Tweening, (in-betweening), is the process of generating intermediate frames between two images to give the appearance that the first image evolves smoothly into the second image. Tweening is a key process in all types of animation, including computer animation. For example, for showing the motion of the square moving from lower left corner to the upper right corner of the frame, the initial and final positions provide the keyframes, while the middle frames are the intermediate frames. The total number of intermediate frames determines the smoothness or quality of the motion. Sophisticated animation software enables you to identify specific objects in an image and define how they should move and change during the tweening process.

One can even use one image for two or three frames of film in a row, rather than using each image only once.

There are many ways of creating an animation, depending on the materials used. The material can be one of the following two types:

(a) Flat (such as drawings or cut-out pieces of paper)
(b) Dimensional (such as clay, puppets, household objects, or even people)

2.24.2 Types of Animation

There are many different types of animation, all useful in different instances. However two basic types of animations are:

1) Frame-based animation
2) Cast-based animation

Frame-Based Animation

Frame-based animation is the simpler of the animation techniques. It involves simulating movement by displaying a sequence of static frames. A movie is a perfect example of frame-based animation. Each frame of the film is a frame of animation. When the frames are shown in rapid succession, they create the illusion of movement. In frame-based animation, there is no concept of an object distinguishable from the background; everything is reproduced on each frame. This is an important point, because it distinguishes frame-based animation from cast-based animation.

Cast-Based Animation

Cast-based animation, which is also called sprite or path animation, is a very popular form of animation and has seen a lot of usage in games. Cast-based animation involves objects that move independently of the background. In this case, an object is something that logically can be thought of as a separate entity from the background of an image. For example, in the animation of a forest, the trees might be part of the background, but a deer would be a separate object moving independently of the background.

Each object in a cast-based animation is referred to as a sprite, and can have a changing position. Almost every video game uses sprites to some degree.

Sprites generally are assigned a position and a velocity, which determine how they move.

2.24.3 Fundamental Principles of Animation

Timing

Timing is the essence of animation. The speed at which something moves, gives a sense of what the object is, the weight of an object, and why it is moving. Something like an eye blink can be fast or slow. If it is fast, a character will seem alert and awake. If it slow the character may seem tired and lethargic.

Ease In and Out (or Slow In and Out)

Ease in and out has to do gradually causing an object to accelerate, or come to rest, from a pose. An object or limb may slow down as it approaches a pose (Ease In) or gradually start to move from rest (Ease Out).

For example, a bounching ball tends to have a lot of ease in and out when at the top of its bounce. As it goes up, gravity affects it and slows down (Ease In), then it starts its downward motion more and more rapidly (Ease Out), until it hits the ground.

Arcs

In the real world, almost all action moves in an arc. When creating animation one should try to have motion follow curved paths rather than linear ones. It is very seldom that a character or part of a character moves in a straight line. Even gross body movements when you walk somewhere tend not be perfectly straight. When a hand/arm reaches out to reach something, it tends to move in an arc as shown in Figure 2.18, for example kicking a ball.

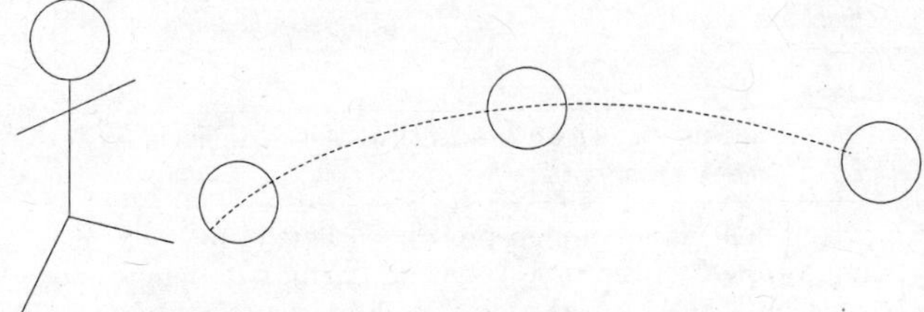

Figure 2.18 Interlaced and progressive scan

Anticipation

Action in animation usually occurs in three sections. The setup for the motion, the actual action and then follow-through of the action. The first part is known as *anticipation*. In some cases anticipation is needed physically. For example, before you can throw a ball you must first swing your arm backwards. The backwards motion is the anticipation, the throw itself is the motion.

Exaggeration

Exaggeration is used to accent an action. It should be used in a careful and balanced manner, not arbitrarily. Find out what the desired goal of an action or sequence is and what sections need to be exaggerated. Exaggerating the important elements makes them stand out and brings them closer to the viewer. The result will be that the animation will seem more realistic and entertaining.

Squash and Stretch

Squash and stretch represent a way of deforming an object such that it shows how rigid the object is. For example, if a rubber ball bounces and hits the ground it will tend to flatten when it hits. This is the squash principle. As it starts to bounce up it will stretch in the direction it is going and revert back to the original shape.

Secondary Action

Secondary action results from the main action. Secondary action creates interest and realism in animation. It should be staged such that it can be noticed but still not overpower the main action.

Follow Through and Overlapping Action

Follow through is the same as anticipation, only at the end of an action. It is usually animated as something goes past its resting point and then coming back to where it would normally be. For example, in throwing a ball, you put your hand back, that is anticipation, it is the preparation for the throwing action itself. Then you throw the arm comes forward for the main action. Follow through is then the arm continuing past the normal stopping point, overshooting it and then coming back. The arm has continued or "followed through" on the action it was doing before returning back to rest.

Overlapping action is an action that occurs because of another action. For example, if a dog is running and suddenly comes to a stop, its ears will probably still keep moving for a bit.

This is overlapping action. It is caused because of the main motion and overlaps on top of the main motion. Overlap contributes to the continuity of a scene.

Straight Ahead Action and Pose-to-Pose Action

There are two basic methods to creating animation. Straight ahead animation is one where the animator draws or sets up objects one frame at a time in order. For example, the animator draws the first frame of the animation, then draws the second, and so on until the sequence is complete. In this way, there is one drawing or image per frame that the animator has setup. This approach tends to yield a more creative and fresh look but can be difficult to time correctly and tweak.

The other approach is Pose-to-Pose animation. Pose-to-Pose is created by drawing or setting up key poses and the drawing or creating in between images. This is the basic computer "keyframe" approach to animation. The basic difference is with Pose-to-Pose you plan out, and know exactly what will happen ahead of time, whereas with Straight Ahead, you are not quite sure how things will turn out until the end. With computers, some people tend to create a hybrid of the two, planning out the overall posed, and then straight ahead animating the stuff in between.

Staging

The concept of staging comes directly from theater and film. It means to arrange things in each frame so that the action is clear and easy to see. If too many things are happening in too many places, the audience would not know where to look. At a given moment a scene has only a few main characters. Staging means to give those characters emphasis and to integrate them with the background.

Appeal

All the characters in an animation should have appeal. Appeal means anything that a person likes to see. It could be quality of charm, design, simplicity, communication or magnetism. Appeal can be gained by correctly utilizing other principles, such as exaggeration in design, avoiding symmetry, using overlapping action, and others.

Personality

Personality determines the success of an animation. The idea is that the animated creature really becomes alive and enters the true character of the role. One character would not perform an action the same way in two different emotional states. No two characters would act the same. It is also important to make the personality of a character distinct, but at the same time be familiar to the audience.

2.25 DESIGN OF AN ANIMATION SEQUENCE

In general, an animation sequence is designed with the following steps:
(a) Storyboard layout
(b) Participating object definition
(c) Keyframe specifications
(d) Generation of in-between frames
The storyboard is an outline of the action (animation). It defines motion as a set of basic events. When creating an animated movie, someone first writes a script for the story. From the script, a series of pictures is drawn to show important moments in the story. The series of pictures is called *storyboard*. Depending on the type of motion to be produced, the storyboard could consist of a high

level sequence of sketches showing the structure and ideas of the animation. Next sound track if any is recorded and a detailed layout is produced with a drawing for every scene in the animation. The detailed lay out and the sound track are then correlated.

☞ *The storyboard is an outline of the action, and the keyframes defined the details of the object motions for selected positions in the animation.*

Each participating object in the action must be given a definition. These objects can be in terms of basic shapes. In addition, we specify the associated movements for each object along with the shape.

A keyframe is a detailed drawing of the scene at a particular instant in the animation sequence. Some keyframes are chosen at extreme or characteristic position in the action. Others are spaced so that the time interval between keyframes is not too large.

☞ *Keyframes, in any animation sequence, can be defined as those frames in which the movements of objects mature from one stage to another.*

The final animation is achieved by filling the gaps between adjacent key frames with in between frames. Inbetween are the intermediate frames between the keyframes. The process of generating in-between is called inbetweening. The number of in-betweens needed depends on the media to be used to display the animation. For instance, a film requires 24 frames per second and graphics displays are refreshed at the rate of 30 to 60 frames per second. Typically, time intervals for the motion are selected so that there are three to five in-between for each pair of keyframes. Depending on the speed specified for the motion, some key frames can be duplicated.

2.26 CEL ANIMATION

Traditional animation, also referred to as classical animation, cel animation or hand drawn animation, is the oldest and historically the most popular form of animation. Cel animation is a traditional form of animation used in the production of cartoons or animated movies where each frame of the scene is drawn by hand. In a cel or frame animation, the entire animation sequence is split up into different frames (in other words, still images).

To create the illusion of movement, each drawing differs slightly from the one before it. The animators drawings are traced or photocopied onto transparent acetate sheets called *cels*, which are filled in with paints in assigned colors or tones on the side opposite the line drawings. The completed character cels are photographed one-by-one onto motion picture film against a painted background by a *rostrum camera*.

When all these images are displayed in sequence, they seem to move. When this kind of shuffling between the pictures is fast enough at around 25 to 30 frames per second, we see a full fledged animated movie. A full length feature film produced using cel animation would often require a million or more drawings to complete.

In object animation, a general picture, which does not change with time, is maintained as a backdrop and an object or two are moved over this background. Here, the motion sequence of the object alone is calculated and generated.

☞ *Object animation is a sequence produced by, movement of an object over a general picture that's maintained as a backdrop.*

☞ *Cel animation is sequence produced by displaying different frames of movements, one after the other rapidly.*

The traditional cel animation process became obsolete by the beginning of the 21st century. Today, animator's drawings and the backgrounds are either scanned into or drawn directly into a computer system. Various software programs are used to color the drawings, and simulate camera movement and effects. The final animated piece is output to one of several delivery media, including traditional 35 mm film and newer media, such as digital video.

2.27 COMPUTER ANIMATION

Computer animation (or CGI or Computer-Generated Image animation) is the art of creating moving images with the use of computers. It is a subfield of computer graphics and animation. Increasingly it is created by means of 3D computer graphics, though 2D computer graphics are still widely used for stylistic, low bandwidth, and faster real-time rendering needs. Sometimes the target of the animation is the computer itself, but sometimes the target is another medium such as film. It also referred to as CGI (Computer-Generated Imagery) or computer-generated imaging), especially when used in films.

☞ *The creation of animated sequences within the computer is called computer animation.*

The term 'Computer animation' categories 2D and 3D animation. '2D' stands for 'two dimensional', is also called 'vector animation' and is typically done in programs like Macromedia Flash and Macromedia Director.

☞ *Flash is vector-based animation tool and Director is authoring multimedia for CD-ROM and the Web.*

The most familiar form of 2D animation is traditional cartoons. Vector animation is also useful in designing interactive interfaces for the Web. 2D animation, is rendered in a two dimensional space. 3D animation, however is rendered in a virtual three dimensional space, using polygons captured by various virtual cameras to film the animation. 3D animation has a variety of applications, from video games to animated films, most commonly, 3D animation is used to render many of the special effects seen in live while both types of computer animation can be accomplished by either frame-by-frame animation or by mathematical interpolation between key frames, the initial steps prior to animating are different. The two separate processes also require different software packages.

For 3D animations, objects (models) are built on the computer monitor (modeled) and 3D figures are rigged with a virtual skeleton. For 2D figure animations, separate objects (illustrations) and separate transparent layers are used, with or without a virtual skeleton. Then the limbs, eyes, mouth, clothes, etc., of the figure are moved by the animator on key frames. The differences in appearance between keyframes are automatically calculated by the computer in a process known as *tweening* or *morphing*. Finally, the animation is rendered.

For 3D animations, all frames must be rendered after modeling is complete. For 2D vector animations, the rendering process is the key frame illustration process, while tweened frames are rendered as needed. For pre-recorded presentations, the rendered frames are transferred to a different format or medium such as film or digital video. The frames may also be rendered in real time as they are presented to the end-user audience. Low bandwidth animations transmitted via the Internet (e.g. 2D Flash, X3D or eXtensible 3D) often use software on the end-users computer to render in real time as an alternative to streaming or pre-loaded high bandwidth animations.

The screen is blanked to a background color, such as black. Then a goat is drawn on the right of the screen. Next the screen is blanked, but the goat is re-drawn or duplicated slightly to the left of its original position. This process is repeated, each time moving the goat a bit to the left. If this process is repeated fast enough the goat will appear to move smoothly to the left. This basic procedure is used for all moving pictures in films and television.

The moving goat is an example of shifting the location of an object. More complex transformations of object properties, such as size, shape, lighting effects and color often require calculations and computer rendering instead of simple re-drawing or duplication.

2.28 COMPUTER-BASED ANIMATION

A computer-based animation is an animation performed by a computer graphical tools to provide visual effects.

2.28.1 Input Process

The computer assistance can be utilized in certain processes involved in an animation. Drawing must be digitized because keyframes in which the entities being animated are at extreme or characteristic positions, must be drawn. This can be done through optical scanning, tracing the drawings with a data tablet or producing the original drawings with drawing program in the first place. The drawings may need to preprocessed to clean up any glitches that arise from optical scanning.

2.28.2 Composition Stage

The composition stage, in which foreground and background figures are combined to generate the individual frame for the final animation that can be performed with image composition technique. Initially, small low resolution frames of an animation are placed in a rectangular array. Then we can use panning and zooming to give the effect of continuity in the frame sequence. The frame buffer can take a particular portion consisting of one low resolution frame, move it to the center of the screen (panning) and then enlarge to fill the entire screen (zooming). This process is repeated for several frames of the animation stored in the single image. The process must be done fast enough to give the effect of continuity. Thus, the low resolution frame when expands would give the sense of animation.

2.28.3 In-between Process

The animation of movement from one position to another needs a composition frames with intermediate position (intermediate frames) inbetween the keyframes. This is called the in-between process. The process of in-betweening is performed in computer based animation through interpolation. The system gets only the start and ending positions. The simplest form of this, is linear interpolation, may result in jerky and unnatural motion between keyframes. Splines are often used instead to smooth out the interpolation between keyframes. Spliner can be used to vary any parameter smoothly as a function of time. Spliner can make an individual point or objects move smoothly in space and time.

2.28.4 Morphing

Morphing (short for metamorphosing) refers to an animation technique in which one image is gradually turned into another (See Figure 2.19). Many of the advanced animation programs support morphing feature.

Figure 2.19 Morphing, in which a cock is gradually converting into a lamb

Another term in connection with morphing is tweening (inbetweeing). It is the process of generating intermediate frames between two images to give the appearance that the first image evolves smoothly into the second image.

Morphing has got the following applications:

(a) Development (of any object) can be simulated (shown artificially) by first obtaining still images at successive stages and then morphing into a child can be shown as a movie using the technique of *morphing*.

(b) Similarly, movement of objects (of animals, humans or cartoon characters) can be simulated. For example, if you take still images at different stages of movement and then apply tweening (using a multimedia software), you can create motion in the object.

(c) Many interesting effects can be created using morphing technique. It is increasingly being used as a special effect on TV and in motion pictures.

(d) Morphing can be used to illustrate evolution in interesting ways. For example, a morph can show how early simple arthropods developed into the diverse insects that exists today.

2.28.5 Application of Animation

Animation is widely used in the entertainment industry (motion, pictures, cartoons, video games), advertising and is being applied in education, in industrial applications, such as control systems and flight simulators for aircraft, and in scientific research. The animations in scientific visualization are generated from simulations of scientific phenomena. The results of simulations may be large data sets representing 2D or 3D data (e.g of fluid flow simulations). These data are converted into images that constitute the animation. The simulation may generate positions and location of physical objects, which have to be rendered in some form to generate animation. For example, simulation of navigation of prototype robot manipulator in robot workspace would give information for animation.

Animation is used in film industry for providing special effects. For example in Hindi movie, chachi 420 the hero is shown being transformed from man to woman by the use of a technique called *morphing*.

Computerized animation and coloring have given a new life to the animation film industry. In animation films of the past, animations were create by using hand drawing technique which was a very tedious and time consuming process. Because of hand-drawing, the quality of animations were also not very good. Using computer programs based on the precise mathematical laws of physics, animators can now create animations that are far more realistic than ever before.

For sales promotion, companies often advertise their products and services on television most of the TV programmes are sponsored by one or more companies and, in turn, they get time slots for advertising their products during the advertising their products during the programme. Several of these advertisements use computer animation to effectively communicate the usefulness of products and services. For example, if you carefully watch the advertisements for detergent soaps/powders, toothpastes, insecticides for mosquitoes and cockroaches, etc., you will see few scenes in them which cannot be videographed. These scenes are produced using computer animation.

Animations are particularly useful to simulate real world situations, such as the flight of a jet airplane.

Animation is being used as an important image generation to design flight simulators for pilot training, to provide facilities respective practice of landing and take offs, through presentation of 3D scenes of the airports and view of cities for day and night landing to the polios. Their scenes change and present a view to the trainee with respect to the speed and position of the aircraft. Similar techniques are also used for training personnel for navigation of ships using ship simulators.

Animation techniques are also used by television broadcast industry for vividly depicting the motion of clouds observed by a satellite.

The sequence of pictures created can also be used to educate or explain to people concept in other areas. This may need creation of realistic images of 3-dimensional objects.

Manufactures of automobiles are interested in the development of technique for displaying crashes in 3-dimension to simulate accidents for example the holograph of a car may collide with the holograph of another vehicle to show how the parses of vehicle will fly in a real crash.

REVIEW QUESTIONS WITH ANSWERS

1. Multiple Choice

1.1 Typical font styles are:
a. bold b. Italics
c. underlined d. All of the above

1.2 Which of the following has replaced NTSC (National Television System Committee)?
a. ATSC b. DVI
c. HDTV d. MPEG2

1.3 How many different colors is a 16-bit image capable of representing?
a. 2 b. 16
c. 256 d. 65,536

1.4 Which picture file format can display more colors?
a. MPS b. JPEG
c. GIF d. All of the above

1.5 Which is the biggest audio file format?
a. WMA b. WAV
c. MP3 d. SWF

1.6 Which image file format can be animated?
a. GIF b. JPEG
c. CDR d. TIFF

1.7 Which one of the following is not a video file extension?
a. MP4 b. AVI
c. QT d. JPG

1.8 What does MPEG stand for?
a. Motion Picture Experts Gang
b. Modern Picture Experts Group
c. Motion Picture Experts Group
d. Modern Picture Experts Gang

1.9 When a program assigns 8 bits to a pixel, that pixel can display one of upto _____ color.
a. 32 b. 64
c. 256 d. 1024

1.10 Music that plays on a computer, such as a radio station, but is never downloaded is known as:
a. P2P
b. Streaming
c. MP3
d. Online

2. State whether the following statements are True or False

2.1 A graphic image file name is tree.eps. This image is bitmap image.

2.2 MIDI data is digitized sound.

2.3 In digital recording, the recording device needs a chip called an analog-to-digital convertor, which digitizes waves into a series of numbers.

2.4 MP3 format has larger file size as compared to WAV file format.

2.5 Vector images use pixels to represent images.

2.6 MIDI is used by the multimedia computer to produce the music.

2.7 RGB typically uses 24 bits to represent a color.

2.8 Adobe Premier, Apple iMovie, are examples of video editing software.

2.9 PNG is a standard used for compression of audio in multimedia.

2.10 Object linking and embedding in Window does not allow to combine video and audio clips.

3. Match the following:

3.1	Used to imitate music and used with MIDI	a.	Gray scale
3.2	The density of pixels on a screen	b.	VIdeo Digitizer

3.3	Graphics that allow each pixel to be shown on a computer as black, white or a shade of gray is known as	c.	Frame
3.4	Changing and merging one computer image into another	d.	Resolution
3.5	Transforming an audio signal into a sound file	e.	Gamma Correction
3.6	Altering the output level of the computer monitor	f.	Quantizing
3.7	Converts analog video signal from video tape into digital data	g.	Megapixel
3.8	One million pixels	h.	Morphing
3.9	Each still image in a motion picture is known as a	i.	Buffer
3.10	Temporary storage space is used for a segment of the file so that data continues to flow smoothly	j.	Sequencing software

4. Fill in the blanks

a. RAM	b. Sound/Music / Audio File	c. Sequential
d. Gray scale	e. Real time	f. 30
g. Bitmapped	h. CAD	i. PostScript
j. Streaming	k. CAM	l. Lossy
m. Resolution		

4.1 Painting programs create ________ graphics.

4.2 ________ graphics allow each pixel be shown on the monitor as black, white, or a shade of gray.

4.3 The clarity of a monitor is known as ________.

4.4 When a digital image is currently being viewed on a computer screen, it is actively loaded into ________.

4.5 A standard page-description language for describing text fonts, illustrations, and other elements of the printed page is called ________.

4.6 MP3 is an extension of a ________file.

4.7 ________ software is used by engineers to design products.

4.8 When a document or media is to be accessed and read from beginning to and, it is known as ________.

4.9 A broadcast/NTSC video requires ________fps for it to play smoothly.

4.10 When something is displayed at the same time as it is created, accessed, or imported, it is known as ________.

Answers

1.	1.1	d	1.2	a	1.3	d	1.4	c	1.5	b	1.6	a
	1.7	d	1.8	c	1.9	c	1.10	b				
2.	2.1	T	2.2	F	2.3	T	2.4	F	2.5	F	2.6	T
	2.7	T	2.8	T	2.9	F	2.10	F				
3.	3.1	j	3.2	d	3.3	a	3.4	h	3.5	f	3.6	e
	3.7	b	3.8	g	3.9	c	3.10	i				
4.	4.1	g	4.2	d	4.3	m	4.4	a	4.5	i	4.6	b
	4.7	h	4.8	c	4.9	f	4.10	e				

Questions with Answers

1. Define anti-aliasing. Describe the advantages of applying 'Anti-aliasing' to graphics.
2. How RIFF file format is different from TIFF file format?
3. Explain the concept of Video on Multimedia.
4. What is the mechanism of digitized sound? How does the computer reconstruct sound wave from a sample data?
5. What is MIDI? In what ways can MIDI be used effectively in Multimedia application?
6. Differentiate between JPEG and MPEG.
7. What is animation? What is frame-by-frame animation? What is meant by persistence of vision with respect to animation?
8. What is tweening? Explain different types of tweening.

Answers to Questions

1. a. *Anti-aliasing* is a method of fooling the eye that a jagged edge is really smooth. It is often referred in games and on graphics. In games, it is normally used in those images that are used for creating a realistic 3D image on the screen. Without anti-aliasing, an image would look stair-stepped, without smooth transitions between colors. In anti-aliasing, there is no loss of details because only the edge pixels change. Advantages of applying antialiasing to graphics:

a. It can smooth out screen fonts.
b. It can round the edges look to have smooth curves.
c. It can significantly improve the clarity of even the poorest quality images and scanned documents.
d. Type can be easier to read due to better quality fonts.
e. Games look a lot prettier and more realistic.

2. Difference between RIFF and TIFF file Formats

a. RIFF: Resource Interchange File Format
TIFF: Tagged Image File Format

b. TIFF format is developed by Aldus (now Adobe) corporation.
RIFF format is jointly developed by IBM and Microsoft.

c. RIFF is a general framework file format for multimedia.
TIFF is used for images.

d. TIFF stores only bitmap data.
RIFF can store other data also.

3. Video is the technology for electronically capturing, recording, processing, storing, transmitting, and reconstructing a sequence of still images representing scenes in motion. Full motion video consists of photographic detailed recording of motion. Like audio, video can also be analog or digital. Digital video is a term which refers to moving pictures that are stored on a computer hard disk for editing or playback. Video deals with the recording of a real life event produced by a device such as digital video recorder. Video data also requires large storage space and needs to meet the real time constraints on retrieval, delivery, and display. Video is an important component of multimedia because it is very useful for illustrating concepts that involve movement.

Today, video places the highest performance demand on any computer system and the digital has replaced analog as the method of choice for making video for multimedia. Video is incorporated into multimedia projects, for many reasons.

(a) The project has certain relevant sequences/material that can be videographed.

(b) The project has certain sequences/material that cannot be produced with the help of animation.

(c) The project has to be made more attractive with video.

(d) The project has live lectures or demonstration or other pre recorded material to be incorporated.

4. The process of converting analog signals to digital signals by way of taking discrete samples, is called Digitization of sound. We can digitize sound from a microphone, a synthesizer, existing tape recordings, live radio and television broadcasts, and popular CDs. Digital, or digitized sound is easier to reproduce and manipulate without loss in quality than analog.
When voice or music is captured by a microphone, it generates an electrical signal. The signal consists of a fundamental sine wave of a certain amplitude and frequency. The amplitude of the signal represents the intensity of the sound, and the frequency represents the pitch of the sound. Sound is made up of continuous analog sine waves that tend to repeat for seconds at a time depending on the music or the voice. The analog sine waveforms are converted to digital format by feeding the analog signal to an analog-to-digital (A/D converter). Once the sound has been digitized, it can be processed like any other binary file.

5. MIDI refers to **M**usical **I**nstrument **D**igital **I**nterface. In computer science, it is a serial interface standard that allows for the connection of music synthesizers, musical instruments and computers.
MIDI files do not store the actual sound, but rather it contains instructions. These instruction include notes and duration needed to recreate the sound and since MIDI files contain instruction rather than data, a synthesizer is required to reproduce the sounds or music. To make MIDI scores, a sequencer software is required. A MIDI keyboard is used for creating musical scores.
As MIDI files take less space than digital audio files which makes it a valuable option in many Multimedia programs.

6. Difference between JPEG and MPEG:
JPEG (Joint Photographic Experts Group) format is one of the most common graphic file format for Web applications. JPEG format is also used to display photographs and other continuous tone images in Hypertext Markup Language (HTML) documents over the World Wide Web and other online services.
On the other hand, MPEG is the acronym for **M**oving **P**ictures **E**xperts **G**roup, a committee that developed the MPEG standard. It is a set of specifications for compressing and playing back full-motion video, including movies and video clips. MPEG rules cover both encoding, for storage on disk and decoding, for digital playback. Viewing a MPEG video on a microcomputer requires a MPEG decoder, which can be hardware, software, or a combination of the two.
MPEG achieves high compression rate by storing only the changes from one frame to another, instead of each entire frame. Although MPEG is a lossy compression method, the loss of video data is generally imperceptible to human eye. For this reason, MPEG generally produces better-quality video than competing formats, such as AVI and QuickTime.

7. Animation is one of the most dynamic form of multimedia. Unlike graphics, animations can provide dynamic movements to the objects. For example, to show a bird flying in the air, all that graphics can provide is a digital photograph of the same. However, with animations, we could actually view the bird flying in the monitor of the PC.
A *keyframe* is simply a frame in which we establish exactly what should appear on stage at particular point. It makes a change in an object's properties from the previous frame. When we associate a change in an object with a new frame, the frame must be a keyframe.
Frame-by-frame animation involves manually creating every frame in an animation. Frame-by-frame animations are useful when you want to change individual parts of an image. Frame-by-frame animation changes the contents of the Stage in every frame and is best suited for complex animation in which an image changes in every frame instead of simply moving across the Stage. Frame-by-frame animation increases file size more rapidly any other animation. In frame-by-frame animation, the values for each complete frame is also stored.
Persistence of vision is the phenomenon where the retina retains an image for a brief split-second (about one twenty-fifth of a second) after the image was actually seen, and lends itself to animation by fostering the illusion of motion when we view images in closely-timed sequence to one another. We do not notice the fractional skips between images because that persistence fills in the momentary gap to make the motion seem seamless. It is also called the retention of a visual image for a short period of time after the removal of the stimulus that produced it.

8. The meaning of the word *tween* is *in-between*. The process of interpolating (fill-in between) two keyframes is called *Tweening*. The space between two keyframes effectively holds the onscreen contents from the first keyframe. For example, suppose that in one keyframe there is an sparrow on the left of the stage. The next keyframe shows the sparrow on the right side of the stage. It fills in-between frames automatically after calculating how to move the first image to the second. All this is done through the tweening. There are three types of tweening. These are:

(a) *Motion Tweening:* Motion tweens are useful for creating animation that consists of continuous motion or transformation of an object. Motion tweens are powerful and simple to create. In a motion tweening, you have to specify the position of the object in the beginning and ending frames and the in-between frames are fills automatically.

(b) *Classic Tweening:* Classic tweens are like motion tweens in that you can create animations that change the properties of an object over time. Classic tweens are a bit more complex to create, however, they provide certain capabilities that some developers desire.

(c) *Shape Tweening:* Shape tweening is a technique for interpolating amorphous (shapeless) changes between shapes in different keyframes. For this, you have to draw a shape at one specific keyframe in the Timeline, and change that shape or draw another shape at another specific keyframe. Then the intermediate shapes for the keyframes in between and Shape tweens make it possible to smoothly morph one shape into another. For example, animation of clouds, water, or fire is perfect for shape tweening.

DESCRIPTIVE TYPE QUESTIONS

1. What are the types of sound objects that can be used in multimedia?
2. Why are standards important for developing multimedia content? What are MPEG Standards?

3. What is the advantage of MIDI over digitized sound?
4. Define the following terms with respect to a video:
Flicker, Anti-aliasing, and Resolution
5. Compare and contrast the main advantages and disadvantages of bitmap graphics and vector graphics.
6. Describe the process of the digitization of an analog sound. Define what a sample is, the frequency of occurrence and how these factors can affect the quality of sound.
7. Define MIDI. List its attribute. Compare and contrast the use of MIDI and digitized audio in multimedia production.
8. What is sound synthesis? What are the applications of sound synthesis?
9. What is color? Explain additive and subtractive colors with example.
10. Explain in brief, different broadcast video standards.
11. Explain any three audio file formats.
12. Explain Hue, Saturation and Brightness in terms of color characteristic.
13. What are the advantages of digital representation of a video?
14. Differentiate between Online Video Editing and Off-line Video Editing.
15. What do you mean by color model? Explain various color models.
16. What is animation? What are different types of animation?
17. What are the steps of designing an animation sequence?
18. What is cel animation?
19. Write applications of animation.

CHAPTER 3

Concepts of Multimedia Editing

3.1 DIGITAL AUDIO

Digital sound or audio is the technology, by which sound signals are represented as a series of binary digital data, i.e., zero and ones, which the computers can understand and comprehend.

3.1.1 Advantages of Digital Audio

Digital audio is the technology, by which sound signals are represented as a series of binary digital data, i.e., zero's and one's which computers can understand and comprehend. Once digitized, the sound can be processed like any other binary files, using the relevant editing and playback software.

Digital audio has its own advantages over it predecessor analog audio.

1. Digital audio is less susceptible to degradation or distortion, because the entire transmission and all other transaction processes take place as electronic signals, avoiding the intervention of air or any other medium. Thus, the quality of the parent signal is maintained throughout.
2. Editing audio with computers makes cutting, pasting and manipulating of parent signals, very easy. Also a lot of special effects like the 'Echo' can be artificially added, without the need of any other hardware. On the other hand audio demanded very expensive hardware and a host of equipments to accomplish the same.
3. Digital audio is of superior quality during reproduction, because of non-intervention of air and other loss incurring mediums.
4. Digital audio can be stored as digital data, in reliable mediums like the CD-ROM (Compact Disk Read Only Memory). Thus extending their life of more than fifty years on an average without losses.

3.2 SOUND QUALITY

In general, the quality of sound has much to do with the effect of a line in ways that have not been fully investigated. Harsh sounds, for instance, like the word harsh itself, may suggest pain or effort. Soft ones, like the word pure, may suggest joy or peace. Specifically, however, the patterns resulting from resemblances between vowel and consonant sounds are based upon traditional or conventional interpretations.

3.2.1 CD Quality

A high quality Compact Disk will play in every drive, every time, with performance and lifetime appropriate to the application. Because the CD format is standardized, we can ensure the quality of a CD by making sure that all parameters are well within the specification. There are two elements to measuring disk quality. These are as under:

(a) **Error Rates:** The easiest way to measure the disk quality is to measure error rates. Most serious defects will cause an increase in error rates. By looking at both the quantity and severity of errors, we can get a pretty good picture of disk quality. Playback errors can be caused by two things: Localized defects, and poor pit geometry.

(b) **Pit Geometry:** In order for a disk to play, the reflected laser beam must generate track-following and focus servo signals so that the player can follow the track and stay focused. Generation of the proper servo signals is completely dependent on the size and shape of the pits on the disk. Without the proper *pit geometry*, the disk will not play reliably.

3.2.2 Radio Quality

Sound can be sent using air as the media. We first convert sound into equivalent electrical signal with the help of a microphone. The electrical energy is amplified and modulated for transmission in the air. The little energy is picked up by a radio receiver and then demodulates it and amplifies the original sound in electrical signal form. This signal is then sent to the loudspeaker which produces the original sound spoken in front of the microphone. The quality will depend on the atmospheric noise and the quality of the hardware. For high quality, we use FM (Frequency Modulation) transmission system. This is limited in range to 40 kms.

3.2.3 Telephone Quality

Telephone instrument sends and receives voice messages. Telephones convert speech to electrical energy, which is sent great distances. All telephones are linked by complex switching systems called central offices or exchanges, where voice change to digital signals and then sent to destination's office. There, it again changes in analog signal to be sent to the destination. In this way, telephone improves the speed and there is no disturbance in voice. Telephones are used for casual conversations, to conduct business, and to help someone in an emergency.

3.3 SOUND SYNTHESIS

In music technology, sound synthesis is the process of generating sound from analog and digital electronic equipment, often for musical, artistic or entertainment purposes. In particular, it refers to the process of generating, combining or mixing sounds from a set of fundamental building blocks or routines in order to create sounds of a greater complexity and richness. Sound synthesis can be used to mimic acoustic sound sources or generate sound that may be impossible to realize naturally.

The process by which a sound card creates music is called the *sound synthesis* or *audio synthesis*. Dialog, music or other sound effects can be achieved either through audio means or through sound synthesis. Captured audio in digital form provides high quality sound reproduction and is useful for dialogue and music sequences.

There are two fundamentals types of sound synthesis technology.

- FM synthesis
- Wavetable synthesis

Let us discuss each of them in brief.

3.3.1 FM Synthesis

FM synthesis is an old and outdated technique. By blending around with a range of frequency modulation, the earlier sound cards managed to produce audio that tried to resemble the original analog sound data. The final output sounded much like 'electronically generated' audio pulses and was not natural. Despite this fact, the cards became popular because of their low cost and better technologies. Later all FM synthesis cards are being replaced by a much superior one called *wavetable synthesis cards.*

3.3.2 Wavetable Synthesis

In wavetable synthesis, the sounds are almost similar to that coming out of original musical instruments. Sound cards with wavetable synthesis technology contain a wide variety of built-in sound samples (i.e., actual recording) of various music instruments. When a note from a particular instrument is played, the card looks up for an equivalent in its wide collection of digital audio samples and reconstructs the sound with that models. Thus, the resulting sounds are much better than their FM synthesis.

3.4 MIDI

MIDI (*Musical Instrument Digital Interface*) is an industry standard electronic communications protocol that enables electronic musical instruments, computers and other equipment to communicate, control and synchronize with each other in real time.

MIDI stores only music or contains instructions rather than actual sound data. These instruction include notes and duration needed to recreate the sound and since MIDI files contain instruction rather than data, a synthesizer is required to hear them. To make MIDI scores, a sequencer software is required. A MIDI keyboard is used for creating musical scores.

☞ *MIDI is the digital standard for connecting computers, musical instruments and synthesizers.*

A MIDI sound file contains MIDI messages. MIDI files have *.mid* extension. A variation of this format is the RIFF (Resource Interchange File Format) MIDI file, which uses *.rmi* extension.

The format of a Standard MIDI File (SMF) contains a header "chunk" at the beginning that defines the type, followed by one or more track chunks. Type 0 files store all tracks in one track chunk. Type 1 files use a separate chunk for each track, with the first chunk storing the tempo.

☞ *Type 0 files use less memory and run faster than type 1. Thus, original MIDI music is maintained in Type 1 format and frequently distributed in Type 0.*

MIDI files distributed for editing are in Type 1 format, since it is difficult to convert from Type 0 to Type 1 using a MIDI sequencer. A less-widely used Type 2 file can contain several Type 0 files.

All music recordings today use MIDI devices. In addition, MIDI is also used to control hardware including recording devices and live performance equipment, such as stage lights and effects pedals.

☞ *MIDI allows computers, synthesizers, MIDI controllers, sound cards, samplers and drum machines to control one another, and to exchange system data.*

A number of music file formats are based on MIDI byte stream. These formats are very compact. A file as small as 10 KB can produce a full minute of music. This is advantageous for applications such as mobile phone ringtones and some video games.

Like vector graphics MIDI files are very compact, however, the sounds produced by the MIDI file depend on the playback device, and it may sound different from one machine to the next. MIDI files are only suitable for recording music. They cannot be used to store dialog. They are also more difficult to edit and manipulate then digitized sound files.

3.4.1 Components of MIDI Interface

A MIDI interface has two different components:

- Hardware connects the equipment. It specifies the physical connection between musical instruments, stipulates that a MIDI port is built into an instrument, specifies a MIDI cable and deals with electronic signals that are sent over the cable.
- A data format encodes the information travelling through the hardware. A MIDI format does not include an encoding of individual samples as the audio format does. Instead of individual samples, an instrument connected data format is used. The encoding includes, besides the instrument specification, the notation of the beginning and end of a note, basic frequency and sound volume.

3.4.2 Comparison of MIDI and Digitized Audio

MIDI was developed to allow musicians to connect synthesizers together. The MIDI protocol is now finding widespread use as a delivery medium to replace or supplement digitized audio in games and multimedia applications.

Advantages of generating sound with a MIDI synthesizer are:

(a) The first advantage is storage space. Data files are used to store digitally sampled audio in PCM (Pulse-Code Modulation) format (such as .WAV files) tend to be quite large. This is especially true for lengthy musical pieces captured in stereo using high sampling rates.

MIDI data files, on the other hand, are very small when compared with sampled audio files. For instance, files containing high quality stereo sampled audio require about 10 MB of data per minute of sound, while a typical MIDI sequence might consume less than 10 KB of data per minute of sound. This is because the MIDI file does not contain the sampled audio data. It contains only the instructions needed by a synthesizer to play the sounds. These instructions are in the form of MIDI messages, which instruct the synthesizer which sounds to use, which notes to play, and how loud to play each note. The actual sounds are then generated by the synthesizer. MIDI is analogous to structured or vector graphics, while digitized audio is analogous to bitmapped images.

(b) For computers, the smaller file size also means that less of the PCs (Personal Computers) bandwidth is utilized in spooling this data out to the peripheral which is generating sound.

(c) Other advantage of utilizing MIDI is to generate sounds to include the ability to easily edit the music and the ability to change the playback speed and the pitch or key of the sound independently. There is not so much of flexibility available in digital audio.

(d) MIDI is more flexible than digital audio files. Each and every note of the instruments that are being played back can be controlled individually. This feature is not at all possible with digital audio. MIDI files sound better than digital audio files.

(e) Due to small size, MIDI files are embedded in Web pages, and play more quickly than their digital equivalent.

(f) MIDI files are much more compact than digital audio files and the size of MIDI files is completely independent of playback quality. MIDI file playback demand lesser RAM (Random Access Memory) and processing power.

(g) Quality of MIDI music is pure because all recordings are done electronically and there is no intervention of external medium like air, which degrades the quality of the resulting digital audio files.

(h) MIDI audio is device dependent, i.e., the playback will be accurate only if the MIDI playback device is identical to the device used for production. Digital audio is consistent in playback quality, i.e., digital data sounds more or less identical regardless of the playback system.

(i) Working with MIDI requires familiarity with musical scores, keyboards and notation as well as audio production.

☞ *MIDI cannot easily be used to playback spoken dialog. Use digitized audio for spoken dialog.*

3.4.3 Disadvantages of MIDI

- Because MIDI data does not represent sound but musical instruments, you cannot be certain that playback will be accurate only if the MIDI playback device is identical to the device used for production.
- Also MIDI cannot easily be used to play back spoken dialog, although expensive and technically tricky digital samplers are available.
- A wider selection of application software and system support for digital audio is available for both the Macintosh and Windows platforms but not for MIDI.
- MIDI files can not be burned onto CD. This is a drawback. But they can be converted into .wav, .aiff, or .mp3 files.

3.5 MUSIC SEQUENCING AND NOTATION

In music, a sequence is a series of short, repeated musical patterns. These patterns usually move up or down a scale. There are harmonic sequences (repeated harmonic patterns) and melodic sequences (repeated melodic patterns). By repeated we mean they have the same underlying structure while being played off of different notes.

In digital audio recording, a sequencer is a program in a computer or stand-alone keyboard unit that puts together a sound sequence from a series (or sequence) of MIDI events (operations). The MIDI sequencer allows the user to record and edit a musical performance without using an audio-based input source. The performance is recorded as a series of events that would ordinarily be played in from a keyboard instrument. The MIDI sequencer does not record the actual audio, but rather the events related to the performance - what note was played at what time, how hard the key was pressed. This data is then played back into a MIDI instrument or sound module. Using this method, the performer can select a piano sound for a musical passage and later decide that the passage would work better as an organ sound. The editor can simply change the sound program on the MIDI keyboard to alter the sound without needing to re-record the entire performance.

Music (musical) notation is any system used to visually represent aurally perceived music through the use of written symbols, including ancient or modern musical symbols. Although many ancient cultures used symbols to represent melodies, none of them is nearly as comprehensive as written language, limiting the knowledge of ancient music to a few fragments. Comprehensive music notation began to be developed in Europe in the Middle Ages and has been adapted to many kinds of music worldwide.

3.6 SOUND EDITING

Sound Editing plays a very important role in all multimedia audio applications. Effective sound editing not only demands a sense of creativity and timing but also a very good understanding of the theme under production of the project. Sound editing was done only in the recording studios with very expensive equipments.

3.6.1 Need for Sound Editing

Need for sound editing arises due to one or more of the following reasons:

(a) With analog audio source, it is difficult to control the external environment.

(b) Every analog audio source is characterized by inconsistency. Even the same person reading out the same sentence after practising ten times may still do mistake while recording the sentence.

(c) It is not possible to add some special effects during recording.

(d) Controlling the audio time duration is very difficult with the original sound sources.

3.6.2 Functions Performed in Sound Editing

Following functions are performed in sound editing:

(i) ***Trimming:*** Every recording is associated with a blank space for a few seconds before and after the required sound. The process of removing blank spaces is called *trimming*. Removal of blank spaces, apart from reducing the audio file size considerably enable perfect item matching and further editing operations easy.

(ii) ***Splicing (Noise Correction):*** The process by which we can remove the unwanted sounds that have crept in during recording.

(iii) ***Reassembling:*** It is the process by which several stray pieces of audio are put together to make a single file. This process is accomplished by 'cutting', 'copying' and 'pasting' sound clips.

(iv) ***Volume Control:*** Increasing or decreasing the volume of whole file or a part of file is called *volume control*. This is very useful at the time of reassembling a file because different sound pieces may have been recorded at various levels.

(v) ***Resampling:*** This is the process of reducing the sound quality from 32-bit to 16-bit or from 16-bit to 8-bit. Reducing the quality of recorded sound decreases the file size. We can do resampling when the original file size is very large. Resampling does not reduce the sound quality, or the changes may be so thin that they are hardly noticeable.

(vi) ***Special Effects (Effect Enhancements):*** Apart from editing the recorded file, we can also apply some special effects to the recorded file. Some special effects which we can apply to the file are as follows:

- *Add Echo:* Add a mild echo effect to the audio file.
- *Reverse:* Reverse the playback of the source file.
- *Mix files:* Mix two sound files one over the other.

(vii) ***Fade-ins and Fade-outs:*** This is the process of smoothing out the beginning and ending of audio files, for gradual transition effects. It also increases or decreases the amplitude of the sound gradually. Time of fading in or out becomes important and it is better to apply this effect after making the selections and not to the entire file.

(viii) ***Equalization:*** Some programs offer digital Equalization (EQ) capabilities, useful for long sections that you wish to fade-in or fade-out gradually. This enveloping helps to smooth out the very beginning and the very end of the sound file.

(ix) ***Time Stretching:*** Advanced programs let you alter the length (in time) of a sound file without changing its pitch. This feature can be very useful, but most time stretching algorithms will severely degrade the audio quality of the file if the length is altered more than a few percentage in either direction.

(x) ***Digital Signal Processing (DSP):*** Digital signal processing uses a specialized processor to convert data from one format to another to a high rate. For digital recording digital sound processors convert musical information into a binary stream of ones and zeros. In this digitized form, the music can be manipulated without risk of distortion. In surround sound systems, DSP provides "steering" to create the acoustical illusion of concert halls, stadiums, or night clubs. A more recent form of digital signal processing is used to provide compression and decompression for audio and video signals.

(xi) ***Reversing Sounds:*** Another simple manipulation is to reverse all or a portion of a digital audio recording. Reverse sound reverses the underlying wave pattern. Unusual and funny patterns can be obtained, particularly with respect to human speech.

3.7 VOICE RECOGNITION SOFTWARE FROM PHILIPS

Voice Recognition, in computer science, is the ability of a computer to understand the spoken word for the purpose of receiving commands and data input from the speaker. *Voice Recognition Software* provides a way for those users who would prefer to talk to their computer rather than typing. Speech recognition software enables user to work faster and more efficiently. Users can create documents, enter data, send e-mail and control their desktop by voice. They also provide digital dictation systems rather than tape-based dictation systems. Now, professionals can use digital dictation machine for recording vital information. This can then be E-mailed to a relevant party for transcription.

Philips gives networked speech recognition product easily available in the market. It offers a range of speech recognition products, including PC-based systems and also central server-based systems. Philips does not include a microphone with its software as do the other software companies. For example, one product of Philips, FreeSpeech98 requires a Pentium/166 MHz processor, 32 MB of RAM and 150 MB of hard disk space. Philips FreeSpeech98 directs the user to read selected text for about 15 minutes.

Three dedicated lines of businesses cover the field:

(a) *Dictation Systems* for speech to text applications.

(b) *Telephony Solutions* for automated information provision (speech to information) over the telephone.

(c) *Voice Control* for embedded speech recognition in products and appliances.

3.8 MONO AND STEREO RECORDING

There are different formats of record and playback sound. Two of the most common formats are monaural, or *mono* and stereophonic, or *stereo*.

Early recordings were made in *mono*, using a single channel to record and playback sound. Broadcasts on AM (Amplitude Modulation) radio are also in mono.

Stereo recording, introduced in the 1960s, uses two channels for sound. In stereo recording, each channel has a different form of the sound. The signals are sent to separate loudspeakers during playback. When played, the sounds from these two separate channels combine in the air and give the illusion of direction that the human ear naturally perceives when hearing sound. A different percentage of each sound might appear at each loudspeaker, giving each sound source its own location between the two loudspeakers.

3.9 IMAGE/GRAPHICS EDITING

Image editing programs come in all shapes and sizes, from a basic bitmap editing program like Windows Paintbrush to professional systems on Silicon Graphics workstations. The common denominator of the hundreds of available program is this: they are all aimed at producing a visual image of some kind. The image may be a simple screen capture or it may be a 3-D realistic rendering of a strand of human DNA-(Deoxyribo Nucleic Acid) but both images are intended to convey some information to a viewer.

Individual programs will vary in complexity and capabilities, but the majority of image editing programs are limited to several categories. A few program do cross over, such as the Canvas program for Macintosh and Windows, which has both bitmap and vector editing capabilities.

3.9.1 Bitmap Editing Programs

Bitmap editing programs are the easiest image editing software to identify and describe. A bitmap is simply a collection of pixels (colored dots) in a gridwork pattern, and any program which allows you to change the pixels in a bitmap is a bitmap editing program. Bitmap editing programs vary in the type and quantity of changes they can make to bitmap images as well as in the variety of file formats they can read and write.

Bitmap editing program are sometimes called "paint-style" programs because some tools (equated with a Paintbrush) are used to "paint" colored pixels on a bitmap grid. You can assign different brush shapes and sizes to the tool and you can also select a specific colour to use. A number of programs allow a variety of painting tools and controls; tools like an airbrush or crayon will produce different patterns of pixels within a bitmap image.

Bitmap editing programs are not limited to painting pixels; they also have many other possible editing tools. For example, the PaintShop Pro and PhotoLab programs.

3.9.2 Vector Editing Programs

Vector editing programs create graphic images using mathematically described objects, such as circles or lines. Vector editing programs are much harder to define and categorize than bitmap editing programs because the variety of objects you can define mathematically is virtually infinite. These editing programs range from the very basic to the imaging systems that run on Silicon Graphics workstations or similar high-end computer platforms. There are separate categories of vector graphics. Some programs can be very simple or basic, while other, more powerful, vector programs are limited to specific types of graphic images. The most powerful vector graphics programs have no limits-they are designed to create any image imaginable.

Powerful vector graphics programs come in a variety of styles and are intended for a wide variety of purposes. Illustration programs, such as CorelDRAW and Adobe Illustrator are used to produce a host of printed material: brochures, book designs, advertising images, product designs, and technical illustrations. CAD (Computer-Aided Design) software can be used to create floorplans, mechanical drawings, or even realistic 3D models. High-end illustration systems can be used to create realistic animated 3D graphics for television or film. In short, virtually any visual image can be created using vector editing software.

3.9.3 Screen Captures

Screen captures are bitmap "snapshots" of your computer screen. They can be used to illustrate a certain feature of a computer program or they can be used as a convenient method of getting an image from your computer screen to a graphic you can edit. For instance, if you have a vector graphic displayed on-screen and you want a bitmap version of the graphic to include in a memo, you can simply capture the image as it is displayed on-screen.

The most recent generation of screen capture programs come with a variety of programs that work together. These programs usually consist of a screen capture utility, a bitmap editing program, and an image management system. The screen capture program converts the computer screen (or a portion of the screen) to a bitmap graphic. The bitmap editing program allows you to change the graphic's colour values or resolution, add borders, or edit out parts of the image. The image management program allows you to organize your bitmap files, view groups of files as thumbnail images, and print groups of files.

PaintShop Pro has a number of screen capture and bitmap editing options, while the ImageCommander program allows you to organize all your graphic files. You can use these programs together to create libraries of graphics that you can organize and access whenever you need a particular image.

3.10 IMAGE EDITING TOOLS

Image editing applications are specialized and powerful tools for enhancing and retouching existing bitmapped images. These applications also provide many of the features and tools of painting and drawing programs, and can be used to create images from scratch as well as images digitized from scanners, video frame-grabbers, digital cameras, clip art files, or original artwork files created with a painting or drawing package.

Here are some features typical or image editing applications and of interest to multimedia developers:

- Multiple windows, which provide views of more than one image at time.
- Conversion of major image-data types and industry-standard file formats.
- Direct inputs of images from scanner and video sources.
- Employment of a virtual memory scheme that uses hard disk space as RAM for images that require large amounts of memory
- Capable selection tools, such as Rectangles, Lassos and Magic wands, to select portions of a bitmap.
- Image and balance controls for brightness contrast, and colour balance.
- Good masking features.
- Multiple undo and restore features.
- Anti-aliasing capability, and sharpening and smoothing controls.
- Color-mapping controls for precise adjustment of colour balances.
- Tools for retouching, blurring, sharpening, lightening, darkening, smudging and tinting.
- Geometric transformations, such as flip, skew, rotate and distort and perspective changes.
- Ability to resample and resize an image.

- 24-bit colour, 8-or 4-bit indexed colour 8-bit gray-scale, black and white, and customizable colour palettes.
- Ability to create images from scratch, using line, rectangle, square, circle, ellipse, polygon, airbrush, paintbrush, pencil and eraser tools, with customizable brush shapes and user-definable bucket and gradient fills.
- Multiple typefaces, styles, and sizes, and type manipulation and masking routines.
- Filters for special effects, such as crystallize, dry brush, emboss, facer, fresco, graphic pen, mosaic, pixelize, poster, ripple, smooth, splatter, stucco, twirl, watercolor, wave and wind.
- Support for third-party special effect plug-ins.
- Ability to design in layers that can be combined, hidden, and reordered.

3.10.1 White Balance Correction

White Balance (WB) is the process of removing unrealistic colour casts so that objects which appear white in person are rendered white in your photo. Proper camera white balance has to take into account the 'colour temperature' of a light source, which refers to the relative warmth or coolness of white light.

Colour temperature is a way of measuring the quality of a light source. It is based on the ratio of the amount of blue light to the amount of red light, and the green light is ignored. The unit for measuring this ratio is in degree Kelvin (K). A light with higher colour temperature (i.e., larger Kelvin value) has "more" blue lights than a light with lower colour temperature (i.e., smaller Kelvin value). Thus, a cooler light has a higher colour temperature.

Human brain can quickly adjust to different colour temperatures. Our eyes, see a white paper as white paper no matter it is viewed under strong sunlight or in a room illuminated with incandescent lights. Unfortunately, colour films can only correctly record the colors in certain range of colour temperatures. Therefore, we have daylight and tungsten films. On the otherhand, digital cameras are very different! Digital cameras usually have built-in sensors to measure the current colour temperature and use an algorithm to process the image so that the final result may be close to what we see with our eyes. But, the algorithm(s) being used may not be accurate enough to make every situation correct. Under some difficult situations when the in-camera algorithm is not able to set the colour temperature correctly or when some creative and special effects are needed, we can instruct the camera to use a particular colour temperature to fulfill our need. This adjustment makes sure the white colour we view directly will also appear white in the image is referred to as *white balance*.

Setting white balance incorrectly may cause a colour shift in the image. For example, suppose the camera is told to use a colour temperature of sunlight to take an image of an indoor environment illuminated mainly by incandescent lights. The camera will expect excessive blue light and less red light, and set its algorithm to be more sensitive to the blue light. However, in an environment illuminated with incandescent lights, colour temperature is low with excessive red light rather than the blue one. As a result, we shall see a reddish or yellowish image.

On the other hand, suppose we set the camera to a low colour temperature (e.g., that of incandescent light) and take a photo under sunlight. Because the white balance is set to incandescent light, the processing algorithm is more sensitive to the blue light. However, in an environment illuminated with incandescent lights, colour temperature is low with excessive red light rather than blue one. As a result, we shall see a reddish or yellowish image.

On the other hand, suppose we set the camera to a low colour temperature (e.g., that of incandescent light) and take a photo under sunlight. Because the white balance is set to incandescent light, the processing algorithm is more sensitive to the red light rather than the blue one. Hence, the resulting image will be bluish.

☞ *Understanding digital white balance can help you avoid colour casts created by your camera's auto white balance, thereby improving your photos under a wider range of lighting conditions.*

3.10.2 Dynamic Range Correction

Dynamic range is a term used frequently in numerous fields to describe the ratio between the smallest and largest possible values of a changeable quantity, such as in sound and light.

The human senses of sight and hearing have a very high dynamic range. A human is capable of hearing (and usefully discerning) anything from a quiet murmur in a soundproofed room to the sound of the loudest rock concert. Such a difference can exceed 100 dB (decibel) which represents a factor of 10,000,000,000 in power. A human can see objects in starlight (although colour differentiation is reduced at low light levels) or in bright sunlight, even though on a moonless night objects receive 1/1,000,000,000 of the illumination they would on a bright sunny day: that is a dynamic range of 90 dB. A human cannot perform these feats of perception at both extremes of the scale at the same time. The eyes take time to adjust to different light levels and the dynamic range of the human eye in a given scene is actually quite limited due to optical glare. The instantaneous dynamic range of human audio perception is similarly subject to masking, so that, for example, a whisper cannot be heard in loud surroundings. Nevertheless, a good quality audio reproduction system should be able to reproduce accurately both the quiet sounds and the loud; and a good quality visual display system should be able to capture both shadow details in nighttime scenes and bright areas of sunny scenes.

In practice, it is difficult to achieve the full dynamic range experienced by humans using electronic equipment. Electronically reproduced audio and video often uses some trickery to fit original material with a wide dynamic range into a narrower recorded dynamic range that can more easily be stored and reproduced. These techniques are called dynamic range compression. For example, a good quality LCD (Liquid Crystal Display) display a dynamic range of around 1000:1 (commercially the dynamic range is often called the "contrast ratio" meaning the full-on/full off luminance ratio), and some of the latest CMOS (Complementary Metallic Oxide Semiconductor) image sensors now have measured dynamic ranges of about 11,000:1 (reported as 13:5 stops, or doublings). Paper reflectance can achieve a dynamic range of about 100:1.

When showing a movie or a game, a display is able to show both shadowy nighttime scenes and bright outdoor sunlit scenes, but, in fact, the level of light coming from the display is much the same for both types of scene (perhaps different by a factor of 10). Knowing that the display does not have a huge dynamic range, the program makers do not attempt to make the nighttime scenes millions of times less bright than the daytime scenes, but instead use other cues to suggest night or day. A nighttime scene will usually contain duller colors and will often be lit with blue lighting, which reflects the way that the human eye sees colors at low light levels.

3.10.3 Gamma Correction

Gamma correction is the adjustment of the brightness and/or contrast in colour on image displayed on computer monitor or on a printer. Adjusting the gamma correction on a image can correct the overall quality of an image.

Gamma correction matters if you have any interest in displaying an image accurately on a computer screen. Gamma correction controls the overall brightness of an image. Images which are not properly corrected can look either bleached out, or too dark. Trying to reproduce colors accurately also requires some knowledge of gamma. Varying the amount of gamma correction changes not only the brightness, but also the ratios of red to green to blue. Gamma correction also plays a big role in making images for the WWW.

Gamma correction is needed because of the nature of CRTs (Cathode Ray Tubes) - the monitors usually used for viewing images). If you have some sort of real live scene and turn it into a computer image by measuring the amount of light coming from each point of the scene, then you have created a "linear" or ungamma-corrected image. This is a good thing in many ways because you can manipulate the image as if the values in the image file were light (i.e., adding and multiplying will work just like real light in the real world). Now if you take the image file and turn each pixel value into a voltage and feed it into a CRT, you find that the CRT does not give you an amount of light proportional to the voltage. The amount of light coming from the phosphor in the screen depends on the voltage something like this:

```
Light_out = voltage ^ crt_gamma
```

So if you just jump your nice linear image out to a CRT, the image will look too dark. To fix this up you have to "gamma correct" the image first. You need to do the opposite of what the CRT will do to the image, so that things cancel out, and you get when you want. So you have to do this to your image:

```
gamma_corrected_image+image^(1/crt_gamma)
```

For most CRTs, the `crt_gamma` is somewhere between 1.0 and 3.0.

3.11 PHOTO RETOUCHING

Photo retouch features let you change images to accomplish a variety of tasks. To improve a composition correct distortions or flaws, creatively manipulate picture elements, add or remove items, sharpen or blur, or merge multiple images. Retouching tools enable us to change or edit pixels in a number of ways.

3.12 VIDEO PRODUCTION

Making video involves working through three general phases:

- *Pre-production* involves writing the script, visualizing scenes by sketching them on a storyboard, and creating a production schedule for shooting the scenes.
- *Production* involves shooting the scenes.
- *Post-production* involves editing the best scenes into the final video program, correcting and enhancing video and audio where necessary. Premiere is designed for efficient editing, correcting, and enhancing of clips, making it a valuable tool for post-production.

3.12.1 Measuring Video Time

Working with video requires precise synchronization, so it is necessary to measure time using numbers. Familiar time divisions– hours, minutes, and seconds– are not precise enough for video editing, because a single second might contain several events.

You can determine how time is divided in your project by specifying the project timebase. For example, a timebase of 30 means that each second is divided into 30 units. The exact time at which an edit occurs depends on the timebase you specify, because an edit can only occur at a time division. Using a different timebase causes the time divisions to fall in different places.

The time divisions in a source clip are determined by the source frame rate. For example, when you shoot source clips using a video camera with a frame rate of 30 frames per second, the camera records the scene every $1/30^{th}$ of a second.

3.13 VIDEO EDITING

Video editing is the process of manipulating and rearranging video shots to create a new work. Editing is usually considered to be one part of the post production process–other post-production tasks include titling, colour correction, sound mixing, etc. Depending on the level of quality you want and the capabilities of your equipment, you may be able to use Video editing software for either online or offline editing. The settings you specify for video capture are different for offline and online editing.

Before you can edit video program, all source clips must be instantly accessible from a hard disk, not from videotape. You can import the source clips from the source videotapes to your computer through a post-production step called *video capture*. You must have a hard disk to store all the clips you want to edit, so to save space, capture just the clips you know you want to use.

3.13.1 Online and Offline Editing

Online editing is the practice of doing all editing on the same computer that will produce the final cut. Today, continuing improvements in the speed of personal computers make online editing increasingly practical for broadcast television or motion-picture film productions. For online editing, you capture clips once at the highest level of quality your computer and its connected hardware can handle.

In offline editing you edit video using lower-quality copies of the original clips and produce the final version on a high-end system using the original clips.

Offline editing requires clips captured with frame-accurate timecode. To do this, use device control to capture clips.

3.14 COMPONENTS THAT AFFECT VIDEO CAPTURE QUALITY

Video capture requires a higher and more consistent level of computer performance. The ability of your computer to capture video depends on the combined performance of the following components:

3.14.1 Video-capture Card

You need video-capture hardware–either a video–capture card or equivalent capability built into your computer. To transfer video between a videotape deck (or other video source) and your computer. Note that a video–capture card is not the same as the video card that drives your computer monitor.

3.14.2 Hard Disk

The hard disk stores the video frames you capture. It must be fast enough to store captured video frames as quickly as they arrive from the video card, otherwise frames will be dropped as the disk falls behind.

3.14.3 Central Processing Unit (CPU)

Your computer's processor handles general processing tasks in your computer. It must be fast enough to process captured frames at the capture frame rate. A faster CPU (Central Processing Unit) or using multiple CPUs in one computer (multiprocessing) is better. However, other system components must be fast enough to handle the CPU speed. Using a fast CPU with slow components is like driving a sports car in a traffic jam.

3.14.4 Codec (Compressor/Decompressor)

Most video-capture cards come with a compression chip that keeps the data within a level your computer can handle. If your video-capture hardware does not have a compression chip, capture using a fast, high-quality codec, such as Motion JPEG (Joint Photographic Experts Group). If you capture using a slow-compressing or lossy codec, such as Cinepak, you will drop frames or lose quality.

3.14.5 Processing Time required by Other Software

If you capture video while several other programs are running (such as virtual memory, network connections, non-essential system enhancers and screen savers), the other programs will probably interrupt the video-capture with requests for processing time, causing dropped frames. Capture video while running as few drivers, extensions, and other programs as possible.

3.14.6 Data Bus

Every computer has a data bus that connects system components and handles data transfer between them. Its speed determines how fast the computer can move video frames between the video-capture card, the processor, and the hard disk.

3.15 LINEAR AND NON-LINEAR VIDEO EDITING

Linear editing means that a project is edited and assembled in a linear fashion from start to finish. Linear editing is most common when working with videotape. Videotape, unlike film, cannot be physically cut into pieces and spliced together in a new order. Instead, the editor must dub or record each desired video clip onto a master tape.

Let's say you have three source tapes, labeled A, B and C. In linear editing, the editor decides which source material he wants to use first, second and third. In this case, he wants to use material from tape C first, then B and A. He starts with tape C. When the desired clip from tape C is done, he stops recording. Then he has to do the same thing for the clips on tapes B and A.

In non-linear editing, however, the editor has the ability to edit any segment of the project in any order he wants. He can cut, copy and paste clips from one part of the project to another just like you can cut, copy and paste text with word processing software.

Linear video editing is the craft of using two videotape machines to create a final video master. It involves copying video from one machine to another with a controlling device. Shots are recorded onto the second machine in their final sequence. Non-linear video editing uses software that allows you to arrange shots and audio on a timeline in which editing does not have to be done in the same sequence as the final video.

3.16 SUBTITLING

Subtitling is an exciting area of translation, and is part of a broader field of audio visual translation which includes dubbing, voice over and audio description. Subtitling is divided into two types: subtitling within the same language, for the deaf and hard of hearing (also called captioning), and subtitling across languages, for foreign-language film and television. Subtitling does not just translate the dialog, but also other meaningful language in films, such as signs, letters, captions and other written words. When a film has lots of written language and dialog happening together, this can result in some very difficult choices for the subtitler.

Subtitling can be defined as the process of providing synchronized captions for film and television dialogue (and more recently for live opera); while dubbing refers to any technique of covering the original voice in an audio-visual production by another voice.

REVIEW QUESTIONS WITH ANSWERS

1. Multiple Choice

1.1 Adding _______ to objects on your slides not only controls the flow of information, but adds interest to your presentation.

a. Background b. Transition

c. Animation d. Popups

1.2 What does GUI stand for?

a. Gaming User Interface b. Graphical User Interface

c. Geometric User Interface
d. Guidance User

1.3 Sound as recorded on a computer is:
a. Analoged
b. Digitized
c. Animated
d. Encoded

1.4 Music that plays on a computer, such as a radio station, but is never downloaded is known as:
a. P2P
b. Streaming
c. MP3
d. Online

1.5 Which of following is a painting program and image editing program?
a. Designer
b. FreeHand
c. Illustrator
d. Photoshop

1.6 Making video involves working through:
a. Pre-production
b. Production
c. Post-production
d. All of the above

1.7 Vector editing programs create graphic images using mathematically described objects, such as:
a. Circles
b. Lines
c. Circles or lines
d. None of these

1.8 In what situation, we use sound editing?
a. Control the external environment
b. Remove inconsistency
c. Add special effects
d. All of the above

1.9 Graphic editing has to be performed:
a. To improve the attributes of existing image
b. To remove unwanted portions of the image
c. To add special effects, not possible with actual photography
d. All of the above

1.10 The scripting language of Flash is called:
a. ActionScript
b. ECMAScript
c. JavaScript
d. RunTime

2. State whether the following statements are True or False

2.1 A bitmap is a simple matrix of the tiny dots that form an image and are displayed on computer screen or printed.

2.2 Vector images can be used for photo-realistic images.

2.3 Most commonly used format for graphics is .BMP or bitmap pictures.

2.4 Use digitized audio for spoken dialog.

2.5 You can digitize sounds from any source, live or pre-recorded.

2.6 Linear video editing is the craft of using two videotape machines to create a final video master.

2.7 Offline editing requires clips captured with frame-accurate timecode.

2.8 Production involves writing the script, visualizing scenes by sketching them on a storyboard.

2.9 Photo retouch features let you change images to accomplish a variety of tasks.

2.10 Digital signal processing uses a specialized processor to convert data from one format to another to a high rate.

3. Match the following:

3.1	Trimming	a.	Digital Signal Processing
3.2	DSP	b.	Removing dead air or blank space
3.3	Scaling	c.	Manipulating and rearranging video shots
3.4	A bitmap	d.	Changing the size of a font
3.5	Converting analog-to-digital signal	e.	A bouncing ball
3.6	4-bits per pixel	f.	A rectangular array of points
3.7	1-bit per pixel	g.	Digitization
3.8	Squash and stretch	h.	16 colors
3.9	Subtitling	i.	2 colors
3.10	Video Editing	j.	Dubbing

4. Fill in the blanks

a. Sequencer
b. FM synthesis
c. MIDI
d. Timeline
e. Production
f. Splicing
g. Sound Editing
h. Masking
i. Trimming
j. Toolbox

4.1 The _____ sequencer does not record the actual audio, but rather the events related to the performance.

4.2 ______ is the process by which we can remove the unwanted sounds that have crept in during recording.

4.3 The process of removing the blank spaces before or after the required signals is called __________.

4.4 The technique of blending around with a range of frequency modulation to produce audio that resembles the original analog sound data is called __________.

4.5 __________ involves shooting the scenes.

4.6 __________ is the process of blocking out selected portions of the image for a particular editing operations.

4.7 ________ holds tools for creating and editing images.

4.8 ________ plays very important role in all multimedia audio applications.

4.9 In time-based tools, elements and events are organized along with a ________.

4.10 The MIDI ________ allows the user to record and edit a musical performance without using an audio-based input source.

Answers

1.	1.1	c	1.2	b	1.3	b	1.4	b	1.5	d	1.6	d
	1.7	c	1.8	d	1.9	d	1.10	a				
2.	2.1	T	2.2	F	2.3	T	2.4	T	2.5	T	2.6	T
	2.7	T	2.8	F	2.9	T	2.10	T				
3.	3.1	b	3.2	a	3.3	d	3.4	f	3.5	g	3.6	h
	3.7	i	3.8	e	3.9	j	3.10	c				
4.	4.1	c	4.2	f	4.3	i	4.4	b	4.5	e	4.6	h
	4.7	j	4.8	g	4.9	d	4.10	a				

Questions with Answers

1. Define the following terms:
   a. Trimming
   b. Splicing
   c. Equalization
2. What are advantages of Digital Audio over Analog Audio?
3. Explain in brief the following:
   a. White Balance
   b. Gamma Correction
   c. Subtitling
4. Explain any four software which are used in multimedia industry.
5. What is difference between online editing and offline editing?
6. Describe in short the advantages and disadvantages of the MIDI audio over digital audio.
7. What is synthesized audio?

Answers to Short Questions

1. a. Every recording is associated with a blank space for a few seconds before and after the required sound. The process of removing blank spaces is called *trimming*. Removal of blank spaces, apart from reducing the audio file size considerably enable perfect item matching and further editing operations easy.
   b. The process by which we can remove the unwanted sounds that have crept in during recording.
   c. Some programs offer digital Equalization (EQ) capabilities, useful for long sections that you wish to fade in or fade out gradually. This enveloping helps to smooth out the very beginning and the very end of the sound file.
2. Advantages of digital audio over analog audio as follow:
   a. Digital audio is less susceptible to degradation or distortion, because the entire transmission and all other transaction processes take place as electronic signals, avoiding the intervention of air or any other medium. Thus, the quality of the parent signal is maintained throughout.
   b. Digital audio is of superior quality during reproduction, because of non-intervention of air and other loss incurring mediums.
   c. Digital audio can be stored as digital data, in reliable mediums like the CD-ROM. Thus extending their life of more than fifty years on an average without losses.
3. (a) ***White Balance:*** White balance (WB) is the process of removing unrealistic colour casts so that objects which appear white in person are rendered white in your photo. Proper camera white balance has to take into account, the 'colour temperature' of a light source, which refers to the relative warmth or coolness of white light.
   (b) ***Gamma Correction:*** Gamma correction is the adjustment of the brightness and/or contrast in colour on image displayed on computer monitor or on a printer. Adjusting the gamma correction on a image can correct the overall quality of an image.
   (c) ***Subtitling:*** Subtitling can be defined as the process of providing synchronized captions for film and television dialogue (and more recently for live opera); while dubbing refers to any technique of covering the original voice in an audio-visual production by another voice.
4. Following are some of the software that are used in multimedia industry:
   a. ***Photoshop:*** Photoshop is most popular program for creating and image editing. You can use Photoshop to alter image like photos, downloaded icons, or scanned artwork. Altering an image includes doing such things as changing the colors within an image, modifying the size and scale of an image, or putting one picture within another.
   b. ***Director:*** Director from Macromedia started out as a multimedia tool for presentations. Macromedia Director is the best solution for creating rich content and applications for CD/DVD-ROM. kiosks, Intranets, and the web. Director allows users to build exceptionally rich content that delivers integrated interactive audio, video, vectors and bitmaps, text, fonts and much more.
   c. ***Premiere:*** Adobe Premier is a powerful program for editing digital video. Premiere helps you to create dynamic video or film, whether you are creating long video programs and motion picture films or short movies for CD-ROM or the Web. Like most editing software, Premiere works by importing video from a source, such as a video tape onto your hard drive, then allowing you to create new edited versions which you can export back to tape, disk or other medium.
   d. ***Flash:*** Adobe flash is a software that creates animations for a web designs. You can create a multimedia enriched content (Flash movies) containing images, sound, video and animation effects with this software. Adding more to this, the Flash software comes with a scripting language, called ActionScript, which provides interactivity to your Flash movies. Flash also comes with number of pre-built components including media components that load Flash video files or MP3 audio to enhance your Website.
5. Online editing is the practice of doing all editing on the same computer that will produce the final cut. Today, continuing improvements in the speed of personal computers make online editing increasingly practical for broadcast television or motion-picture film productions. For online editing, you capture clips once at the highest level of quality your computer and its connected hardware can handle.
   In offline editing you edit video using lower-quality copies of the original clips and produce the final version on a high-end system using the original clips.
6. Advantages of MIDI
   a. MIDI files are much more compact than digital audio files.
   b. MIDI files are small; they donot take up as much RAM, disk space, and CPU resources.
   c. The size of MIDI file is completely independent of playback quality.
   d. In some cases, MIDI files may sound better than digital audio files if the MIDI sound source you are using is of high quality.
   e. The length of a MIDI file can be changed (by varying its tempo) without changing the pitch of the music or degrading the audio quality.
   f MIDI files are embedded in Web pages, load and play time are faster.

Disadvantages of MIDI

a. Because MIDI data is not sound, you can be certain that playback will be accurate only if the MIDI playback device is identical to the device used for production.
b. MIDI cannot easily be used to play back spoken dialog, although expensive and technically tricky digital samples are available.
c. A wider selection of application software and system support for digital audio is available for both the Macintosh and Windows platforms but not for MIDI.
d. Midi files can not be burned onto CD. This is a drawback. But they can be converted into .wav, .aiff, or .mp3 files.

7. In music technology, sound synthesis is the process of generating sound from analog and digital electronic equipment, often for musical, artistic or entertainment purposes. In particular, it refers to the process of generating, combining or mixing sounds from a set of fundamental building blocks or routines in order to create sounds of a greater complexity and richness.

DESCRIPTIVE TYPE QUESTIONS

1. What do you mean by sound editing? Explain different functions performed in sound editing.
2. How is bitmap editing program is different from vector editing program?
3. Explain different components that affect video capture quality.
4. Explain different phases of video production.
5. What is photo retouching?
6. How mono recording is different from stereo recording?
7. What do you mean by music sequencing and notation?
8. What is codec?
9. Write a short note on image/graphic editing programs.
10. Explain different image editing program.
11. What is synthesized audio? Explain with example.
12. Compare MIDI with digitized audio.
13 What is MIDI? How does it help in the creation of multimedia applications?

CHAPTER 4

Introduction to Compression Technology

4.1 COMPRESSION TECHNOLOGY

Multimedia files are usually very large in size. Therefore, for the purpose of the storage and transmitting large-sized multimedia files on the Internet, the file sizes need to be reduced. Files which contain text and other files may also sometimes need to be encoded or compressed for the purpose of sending e-mail and also for other multimedia applications.

In the field of computer science, the term data compression is also known as *source coding*. It allows the file storing in less space and, if there is need to transmit the data or file, it will send more efficiently and at low cost.

4.1.1 Concept of Lossy and Lossless Compression

If decompressed data is the same as the original data, it is referred to as *lossless compression*, otherwise the compression is *lossy* because there is loss of originality in the reproduced data.

In *lossless* compression, all of the information–and thus all of the quality–in the original clip is preserved after compression. However, preserving the original level of quality limits the degree to which you can lower the data rate and file size, and the resulting data rate may be too high for smooth playback. Lossless codecs, such as Animation (at the best quality setting) are used to preserve maximum quality during editing or for still images where data rate is not an issue.

But, in *lossy compression*, some of the original data discards during compression. For example, if the pixels making up a sky actually contain 78 shades of blue, a lossy codec set for less than best quality may record 60 shades of blue. Lossy compression allows much lower data rates and file sizes than lossless compression. Video are commonly used for final production of video delivered using CD-ROM (Compact Disk Read Only Memory) or the Internet. In case of lossy compression, the desired quality level of the decompressed data is application dependent.

4.2 BASIC IMAGE COMPRESSION

Image compression is minimizing the size in bytes of a graphics files without degrading the quality of the image to an unacceptable level. The reduction in file size allows more images to be stored in a given amount of disk or memory space. It also reduces the time required for images to be sent over the Internet or download from Web pages.

> ☞ *Image compression is the application of data compression on digital images. In effect, the objective is to reduce redundancy of the image data in order to be able to store or transmit data in an efficient form.*

Computer programmers are constantly working on new methods of using less computer memory to do the same amount of work.

> ☞ *Whenever a computer program or mathematical algorithm is used to reduce the amount of memory a computer file uses, that file is said to be compressed.*

Computer files of every type have some repeating elements. The same information appearing over and over. For example, files that contain only text will have many words and characters repeated over and over. There are various compression methods, and each is designed to work best with a particular type of data, but they all rely on replacing repeating elements with more efficient data storage.

There are many different organizational methods you can use to reduce the total amount of space you need to record the data. Data compression can be categorized in two ways. Compression applied to an entire file or compression incorporated within a file structure.

When an entire file is compressed, the compression program takes all the data, applies a particular compression algorithm to the data, and creates a new file. There is one drawback, the file cannot be used by any software until it is uncompresses back to its original state. So entire file compression is useful for long-term storage or transportation, but inconvenient for everyday use.

In DOS (Disk Operating System) and Windows computers, ZIP (Zone Improvement Plan) and ARC (ARChive) are two common compression formats. To uncompress all these formats, the computer needs software that is especially designed to read the compressed files.

Compression can also be incorporated into, and done within, the actual structure of a computer file, so any software designed to read the file format will not be affected by the compression. This makes internal file compression extremely useful, especially when you are dealing with computer that take up large amounts of computer memory.

Image compression can be *lossy* or *lossless*. Lossless compression is sometimes preferred for artificial images, such as technical drawings, icons or comics. This is because lossy compression methods, especially when used at low *bit rates*, introduce *compression artifacts*. Lossless compression methods may also be preferred for high value content, such as medical imagery or image scans made for archival purposes. Lossy methods are especially suitable for natural images, such as photos in applications where minor (sometimes imperceptible) loss of fidelity is acceptable to achieve a substantial reduction in bit rate. The lossy compression that produces imperceptible differences can be called *visually lossless*.

Compressing an image is significantly different than compressing raw binary data. Of course, general purpose compression program can be used to compress images, but the result is less than optimal. This is because images have certain statistical properties which can be exploited by encoders specifically designed for them. Also, some of the finer details in the image can be sacrificed for the sake of saving a little more bandwidth or storage space. This also means that lossy compression techniques can be used in this area.

Lossless compression involves with compressing data which, when decompressed, will be an exact replica of the original data. This is the case when binary data, such as executables, documents etc. are compressed. They need to be exactly reproduced when decompressed. On the other hand, images (and music too) need not be reproduced 'exactly'. An approximation of the original image is enough for most purposes, as long as the error between the original and the compressed image is tolerable.

☞ *A text file or program can be compressed without the introduction of errors, but only up to a certain extent. This is called lossless compression. Beyond this point, errors are introduced. In text and program files, it is crucial that compression be lossless because a single error can seriously damage the meaning of a text file, or cause a program not to run.*

In image compression, a small loss in quality is usually not noticeable. There is no "critical point" up to which compression works perfectly, but beyond which it becomes impossible. When there is some tolerance for loss, the compression factor can be greater than it can when there is no loss tolerance. For this reason, graphic images can be compressed more than text files or programs.

Image compression is minimizing the size in bytes of a graphics file without degrading the quality of the image to an unacceptable level. The reduction in file size allows more images to be stored in a given amount of disk or memory space. It also reduces the time required for images to be sent over the Internet or downloaded from web pages.

There are several different ways in which image files can be compressed. For Internet use, the two most common compressed graphic image formats are the JPEG (Joint Photographic Experts Group) format and the GIF (Graphics Interchange Format) format. The JPEG method is more often used for photographs, while the GIF method is commonly used for line art and other images in which geometric shapes are relatively simple.

Other techniques for image compression include the use of fractals and wavelets. These methods have not gained widespread acceptance for use on the Internet. However, they offer higher compression ratios than the JPEG or GIF methods for some types of images. Another new method that may in time replace the GIF format is the PNG (Portable Network Graphics) format.

☞ *A compression technique that preserves all the original information in an image or other data structure is called losseless compression. PKZIP (a file archiving computer program which was originally written by Phil Katz) and Microsoft CAB (a compressed file format which stands for Cabinet) files are popular applications of lossless compression.*

☞ *A compression technique that achieves optimal data reduction by discarding redundant and unnecessary information in an image. MPEG, and JPEG are popular examples of lossy compression.*

4.3 IMAGE TRANSMISSION

Image transmission takes into account transmission of digital images through computer networks. Image size depends on the image representation format used for transmission. There are several possibilities.

1. Raw image data transmission
   In raw image data transmission, the image is generated through a video digitizer and transmitted in its digital format. The size can be computed as:
   size = spatial_resolution × pixel_quantization
2. Compressed image data transmission
   In compressed image data transmission, the image is generated through a video digitizer and compressed before transmission. JPEG is the standard compression techniques for still images. The reduction of image size depends on the compression method and compression rate.
3. Symbolic image data transmission
   In symbolic image data transmission, the image is represented through symbolic data representation as image primitives (such as 2D or 3D geometric representation), attributes and other control information. Image size is equal to the structure size, which carries the transmitted symbolic information of the image.

4.4 JPEG

JPEG (Joint Photographic Experts Group) format is one of the most common graphic file format for Web applications. JPEG format is also used to display photographs and other continuous tone images in HyperText Markup Language (HTML) documents over the World Wide Web and other online services.

The JPEG format was created by a group of photographic experts to store full-color spectrum, continuous-tone images that is, for images not restricted to dual-tone (black and white) only. This standard allows generation of compressed files for Grayscale images, photographic images, and still video which can be utilized by various multimedia storage and communication applications. JPEG images are of much higher fidelity as well as in higher compressed form than images of GIF format. However, download speed, over the Internet, is much lower with JPEG files. That is, it takes longer time to download graphic files that use JPEG format than those that use GIF format.

☞ *When you create a JPEG image or convert an image into JPEG, you are asked to specify the quality of the image you want. Since the higher quality requires larger memory space, one can make a compromise between image quality and filesize.*

4.4.1 JPEG Compression

For bitmap graphics files, a relatively recent form of compression has been developed which can provide much greater compression ratios than other formats, particularly for photographic quality bitmaps. This format, developed by the Joint Photographic Experts Group, is called JPEG and is usually given the JPG file extension on DOS-based computers. You do not need a specific program to uncompress the JPEG file format, but you do need a recent version of a bitmap editing program that supports the file format, such as PaintShop Pro.

4.4.2 Lossless vs. Lossy Compression

JPEG compression methods have given rise to two new computer graphics terms. lossless and lossy. Lossless compression is any compression in which no original image data is discarded (lost), and images which have been compressed and then restored are–pixel by pixel–precisely the same as the original image. Lossy compression, on the other hand, actually discards (loses) some original image data when the file is compressed. JPEG is capable of both lossy and lossless compression, and the compression amounts achieved can be dramatic (lossy JPEG files are often less than 5% of the original file size).

Images compressed using the lossy method do not necessarily look much worse than images compressed with the lossless method. JPEG takes advantages of the fact that the human eye is very sensitive to variations in apparent brightness, or intensity, and less sensitive to variations in hue or tone. JPEG stores more information about changes in brightness between pixels than it does about color changes between pixels. Since your eye is less likely to notice the minor differences in pixel colors on a pixel-by-pixel scale, the overall image appears unchanged.

4.4.3 JPEG Compression at Work

JPEG compression works best with photographic quality images, unlike other compression methods, which work best with images that contain large areas of solid colors or repeating patterns. Compression that retains all the data from the original image is helped by repeating patterns, since these pixel patterns can be stored once and then replicated as many times as needed to recreate the image.

Lossy compression, on the other hand, examines grouping of pixels (for example, a 9 x 9 square of pixels) to determine the variations between them. Then it stores values for the variation between the pixels rather than for the pixels themselves.

Lossy compression tends to make sharp lines soften or blur slightly and makes variations appear in areas of previously solid color. Photographic quality images, by their nature, tend not to have straight lines or solid areas of color, so these effects are not as noticeable.

4.4.4 JPEG 2000

JPEG 2000 is a file format that provides greater flexibility than the standard JPEG format. Using JPEG 2000, you can produce images with better compression and quality for both Web and print publishing. Unlike traditional JPEG files, which are lossy. The JPEG 2000 format supports optional lossless compression. The JPEG 2000 format also supports using a Region of Interest (ROI) to minimize file size and preserve quality in critical regions of an image.

4.5 BASIC OF AUDIO COMPRESSION

Audio compression is a form of *data compression* designed to reduce the size of audio files. The process of reducing the volume of data by applying a compression technique is called *compression* and the resulting data is called *compressed data*. Compression allows the audio storing in less space and, if there is need to transmit the signal, it will send more efficiently and at low cost.

Audio files consist of analog signals of varying frequencies. The audio signals are converted to digital form and then processed, stored or transmitted. Sounds, including music and speech, are formed of analog sine waves that tend to repeat for seconds at a time. This repetitive nature of audio signals makes audio signals ideal for compression.

Audio compression algorithms are implemented in computer software as audio *codecs*. Generic data compression algorithms perform poorly with audio data, reducing file sizes much below 87% of the original, and are not designed for use in real time. Consequently, specific audio "*lossless*" and "*lossy*" algorithms have been created. Lossy algorithms provide far greater compression ratios and are used in mainstream consumer audio devices.

In both lossy and lossless compression, information redundancy is reduced, using methods, such as coding, pattern recognition and linear prediction to reduce the amount of information used to describe the data.

4.5.1 Lossless Audio Compression

If the decompressed data is the same as the original data, it is referred to as *lossless compression*.

As file storage and communication bandwidth have become less expensive and more available, the popularity of lossless formats has increased sharply. Because people are choosing to maintain a permanent archive of their audio files. The primary users of lossless compression have been audio engineers, audiophiles and those consumers who want to preserve an exact copy of their audio files, in contrast to the irreversible changes from lossy compression techniques. Compression ratios are similar to those for lossless data compression (around 50-60% of original size).

It is difficult to maintain all the data in an audio stream and achieve substantial compression. First, the vast majority of sound recordings are highly complex, recorded from the real world. As one of the key methods of compression is to find patterns and repetition therefore more chaotic data, such as audio does not compress well.

Lossless audio codecs have no quality issues, so the usability can be estimated by:

- Speed of compression and decompression
- Degree of compression
- Software and hardware support
- Robustness and error correction

4.5.2 Lossy Audio Compression

If the decompressed data is not same as the original data, then the compression is called lossy, because there is loss of originality in the reproduced data.

Lossy audio compression is used in an extremely wide range of applications. In addition to the direct applications (MP3 players or computers), digitally compressed audio streams are used in most video DVDs; digital television; streaming media on the Internet; satellite and cable radio; and increasingly in terrestrial radio broadcasts. Lossy compression typically achieves far greater compression than lossless compression (data of 5 percent to 20 percent of the original stream, rather than 50 percent to 60 percent), by discarding less-critical data.

The innovation of lossy audio compression was to use psychoacoustics to recognize that not all data in an audio stream can be perceived by the human auditory system. Most lossy compression reduces perceptual redundancy by first identifying sounds which are considered perceptually irrelevant, that is, sounds that are very hard to hear. Typical examples include high frequencies, or sounds that occur at the same time as louder sounds. Those sounds are coded with decreased accuracy or not coded at all.

Because data is removed during lossy compression and cannot be recovered by decompression, some people may not prefer lossy compression for archival storage.

4.5.3 MP3 (Moving Pictures Expert Group Layer–3)

MP3 (Moving Pictures Expert Group Layer - 3) represents an audio coding format for digital audio which uses the structure of lossy data compression. The functions involve in digital audio compression are to transfer and playback of music on almost each digital audio players. Lossy compression algorithm is used in MP3 to lessen the amount of data and information required in audio recording. The MP3 files are created of 128 KB/s which are about 1/11 of the Compact Disk (CD) file. This CD file is created with the help of original audio source file. The MP3 file uses the function of perpetual coding in which the compression works by dropping accuracy of selected part of sound that are considered to be beyond the acoustic and hearing resolution ability of a most persons.

4.5.4 MP4 (Moving Pictures Expert Group Layer–4)

MP4, short for MPEG-4, is a multimedia container format standard specified as a part of MPEG-4. It is most commonly used to store digital video and digital audio streams, as well as other data such as subtitles and still images. Since MP4 is a container format, it does not have a standard method of coding the audio or video information. Instead, codecs dictate how the audio or video will be coded and possibly compressed.

4.6 BASICS OF VIDEO COMPRESSION

A compression/decompression chip or software reduces the amount of data needed to re-create the video signals. As an example, the software compression for Microsoft Video for Windows looks for redundant information. Here, the background is a large expanse of a single color, blue. Rather than save the same information for each pixel that makes up the background, compression saves the color data for that exact shade of blue only once, along with directions for where to use the color when the video is replayed.

Video for Windows saves more space when it writes the video to disk by interweaving the data for the picture with the audio in a file format called .avi (audio/video interleave). To replay the video, the compressed and combined video and audio data is either sent through a compression/decompression chip or processed by software. Either method restores areas that had been eliminated by compression. The combined audio and video elements of the signal are separated and both are sent to a Digital-to-Analog converter (DAC), which translates that binary data into analog signals that go to the screen and speakers.

Instead of being recorded, the compressed video and audio signals may be sent over special telephone lines, such as an Integrated Services Digital Network (ISDN) line, that transmit the data in a digital form rather than as the analog signal used by ordinary phone lines. A similarly equipped PC (Personal Computer) at a remote location receives the digital signals, decompresses them, and converts them to the analog signals needed to control the display and audio playback.

Advanced forms of compressing both recorded video and videoconferencing use a sampling process to cut down on the amount of data that must be recorded or transmitted. One method, used by .avi, makes a record of one complete video frame, and then records only the differences–*the delta*– in the frames that follow. Each frame is re-created by combining the delta data with the data for the frame that preceded it.

Motion Pictures Expert Group (MPEG) compression, which is effective enough to produce full-screen video, only records key frames and then predicts what the missing frames look like by comparing the changes in the keyframes.

4.7 VIDEO COMPRESSION

Compression is a digital process that allows data to be stored or transmitted using less than normal number of bits.

In Visual recording and transmission, video compression is a technique used to reduce the amount of data in a video file, to limit the amount of storage space or bandwidth it requires. It is common in online mediums and in broadcasting. Video compression works on the same theoretical basis as other types of file compression, and even cryptography, which is that one piece of data can be used and re-used to represent multiple pieces of data.

Literally speaking, video compression is a way of making video files smaller. More specially, video compression is a method by which the pixels that are not easily observable to human eyes are ignored or assimilated into a adjacent ones. Video decompression or *decoding* is a method by which original pixels are recovered to the original or near-original state. Lossy compression refers to the data reduction by which a decoded video cannot be recovered to the original state. In contrast, lossless compression refers to the data reduction by which a decoded video can be recovered to the original state.

Specifically, video compression assumes an uncompressed piece of video contains much more data than is needed to satisfactorily convey it. Compression technology therefore strives to achieve an optimal trade-off that balances data reduction with quality. From a technical standpoint, most types of video compression work by comparing a single frame of video to the frames immediately before it and after it, and saving only the pieces of the frame that are substantially different. The level of compression, therefore, can be adjusted by limiting or expanding just how much difference the compression software looks for. Compression works best when only small sections of the video are changing at a time. Fast-moving objects and events, such as explosions, are very hard to compress, due to their constantly changing composition.

With most means of video compression, the higher the level of compression, the longer it can take for video player hardware to decode the data. This can result in visual glitches. One of these, and a common pitfall of over-compression, is known as *artifacting,* a phenomenon wherein small, static chunks from previous frames of video remain on the screen over top of the moving image. Artifacting is particularly common in video files formatted for the Internet and mobile devices, where visual quality is a secondary priority behind file size.

In mediums, such as DVD-Video (DVDs), in which optimum visual quality is the main objective, a video can still be greatly compressed and remain reasonably sharp. New technologies such as Blu-ray, which have much greater capacities than DVDs, require less compression and can therefore present a video in even greater quality. Ongoing advances in both storage and transmission technologies continue to reduce the need for extreme levels of compression, and shift the emphasis towards providing greater quality.

Video compression algorithms ("codecs") manipulate video signals to dramatically reduce the storage and bandwidth required while maximizing perceived video quality. To compress the file and reduce its size, it needs to be filtered through a specialized software called a Codec, which is short for compression/decompression or Coder/Decoder. The software reads the media data and applies mathematical algorithm to reduce its size. The algorithms find redundant information within the media files. Redundant information are those which can either be discarded without affecting the media quality by appreciable measures, or data that can be expressed in a more compact form. In either case this leads to a reduction in file size, but the actual amount of reduction depends on a large number of factors involving both the media data and the Codec used.

Understanding the operation of video codecs is essential for developers of embedded systems, processors, and tools targeting video applications. For example, understanding video codecs' processing and memory demands is key to processor selection and software optimization.

4.8 VIDEO COMPRESSION TECHNOLOGY.

At its most basic level, compression is performed when an input video stream is analyzed and information that is indiscernible to the viewer is discarded. Each event is then assigned a code commonly occurring events are assigned few bits and rare events will have codes more bits. These steps are commonly called signal analysis, quantization and variable length encoding respectively. There are four methods for compression, Discrete Cosine Transform (DCT), Vector Quantization (VQ), fractal compression, and Discrete Wavelet Transform (DWT).

Discrete cosine transform is a lossy compression algorithm that samples an image at regular intervals, analyzes the frequency components present in the sample, and discards those frequencies which do not affect the image as the human eye perceives it. DCT is the basis of standards, such as JPEG and MPEG.

Vector quantization is a lossy compression that looks at an array of data, instead of individual values. It can then generalize what it sees, compressing redundant data, while at the same time retaining the desired object or data stream's original intent.

Fractal compression is a form of VQ and is also a lossy compression. Compression is performed by locating self-similar sections of an image, then using a fractal algorithm to generate the sections.

Like DCT, discrete wavelet transform mathematically transforms an image into frequency components. The process is performed on the entire image, which differs from the other methods (DCT), that works on smaller pieces of the desired data. The result is a hierarchical representation of an image, where each layer represents a frequency band.

4.9 MPEG

Motion Pictures Expert Group (MPEG) compression, which is effective enough to produce full-screen video, only records key frames and then predicts what the missing frames look like by comparing the changes in the keyframes.

4.9.1 MPEG-1

MPEG standards address the issues of video coding for entertainment and broadcast purposes. The first public standard of the MPEG committee was the MPEG-1. It was released in 1993. MPEG-1 video compression is based upon the same technique that is used in JPEG. In addition to that, it also includes techniques for efficient coding of a video sequence. MPEG-1 is optimized for coding of video and associated audio for digital storage media, such as CD-ROM. It can be also applied to other storage or communication systems.

4.9.2 MPEG-2

MPEG-2 enhances the techniques of MPEG-1 to support video coding for a range of video communication applications, including broadcast digital television and higher quality at the expense of a higher bandwidth usage. MPEG-2 also provides more advanced techniques to enhance the video quality at the same bit-rate. DVD movies are compressed using the techniques of MPEG-2.

4.9.3 MPEG-3

It is the next version of the MPEG standard. It was designed to handle HDTV, (High Definition Television) however, it was discovered that the MPEG-2 standard could be slightly modified and then achieve the same results as the planned MPEG-3 standard.

4.9.4 MPEG-4

The next generation of MPEG is MPEG-4, which is based upon the same technique as MPEG-1 and MPEG-2. Key aspects of this newly proposed MPEG-4 standard include independent coding of objects in a picture frame, the ability to interactively composite these objects into a scene at the display, the ability to combine graphics, animated objects in the scene, and the ability to transmit scenes in higher dimensionality formats (e.g. 3D). Also, inherent in the MPEG-4 standard is the concept of video scalability, both in the temporal and spatial domains, in order to effectively control the video bit rate at the transmitter, in the network, and at the receiver so as to match the available transmission and processing resources.

4.9.5 H.264

H.264 is the latest generation standard for video encoding. It provides good video quality at substantially lower bit rates than previous standards and with better error robustness. The H.264 standard supports motion video coding for video conferencing and videotelephony applications. It is optimized for video communications at the bit rates supported by ISDNs (Integrated Services Digital Networks).

4.9.6 MPEG-7

MPEG-7 is a different kind of standard. As it is a multimedia content description standard, it does not deal with the actual encoding of moving pictures and audio. But, the representation that is defined within MPEG-4, i.e., the representation of audio-visual data in terms of objects, is very well-suited to the MPEG-7 standard. With MPEG-7, the content of the video is described and associated with the content itself. For example, to allow fast and efficient searching in the material. It is relevant for video surveillance since it could be used to tag the contents and events of video streams for more intelligent processing in video management software or video analytics applications.

4.9.7 MPEG-21

MPEG-21 is a standard that defines means of sharing digital rights, permissions, and restrictions for digital content. It is an eXtensible Markup language or XML-based standard, which is developed to counter illegitimate distribution of digital content. MPEG-21 is not particularly relevant for video surveillance situations.

4.10 VIDEO COMPRESSION PRINCIPLE

The video compression principle that is employed in MPEG system using I-, P-and B-frames. MPEG-1 has several frame/picture types that serve different purposes.

4.10.1 I-Frames

I-frame an abbreviation for Intra-frame, is so-called because it can be decoded independently of any other frames. They may also be known as I-pictures, or keyframes due to their somewhat similar function to the key frames used in animation. I-frames can be considered effectively identical to baseline JPEG images.

I-frame only compression is very fast, but produces very large file sizes: a factor of 3x (or more) larger than normally encoded MPEG-1 video, depending on how temporally complex a specific video is.

4.10.2 P-frames

P-frame is an abbreviation for Predicted-frame. They may also be called forward-predicted frames, or inter-frames.

P-frames exist to improve compression by exploiting the temporal (over time) redundancy in a video. P-frames store only the difference in image from the frame (either an I-frame or P-frame) . immediately preceding it (this reference frame is also called the *anchor frame*).

A P-frame can contain any number of intra-coded blocks, in addition to any forward-predicted blocks. If a video drastically changes from one frame to the next (such as a scene change), it is more efficient to encode it as an I-frame.

4.10.3 B-frames

B-frame stands for bidirectional-frame. They may also be known as backwards-predicted frames or B-pictures. B-frames are quite similar to P-frames, except they can make predictions using both the previous and future frames (i.e., two anchor frames).

A B-frame can contain any number of intra-coded blocks and forward-predicted blocks, in addition to backwards-predicted, or bidirectionally predicted blocks.

4.11 CHOOSING A VIDEO COMPRESSION METHOD

The goal of data compression is to represent the same content using less data. You can specify a compressor/decompressor, or codec, that manages compression. A codec is the algorithm used to compress (code) a video for delivery and then decode it in real time for fast playback. Different codecs are optimized for different methods of delivery, for example, from a hard drive, from a CD-ROM, or over the Web. Real-time video compression algorithms, such as MPEG, Indeo, JPEG and Cinepak are available to compress digital video information at rates that range from 50:1 to 200:1. In addition to compressing video data, streaming technologies are being implemented to provide reasonable quality low bandwidth video on the Web. By starting playback of a video as soon as enough data has transferred to the user's computer to sustain this playback. Users do not have to be wait for large file to downloaded.

A codec may use one or more strategies for compression because no single method is best for all situations. The following list describes the most common strategies used by codecs and the kinds of video they are intended to compress:

4.11.1 Spatial (space) Compression

Spatial compression looks for ways to compact a single frame by looking for pattern and repetition among pixels. For example, instead of describing each of several thousand pixels in a picture of a blue sky, spatial compression can record a much shorter description, such as "All the pixels in this area are light blue." *Run-length encoding* is a version of this technique that is used by many codecs. Run-length Encoding (RLE) is a very simple form of data compression in which runs of data (that is, sequences in which the same data value occurs in many consecutive data elements) are stored as a single data value and count, rather than as the original run. This is most useful on data that contains many such runs, for example, relatively simple graphic images, such as icons, line drawings, and animations. It is not recommended for use with those files that donot have many runs as they could potentially double the file size.

In run-length method, repeated symbols in a string are replaced with the symbol and the number of instances it is repeated. For example, "aaabbbbcccccaaabbbb" is expressed as "a3b4c5a3b4".

Codecs that use spatial compression, such as QuickTime Animation or Microsoft RLE, work well with video containing large solid areas of color, such as cartoon animation.

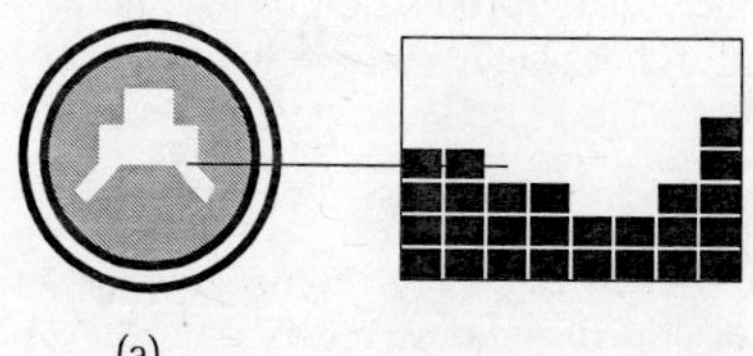

(a)

Digital image consumes a lot of disk space when stored without compression

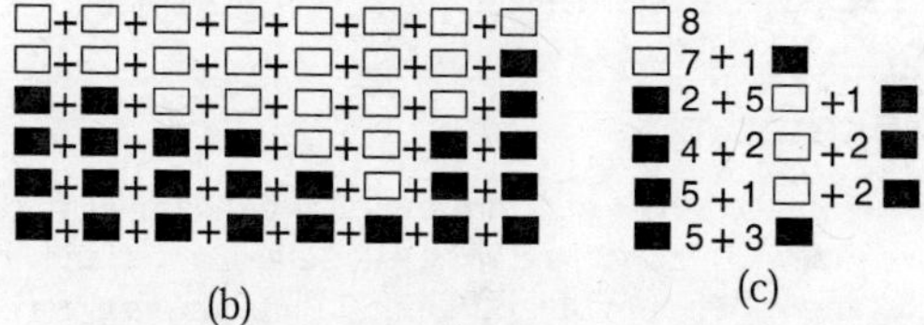

(b) (c)

Applying run-length encoding stores the same frame data in much less space

Figure 4.1

Figure 4.1 shows the techniques used in compressed data. Compression is useful because it helps reduce resource usage, such as data storage space or transmission capacity. Codecs use the spatial compression techniques, such as QuickTime Animation or Microsoft RLE which works well with digital images. Figure 4.1 (a) shows that digital images are composed of pixels, which consume a lot of disk space when stored, without compression whereas Figures 4.1 (b) and 4.1 (c) show that run-length encoding technique is applied to store the same frame data in much less space.

☞ *In general, as you increase spatial compression, the data rate and file size decrease, and the picture loses sharpness and definition. However, some forms of run-length encoding preserve picture quality completely, but require more processing power.*

Common formats for run-length encoded data include TGA (Truevision Graphics Adapter), PackBits, PCX (Personal Computer eXchange) and ILBM (InterLieaved BitMap).

Run-length encoding performs lossless data compression and is well suited to palette-based iconic images. It does not work well at all on continuous-tone images, such as photographs, although JPEG uses it quite effectively on the coefficients that remain after transforming and quantizing image blocks.

Run-length encoding is used in fax machines (combined with other techniques into Modified Huffman coding). It is relatively efficient because most faxed documents are mostly white space, with occasional interruptions of black.

Data that have long sequential runs of bytes (such as lower-quality sound samples) can be RLE compressed after applying a predictive filter, such as delta encoding.

4.11.2 Temporal (time) Compression

Temporal compression compacts the changes during a sequence of frames by looking for patterns and repetition over time. In some video clips, such as clip of a television announcer, temporal compression will notice that the only pixels that change from frame to frame are those forming the face of the speaker. All the other pixels do not change (when the camera is motionless). Instead of describing every pixel in every frame, temporal compression describes only the pixels that are different from the previous frame. This technique is called *frame differencing*. When most of the pixels in a frame are different from the previous frame. It is preferable to describe the entire frame again. Each whole frame is called a *keyframe*, which sets a new starting point for frame differencing.

☞ *Temporal compression works best when large areas in the video do not change, and is less effective when the image constantly changes, such as in a music video.*

4.11.3 Lossless and Lossy Compression

If decompressed data is the same as the original data, it is referred to as *lossless compression*, otherwise the compression is *lossy* because there is loss of originality in the reproduced data.

Some codecs use *lossless* compression, which ensures that all of the information–and thus all of the quality–in the original clip is preserved after compression. However, preserving the original level of quality limits the degree to which you can lower the data rate and file size, and the resulting data rate may be too high for smooth playback. Other compression methods use lossy compression, which discards some of the original data during compression. For example, if the pixels making up a sky actually contain 78 shades of blue, a lossy codec set for less than best quality may record 60 shades of blue. Lossy compression allows much lower data rates and file sizes than lossless compression. Videos are commonly used for final production of video delivered using CD-ROM or the Internet. Lossless codecs, such as Animation (at the best quality setting) are used to preserve maximum quality during editing or for still images where data rate is not an issue. In case of lossy compression, the desired quality level of the decompressed data is application dependent.

Videoconferencing uses lossy compression. Within each frame, differences that are unnoticeable or nearly so are discarded. A slight variation in the background here, for example, is sacrificed so that the system will not have to handle the information needed to display that difference. Monitors can display more colors than the human eye can distinguish. By discarding minor differences, lossy compression saves time and memory without any discernible change in image.

4.11.4 Asymmetrical and Symmetrical Compression

The code you choose affects production workflow, not just in file size or playback speed, but in the time required for a code to compress a given number of frames. Fast compression helps video production, and fast decompression makes viewing easier, but many codecs take far more time to compress frames than to decompress than during playback. This is why a 30-second clip may take a few minutes to process before playback. In a compression technique, if the time required to compress and to decompress are roughly same, it is referred to as symmetrical compression. In asymmetrical compression, the time taken for compression is usually much longer than decompression. Symmetrical techniques are used in those applications that require data to be digitized and compressed in real time, such as video conferencing. On the otherhand, asymmetrical techniques are used in those applications in which the data are compressed once and decompressed several time, such as in video-on-demand applications.

4.12 VIDEO RECORDING AND TAPE FORMATS

4.12.1 Ampex

The word Ampex is the name of a company based in California which manufactures audio instruments and expands to Alexander M Pontaiff Excellence. It became a leader in magnetic recording in the 1950's in both audio and video. The company invented the quadruplex format that was used in the broadcast industry for decades for recording televisions programs onto magnetic tape.

In 1967, ABC (American Broadcast Corporation) used Ampex recorders for the first time to display instant slow motion replay of sporting events. Ampex in that year also invented the portable broadcast video recorder which enabled broadcast quality video to be shot in outdoor locations.

In 1970, Ampex introduced the first robotic library system which enabled TV stations to re-sequence TV commercials instantaneously. The Ampex recording system is now obsolete. All modern day recordings are being done in digital format.

4.12.2 VERA

VERA (Vision Electronic Recording Apparatus) was an early videotape format developed by the BBC (British Broadcasting) beginning in 1952. It used very high tape speeds of about 200 inches/second to record the high frequencies recorded by video signals.

VERA was capable of recording about 15 minutes of 405-line black and white video per reel. Development began in 1952, but VERA was not perfected until 1958, by which time it had already been rendered obsolete by the Ampex quadruplex video recording system.

4.12.3 U-matic

U-matic is a videocassette format first shown by Sony in prototype in October 1969, and introduced to the market in September 1971. It was among the first video formats to contain the videotape inside a cassette, as apposed to the various open-reel formats of the time. Unlike most other cassette-based tape formats, the supply and take-up reels in the cassette worked in opposite directions during playback, fast-forward and rewind: one reel would run clockwise while the other would run counter-clockwise.

In the early 1980s, Sony introduced the semi backwards-compatible High-band or BVU (Broadcast Video U-matic) format, and the 'original' U-matic format became known as 'Low-band'. This high-band format had an improved color recording system and lower noise levels.

Sony made final improvements to the BVU format and called it BVU-SP (superior performance). Superior performance, is the further enhanced variation on the format which uses chrome tape for better video response and lower noise.

In 1990s, it was made absolute by sony betacam-SP. U-matic is no longer used in mainstream production but would be remembered as a cheap and robust facility processed by almost all TV stations in the world.

4.12.4 Betamax

Betamax (sometimes called Beta) is a home videocassette tape recording format developed by Sony, released on May 10, 1975. The cassettes contain 1/2-inch (12.7 mm)-wide videotape in a design similar to the earlier, professional 3/4-inch (19.05 mm) U-matic format. The format is generally considered obsolete, though it is still used in specialist applications by a small minority of people.

4.12.5 Betacam

Betacam is a family of half-inch professional videotape products. It was developed by Sony in 1982. All Betacam variants from (plain) Betacam to Betacam SP and Digital Betacam, use the same shape cassettes, meaning *vaults* and other storage facilities do not have to be changed when upgrading to a new format. The cassettes come in two sizes: S and L. Betacam cameras can only load S tapes, while VTRs can play both S and L tapes. The cassette shell and case for each Betacam cassette is colored differently depending on the format, allowing for easy visual identification. There is also a mechanical key that allows a video tape recorder to tell which format has been inserted.

The format supplanted the three-quarter inch U-matic format, which Sony had introduced in 1971. In addition to improvements in video quality, the Betacam configuration of an integrated camera/recorder led to its rapid adoption by electronic news gathering organizations.

Video Home System (VHS)

The Video Home System, (VHS) is a recording and playing standard for Video Cassette Recorders (VCRs), developed by JVC and launched in 1976. VHS became a standard format for consumer recording and viewing in the 1980s. VHS initially offered a longer playing time than the betamax system, and it also had the advantages of a far less complex tape transport mechanism. Early VHS machines could rewind and fast-forward the tape considerably faster than a betamax VCR.

A VHS cassette holds a macimum of about 430 m of tape at the lowest acceptable tape thickness, giving a maximum playing time of about 3.5 hours for NTSC (National Television System Committee) and 5 hours for PAL (Phase Alternating) at "standard" (SP) quality.

VHS tapes have approximately 3 MHz of video bandwidth, which is achieved at a relatively low tape speed by the use of helical scan recording of a frequency modulated luminance (black and white) signal, with a down-converted "color under" chroma (color) signal recorded directly at the baseband. Because VHS is an analog system, VHS tapes represent video as a continuous stream of waves, in a manner similar to analog TV broadcasts. The waveform per scan-line can reach about 160 waves at max, and contains 525 scanlines from top of the screen to bottom of the screen in NTSC (480 visible). PAL variants have 625 scanlines (576 visible). In modern-day digital terminology, VHS is roughly equivalent to 333 x 480 pixels.

In 1987 JVC introduced the new format called super VHS.

S-VHS (Super VHS) was an improved backward compatible version of the VHS introduced in 1987. S-VHS is an analog video standard with improved video bandwidth. S-VHS improved the luminance resolution to 400 horizontal per picture height (versus 250 for VHS/Beta and 500 for DVD). The audio-system (both linear and AFM or Audio Frequency Modulation) is the same. S-VHS made little impact on the home market, but gained dominance in the camcorder market due to its superior picture quality.

VHS-C (Video Home System-Compact) is a compact version of the VHS used for portable recorders. Since VHS-C tapes are based on the same magnetic tape as full size tapes, they can be played back in standard VHS-players using a mechanical adapter, without the need of any kind of signal conversion.

Super VHS or S-VHS was developed by JVC in 1987. S-VHS provided an improved luminance and chrominance quality, yet S-VHS recorders were compatible with VHS tapes.

Video Cassette Recorder (VCR)

Video Cassette Recording (VCR) was an early domestic video format designed by Philips. It was the first successful home *videocassette recorder* system.

The VCR, is also called Video Tape Recorder (VTR), is a device used to records and play audio and video information using removable cassettes containing magnetic tape. Before the advent of the VCR, reel-to-reel tape was mainly used for recording video. In the early 1970s the concept of a cassette was introduced by philips with its Video Compact Cassette (VCC), however the system was expensive and never became popular. Towards the late 1990s, the VCR has been started being superseded by digital media like DVD.

4.12.6 Video 2000

Video 2000 also known as video compact cassette, or VCC was a consumer VCR system and videotape standard developed by philips. Distribution of video 2000 products began in 1979 and ended in 1988. Video 2000 uses double-sided cassettes. The cassette was slightly larger than VHS and could record four hours of video on each side. Technically it was superior to both VHS and Betamax.

4.12.7 Compact Video Cassette (CVC)

Compact Video Cassette (CVC) was the one of the first videocassette formats to use a tape smaller than its earlier predecessors of VHS and Betamax, and was developed by Funai Electronics of Japan. The first model of VCR for the format was the Model 212, introduced in 1980 by both Funai and Technicolor. The two companies had created a joint venture to manufacture and introduce the format to the home video market. The system, which included the VCR and a handheld camera, was very small and lightweight for its time.

The CVC format had been used a cassette slightly larger than an audio cassette and was loaded with 1/4" videotape. Unlike most other video cassette formats that have two spools fixed in diameter, the cassette size was able to be made smaller by reusing the space vacated by one spool as the other spool filled up, similar to a standard audio cassette.

4.12.8 Camcorder

Camcorder (video camera recorder) is an electronic device that combines a video camera and a video recorder into one unit. In order to differentiate a camcorder from other devices that are capable of recording video, like cell phones and compact digital cameras, a camcorder is generally identified as a portable device having video capture and recording as its primary function. The earliest camcorders employed analog recording onto videotape. Since the 1990s digital recording has become the norm, but tape remained the primary recording media. Starting from early 2000s tape as storage media is being gradually replaced with tapeless solutions like optical disks, hard disk drives and flash memory. All tape-based camcorders use removable media in form of video cassettes. Camcorders that permit using more than one type of media, like built-in hard disk drive and memory, are often called *hybrid camcorders*.

4.12.9 Video 8

It is a video cassette recorder system used with video cameras. The tapes were 8mm thick and recorded video in analog format. The tapes were the size of audio cassettes making them portable and popular for use with cameras. The video quality is better than VHS and is one of the dominant formats for video cameras. The tapes came in two versions 60 minutes and 120 minutes.

Digital Video, MINIDV, DVCAM

Digital Video (DV) is a type of video recording system that works by using a digital rather than an analog video signal. Starting in the late 1970s to the early 1980s, several types of video production equipment, such as Time Base Correctors (TBC) and Digital Video Effects (DVE) units were introduced that operated by taking a standard analog video input and digitizing it internally. This made it easier to either correct or enhance the video signal, as in the case of a TBC, or to manipulate and add effects to the video, in the case of a DVE unit. The digitized and processed clip from these units would the be converted back to standard analog video.

MiniDV is one of three common digital formats used in sound and picture recording. Using digital technology, MiniDV captures video and audio on high-density cassette tapes. This format is very popular, as it delivers sound and video that is decidedly sharp and high quality.

The MiniDV format is one of the most commonly used formats for camcorders. Leading manufacturers like Sony, Panasonic, JVC (Japan Victor Company), Sharp, Canon, and many others offer MiniDV comcorders. These camcorders deliver video that is much clearer than analog camcorders. They also offer stronger color reproduction. MiniDV camcorders are lightweight and compact, many featuring extras like MPEG and night recording.

Usually, MiniDV camcorders can be connected to a television or VCR for display or copying purposes. MiniDV tapes are tiny, only a fraction of the size of other Digital Video (DV) cassettes. They are commonly used for both personal and semiprofessional-quality video. The tapes are available in recording lengths of 30, 60 and 80 minutes.

Among digitally recorded cassette tapes, MiniDV tapes are the most widely used. These tapes offer easy compatibility for playback on almost any type of DV-compatible device. In fact, MiniDVs can even be used for playback on devices intended for DVCAM (Digital Video Camera) and DVPRO tapes. This is because the tapes are identical to DVCAM and DVPRO tapes, with the exception of the recording format.

DVCRRO, DVCPROP2

Panasonic's DVCPRO (Digital Video Cassette Professional (Panasonic)) is another variant of the DV technology which uses another tape type. It always uses 4:1:1 color sub-sampling and 48 KHz/16 bit audio recording. This was referred to as DVCPRO25 (where the 25 stands for 25 Mbps) and has a bitrate of 25 Mbps.

When recorded to tape, DVCPRO uses wider track pitch-18 μm vs. 10 μm of baseline DV, which reduces the chances of dropout errors when video is recorded to tape. Two extra longitudinal tracks provide audio cue and for timecode control. Tape is transported 80% faster compared to baseline DV, resulting in shorter recording time. Long Play mode is not available.

Another variant called DVCPROP2, introduced by Panasonic in 2004, uses recording of DV/DVCRO25/DVCPRO50 streams on a PCMCIA (Personal Computer Memory Card International Association) compatible Flash memory cards instead of tapes. The card called P2 is capable of holding 2 GB of data and the cameras had multiple slots for cards. Cards are recorded in sequence and when a card is full, it can be swapped out while another card is recording.

D-1

Digital video was first introduced commercially in 1986 with the Sony D-1 format, which recorded an uncompressed standard definition component video signal in digital form instead of the high-band analog forms that had been commonplace until then. Due to the expenses, D-1 was used primarily by large television networks. It would eventually be replaced by cheaper systems using compressed data, most notably Sony's Digital Betacam, still heavily used as a field recording format by professional television producers, that made it in studios at their company.

D2 & D3

The D2 format was developed primarily by Ampex and Sony, while D3 format was developed primarily by Panasonic. Their major advantage over a component digital format is the lower cost in equipment, although this equipment is expensive enough to find a market only at the professional level and has not been used much in multimedia production.

D2 is an NTSC composite format. This format is well-suited as a "workhorse" in the broadcast environment, for handling program and commercial playbacks, as well as satellite recordings, since all of it is received by the station as NTSC video. D2 was designed to be a direct plug-in replacement for 1-inch and Betacam recorders, while D-1 needs to work in a completely non-NTSC environment. D2 operates at the same 4x subcarrier (14.31818 MHz) sampling rate as most TBCs and frame syncs and some existing equipment has been adapted to plug directly into the D2 machines.

D3 uses 1/2" tape instead of the 19mm (3/4") tape used in D1 and D2. It also uses a different error correction system, a different modulation coding system (for recording), and a low-tension, low-friction transport. D3 is plug-in compatible with D2 - it is a composite format. In addition, D3 uses a flying erase head for insert editing - D2, in contrast, just records over previous material, which, in fact, works out because of the nature of digital recording. This machine is now obsolete.

D5

D5 is D3 playback compatible, but offers 10-bit processing (which some say improves the quality of the recording), and is a composite and component VTR. This machine is now largely obsolete.

D6

D6 is a digital HDTV recorder that records 64 minutes of 1.2 GB/sec video on a D1 large-shell cassette. Luminance sampling is 72 MHz and chroma sampling is 36 MHz. Sampling happens on a 8-bit level.

D7

D7 is the standard for Panasonic and DVCPRO, which is a 4:1:1 component machine with 8-bit recording and 5:1 compression using DCT (Direct Cosine Transform). This format is also compatible with the many MiniDV camcorders out there.

D9 is the proposed standard for Digital-S, the format form JVC that is to replace S-VHS. Digital-S uses full 4:2:2 sampling, with 8-bit recording and a 3:3:1 DCT compression scheme, in a 1/2" tape in a shell that look like an S-VHS cassette. The specification calls for four channels of audio, even though only two are used in current machines. Its video inputs accept composite, component, digital component, digital composite and S-Video. The machine will playback your existing S-VHS library.

D10

It is a digital component system, which will record and playback MPEG encoded video. It will also play back all Betacam formats (digital or analog) except for HDCAM (High Definition Camcorder), making it a possibly excellent replacement for existing "workhorse" VTR playback and record applications, such as master control, satellite feedroom recordings and so on.

MicroMV

MicroMV was a proprietary videotape format introduced in 2001 by Sony. This cassette is physically smaller than a Digital 8 or DV cassette. In fact, MicroMV is the smallest videotape format – 70% smaller than MiniDV. Each cassette can hold up to 60 minutes of video.

The MicroMV format does not use the highly popular DV format. Instead, it uses 12 Mbit/s MPEG-2 compression, like that used for DVDs and HDV. Footage recorded on MicroMV format initially could not be directly edited with mainstream DV editing software, such as Adobe Premiere or Apple Final Cut Pro; instead Sony supplied its own video editing software MoiveShaker (for Windows PCs only.

MicroMV has not been a successful format. Sony was the only electronics manufacturer to sell MicroMV cameras. As of January 2006, Sony does not offer any new MicroMV camcorder models.

LaserDisc

The LaserDisc (LD) is an obsolete home video disk format, and was the first commercial optical disk storage medium. Initially marketed as Discovision in 1978, the ethnology was licensed and sold as Reflective Optical Videodisc, Lase Videodisc, Laservision, Disco-Vision, DiscoVision, and MCA DiscoVision until Pioneer Electronics purchased the majority stake in the format and marketed LaserDisc in the mid to late 1980s.

While the format itself produced a consistently higher quality image than its rivals, the VHS and Betamax systems.

VCD

VCD stands for 'Video Compact Disk' and basically it is a CD that contains moving pictures and sound. A VCD has the capacity to hold up to 74/80 minutes (on 650MB/700MB CDs, respectively) of full-motion video along with quality stereo sound. VCDs use a compression standard called MPEG to store the video and audio. A VCD can be played on almost all stand alone DVD players and of course on all computers with a DVD-ROM (Digital Versatile/Video - Read Only Memory) or CD-ROM drive with the help of a software based decoder/player. The quality of a VCD is about the same, but usually better than VHS tape-based Movies.

DVD-Video

DVD-Video is a consumer video format used to store digital video and DVD disks, and is currently the dominant consumer video format in Canada, Europe and Australia. Disks using the DVD-Video specification require a DVD drive and a MPEG-2 decoder (e.g., a DVD player, or a DVD computer drive with a software DVD player). Commercial DVD movies are encoded using a combination of MPEG-2 compressed video and audio of varying formats.

REVIEW QUESTIONS WITH ANSWERS

1. Multiple Choice

1.1 In a video camera, CCD stands for:
a. Charge Coupled Device
b. Carbon Crystal Digitizer
c. Color Coding Data
d. None of the above

1.2 Codec (Coder/Decoder) is the algorithm used to:
a. Compress a video for delivery
b. Decode it in real time for fast playback
c. Both (a) and (b)
d. None of the above

1.3 Which of the following is not a television signal format?
a. PAL b. MPEG
c. SECAM d. HDTV

1.4 B-frame stands for
a. Bidirectional-frame
b. Binary-frame
c. Binomial-frame
d. Betacam-frame

1.5 Which format is used in digital cameras?
a. MPEG-1 b. MPEG-2
c. MPEG-4 d. SWF

1.6 Usually, __________ video is transferred through FireWire.
a. Analog b. Digital
c. Bit-mapped d. Digitized

1.7 What is the process that condenses files to be stored in less space and therefore, sent faster over the Internet?
a. Data condensation b. Data compression
c. Zipping d. Defragmentation

1.8 'Zipping' a file means:
a. Encrypting it b. Decrypting it
c. Compressing it d. Transmitting it

1.9 Which is the biggest audio file format?
a. WMA b. WAV
c. MP3 d. SWF

1.10 When an MP3 stores a file what does it get rid of?
a. Deletes The Frequencies The Human Ear Cannot Hear
b. Deletes the song information
c. Deletes the bits on the end of a song that has no music
d. Deletes the bytes on the end of a song that has no music

2. State whether the following statements are True or False

2.1 Codec is the algorithm used to compress (code) a video for delivery and then decode it in real time for fast playback.

2.2 JPEG is a lossy image compression method.

2.3 Spatial redundancy indicates that much of the information in an image is repeated.

2.4 The quantization in JPEG is aimed at reducing the total number of bits needed for a compressed image.

2.5 Sony's D1 format was the first digital video format introduced in 1987.

2.6 Codec can be hardware-based, software-based, or both.

2.7 A WAV file format has a smaller file size than a MP3 file format.

2.8 Object linking and embedding in window does not allow to combine video and audio clips.

2.9 PNG is a standard used for compression of audio in multimedia.

2.10 GIF is a format commonly used on MS-DOS and MS-Windows computers.

3. Match the following:

3.1	MPEG	a.	AVI
3.2	MPEG-1	b.	FLAC
3.3	MPEG-2	c.	Compressed format
3.4	MPEG-4	d.	Designed for CD-ROM based applications
3.5	NTSC	e.	Designed for DVD applications
3.6	Compression Format	f.	Efficient method of object oriented content based storage and retrieval of multimedia content
3.7	A Microsoft supported video format	g.	TV broadcasting standard

3.8	Lossless compression	h.	ZIP
3.9	Digital betacam	i.	Original data is not changed permanently during compression
3.10	A lossless compression Codec	j.	Video recording format

4. Fill in the blanks

a. MP4	b. MPEG decoder	c. Data Compression
d. MPEG-2	e. MPEG-4	f. PNG
g. Optical	h. Bit rate	i. RAM
j. Lossless		

4.1 Viewing a MPEG video on a microcomputer requires a ________.

4.2 When using a(n) ________ compression system, a file can be compressed and decompressed without loss of data.

4.3 ________ video file format is generally used in a multimedia project in order to ensure that the video clip's file size is as small as possible.

4.4 The process that condenses files so they can be stored in less space and transmitted over the Internet at a faster rate is called ________.

4.5 ________ video compression is used to deliver high quality picture in DVD movies.

4.6 ________ is used for both streaming and downloadable web content.

4.7 DVD is ________ disk storage media format.

4.8 MPEG-1 uses fixed ________.

4.9 ________ is a lossless file format.

4.10 When a digital image is currently being viewed on a computer screen, it is actively loaded into ________.

Answers

1.	1.1	a	1.2	c	1.3	b	1.4	a	1.5	a	1.6	b
	1.7	b	1.8	c	1.9	b	1.10	a				
2.	2.1	T	2.2	T	2.3	T	2.4	T	2.5	T	2.6	T
	2.7	F	2.8	F	2.9	F	2.10	F				
3.	3.1	c	3.2	d	3.3	e	3.4	f	3.5	g	3.6	h
	3.7	a	3.8	i	3.9	j	3.10	b				
4.	4.1	b	4.2	j	4.3	a	4.4	c	4.5	d	4.6	e
	4.7	g	4.8	h	4.9	f	4.10	i				

Questions with Answers

1. Explain briefly the following terms:
   a. Compression Ratio
   b. Camcorder
2. a. What are the main differences between the target media for JPEG and GIF compression?
   b. Differentiate between JPEG and MPEG.
3. Why must multimedia content be compressed and decompressed for use on the Web?
4. Briefly explain about the different techniques used for video compression.
5. What is the purpose of streaming audio and video files?
6. Why will it be more appropriate to use JPEG images instead of GIF images for transmitting content over Internet? Also differentiate between lossy compression and loss less compression.
7. What is the key difference between I-frame, P-frame and B-Frame in MPEG-2 video compression?
8. What is Codec? Explain how a Codec functions.

Answers to Short Questions

1. a. *Data compression ratio* quantifies the reduction in data representation size produced by a data compression algorithm. The data compression ratio is identical to the physical compression ratio used to measure physical compression of substances.

$$\text{Compression Ratio} = \frac{\text{Compressed size}}{\text{Uncompressed size}}$$

Thus a representation that compresses a 100 MB file to 25 MB has a compression ratio of 25/100 = 0.4.

For signals of indefinite size, such as streaming audio and video, the compression ratio is defined in terms of uncompressed and compressed data rates instead of data sizes.

The higher the compression ratio is, the smaller is the bandwidth consumption.

b. *Camcorder* (video camera recorder) is an electronic device that combines a video camera and a video recorder into one unit. In order to differentiate a camcorder from other devices that are capable of recording video, like cell phones and compact digital cameras, a camcorder is generally identified as a portable device having video capture and recording as its primary function. The earliest camcorders employed analog recording onto videotape.

2. a. Difference between JPEG and GIF compression:

JPEG: JPEG is the standard compression technique for still images which is developed by the Joint Photographic Experts Group.

JPEG is capable of both lossless and lossy compression. Lossless compression is any compression in which no original image data is discarded (lost), and images which have been compressed and then restored are–pixel by pixel–precisely the same as the original image. Lossy compression, on the other hand, actually discards (loses) some original image data when the file is compressed.

GIF: A Graphics Interchange Format (GIF) format is another type of compression technique. GIF method is commonly used for line art, black and white graphics, sharp transitions, or text-based images in which geometric shapes are relatively simple. The compression scheme used in GIF is lossless, which means file size is reduced without harming the quality of the image. Images compressed with GIF are limited to 256 colors maximum, therefore, this format is not well-suited for photos. GIF files also allow transparency and animation, making them quite popular among Web designers seeking to create unique effects for their sites.

b. **Difference between JPEG and MPEG:**

JPEG: JPEG (Joint Photographic Experts Group) format is one of the most common graphic file format for Web applications. JPEG format is also used to display photographs and other continuous tone images in HyperText Markup Language (HTML) documents over the World Wide Web and other online services.

JPEG images are of much higher fidelity as well as in higher compressed form than images of GIF format. However, download speed, over the Internet, is much lower with JPEG files. That is, it takes longer time to download graphic files that use JPEG format than those that use GIF format.

MPEG: On the other hand, MPEG is the acronym for Moving Pictures Experts Group, a committee that developed the MPEG standard. It is a set of specifications for compressing and playing back full-motion video, including movies and video clips. MPEG rules cover both encoding, for storage on disk and decoding, for digital playback. Viewing a MPEG video on a microcomputer requires a MPEG decoder, which can be hardware, software, or a combination of the two.

MPEG achieves high compression rate by storing only the changes from one frame to another, instead of each entire frame. Although MPEG is a lossy compression method, the loss of video data is generally imperceptible to human eye. For this reason, MPEG generally produces better-quality video than competing formats, such as AVI and QuickTime.

3. Multimedia files are usually very large in size. Therefore, for the purpose of the storage and transmitting large-sized multimedia files on the Web, the file sizes need to be compressed. So, that the compressed files will decrease the average page load size, therefore, decreasing bandwidth usage. This makes it much more convenient for viewers to access the file with faster loading as well as making the usage of your Web server resources more efficient.

4. Video compression is a technique which is used to reduce the amount of data in a video file, to limit the amount of storage space or bandwidth it requires. Video compression works on the same theoretical basis as other types of file compression.

Literally speaking, video compression is a way of making video files smaller. More specially, video compression is a method by which the pixels that are not easily observable to human eyes are ignored or assimilated into a adjacent ones. Video decompression or decoding is a method by which original pixels are recovered to the original or near-original state.

Video Compression Techniques:

Spatial Compression: The spatial compression technique is used to reduce digital video file sizes by compressing the pixels within each frame independently. This technique is also known as the 'intra-frame' technique. The spatial compression technique involves removing or reordering information about a field of colored pixels to keep file space.

Temporal Compression: The temporal compression technique is used to reduce digital video file sizes by compressing frames as a group. This technique is also known as the 'inter-frame' technique. The technique involves in temporal compression is to compare one still frame with an adjoining frame and, instead of saving all the information about each frame into the digital video file, only saves information about the differences between frames (frame differencing). This type of compression relies on periodic keyframes. At each keyframe, the entire still image is saved, and these complete images are used as the comparison frames for frame differencing.

Lossy and Lossless Compression: There are two categories of compression techniques used with digital graphics, lossy and lossless. Both use different techniques to compress files; but both have the same aim. Lossy compression techniques include DCT (Discrete Cosine Transform), Vector Quantization and Huffman coding whereas the lossless compression techniques include RLE (Run-Length Encoding), string-table compression, LZW (Lempel Ziff Welch) and zlib.

5. *Streaming* is a method of delivery of sound and video files over the web. The computer begins playing the file when sufficient data for playback has been downloaded and it continues to receive the rest of it, keeping ahead so playback does not pause or break up.

Audio/video streaming allows the user to listen or view video files on the Internet in real time, with no need to download an entire file before playback. It is entirely different from when user has to download files to listen to it. In streaming, both the client and server cooperate for uninterrupted motion. The client side stores a few seconds of audio/video in a buffer (files created by buffering are temporary, and are gone when playback is complete) before it starts sending it to the screen and speakers. Throughout the session, it continues to receive data ahead of time.

Purpose of Streaming Audio/Video Files:

(a) A file with streaming cannot be copied, downloaded, or edited. Therefore, illegal act of piracy or copyright infringement is not possible. Streaming will keep sources secured in the Website.

(b) Audio/video media can be used in online advertising, live Web casts, and e-learning training and solutions. Connecting media to the computer is easier with streaming.

(c) It is also beneficial for people who work overseas and wanted to listen to their favorite local artists. Players like Windows Media Player work well with streaming.

6. JPEG (Joint Photographic Experts Group) format is one of the most common graphic file format for Web applications. JPEG format is also used to display photographs and other continuous tone images in hypertext markup language (HTML) documents over the World Wide Web and other online services.

There are several advantages of JPEG images that make it more appropriate instead of GIF images for transmitting content over Internet. These are as under:

(a) JPEG images are of much higher fidelity as well as in higher compressed form than images of GIF format. It allow you to save a good quality picture with a small file size.

(b) JPEG is more capable than GIF for storing full-color or grey-scale images of "realistic" scenes. Any continuous variation in color, such as highlighting or shading will be represented more faithfully and in less space by JPEG than by GIF.

(c) JPEG format compresses files and lets you choose compression versus quality. When you create a JPEG image or convert an image into JPEG, you are asked to specify the quality of the image you want. Since the higher quality requires larger memory space, one can make a compromise between image quality and file-size.

(d) JPEG format allow you to preserve the vibrancy of the colors with a minimal loss of quality while printing the photographs.

(e) With the help of JPEG format, the degree of lossiness can be varied by adjusting compression parameters. This means that the image maker can trade off file size against output image quality.

If decompressed data is the same as the original data, it is referred to as *lossless compression*, otherwise the compression is *lossy* because there is loss of originality in the reproduced data.

In *lossless* compression, all of the information–and thus all of the quality–in the original clip is preserved after compression. However, preserving the original level of quality limits the degree to which you can lower the data rate and file size, and the resulting data rate may be too high for smooth playback. Lossless codecs such as Animation (at the best quality setting) are used to preserve maximum quality during editing or for still images where data rate is not an issue.

But, in *lossy compression*, some of the original data discards during compression. For example, if the pixels making up a sky actually contain 78 shades of blue, a lossy codec set for less than best quality may record 60 shades of blue. Lossy compression allows much lower data rates and file sizes than lossless compression. Video are commonly used for final production of video delivered using CD-ROM or the Internet. In case of lossy compression, the desired quality level of the decompressed data is application dependent.

7. The three major picture types used in the different video algorithms are I, P and B. They are different because of the following characteristics:

   I-frames are the least compressible but donot require other video frames to decode.

   P-frames can use data from previous frames to decompress and are more compressible than I-frames.

   B-frames can use both previous and forward frames for data reference to get the highest.

8. To compress the file and reduce its size, it needs to be filtered through a specialized software called a *CODEC*, which is short form of compression/decompression or Coder/Decoder. It is an algorithm used to compress (code) a video for delivery and then decode it in real time for fast playback. Different codecs are optimized for different methods of delivery. For example, for a hard drive, for a CD-ROM, or for the web. A codec may use one or more strategies for compression because no single method is best for all situations.

   Codec software reads the media data and applies mathematical algorithm to reduce its size. The algorithms find redundant information within the media files. Redundant information are those which can either be discarded without affecting the media quality by appreciable measures, or data that can be expressed in a more compact form. In either case, this leads to a reduction in file size, but the actual amount of reduction depends on a large number of factors involving both the media data and the CODEC used.

DESCRIPTIVE TYPE QUESTIONS

1. What is video. How video works?
2. What is difference between analog and digital video?
3. What is the difference between Spatial compression and Temporal compression?
4. What are the hardware and software requirements for audio and video?
5. What is video conferencing? Explain the difference between video conferencing and document conferencing?
6. Differentiate between Analog and Digital Video.
7. Explain the following video recording and tape formats:
   (a) MiniDV
   (b) VCD
   (c) DVD-Video
8. Differentiate between MP3 and MP4.
9. How lossy compression is different from lossless compression?
10. Briefly explain about the different techniques used for video compression.
11. Explain the following:
    (a) MPEG-1 (c) MPEG-4
    (b) MPEG-2 (d) MPEG-21

CHAPTER 5

Multimedia Application Design

5.1 INTRODUCTION TO SYSTEM DEVELOPMENT LIFE CYCLE (SDLC)

The process of developing and using a system follows a typical set of steps. Just as all living beings follow a life cycle, so also all systems follow a "*life cycle*".

System development is a birth-to-mature process called System Development Life Cycle (SDLC). A system project begins (is born) with a decision to analyze user requirements. The project is completed (matures) once a usable software product is produced and implemented or released. Thus the system development life cycle consists of system analysis, design and implementation.

The entire process from the need of the system being felt till the system is used and ultimately declared absolutely reliable forms the life cycle of the system.

☞ *The period of time that begins when a system is conceived and ends when a system is fully operational for use and gets maintained is called the development life cycle of a system.*

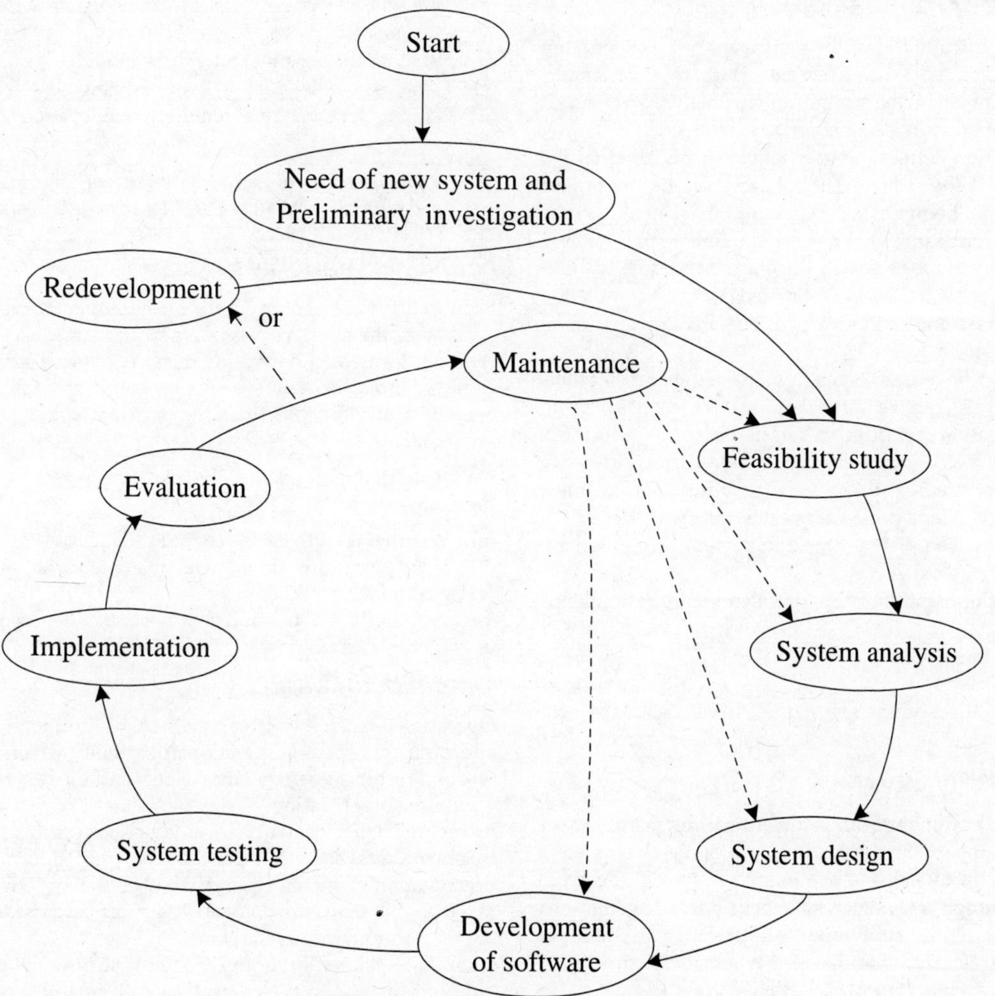

Figure 5.1 Activities involved in SDLC

5.2 VARIOUS PHASES OF THE SYSTEM DEVELOPMENT LIFE CYCLE

The basic idea of SDLC is that there is a well-defined process by which a system is conceived, developed and implemented. The system development starts when management of an organization or sometimes system development personnel realizes that a particular business system needs improvement. The system development life cycle as shown in Figure 5.1. consists of the following activities:

(a) Preliminary investigation
(b) Feasibility study
(c) System analysis
(d) System design
(e) Development of software
(f) System testing
(g) Implementation and Evaluation
(h) Maintenance

5.2.1 Preliminary Investigation (Problem Formulation)

One of the most difficult tasks of the system analyst is identifying the real problem of the existing system. Without clear understanding of the problem in the system, any further work done will lead to wastage of effort at a later stage.

Problem definition defines the user requirements, or what the user expects out of the system. This phase also sets the project boundaries, which define what parts of the system can be changed by the project and what parts are to remain without any change. This also includes a rough idea of the resource requirements for the project as well as the estimated start and completion dates for each phase and the number of persons expected to be involved in each phase.

All projects that have been requested are not always feasible. Some organizations receive so many project requests from employees that only a few of them can be pursued. Even those projects that are feasible and desirable should be put into a schedule. The management decides the requests, that are most important and only after a project request is approved, the cost of the project, priority, completion time and personnel required are estimated.

In system development life cycle, problem identification helps in:

(a) Pinpointing the problems.
(b) Setting proper system goals.
(c) Determining the boundaries of the project by taking into consideration the limitations of the available resources.

5.2.2 Feasibility Study

A feasibility study is undertaken to determine the possibility of either improving the existing system or developing a completely new system. This study helps to obtain an overview of the problem and to get rough assessment of whether feasible solutions exist. Since the feasibility study may lead to the commitment of large resources, it is important that it is conducted competently and that no fundamental errors of judgement are made.

☞ *Feasibility studies are used as a basis for deciding whether to proceed with, postpone or cancel the project.*

The purpose of feasibility study is to determine whether the requested project is successfully realizable and feasible. There are three aspects of feasibility study, namely

(a) Technical feasibility
(b) Economic feasibility
(c) Operational feasibility

Technical Feasibility

Technical feasibility centres around the required/existing computer system (hardware/software) and to what extent it can support the proposed application. For example, if the current computer is operating at 80% capacity, then running another application could overload the system or require additional hardware. This involves financial consideration to accommodate technical enhancement. If the budget is a serious constraint (limitation) then the project is judged as not feasible.

This study should answer the following questions:

(a) Whether the project can be carried out with the existing equipment?
(b) Whether the existing software is enough?
(c) Can the work be done with the existing personnel?
(d) If a new technology is required, how best can it be implemented?

☞ ***Technical feasibility*** *is concerned with specifying equipment and software that will successfully support the required task.*

Economic Feasibility

Economic feasibility study is the most frequently used method for evaluating the effectiveness of a new system. Cost-benefit analysis is performed to determine the benefits and savings that are expected from the new system and compare them with costs. If benefits outweigh costs, then the decision is made to design and implement the new system.

By conducting this study the analyst can ascertain the following:

(a) Whether the project is economically feasible?
(b) If enough funds are not available, then what are the sources of funds?
(c) Whether there are sufficient benefits when compared to the costs incurred?

Operational Feasibility

Operational feasibility is concerned with human, organizational and political aspects. Operational feasibility covers two aspects. One is a technical performance aspect and the other is acceptance within the organization.

Technical performance includes issues, such as determining whether the system can provide the right information for the organization's personnel, and whether the system can be organized so that it always delivers this information at the right place and at right time.

Operational feasibility must determine how the proposed system will fit in with the current operations and what, if any, job reconstruction and re-training will be needed to implement the system.

The evaluation must then determine the general attitudes and job skills of existing personnel and whether any such restructuring of jobs will be *acceptable to the current users.*

The analyst should determine:

(a) Whether the system can be used if it is developed and implemented?
(b) Will there be resistance from users that will cripple the possible application benefit?

☞ *The feasibility study is carried out by a small group of people who are familiar with information systems technique.*

5.2.3 System Analysis

The analysis phase is the detailed understanding of all important facts of the business area under investigation. The relationships of the various system components among themselves and with environment are studied and understood. This requires data collection from a variety of sources. For this, questionnaires, forms, interviews, study of existing documents, records, etc., are used. The analyst must try to answer the following set of questions:

(a) What is being done in the organization?
(b) How is it being done?
(c) What is the volume of the transactions?
(d) How frequently do the transactions occur?
(e) What are the problems that may arise?
(f) If a problem arises, how will it be solved?
(g) What could cause such a problem?

To answer these questions, the system analyst must consult a variety of persons. He has to understand the whole details about the business, the processes involved in it and the problems faced by the staff. He should also identify the reasons for the problems that have occurred and the preventive measures to avoid them.

The analyst must have a detailed study of the manuals and reports about the organization. Further he should have a direct observation of the activities in the organization and collect a sample of the forms and documents to understand the whole system.

5.2.4 Development of Prototype

A prototype is a model of the final system. The purpose of a prototype is to allow the user to see something concrete. It is very difficult to form an idea of the features of a system from a set of written specifications, particularly for the user. The prototype shows the user how some part of the system will look. The system that is developed at a high cost may fail in certain situations. To avoid this, the analyst should design a mini-system similar to the one to be developed. This prototype acts as a test system. If this system is successful, the analyst can start designing the actual system.

5.2.5 System Design

In the system design process, the primary objective is to identify user requirements and to build a system that satisfies these requirements. Design of system is largely the logical design. The logical design can be sketched on a paper or on a computer terminal. The design, also including the physical design elements, describes the data to be inputted, the processes involved in the manipulation of data and the output.

(a) The analyst should specify the file structures, storage devices, etc.
(b) The database is also designed in this phase.
(c) Hardware cost, capability, speed, error rates, and other performance characteristics are specified.
(d) Changes to be made in the organizational structure of the firm are outlined.
(e) Input, output, files, forms and procedures are planned.
(f) Finally, standards for testing, documentation and system control are formulated.

☞ *The most challenging and creative part of the system development life cycle is the design of the system.*

5.2.6 Development of Software

Development is the phase where detailed design is used to actually construct and build the system. In this phase, the system is actually programmed. Now, the analyst should decide whether to buy a commercial software or to develop new customized programs with the help of programmers. The choice depends on the cost of the software and the cost of programming such software. In large organizations the work is entrusted to programmers, whereas in small organizations, the job is assigned to outside organizations.

Programmers are also responsible for documenting the programs. The documents should include comments that provide explanation of the procedures coded in the programs.

5.2.7 System Testing

Testing is the process of making sure that the programs perform the intended tasks. Once the system is designed it should be tested for validity. During system testing, the system is used experimentally to ensure that the software does not fail, i.e., it will run according to its specification and in the way users expect it to.

The system is tested with special test data and the results are examined for their validity. Some of the users may be permitted to operate on the system so that the analyst can ascertain that the system can work in the specified environment.

5.2.8 Implementation and Evaluation

Implementation

Implementation is the final phase of development. It consists of installing hardware, programs, collecting data and organizing people to interact with and run the system.

In the implementation phase, user actually starts using the system. This phase therefore involves training the users for using the system and also providing them friendly documentation to refer to.

Implementation can be done in two ways. One way is by implementing the new system along with the old system and make them run in parallel. The other method is to replace the entire system. In large organizations, the new system can be implemented in certain areas as a pilot project and if satisfactory results are obtained, it can be implemented to other areas also.

Evaluation

Once the system is implemented, it should be evaluated. *Evaluation* is the process of verifying the capability of a system, after it is put in operation, to see whether it is meeting the objectives or not. Evaluation is an important aspect, due to the following reasons:

(a) To assess the system, i.e. how the system is functioning, what the response time, overall reliability and level of utilization is etc.
(b) To find the limitations in the system.
(c) To identify whether the new system developed would be beneficial to the organization under operating conditions.
(d) To judge the attitude of different persons in the organization regarding the newly developed system.
(e) Evaluation of cost, time and effort taken for the overall project.

5.2.9 Maintenance

Maintenance is the process of incorporating changes in the implemented existing system for proper utilization. This involves enhancement, adaptation and correction.

Enhancement

Enhancement implies adding new functions or additional capabilities to the system.

Adaptation

Adaptation implies customizing the software to run in the new environment.

Correction

Correction implies correcting the bugs in the existing software.

5.3 MULTIMEDIA APPLICATION DESIGN

Multimedia system development process involves a number of steps like traditional software system development and is known as Multimedia System Development Life Cycle (MSDLC). Creating a multimedia application is a complex and abstract process. It can be categorized into a design phase and an implementation phase. In the design phase, the content writer and visual artists are involved with paper work for specifying what should be the content of the presentation keeping in mind the target audience, how the content should be arranged, what should be the screen designs, how the user should navigate from one frame to the next etc. During implementation phase the production team uses appropriate editing and authoring software to build up the presentation according to the designs.

A typical software project which uses various multimedia technologies and interactivity with specific aim of disseminating explicit information to a well-defined homogeneous or heterogeneous market segment can be called as a *multimedia project*. There are four basic stages in any multimedia project:

(i) ***Planning and Costing:*** The first task is to choose a topic on which we need to create the project. A project always begins with an idea or a need that we can refine by outlining its messages and objectives. In general, one can select any topic, which can be explained and demonstrated using various media types. Before developing the project, plan what writing skills, graphics, music, video and other multimedia expertise will be required. In addition, estimate the time needed to do all elements, and prepare a budget to get the estimate of cost.

To develop a multimedia presentation or program, it is valuable to understand precisely who the user is. To compose a multimedia program the developer should consider the following:

(a) Level of understanding of the audience
(b) Expectation of the users
(c) Goal of presentation (training/entertainment)
(d) Allocated time
(e) Type of presentation required (text, graphics, sound, video, animation or combination)
(f) Interactive/non-interactive presentation
(g) Impact of the presentation to the audience (instant or long-term).

Having all these details firmly in hand will help the multimedia developer to create a successful product.

(ii) ***Designing and Producing:*** Typically, the design phase consists of storyboarding, flowcharting, prototyping, and user testing as well as a parallel production of media. Perform each of the planned tasks to create a finished product.

Most common way to start design is by composing an outline of the sequences and locks of information that will appear on the screen. This determines the amount of information-text, graphics, clickable objects which will be presented on each screen. It is also the time to establish a navigation methodology for the user. The developer has to decide whether there will be a navigation bar with arrows leading from scene to scene, or there will be text or objects that the users should click to jump argon the entire program.

Once the subject matter has been chosen, the next step is to write a story. A story describe, the overall content of the project. Once the overall subject matter has been finalized, the next step is to create a *script*. While story focuses on 'what' is communicated to his/her audience, a script emphasizes 'how' the content should be displayed to the user.

Once the script has been prepared, the next step is to prepare storyboard. The storyboard depicts what should be the layout of the project. The storyboard will decide which element has to come from the right side, which one from the left side, how they will combine and form the compound. A storyboard depicts the initial idea content of a multimedia concept in a series of sketches. The storyboard can be used for a great deal of animation or many different scenes. Used by film directors for productions ranging from 30 second television commercials to feature-length motion pictures, the storyboard consists of sketches of the scenes and actions. Mapping out a storyboard helps the author to recognize gaps in logic. Some multimedia authoring programs provide facilities for drawing and organizing the frames of a storyboard.

After that a flowchart organizes the storyboard by inserting navigation information – the multimedia concept's structure and user interaction.

Tools Selection is one of the important step in Multimedia Development Life Cycle. Multimedia product requires many type of software tools, for instance, creating text often requires a work processor; working with digital images requires graphics software; using video requires a video-capture program and editing software; sound often requires its own editing software. All of this software is used to generate the content. When the content is ready, it needs to be assembled in a process called multimedia *authoring*. Authoring is a process of assembling the content into the multimedia software development environment following the map provided by the storyboard. Two kinds of authoring that occur:

(a) Content assembly - the content is put together and linked to other content.

(b) Functional programming - software is created to provide specific behavior.

This process requires still another type of software, which can understand different types of media, combine them, control the sequences in which they appear, and create navigational tools for the user interface.

There are many elaborate ways to categorize navigation schemes, but a fairly simple list is sufficient to get the general idea. Sequential navigation is like a slide show, allowing the user to move forward or backward through a sequence. Hierarchical navigation provides links to specific sections of the title, and then to subsections, so that the user may choose when to view the material for a given section even though random access to every single screen may not be possible. This type of navigation is suitable for giving access to structures, orderly information. A third type of navigation is associative navigation, which includes links to screens that are related in some way to the current screen, but not as a continuation of the same thought (as the next screen in a sequence would be) or as a generalization or dissection of the current idea (as would be the case in hierarchical navigation). Associative links result in Web-like networks like the World-Wide Web (WWW).

The tools used for multimedia depends largely on the variety of media to be included. For a simple text-and-graphics slide show type of presentation, a presentation software program should be enough. One could enliven the offering by adding pre-existing graphics form the hundreds of commercially available CD-ROM collections of Clip Art, clip sound, and clip video. These clop collections store small fields in the proper file formats for use in wide range of multimedia programs.

A user can use sophisticated sound edition program, to splice together segments or add sound effects electronically, for example, echoes to the sounds. Users can do the same kind of electronic editing for video.

The most popular programs for combining the elements of a multimedia presentation is Macromedia Director. In Director, the multimedia author assembles each element-text, graphics, sound, and video into separate "tracks". The program helps the author to synchronize all the elements. For instance, a crash sound effect is heard when the two animated object collide. The director generates files that contains the entire multimedia presentation ready for distribution on disk or CD-ROM, or to be played over an integrative television or though the Internet.

After creation of all the contents, it is required to put them all together. For a complex product created with the use of a sophisticated tool, such as director, the multimedia authoring generally is performed by a skilled multimedia developer or programmer. Sometime your are asked to develop the prototype of the real system to the user. Prototyping a product may be used to sell the concept or test the idea for capabilities before producing the real one.

Next step of project design is implementation. Implementation means actually creating the physical presentation using required hardware and software.

☞ *The authoring process will implement the desired feature set using the prescribed tool. If the tool is inadequate, the project may fail.*

(iii) ***Testing and Feedback:*** After implementation phase is completed; an important step of testing and feedback should be done for improving the quality of the project. This step involves distributing whole or part of the presentation to sections of the target audience or experts and getting feedback from them about the possible areas which will need improvement.

During the test the developer should consider the following points:

(a) Is it product to read (in case of descriptive text)?

(b) Is it user friendly?

(c) Is it interactive and easy to navigate?

☞ *Always test your programs to make sure they meet the objectives of your project, they work properly on the intended delivery platforms, and they meet the needs of your client or end user.*

Alpha testing and Beta testing occur at different stages of development.

(a) Alpha testing - The product is evaluated relatively early in the development phase, mainly to review the application concept, format, user interface, and page layout. Alpha testing is usually done in-house or with end users who agree to keep their comments and experiences confidential.

(b) Beta testing - The product is evaluated just prior to final release mainly to find bug and content mistake.

(iv) ***Delivery and Maintenance:*** The final phase in the production schedule is the delivery of the application to the intended client. Usually the runtime version of the application files are copied onto a CD-ROM and physically handed over to the customer. Following tasks are involved for releasing the product to the end user:

(a) Documentation for the product in written including user and installation guide and troubleshooting instruction.

(b) Mass production of CD-ROM.

(c) Packing of product.

(d) Marketing the product.

(e) Mass production of hardware.

(f) Installation of the software.
(g) Training of personnel to use the software.

Maintenance is the process in which a product can evolve and grow with emerging technology or to meet user demands. You can either complete redistribution of the product or distribution of portions of the product to replace faulty or deficient segment of software or data. Depending on the extent of the rework, maintenance activities may be accomplished a new development cycle for planing through authoring and evaluation.

5.4 ISSUES IN MULTIMEDIA APPLICATION DESIGN

There are various issues in Multimedia authoring. Issued involved:

1. Content Design
2. Technical Design
3. Visual Design

Let us discuss each of them in brief.

5.4.1 Content Design

It refers to all types information, in all possible forms of media collected for the specific title under production. General content design and development encompasses data collection, data analysis and filtering, data arrangement and sequence, and data verification.

The sources of information vary, depending upon the project under production. Libraries, magazines, expert discussions, video interviews and the Internet are some of the sources from where data can be collected.

All the data collected from different sources are not useful, so collected data must be edited or modified and unwanted data should be removed or filtered from the collected data. Filtering process is generally undertaken by field expert in coordination with project manager and designer.

Filtered data must be arranged in proper logical sequence. This forms the backbone of the storyboard that is going to be developed.

The *storyboard* is an outline of the action. The storyboard depicts what should be the layout of the project. The storyboard will decide which element has to come from the right side, which one from the left side, how they will combine and form the compound. A storyboard depicts the initial idea content of a multimedia concept in a series of sketches. For example, while creating an animated movie, someone first writes a script for the story. From the script, a series of pictures is drawn to show important moments in the story. The series of pictures is called *storyboard.* Depending on the type of motion to be produced, the storyboard could consist of a high-level sequence of sketches showing the structure and ideas of the animation. Advantages of using Storyboard are:

(a) For a Website developer, it will be very helpful to check that all navigational links are correct or not.

(b) It will display the overall picture of what the Website will look like which enables the developer to improve the quality by identifying and flaws or faults in the design.

(c) It allows for the best possible design to be reached by constantly overviewing the overall picture.

☞ *A Storyboard enables designers and producers to pre-visualize their work before commencement.*

Data verification is one of the important steps. It is very intelligent decision, to proceed the verification process, with somebody not involved with data collection. Authentically of information collected can be checked up with alternate resources, if any. The verified data, arranged in proper sequence is the final data that are distributed to the designers involved in the project.

5.4.2 Technical Design

Technical parameters that affect the design and delivery of multimedia applications are discuss below:

(a) **Video Mode and Computer Platform** : There are many "portable", "cross-platform" software and "run-time modules", but many of them lose quality / performance during the translation.

Some authoring programs are available on several platforms and provide tools for transforming and converting files and programs from one to the other. Care should be taken when considering cross-platform development because of significant performance differences in hardware peripherals and devices.

Run-time software is often included in authoring software to explain the distribution of your final product by packaging playback software with your content. Advanced authoring programs provide specialized packaging and run-time distribution for use with devices such as CD-ROMs.

Care must be taken when using run-time players for advanced authoring systems that all specialized DLLs (Dynamic Link Libraries), run-time modules for other programs and non-system fonts used in the presentation are packaged together when the final product is distributed.

(b) **Memory and Disk Space Requirement** : Memory system is considered as a major power bottleneck for multimedia applications. Most multimedia applications use stream type of data structures with regular access patterns. This technique requires extra hardware prediction logic, and hardware prefetching technique to achieve significant performance improvement especially if large graphics, video and audio files are to be open. Fast memory technique is also required for multimedia applications because a large number of media objects are retrieved by users in a very fast way. Multimedia applications also require vast disk space to minimize user frustration because users download complex graphics, animations, movies, videos, data and information using the Internet and the downloading process requires specifying the graphics and boards as well as the processor, memory and disk space, communication bandwidths.

(c) **Delivery** :It includes Live Presentation, type of graphics card, video memory (1 MB, 2 MB, 4 MB, etc.), access time of hard disk (important for real-time video), type of sound card (support for General MIDI or Musical Instrument Digital Interface, audio-video software, Delivery by CD-ROM, Electronic Delivery (ftp (File Transfer Protocol), WWW, etc.).

5.4.3 Visual Design

There are factors that should be considers in the visual design of a multimedia presentation:

(a) **Themes and Styles** : A multimedia presentation should have a consistent theme/style, it should not be confusion with multiple themes. The choice of theme/style depends on the styles and emotions of your audience. For example, Cartoon theme should be interesting and entertaining and must be consistent with the character's personality.

(b) **Graphic Styles** : Some color schemes (e.g., natural and floral for outdoor scenes) and art styles (e.g., oil paints, watercolors, color pencils, pastels) are best combined with a certain theme/style. While using color schemes do not use too many colors, be consistent with the use of color, use colors to separate ideas and signal changes. Use large fonts (e.g., 18 to 36 points), no more than 6-8 lines per screen depends on the application.

(c) **Pace and Running Length** : Allow a block of text to be slowly read twice. Transition time should be taken into account for the total running time.

(d) **Animation Style** : Only animate when it has a specific purpose or is necessary for the application.

(e) **Basic Layout** : Make sure that the information delivery path in the layout is smooth, not irregular or jumpy i.e., what naturally comes first, should be placed first, e.g. 1990 before 1995, use headlines/subtitles, additional shapes, buttons, fonts, backgrounds and textures to enhance the visual appearance.

5.5 INTERACTIVITY

In a multimedia system, if the user has the ability to control what elements are delivered and when, the system is called an *interactive system*. Interactivity allows the viewer to navigate through a presentation in their own way and at their own pace. Users can jump from topic-to-topic and skipping areas of little interest

(a) Traditional mass media include television, film, radio, and newspapers. These are called mass media, since the communication processes are one way, originating from a source and being delivered to a mass audience. These technologies also combine audio, video, graphics, and text, but in a way that is inflexible. For example, a film has a predefined beginning, middle, and end, irrespective of the audience watching it.

(b) With the power of the computer, the same media could be manipulated by the audience. In this manner, the audience does not need to remain passive, but becomes the user of the system. Thus, the key difference between mass media and multimedia is the shift from audience to users, and one-way communication to two-way communication. This is accomplished through interactivity.

To communicate with the system, the user can use a variety of devices, such as the keyboard, mouse, tracking ball, touch screen, and pen-based mouse. Thus while designing a multimedia application; we have to decide the level of interactivity we wish to provide to the user of the system.

5.6 GUIDELINES TO DEVELOP MULTIMEDIA PROJECT

Follow the following points while developing multimedia project:

1. Investigate how users use the system and make it more efficient. This involves releasing a beta version to a number of representative users, and including their input, probably redesigning the interface. Provide shortcuts for all the common queries.
2. Scrolling is evils avoid it at (almost) all costs. After all, scrolling is inherently sequential and introduces from the window. Use hypertext for instant access to relevant information.
3. Screen space is valuable and very expensive use it wisely.
4. Fancy slide transitions (Zooming in/out, Page turning, Fading in/out, etc.) are visually nice but expensive in terms of resources (both production and minimal system replay requirements). Use them only if you can afford them.
5. Focus on functionality and quality of the material.
6. Always offer specialized help there is no substitute for it when users really need it.

5.7 SAMPLE MULTIMEDIA PROJECTS

Multimedia application development requires structured and methodical process to seamless blend the technology with the creative thinking. Each of the multimedia development process requires the development of content and functionality that is similar to other production process, such as book, music, film and video and software development.

Multimedia project depends on three components:

Producer - The creator of the product. Responsible for managing the budget, resources, tools, and schedule.

Consumer - The sponsor. Define the need, skills of end users and the benefit of the product.

Product - Including content - form, pictures, audio, video, function - How the product works with Technology.

Five samples help you understand how to apply a structured process to multimedia development. Let us discuss each of them

Commercial - A profit game product which will be developed and produced.

Kiosk - A standalone information delivery system located in a shopping mall. Updated periodically.

Briefing - A corporate technical presentation that will be used a limited number of times.

Trainer - A computer-based training system for individuals to learn new processes and products.

Web site - A multimedia-based WWW application for corporate customers.

REVIEW QUESTIONS WITH ANSWERS

1. Multiple Choice

1.1 The first step in the SDLC:

a. Preliminary investigation and analysis
b. System design
c. Database design
d. None of these

1.2 The detailed study/investigation of the present system is frequently referred to as :
a. System planning b. System analysis
c. Feasibility study d. None of the above

1.3 The System Development phase associated with creation of test data is :
a. Systems analysis b. Physical design
c. System acceptance d. Logical design

1.4 Prototype is a :
a. Minimodel of the existing system
b. Minimodel of the proposed system
c. Working model of the existing system
d. None of the above

1.5 System quality pertains to:
a. Reliability b. Efficiency
c. Maintainability d. All the above

1.6 Historically, the term "hypertext" was used when textured information was linked in ____ ways.
a. Sequential b. Real time
c. Non-sequential d. Linear

1.7 A multimedia project is said to be _______ and user-interactive when users are given navigational control.
a. Hypertext b. Linear
c. Non-linear d. Plug-in

1.8 Types of audio in multimedia applications:
a. Music
b. Sound effects
c. Narration
d. All of the above

1.9 Types of interactive multimedia applications:
a. Menu b. Simulations
c. Hypermedia d. All of the above

1.10 Technical parameters that affect the design and delivery of multimedia applications:
a. Video Mode and Computer Platform
b. Memory and Disk Space Requirement
c. Delivery
d. All of the above

2. State whether the following statements are True or False

2.1 A prototype is a model of the final system.

2.2 Deployment means releasing the product to the end user.

2.3 Evaluation is the process that tests and assesses a Multimedia product to make sure it is what was ordered and it does what it supposed to do.

2.4 Authoring is a process of assembling the content into the multimedia software development environment following the map provided by the storyboard.

2.5 Storyboarding involves a complex effort to develop panels for screen layouts that describe content, flow and format.

2.6 Hardware selection is an implementation activity.

2.7 The results of the feasibility study are forwarded to corporate management along with a recommendation to continue or discontinue the project.

2.8 Maintenance is the process of incorporating changes in the existing system.

2.9 Once a new system is implemented, no subsequent evaluation of its performance is necessary.

2.10 Output of each phase must be verified and validated before starting with the next phase.

3. Match the following:

3.1	Prototype	a.	'How' the content should be displayed to the user
3.2	Installation procedure	b.	Immediate change to next image
3.3	Non-linear	c.	Zooming in/out
3.4	Linear	d.	Generally menu-driven systems intended to be easy to use by the multimedia developer.
3.5	Simple branching	e.	Supports a go-to based on the result of IF-THEN decision
3.6	Conditional branching	f.	Ability to go to another section of the multimedia production
3.7	Authoring systems	g.	Users just sit and watch as if it is a movie.
3.8	Fancy slide transitions	h.	Users are given the navigational control and can browse the contents
3.9	Script	i.	Documentation
3.10	Cut	j.	Model

4. Fill in the blanks

a. API b. CBT c. Review
d. Fade e. Dissolve f. Prototyping
g. Analysis activity h. Flexibility i. Enhancement
j. Testing

4.1 __________ is the process of making sure that the programs perform the intended tasks.

4.2 __________ implies adding new functions or additional capabilities to the system.

4.3 __________ refers to the capability of the system to adapt to changing environmental factors.

4.4 The next major step before system design and after feasibility study is __________.

4.5 __________ is the creating, developing and refining a working model of the final Operational System.

4.6 ______ is an application program interface, set of routines, protocols, and tools for building software applications.

4.7 ______ a type of education in which the student learns by executing special training programs on a computer.

4.8 In _________ stage of testing, you make sure the project works as designed.

4.9 _______ is a metaphor for a complete change of scene.

4.10 In _________ the current image distorts into an unrecognizable form before the next clear image appears.

Answers

1.	1.1	a	1.2	b	1.3	c	1.4	b	1.5	d	1.6	c
	1.7	c	1.8	d	1.9	d	1.10	d				
2.	2.1	T	2.2	T	2.3	T	2.4	T	2.5	T	2.6	T
	2.7	T	2.8	T	2.9	F	2.10	T				
3.	3.1	j	3.2	i	3.3	h	3.4	g	3.5	f	3.6	e
	3.7	d	3.8	c	3.9	a	3.10	b				
4.	4.1	j	4.2	i	4.3	h	4.4	g	4.5	f	4.6	a
	4.7	b	4.8	c	4.9	d	4.10	e				

Questions with Answers

1. Write short notes on the following:
   a. System Development Life Cycle (SDLC)
   b. Multimedia System Development Life Cycle (MSDLC)
2. What is significance of storyboard in Multimedia project?
3. Differentiate between System Analysis and System Design.
4. What do you mean by implementation and evaluation?
5. Write a short note on interactivity.

Answers to Short Questions

1. a. System development is a birth-to-mature process called System Development Life Cycle (SDLC). A system project begins (is born) with a decision to analyze user requirements. The project is completed (matures) once a usable software product is produced and implemented or released. Thus the system development life cycle consists of System analysis, design and implementation.

   b. Multimedia system development process involves a number of steps like traditional software system development and is known as Multimedia System Development Life Cycle (MSDLC). Creating a multimedia application is a complex and abstract process. It can be categorized into a design phase and an implementation phase. In the design phase the content writer and visual artists are involved with paper work for specifying what should be the content of the presentation keeping in mind the target audience, how the content should be arranged, what should be the screen designs, how the user should navigate from one frame to the next etc. During implementation phase the production team uses appropriate editing and authoring software to build up the presentation according to the designs.

2. A storyboard depicts the initial idea content of a multimedia concept in a series of sketches.
   The storyboard can be used for a great deal of animation or many different scenes. Used by film directors for productions ranging from 30 second television commercials to feature-length motion pictures, the storyboard consists of sketches of the scenes and actions. Mapping out a storyboard helps the author to recognize gaps in logic. Some multimedia authoring programs provide facilities for drawing and organizing the frames of a storyboard.

3.

System Analysis		System Design
System analysis is the examination of the problem.		System design is the creation of the information system which is the solution to the problem.
It is concerned with identifying all the constraints and influences.		It is concerned with the coordination of the activities, job procedures and equipment utilization in order to achieve system goals.
It deals with data collection and a detailed evaluation of present system.		It deals with general design specification, detailed design specifications, output, input, files and procedures. It also deals with program construction, testing and user acceptance.
It portrays logical model of the system through Data Flow Diagrams and Data Dictionaries.		It provides technical specifications and reports with which the problem can be tackled.

4. Implementation is the final phase of development. It consists of installing hardware, programs, collecting data and organizing people to interact with and run the system.
   In the implementation phase, user actually starts using the system. This phase therefore involves training the users for using the system and also providing them friendly documentation to refer to.
   Once the system is implemented, it should be evaluated. Evaluation is the process of verifying the capability of a system, after it is put in operation, to see whether it is meeting the objectives or not.

5. In a multimedia system, if the user has the ability to control what elements are delivered and when, the system is called an interactive system. Interactivity allows the viewer to navigate through a presentation in their own way and at their own pace. Users can jump from topic-to-topic and skipping areas of little interest.

DESCRIPTIVE TYPE QUESTIONS

1. Explain basic stages in any multimedia project.
2. Differentiate between alpha testing and beta testing.
3. What are the factors that should be considered in the visual design of a multimedia presentation.

4. What are technical parameters that affect the design and delivery of multimedia applications.
5. Write a short note on Implementation and Evaluation.
6. What is meant by software life cycle and what is its importance?
7. What are the important factors to be considered when choosing a subject matter for a presentation?
8. Why is specifying the target audience important?
9. How script is different from storyboard?
10. What is the importance of a storyboard in the design phase of a multimedia production?
11. Why is interactivity in multimedia presentation is important?

CHAPTER 6

Multimedia Authoring and Publishing

6.1 MULTIMEDIA AUTHOURING BASICS

Multimedia authoring refers to the process of developing a multimedia project (both media handling and integration) using specialized packages and utilities exclusively meant for this purpose.

Authoring tools are software packages with standard user interface elements that are used to produce contents for web publishing. Authoring software provides an integrated environment for binding together content and functions of your project, and typically includes everything needed to create, edit and import specific types of data, assemble raw data into playback sequence and provide a structured method or language for responding to the user input. Authoring tools enable, encourage, and assist users ("authors") in the creation of accessible Web content through prompts, alerts, checking and repair functions, help files and automated tools.

☞ *The term "authoring tool" refers to the wide range of software used for creating Web contents.*

Multimedia authoring tools provide the important framework you need for organizing and editing the elements of your multimedia project, including graphics, sounds, animations, and video clips.

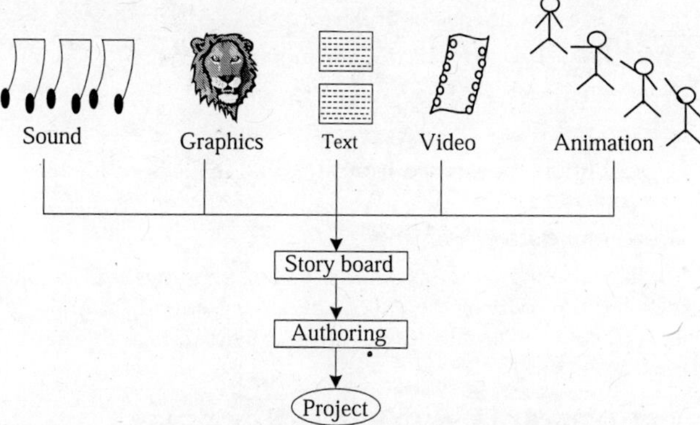

Figure 6.1 Authoring integrates all media/contents developed for the project

Authoring tools must also ensure that the author can navigate a document efficiently while editing.

Some Authoring Tools for Web editor graphics are:

- Editing tools especially designed to produce Web content, such as MS FrontPage, MS Visual InterDev.
- Tools that provide the option of saving material in a Web format, such as word processors (For example, MS Word), or DTP packages (for example, Adobe PageMaker).
- Tools that transform documents into Web formats (e.g., filters to transform desktop publishing formats to HTML).
- Tools that produce multimedia, especially where it is intended for use on the Web (e.g., video production and editing suites). For example, Macromedia Flash.
- Tools for site management or site publication that automatically generate Websites dynamically from a database, such as MS Access.

6.2 AUTHORING TOOL FEATURES

Many authoring tools have a set of common features for dealing with content, presenting data, obtaining input from the user and controlling the execution of the product. Features of multimedia authoring tools are as mention below.

6.2.1 Editing Features

The elements of multimedia - image, animation, text, digital audio and MIDI music and video clips - need to be created, edited and converted to standard file formats and the specialized applications. Authoring systems typically include the ability to create, edit and import specific types of data; assemble raw data into a playback sequence or cue sheet and provide structured method or language for responding to user input.

6.2.2 Organizing Features

The organization, design and production process for multimedia involves storyboarding and flowcharting. Some authoring tools provide a visual flowcharting system or overview facility for illustrating your project's structure. Multimedia authoring tools provide the important framework you need for organizing and editing the elements of multimedia like graphics, sounds, animations and video clips. Storyboards or navigation diagrams too can help organize a project.

6.2.3 Programming Features

An authoring language is a programming language used to create tutorials, computer-based training courseware, Websites, CD-ROMs and other interactive computer programs. Authoring systems (packages) generally provide high-level visual tools that enable a complete system to be designed without writing any programming code. Authoring tools that offer a very high - level language or interpreted scripting environment for navigation control and for enabling user inputs, such as Macromedia Director, Macromedia Flash.

The scripting language included in authoring tools to provide a wide variety of other actions. With script you can perform computational tasks; sense and respond to user input; create character, icon and motion animation; launch other application; and control external multimedia devices. Program controlled code or scripting with the application controls program execution. Execution, in some cases, may be fixed or altered by the user.

6.2.4 Interactivity Features

Interactivity is, in essence, a stimulus/response relationship, and one way we can categorize our options is by listing stimuli the user can provide and then the responses we can make happen. Authoring tools are used for designing interactivity and the user interface, for presentation your project on screen and assembling multimedia elements into a single cohesive project. Simple interactive authoring tools provide the critical features of being able to interactively navigate through a product. Multimedia authoring is creation interactive applications. Interactivity empowers the end users of your project by letting them control the content and flow of information. There are three common classifications of interactivity:

(a) A linear presentation is one in which the author decides the sequence and manner in which information is presented. The user controls only the pace.

(b) A branching program is one in which the user has some control over the sequence of presentation by selecting from a group of choices, such as from a main menu. The author still maintains the control of deciding what to include in the choices available at any point in the program.

Authoring tools should provide one or more levels of interactivity:

(i) Simple branching, which offers the ability to go to another section of the multimedia production.

(ii) Conditional branching, which supports a go-to based on the result of IF-THEN decision or events.

(iii) A structured language that supports complex programming logic, such as nested IF-THENs, subroutines, event tracking and message passing among objects and elements.

(c) Hypermedia can be thought of as a Web of interrelated information in which the user is in almost complete control of the pace and, to a somewhat lesser extent, the sequence and content of the presentation. Links provide for random access of information.

Several tools are used for developing interactive multimedia. These are:

(a) Authoring systems

(b) Authoring languages

(c) Generic languages (e.g. C, C++, Java)

Authoring systems are generally menu-driven systems intended to be easy to use by the multimedia developer. Multimedia and its Application Environment where whatever multimedia developer wishes to do is either selected from a menu or entered into the computer in a straightforward, well-prompted way. Authoring languages are specially designed programming languages, and have some distinct advantages over generic languages. They have been created specifically for the training/educational field, and as such provide appropriate commands and structures to cater for the types of presentation and interaction involved in CBT.

6.2.5 Performance Tuning Features

Complex multimedia projects require extra synchronization of events. Accomplishing synchronization is difficult because performance varies widely among the different computers used for multimedia development and delivery. Some authoring tools allow you to lock a production's playback speed to specified computer platform, but other provides no ability what so ever to control performance on various systems.

6.2.6 Playback Features

When you are developing multimedia project, your will continually assembling elements and testing to see how the assembly looks and performs. Your authoring system should let you build a segment or part of your project and then quickly test it as if the user were actually using it.

6.2.7 Delivery Features

Delivering your project may require building a run-time version of the project using the multimedia authoring software. A run-time version allows your project to play back with out requiring the full authoring

6.2.8 Cross-Platform Features

It is also increasingly important to use tools that make transfer across platforms easy. For many developers, the Macintosh remains the multimedia authoring platform of choice, but 80% of that developer's target market may be Windows platforms.

6.2.9 Internet Playability

Due to the Web has become a significant delivery medium for multimedia, Authoring systems provide a means for converting their output to be delivered within the context of HTML or DHTML.

In short, Multimedia authoring tools have following features:

- Building the Interface
- Specify screen dimensions and background color
- Create links that go to "next" and "previous" screens
- Create links that go to non-adjacent screens
- Specify transitions
- Define button appearance, icon, style and make invisible buttons (hot spots)
- Draw simple screen elements
- Media handling, such as import sound, graphics, video so they become part of the executable access sound, graphics, and video as external files at run time synchronize different media

6.3 MULTIMEDIA AUTHORING SYSTEMS

Multimedia authoring system is a set of software tools for creating multimedia applications embedded in an authoring environment. Authoring systems typically include the ability to create, edit and import specific types of data; assemble raw data into a playback sequence and provide structured method or language for responding to user input.

☞ *A person who creates applications for multimedia integration, for example, presentation is called an author and the development work is called authoring.*

Authoring systems for multimedia applications are designed with the following two primary targets in mind. Professionals who prepare documents, audio or sound tracks and full motion video clips for wide distribution; and average business users preparing documents, audio recordings or full motion video clips for stored message or presentations. The key differences between the uses of these two types of authoring systems for creating multimedia objects pose different sets of requirements for the authoring systems. For example, professional authoring is usually performed at centralized professional authoring workstations in some kind of media laboratory or studio which includes professional quality video cameras and sound equipment. Individual adhoc authoring on the other hand, is performed at the user's desktop using non-professional cameras and sound and light equipment. Quality standards are very important in both cases.

6.3.1 Need of Authoring Systems

Authoring tools provide the important framework you need for organizing and editing the elements of your multimedia project including graphics, sounds, animations, and video clips. Authoring tools are used for designing interactivity and the user interface, for presenting your project on screen, and for assembling diverse multimedia elements into a single cohesive product. With multimedia authoring software, you can make video productions, animations, games, interactive Websites, demo disk, presentations, kiosk application, interactive training, Computer-based training, Dictionaries (Tells how to pronounce difficult word), Encyclopedias (important sound and video clips), Business presentations, Web applications, Advertisement, etc. Authoring systems are useful for development of CD-ROM information products online documentation products, online documentation and help systems and sophisticated multimedia enhanced publications.

6.4 AUTHORING TOOLS

The tool set for building multimedia projects contains one or more authoring systems, the tools for creating and editing multimedia elements and the tools for housekeeping tasks such as capturing images from the screen, translating file formats and moving files among computers.

6.4.1 Tools for Creating and Editing

Here, we have painting and drawing tools as well as 3-D modelers. Painting software like Fractal Design Painter is dedicated to producing crafted bitmap images. Drawing software like CorelDRAW and Canvas is dedicated to producing vector-based linear art that can be easily printed using PostScript or another mark up system, such as Quick Draw on the MAC computer. Some software applications combine both drawing and painting capabilities, but many authoring systems import only bit mapped images.

6.4.2 3D Modeling and Animation Tools

With 3-D modeling software, objects rendered in perspective appear more realistic as we can choose the right lighting and perspective for final rendered image. Powerful modeling packages, such as Macromedia's Extreme 3D, Auto Desk's 3D Studio Max, Strata Vision's 3D, Specular's Logo Motion and Infini-D, and Caligari's true Space are also bundled with assortments of pre-rendered 3-D clip art objects such as people, furniture, buildings, cars, airplanes, trees and plants. There are also specialized applications for creating and animating 3-D text like Fontographer, Type-Designer, Font Manager, Making Pretty Text, Font Chameleon.

6.4.3 Image and Editing Tools

Image editing applications are specialized and powerful tools for enhancing the existing bitmapped images. These applications also provide tools for painting and drawing that can be used to create images from scratch as well as images digitized from scanners, video frame grabbers, digital cameras, Clip Art files, or original artwork files created with a painting or a drawing package. Image editing programs usually support plug-in modules from third party developers. These modules can be used to create special effects.

6.4.4 Optical Character Recognition (OCR) Software

A scanner is typically used to convert printed matter into electronic text files in the form of bitmaps. OCR software then turns bit-mapped characters into electronically recognizable ASCII text. The software breaks the bitmap image into chunks according to whether it contains text or graphics by examining the texture and density areas of the bitmap and by detecting edges. The text areas are then converted into ASCII characters using probability and expert systems.

6.4.5 Sound Editing Programs

Sound editing tools for both digitized and MIDI sound allow operations like cut, paste and edit on segments of it with great precision in real time. Using sound editing software, we can make our own sound effects and install them as system beeps that indicate an error warning or special activity. Both MAC and Windows systems provide system sounds, which are available as soon as we install the operating system. For digital waveform sounds, Windows ships with the Sound Recorder program that provides some rudimentary features for sound editing; most soundboards for PCs include editing software, such as Creative Lab's Wave Studio.

When dealing with MIDI sound, we need to know about tempos, clefs, notations, keys and instruments and understand the way music is sequenced. Many MIDI applications provide both sequencing and notations capabilities.

6.4.6 Animation, Video and Digital Movies

Animations and digital video movies are sequences of bitmapped graphic scenes called frames, rapidly played back. We can generate animation without the authoring system by rapidly changing the location of objects. Most authoring tools adopt either frame or object-oriented approach to animation, but rarely both. Movie-making tools , such as QuickTime from MAC and Microsoft Video for Windows, also known as Audio Video Interleaved (AVI), technology can be used to create, edit, and present digitized motion video segments in a small window. Movie making tools, such as Premiere, VideoShop and Media Studio Pro let the user edit and assemble video clips captured from camera, tape or other digitized movie segments, animations, scanned images and audio clips obtained from digitized audio or MIDI files. The completed clip with added visual effects can be played back.

Both QuickTime and AVI* provide a methodology for interleaving or blending audio data with video data so that sound remains synchronized with the video. Both technologies allow data to stream from disk into memory in a buffered and organized manner.

6.5 TYPES OF AUTHORING TOOLS

Multimedia authoring tools provide the important framework needed for organizing and editing the elements that include graphics, sounds, animations and video clips. Authoring tools are used for designing interactively and provide the user interface for assembling multimedia elements into a cohesive project that can be presented on the screen. Authoring software provides an integrated environment for binding together the content and the functions in the multimedia project. Authoring systems should have the ability to create, edit, and import specific types of data, assemble raw data into playback sequence or a cue sheet; and should provide a structured method or language for responding to user input. With multimedia authoring software, we can generate video productions, animations, games, demo disks and interactive guided tours, presentations, interactive training, simulations, prototypes, and technical visualizations.

Multimedia authoring, is the final stage of multimedia project production. It is here, by making use of various packages and programming environments, that the producer actually integrates all types of contents of the project. It is the most important phase of multimedia project design and development, because the output of this phase will be replicated and introduced in the market. All alterations, modifications, revisions, reconsiderations and redesigning ends with this phase. Any delay during the authoring stage will result in overall delay of the project.

When a multimedia application is produced via an authoring system the author goes through several stages.

The various authoring tools are categorized into:

(a) Card or page-based authoring tools
(b) Icon-based authoring tools
(c) Time-based authoring tools
(d) Object-oriented authoring tools

This categorization is based on the approach used for sequencing or organizing multimedia elements and events. Every authoring tool, package environment or platform, uses some fundamental methodology for developing the multimedia project. Some tools, even offer the flexibility to switch over from one methodology to another whenever the need arises.

6.5.1 Card or Page Based-Authoring Tools

In these authoring systems, multimedia elements are organized as pages of a book or a stack of cards. Every page of the book may contain many media elements including sounds, video and animations. As the user or consumer proceeds with the project, the pages progress in sequence, as determined by the user interaction.

Individual pages can be linked so that it is possible to move over from one page to another related page. This type of authoring methodology is best-suited for those projects, whose contents can be arranged as individual sequences or frames–one independent of another, as far as possible or when the bulk of content consists of elements that can be viewed individually like the pages of a book or cards in card file. Since the educational software is based on page based tools these are very useful in developing educational applications. Toolbook is an example of page-based multimedia development software.

☞ *The authoring systems in this category are hypercard, supercard, media object, and Tool book.*

6.5.2 Icon-based Authoring Tools

In these authoring system, multimedia elements and interactions cues are organized as objects in a structural framework or process. Icon-based, event-driven tools simplify the organization of your project and typically display flow diagrams of activities along branching paths. In these authoring systems, multimedia elements and events are organized as a structure or flowchart. The structure or flowchart is built from events, tasks and decisions by dragging appropriate icons from a library. These icons include menu choices, graphic images, sounds and computations. The flowchart depicts flow of activities along its branching paths. When the structure is built up, we can add text, graphics, animation, sounds and video movies. We can also edit the structure by rearranging and fine-tuning the icons and their properties. The authoring tools in this category are Authorware Professional, Icon Author and Quest, both from Windows. In complicate structures, this charting is particularly useful during development.

☞ *Icon-based tools allow each and every event and elements belonging to a particular multimedia project, to be arranged sequentially in the form of icon. Icons makes it possible to the access to the contents and control.*

6.5.3 Time-based Authoring Tools

Time-based Authoring tools allow the designer to arrange various media elements and events of the multimedia project sequentially along a well-defined time line. As the time advances, from zero seconds (which will the starting point of the project) the events also begin to occur, one after the another. The event may include media files updation and playback as well as transition of information, from one portion to another. The speed at which these transitions occur, can also be accurately controlled. These tools take the help of a software times which is a typical clock that starts at the beginning of the project and graduates minute after minute. The events happen, one after another following this time. This type of authoring methodology can be very well-adopted for those projects wherein the information flow can be directed from beginning to end much like the movies. Macromedia's Director is an example for multimedia authoring system that makes use of this methodology.

☞ *Time-based authoring software includes, a time line where the pages or data components are inserted and display of different components can be controlled either by assigning a duration to each page or manually. This produces very successful animations and effects.*

6.5.4 Object-Oriented Authoring Tools

In these authoring systems, multimedia elements and events are organized as objects in a hierarchical order with parent and child relationships. The objects are ordered according to the properties or modifiers assigned to them and messages are passed among these objects. For example, a dog is defined by barking and jumping modifiers and a teenager object like a girl may be programmed to take out the trash every Friday evening on getting a message from Dad. Objects take care of themselves, i.e., given a message they do their thing without external procedures and programming. Object-oriented tools are particularly useful for games that contain many components with many characteristics and for simulating real life situations, events and their constituent properties.

Java is also an object-oriented programming environment. Borland's JBuilder allows you to create Java solutions in an icon-based environment.

Increasingly Lingo, the scripting language used in Director, and the equivalent in Flash and Authorware, take an object-oriented approach.

Mark up Tools

These are primarily used to mark up documents so that they can be viewed in Web browsers. Some examples of mark up tools systems include: HTML, VRML, XML, SMIL.

Applications , such as Macromedia Dreamweaver allow you create Web pages without learning the underlying html.

6.6 METAPHORE

Authoring is the process of creating multimedia applications. Metaphors are methodologies employed to create multimedia applications. Most authoring programs use one of several authoring metaphors, also known as *authoring paradigm.*

6.6.1 Different Metaphors

Authoring tools used different metaphors for sequencing and organizing multimedia elements and events. On this basis, they can be classified into following categories:

- Scripting language metaphor
- Slide show metaphor
- Hierarchical metaphor
- Network metaphore
- Iconic/flow-control metaphor
- Frames metaphor
- Timeline metaphor

Scripting Language Metaphor

Scripting language metaphor use a special language to enable interactivity (buttons, mouse, etc.), and to allow conditionals, jumps, loops, functions/macros, etc.

Slide Show Metaphor

Slide show metaphor associates the authoring task with a slide show. This is used by Microsoft PowerPoint. Each screen of the presentation is shown as a slide object that can be separately created, edited and arranged. This metaphor is excellent for creating linear presentations, it is not very efficient when random interactivity is needed.

Hierarchical Metaphor

Hierarchical Metaphor is user-controllable elements which are organized into a tree structure, often used in menu-driven applications. It has restriction that one must move between objects via the paths in the hierarchy. For some kinds of applications one would like to have a more free environment that has no restrictions on where you go.

Network Metaphor

The network metaphor is an interactive application that allows the user to move from any object in the application to any other object without restriction.

Iconic/Flow-control Metaphor

An authoring metaphore that is particularly suited to authoring by non-programmers. Here an application is built by dragging icons from an icon palette into the application workspace and connecting them to create the logic of the application.

In these authoring systems, multimedia elements and interaction cues or events are organized as objects in a structural framework. Icon-based, event driven tools simplify the organization of a project and typically display flow diagrams of activities along branching paths. Some examples of icon-based systems include: Authorware Professional (Windows), IconAuthor (Windows)

Frames Metaphor

Iconic/Flow-control Metaphor; however links between icons are more conceptual, rather than representing the actual flow of the program. Flowchart consists of modules composed of frames. Frames are constructed from objects, , such as text, graphics, audio, animations and video, all of which can respond to events.

Timeline Metaphor

The timeline metaphor uses horizontal lines to represent flow of time. The developer is required to place the objects and controls on one or more timelines and specify their attributes and interaction with each other. The timeline spread over a temporal units called frames. Navigational and other codes can be attached to frames as well as media objects. Macromedia's Director authoring tool uses this kind of metaphore. This kind of structure is especially useful when the presentation deals with a lot of animation or other dynamic activity.

6.7 SOME USEFUL EDITING AND AUTHORING TOOLS

6.7.1 Adobe Photoshop

Adobe Photoshop is a graphic program that has set the standard for image manipulation. One of the excellent features of Photoshop is the Toolbox that places all the drawing tools in left next to the picture so that you can use them quickly and easily. You can also use it to create original art.

6.7.2 Adobe Premiere

Adobe Premiere is a powerful program for editing digital video. Premiere helps you create dynamic video or film, whether you are creating long video programs and motion picture films or short movies for CD-ROM or the Web. Like most editing software, Premiere works by importing video from a source, such as a video tape onto your hard drive, then allowing you to create new edited versions which you can export back to tape, disk or other medium. The major features of Adobe Premiere are:

- Capture high quality video from your DV camcorder.
- Organize your audio and video clips and edit them into a complete production.
- Enhance your work with transitions and effects, titles and animations.
- Save and share your productions as digital video files.
- Output streaming media formats to share on the Web.

Making video involves working through three general phases:

- *Pre-production* involves writing the script, visualizing scenes by sketching them on a storyboard, and creating a production schedule for shooting the scenes.
- *Production* involves shooting the scenes.
- *Post-production* involves editing the best scenes into the final video program, correcting and enhancing video and audio where necessary. Premiere is designed for efficient editing, correcting, and enhancing of clips, making it a valuable tool for post-production.

6.7.3 Flash

Adobe Flash is a software that creates animations for a Web designs. You can create a multimedia enriched content (Flash movies) containing images, sound, video and animation effects with this software. Adding more to this, the Flash software comes with a scripting language, called ActionScript, which provides interactivity to your Flash movies. Flash also comes with number of pre-built components including media components that load Flash video files or MP3 audio to enhance your Website.

Flash is basically a vector-based software that provides you with drawing tools to create vector objects. The drawing created in Flash can be saved as GIF files. Flash enables you to create animations on the objects of your movie. It creates animation using a process called *tweening*. Flash movies can be controlled by adding interaction to them. You can create or use an in-built button component as an interface element. For example, you can click a button to start or stop the movie. You can also add digital sound and video as the contents of your Flash movie.

HTML and Adobe Flash are two popular technologies that are used for creating valuable and attractive content on the World Wide Web. Although, HTML aims to replace other Rich Internet Application (RIA) platforms, , such as Adobe Flash or Microsoft Silverlight, especially by taking advantage of its capability to render multimedia content without requiring a plugin or "player" application installed. But, Adobe Flash is a multimedia platform and a RIA (Rich Internet Applications) tool used for adding vivid animation and interactivity to ads, games and various types of Web pages.

Here are the some of the advantages of Adobe Flash that make it very popular over HTML:

(i) ***Emerging Technology:*** Being still under development, HTML lacks the reliability of Flash. Features could be changed on the long run, which means that using it will require more maintenance effort than a Flash-based approach.

(ii) ***Lower Performance than Flash:*** On most Windows platforms, HTML applications run slower than applications developed using Flash. As a consequence, using heavy graphics (animations and complex visual effects) in a HTML application could pose certain performance issues.

(iii) ***Lower Capabilities of generating 3D Content and Visual Effects:*** HTML does not provide native support for animations, so developers have to rely on other technologies (for example JavaScript) to create animated content. But, Flash, which is mainly focused on creating graphic content and animations, HTML5 is mainly focused on structuring and presenting content for the Web, which means that it provides a limited support for creating complex visual effects.

(iv) ***Depends on the Browser on which it is Run:*** Since HTML5 is a Web standard, and each browser implements it in its own way, the same content can be rendered differently on different browsers. For example, a visual effect can be displayed correctly on one browser, while it might not be displayed at all (or displayed totally different) on another.

(v) ***Reduced Online support and Fewer Development Tools:*** Being an emerging technology, currently there are not too many development tools available. Also, there is a reduced online support and documentation for HTML5. As a consequence, the development process for HTML5 applications is not as fluent as Flash development.

HTML5 is widely regarded as a technology of the future, however it is still under development and it does not provide the reliability of Flash. Even if developing animations and complex visual effects with HTML is feasible from a technical point of view, still the development process is not as fluent as Adobe Flash development.

6.7.4 Macromedia Director

Director is the premier multimedia authoring package available for Windows and Macintosh computers, developed and published by Macromedia Inc., a public company formed in 1992.

Director is used to collect various types of media (, such as text, image and sound) and you can develop high performance multimedia content and applications for CDs, DVDs, Kiosks, and the Internet. Director has become a key development tool for the World Wide Web. It help reduce the size of projects created by Director for the Internet. Macromedia developed shockwave. Director movies are shocked, or compressed before being distributed on Web sites. Users can then playback these films by using shockwave plug-in.

Before we start using Director, let us imagine that you are charged with making a movie for a major Hollywood Studio. First, you want to know what the movie is about and what is going to happen in the movie. Think of this as the movie definition, or synopsis. After you define what the movie is about, you determine where you are going to film the movie. The right locations can make the movie great.

The actors you want in the movie are also very important. A good cast can help turn a movie into a blockbuster. Do not forget the props the actor will use, they are part of cast too.

Finally, you need a strong script. A script defines what happens and when. The script determines everything from the dialogue and the stage directions to the surrounding enviornment. Director uses all these same ideas and enables you to use them to create a multimedia project. This is similar to the way a real director makes a movie.

All the parts that make up a project in Director are called a *movie*. A movie contains the information needed to play the project for an end user. All Director projects starts with a movie. The movie is the main file stored on disk. A Director movie has the filename extension .dir.

A projector is created from a movie file for playback on the end user's computer. It can also be shocked, or compressed, into a shockwave movie for distribution on the Internet.

☞ *The process of using director to create a movie is often referred to a author mode. Similarly, when a director movie is playing back inside a projector, it is called projector mode, it is called plugin mode inside the browser.*

6.7.5 Lingo

Lingo is a scripting language used in Director. You can make movies more interactive by using Lingo scripting language. It can perform the tasks, such as creating objects and animating the objects in Director. There are two types of syntaxes used in Lingo programming language, which are:

- **Verbose Syntax**: Enables you to write the programs in an English sentence.
- **Dot Syntax**: Enables you to write the programs in which the word are replaced with dots and brackets.

Lingo has limited functionality in Director but using Xtras can extend its functionality. Xtras are the code modules, which can add extended functionality and special capabilities to Director. When you create any Xtra, you can put it in Xtras folder in the Director folder. When Director is launched, the Xtras folder is scanned and the commands and functions of the Xtras are integrated into Director.

6.7.6 Dreamweaver

Dreamweaver is the most popular professional Web creation tool. It is also a popular tool for independent Web developers who work on Websites for their clients. As a cross-platform tool, Dreamweaver works virtually identically on Macintosh and Windows-based computers and is popular on both platforms. The foundation of Dreamweaver, and Web development, is the HyperText Markup Language (HTML). A language used to describe the structure of content so that it can be viewed over the Web in a Web browser. The modern version of HTML called XHTML (Extensible Hypertext Markup Language). Dreamweaver writes the XHTML for you, so you do not need to know how to write XHTML to get started using Dreamweaver. This chapter describes an overview of Dreamweaver CS5 and helps you get started with the Dreamweaver application.

6.8 MULTIMEDIA DEVELOPMENT TEAM

A successful project production starts with the right team and ends with the same. High-quality interactive multimedia applications are the products of a production team. A multimedia team will produce fine-quality high-end applications, such as games, information kiosks, commercial training and educational applications. They are usually produced by a specialized team.

6.8.1 Project Manager

The project manager takes the overall responsibility of developing the product. He is the top man, as far as the team is concerned and is responsible for the total quality as well as timely delivery of the project. Responsibilities of the project manager includes:

- Develop the multimedia concept of the topic chosen for the project.
- The Project Manager will understand the complete process for the semester including familiarity with the roles of all participants.
- The Project Manager will have exposure to existing media based productions as well as technical skills with all production tools to oversee correct technical procedures and efficiency in the development process.
- The Project Manager must be familiar with the project vision and purpose from the client and have a realistic vision for the end product.
- The Project Manager will review pre-production timelines, content at all stages, understand the system for content management. They will establish a level of quality for the project and evaluate content based on that standard throughout the semester. The Project Manager will have authority to reject substandard content and evaluate design ideas based on practicality and attainability.
- Monitoring the process of the project in all it's phases, on day-to-day basis.
- A very important part of the project manager's duties is to keep the project in perspective, to meet the end of semester deadline.

6.8.2 Project Director

The Director will understand the complete process for the semester including familiarity with the roles of all participants. The Director will work with the Project Manager to outline development team tasks throughout the production process. Responsibilities of the project director includes:

- The Director will have exposure to existing media-based productions as well as technical skills with all production tools to oversee correct technical procedures and efficiency in the development process.

- The responsibility of the Director is to manage and organize the work that is produced by the other technical groups (graphics, audio, video, animation). The directors absorb a variety of ideas and pull them into a working plan. Directors are the collectors and organizers of content.
- The Director may be the first to see what areas are weak and need additional participation. They may also see problems as they occur so the problems can be addressed to the Project Manager and class Instructor.

6.8.3 Technical Engineers

- The Technical Engineer understands file types and playback optimization, has familiarity with hardware/software and assists in defining project specifications.
- The Technical Engineer attends to problem-solving any technical issues that arise during the production process and works with the development team in maintaining correct procedures and standards throughout the development process.
- The Technical Engineer will track project development for functionality and media specifications and test product functionality throughout the process. They will be responsible for CD-ROM and/or DVD production, ftp (File Transfer Protocol), and Web delivery.

6.8.4 Scriptwriters

- The Scriptwriters will work closely with the Client, Project Manager, and Graphic Designer and the entire development team to develop a written project script.
- The Scriptwriter will perform project research as needed and write the script for stories, dialogs.
- The Scriptwriter will be familiar with and follow modified scriptwriting techniques from the television and motion picture industries.
- The Scriptwriter will also perform tasks as copy editor for text content throughout the production process.

6.8.5 2D and 3D Animators

- The Animators will work closely with the graphic designers and audio technicians to develop animations (titles, characters, etc.).
- Assist in establishing standards for file formats, compression types and ratios, window dimensions, resolution, colors, frame rates, and font selection.
- They develop the animation sequences involved in the project, in coordination with the media content developers.
- They decide which type of animation, i.e., 2D or 3D must be adopted for the specific sequences and develop them accordingly.

6.8.6 Graphic Designers

- The graphic designers will follow the written script to develop interface designs, color schemes, and create graphics (from storyboards to final) navigation graphics, fonts and text formatting, photo collages, 3D objects, logos, artwork, backgrounds, animation, and establish an overall visual "feel" while maintaining visual continuity throughout production.
- They will provide ideas in thumbnail and storyboard form and follow through with finished artwork ready for production to begin.
- The graphic designers will be assigned specific tasks throughout the development process and need to meet timeline and production specifications as outlined and follow the file management system for content submissions.
- The Graphic Designers need to understand resolution, file types, copyright limitations and be familiar with Photoshop, Illustrator, and the drawing and text tools in Authorware.

6.8.7 Interactivity Designers

- The Interactivity Designers will design project interactivity and develop navigational flowcharts. They will develop scripting specific to project interactivity and navigation and perform Authorware programming as needed.

6.8.8 Programmers/Compilers

- The programmer role is to write the program code lines or scripts using the authoring tools.
- Combines the multimedia elements into a multimedia program.
- The programmers/compilers tasks will overlap those of the Interactivity Designers and they will work closely throughout the production process.
- The Programmers/Compilers will transfer existing data to files for Authorware as needed, assemble parts into Authorware movies (put the puzzle together), and perform extensive project testing. The programmers will do exactly that programming with Authorware variables, functions, and other use of the calculations.

6.8.9 Photographers

- The Photographers will acquire photo content as needed. They will perform image editing scanning and image enhancement/manipulation/montage function while maintaining visual continuity as established by the graphic designers.

6.8.10 Video Technicians

- Video technicians will provide video content as needed. This includes interviews and special effects video as needed. They are responsible for capturing, editing, video digitizing, add effects, compression, etc.

6.8.11 Audio Technicians

- Audio technicians will provide audio content as needed. This includes sound effects, music, and voice overs as needed. They will perform audio editing, sound effects, compression, format to input to Authorware.
- They develop the digital audio clips, including the voice overs as directed by the media designer's report.
- Edit the raw audio data and convert them suitably, so that they can be embedded in the project.

REVIEW QUESTIONS WITH ANSWERS

1. Multiple Choice

1.1 The free add-on program to PowerPoint that makes it possible to publish video presentations to the Web is called:
a. Adobe Flash b. Producer
c. FrontPage d. Director MX

1.2 Authoring tools help you to:
a. Write a storyboard
b. Search the Internet
c. Control the presentation of multimedia elements
d. All of the above

1.3 A multimedia project is said to be _______ and user-interactive when users are given navigational control.
a. Hypertext b. Linear
c. Non-linear d. Plug-in

1.4 A specialized program used to create multimedia presentations is a _______.
a. Web authoring program
b. Desktop publishing program
c. Multimedia authoring program
d. Illustration program

1.5 Which of following is a painting program and image editing program?
a. Designer b. FreeHand
c. Illustrator d. Photoshop

1.6 Which kind of authoring system is Adobe Flash?
a. Card-based b. Page-based
c. Time-based d. con-based

1.7 Elements are organized as pages of a book or a stack of cards in an _________ authoring system.
a. Card-based b. Icon-based
c. Time-based d. None of the above

1.8 Page-based authoring system contains media object(s):
a. Buttons
b. Text fields
c. Graphic objects
d. All of the above

1.9 To make a good multimedia you need:
a. Hardware and software b. Good ideas
c. Talent and skill d. All of the above

1.10 A scripting language is considered as:
a. A subset of HTML
b. A form of BASIC
c. A very high-level language
d. A very low-level language

2. State whether the following statements are True or False

2.1 Authoring is the name of the function for integrating multimedia elements, programmatically and/or without programming.

2.2 Adobe Premier, Apple iMovie, are examples of video editing software.

2.3 Multimedia production process involves not only the production of individual components but also integration of those components using an authoring tool.

2.4 With multimedia authoring software, you can make games and interactive Web sites.

2.5 Director is a popular 3D animation and interactive multimedia authoring tool.

2.6 Macromedia's Director is a powerful and complex authoring tool with feature Interactive multimedia applications.

2.7 Flash is a simple authoring tool that facilitates the creation of interactive movies.

2.8 Hierarchical metaphor is user-controllable elements which are organized into a tree structure.

2.9 Java is also an object-oriented programming language.

2.10 Scripting language metaphor uses a special language to enable interactivity and to allow conditionals, jumps, loops, functions/macròs, etc.

3. Match the following:

3.1	Can combine clips into coherent scenes, splice together scenes, and insert visual transitions	a.	Authoring tool for Internet and WWW
3.2	FrontPage	b.	Multimedia authoring software
3.3	Popular software for creating 2D animation for use in Web pages	c.	ActionScript
3.4	Programming/Scripting language for Flash	d.	Flash
3.5	Lingo	e.	Industry standard digital image software
3.6	Photoshop	f.	Script editor for debugging the user code
3.7	Elements and events organized along a timeline	g.	Stage
3.8	A big white rectangular area	h.	Time-based
3.9	VCD stands for	i.	Alphanumeric characters
3.10	Text	j.	Video Compact Disk

4. Fill in the blanks

a. Authoring b. Timeline c. Lingo
d. Copyright e. 3D modeling software f. Icon-based
g. ActionScript h. Cast i. Cast-based
j. Flash

4.1 _______is the name of popular software used to create 2D animation for use in Web pages.

4.2 _______is the name of the programming/scripting language of Flash.

4.3 _______, photographs, drawings, text or company logos should not be used without permission.

4.4 _______ is used for integrating multimedia elements, programmatically or by using application software, to create a multimedia project.

4.5 In time-based tools, elements and events are organized along with a _______.

4.6 Software that can create art that a designer can rotate, view from a variety of angles, and take two-dimensional "snapshots" of the best views is known as _______________ .

4.7 The __________ is a multimedia database containing still images, sound files, text, palettes, quickdraw shapes, programming scripts, etc.

4.8 Director utilizes __________, a full featured object oriented scripting language, to enable interactivity and programme control.

4.9 Multimedia elements and interaction events are organized as objects in a structural framework or process in an __________ authoring system.

4.10 _________ tools are best used with elements that can be viewed individually like the pages of a book.

Answers

1.	1.1	b	1.2	d	1.3	c	1.4	c	1.5	d	1.6	c
	1.7	a	1.8	d	1.9	d	1.10	c				
2.	2.1	T	2.2	T	2.3	T	2.4	T	2.5	F	2.6	T
	2.7	T	2.8	T	2.9	T	2.10	T				
3.	3.1	b	3.2	a	3.3	d	3.4	c	3.5	f	3.6	e
	3.7	h	3.8	g	3.9	j	3.10	i				
4.	4.1	j	4.2	g	4.3	d	4.4	a	4.5	b	4.6	e
	4.7	h	4.8	c	4.9	f	4.10	i				

Questions with Answers

1. What is Flash? What are the advantages of using Flash over HTML?
2. What is Lingo?
3. What is the use of authoring tool in multimedia development?
4. What is authoring system? Explain the features of Macromedia Director.
5. Give a definition of multimedia authoring system. What key features should such a system provide?
6. Write short notes on the following:
   (a) Card- and page-based tools
   (b) Icon-based authoring tools
   (c) Time-based authoring tools
   (d) Object-oriented tools

Answers to Short Questions

1. Adobe Flash is a software that creates animations for Web designs. You can create a multimedia enriched content (Flash movies) containing images, sound, video and animation effects with this software. Adding more to this, the Flash software comes with a scripting language, called ActionScript, which provides interactivity to your Flash movies. Flash also comes with number of pre-built components including media components that load Flash video files or MP3 audio to enhance your Web site.

   Here are the some of the advantages of Adobe Flash that make it very popular over HTML:

   a. ***Emerging technology:*** Being still under development, HTML lacks the reliability of Flash. Features could be changed on the long run, which means that using it will require more maintenance effort than a Flash-based approach.

   b. ***Lower performance than Flash:*** On most Windows platforms, HTML applications run slower than applications developed using Flash. As a consequence, using heavy graphics (animations and complex visual effects) in a HTML application could pose certain performance issues.

   c. ***Lower capabilities of generating 3D content and visual effects:*** HTML does not provide native support for animations, so developers have to rely on other technologies (for example JavaScript) to create animated content. But, Flash, which is mainly focused on creating graphic content and animations, HTML5 is mainly focused on structuring and presenting content for the Web, which means that it provides a limited support for creating complex visual effects.

   d. ***Depends on the browser on which it is run:*** Since HTML5 is a Web standard, and each browser implements it in its own way, the same content can be rendered differently on different browsers. For example, a visual effect can be displayed correctly on one browser, while it might not be displayed at all (or displayed totally different) on another.

   e. ***Reduced online support and fewer development tools:*** Being an emerging technology, currently there are not too many development tools available. Also, there is a reduced online support and documentation for HTML5. As a consequence, the development process for HTML5 applications is not as fluent as Flash development.

2. *Lingo* is a scripting language used in Director. You can make movies more interactive by using Lingo scripting language. It can perform the tasks, such as creating objects and animating the objects in Director.

3. *Authoring tools* are the software packages with standard user interface elements that are used to produce contents for Web publishing. Authoring software provides an integrated environment for binding together contents and functions of the project. It typically includes everything needed to create, edit and import specific types of data, assemble raw data into playback sequence and provide a structured method or language for responding to the user input. Authoring tools enable, encourage, and assist users ("authors") in the creation of accessible Web content through prompts, alerts, checking and repair functions, help files and automated tools.
   Multimedia authoring tools provide the important framework you need for organizing and editing the elements of your multimedia project, including graphics, sounds, animations, and video clips. Authoring tools must also ensure that the author can navigate a document efficiently while editing.

4. Multimedia authoring system is a set of software tools for creating multimedia applications embedded in an authoring environment.

   Features of Macromedia Director

   Director is the premier multimedia authoring package available for Windows and Macintosh computers, developed and published by Macromedia Inc., a public company formed in 1992.
   Director is used to collect various types of media (such as text, image and sound) and you can develop high performance multimedia content and applications for CDs, DVDs, Kiosks, and the Internet.
   Director allows users to build exceptionally rich content that

delivers integrated interactive audio, video, vectors and bitmaps, text, fonts and much more. Director fully integrates with Macromedia Flash MX, so you can fully realize the potential of both applications by combining them together.

5. *Multimedia authoring* refers to the process of developing a multimedia project (both media handling and integration) using specialized packages and utilities exclusively meant for this purpose.

Authoring systems for multimedia applications are designed with the following two primary targets in mind. Professionals who prepare documents, audio or sound tracks and full motion video clips for wide distribution; and average business users preparing documents, audio recordings or full motion video clips for stored message or presentations. The key differences between the uses of these two types of authoring systems for creating multimedia objects pose different sets of requirements for the authoring systems. For example, professional authoring is usually performed at centralized professional authoring workstations in some kind of media laboratory or studio which includes professional quality video cameras and sound equipment. Individual adhoc authoring on the other hand, is performed at the user's desktop using non-professional cameras and sound and light equipment. Quality standards are very important in both cases.

6. (a) Card- and page-based tools : In these authoring systems, elements are organized as pages of a book or a stack of cards. The authoring system lets you link these pages or cards into organized sequences. You can jump, on command, to any page you wish to in a structured navigation pattern. Card- and page-based systems allow you to play audio, video and animations. Some examples of card- and page-based systems include: HyperCard (Macintosh), SuperCard (Macintosh), ToolBook (Windows), Visual BASIC (Windows).

Card- and page-based systems are best suited to applications where the bulk of the content consists of elements that can be viewed individually.

(b) Icon-based authoring tools : In these authoring systems, multimedia elements and interaction cues or events are organized as objects in a structural framework.

Icon-based, event driven tools simplify the organization of a project and typically display flow diagrams of activities along branching paths.

Some examples of icon-based systems include: Authorware Professional (Windows), IconAuthor (Windows)

Icon-based, event-driven systems are suited to a wide range of applications and offer a high-level of support when developing packages with complex navigation structures.

(c) Time-based authoring tools : In these authoring systems, elements are organized along a time-line with resolutions as high as 1/30th second, or even higher in specialist applications.

Sequential organized graphic frames are played back at a speed you can set. Other elements, such as audio events, are triggered at a given time or location in the sequence of events.

(d) Object-Oriented tools : Most authoring tools now seek to demonstrate they include object-oriented abilities. Similarly object-oriented tools have all been forced to develop iconic graphical interfaces and other abilities to quickly create multimedia components.

In OO tools, multimedia elements and events become objects that live in a hierarchical order of parent and child relationships - attributes and abilities are inherited. Messages passed among these objects order them to do things according to the properties or modifiers assigned to them. Object-oriented tools are particularly useful for games that contain many components with many 'personalities' and for simulating real-life situations, events, and their constituent objects.

DESCRIPTIVE TYPE QUESTIONS

1. What is a multimedia authoring tool and what are its main features?
2. What is authoring tool? Explain different types of authoring tool with the help of examples.
3. What role is played by 2D and 3D Animators?
4. What is an authoring metaphor? Why is it required?
5. Explain features of some major authoring metaphor.
6. Discuss role of Technical Engineers and Scriptwriters.
7. Write short note on Adobe Premiere.

Sample Paper–1

Total Time : 3 Hours

Total Marks 100
(Part One - 40 Part Two - 60)

PART – ONE

1. Multiple Choice

1.1 ____________ refers to any type of application or presentation that involves more than one type of media, such as text, graphics, video, animation, and sound.
a. An executable file b. Desktop publishing
c. Multimedia d. Hypertext

1.2 Hypertext is
a. used to link document
b. a search engine
c. includes sound and video
d. requires plug-in to be view by a browser

1.3 __________ audio/video refers to on-demand requests for compressed audio/video files.
a. Streaming live b. Streaming stored
c. Interactive d. None of the above

1.4 You are preparing a multimedia presentation to be posted on your organization's website. You want to include images that you have gathered from the internet. What legal restriction must you consider before including these images?
a. Copyright b. Relevance
c. Resolution d. size

1.5 Which one of these is a video file
a. frogs.avi b. horse.jpg
c. cat.mp3 d. All of the above

1.6 Authoring tools help you
a. Write a storyboard
b. Search the Internet
c. Control the presentation of multimedia elements
d. All of the above

1.7 Which of the following is a common sans serif font?
a. Arial b. Courier
c. Times d. All of the above

1.8 A multimedia project is said to be __________ when users are NOT given navigational control.
a. Hypertext b. Linear
c. Nonlinear d. Plug-in

1.9 Dynamic web pages are created using:
a. HTML b. CGI Scripts
c. Microsoft Word d. TCP/IP

1.10 Hypermedia structures are navigated through
a. keys b. buttons
c. panels d. None of these

2. State whether the following statements are TRUE or FALSE.

2.1 Animation is used to create movements on the screen.
2.2 On the Internet, only hypertext hyperlinks are hot.
2.3 Animation can be used to emphasize the three-dimensional nature of objects.
2.4 Most commonly used format for graphics is .BMP or bitmap pictures.
2.5 If the sequence and timing of these multimedia elements can be controlled by the user, then one can name it as Non-Interactive Multimedia.
2.6 Bitmaps are represented at the level of pixels.
2.7 Colour models help us in recognizing and expressing information related to colour.
2.8 Loudness of sound waves is measured in a unit called decibel.
2.9 Translation involves moving an object in straight lines in any direction on the screen.
2.10 Macromedia's Director is a powerful and complex multimedia authoring tool.

3. MATCH words and phrases in Column X with the nearest in meaning in Column Y.

	X		Y
3.1	Dots on the screen arranged in rows.	A	Clip art
3.2	The creation of motion from still pictures	B	ASCII
3.3	Previously drawn images that artists can legally use in their own work	C	Authroing Software
3.4	Computer-generated worlds that created the illusion of immersion	D	GUI
3.5	A motion picture compression system.	E	Video conferencing
3.6	Standard character set for text files	F	Pixels
3.7	Programs used to create full, multimedia productions, such as simulations and tutorials	G	MPEG
3.8	A computer interface using point-and-click mouse actions	H	Virtual worlds

3.9 Transporting real-time voice and video over telecommunications services — I Animation
3.10 Copying files in CDs — J. Burning

4. **FILL IN THE BLANKS in the following questions by choosing the most appropriate word or phrase from the following list.**

a	Non-sequential	b	Morphing
c	digitized	d	lossless
e	RAM	f	Virtual reality
g	256	h	Resolution
i	pixels	j	Burning

4.1 The clarity of a monitor is known as ________.

4.2 When a program assigns 8 bits to a pixel, that pixel can display one of up to ________ colours.

4.3 When sound is digitally recorded, it is said to be ________.

4.4 When a video clip merges and transforms into another image it is known as ________.

4.5 The process of copying files to a CD is known as ________.

4.6 Historically, the term "hypertext" was used when textual information was linked in ________ ways.

4.7 When using a(n) ________ compression system, a file can be compressed and decompressed without loss of data.

4.8 When a digital image is currently being viewed on a computer screen, it is actively loaded into ________.

4.9 A simulated experience generated by computer, like visiting the surface of the sun or experiencing life inside a human blood cell, is called ________.

4.10 A ________ is a single point in a graphic image.

Answers to Objective Type Questions

1.	1.1	c	1.2	a	1.3	b	1.4	a	1.5	a
	1.6	c	1.7	a	1.8	b	1.9	a	1.10	b
2.	2.1	T	2.2	F	2.3	T	2.4	T	2.5	F
	2.6	T	2.7	T	2.8	T	2.9	T	2.10	T
3.	3.1	f	3.2	i	3.3	a	3.4	h	3.5	g
	3.6	b	3.7	c	3.8	d	3.9	e	3.10	j
4.	4.1	h	4.2	g	4.3	c	4.4	b	4.5	j
	4.6	a	4.7	d	4.8	e	4.9	f	4.10	i

PART – TWO

(Answer any four questions)

5. (a) What is multimedia? What are its advantages?
   (b) What is meant by the terms multimedia and hypermedia? Distinguish between two concepts.

6. (a) Explain the use of the following hardware components in multimedia.
   (i) Scanner
   (ii) Soundcard
   (b) What are the characteristics of multimedia presentation?

7. (a) What are the 3 characteristics of colour?
   (b) What are capabilities and limitations of bitmap images?

8. (a) What are the advantage of MIDI over digitized sound?
   (b) What is the distinction between lossless and lossy compression?

9. (a) What is animation? What are different types of animation?
   (b) What is colour? What is additive and subtractive colour?

Sample Paper–2

Total Time : 3 Hours **Total Marks 100**
(Part One - 40 Part Two - 60)

PART – ONE

1. Multiple Choice

1.1 Which of the following is not a technology likely to previal as a delivery means for interactive multimedia files.
a. Glass fiber b. radio/cellular
c. Floppy disk d. CD-ROM/DVD-ROM

1.2 VR stands for
a. Virtual reality b. Visual reponse
c. Variable rate d. None of the above

1.3 D.V.D stands for
a. Digital versatile disk
b. Duplicated video disk
c. Density variable disk
d. Double view disc

1.4 Multimedia becomes interactive multimedia when
a. the user has some control over what information is viewed and when it it viewed
b. the information is displayed by a computer with a touchscreen or other input device
c. quizzes and tests with evaluations and scoring are included
d. None of the above

1.5 Interactive multimedia becomes hypermedia when
a. The informaton is available on the web either the Internet or a local area network.
b. It includes a structure of linked elements through which a user can navigate and interact.
c. quizzes and tests with evaluations and scoring are included.
d. None of the above

1.6 A printed page might be presented in which of these orientations
a. Portrait
b. Landscape
c. Both (a) and (b)
d. None of the above

1.7 Compression method that does not lose data or quality.
a. lossless b. lossy
c. both (a) and (b) d. None of the above

1.8 Which is multimedia element(s)
a. Text and sound b. graphics and animation
c. Video d. All of the above

1.9 Which is true about vector images
a. vector images are most appropriate for lines, boxes and circles etc.
b. vector images require a plug-in for display on a web page.
c. vector images cannot be used for photo-realistic images.
d. All are true

1.10 Which is true about MIDI files
a. MIDI files are much more compact than digital audio files.
b. MIDI files embedded in web pages load and play more quickly than their digital equivalents.
c. Both (a) and (b)
d. None of the above

2. State whether the following statements are TRUE or FALSE.

2.1 Use digitized audio for spoken dialog.
2.2 You can digitize sounds from any source, live or prerecorded.
2.3 MIDI data is device independent.
2.4 Lingo is programming language of Macromedia Director.
2.5 Palettes are mathematical tables that define the colour of a pixel displayed on a screen.
2.6 Path animation is motion created by moving an object along a determined path.
2.7 Quantization is rounding off the value of each sound samples to the nearest integer.
2.8 Plug-ins allow you to view the file without downloading first.
2.9 Shockwave creates highly-compressed interactive animations and movies.
2.10 TIFF is a graphic image file format.

3. MATCH words and phrases in Column X with the nearest in meaning in Column Y.

	X		Y
3.1	MP3	A	Compressed graphics file format
3.2	JPEG	B	A CD quality audio file format
3.3	QuickTime	C	Resource interchange File Format
3.4	RIFF	D	A video file format
3.5	Hypermedia	E	Graphic Image file format
3.6	TIFF	F	Media which links text, sounds, graphics, movies and/or animations
3.7	AIFF	G	Device independent

3.8 MIDI — H A macintosh audio format

3.9 Bandwidth — I Frequency at which samples of a sound are taken.

3.10 Sampling rate — J bps

4. ***FILL IN THE BLANKS*** **in the following questions by choosing the most appropriate word or phrase from the following list.**

a	Bandwidth	**b**	burner
c	tweening	**d**	wave
e	Audio resolution	**f**	hypermedia
g	2D animation	**h**	S-VHS
i	Streaming latency	**j**	dependent

4.1 _________ are used for reading and making CD and DVD.

4.2 Multimedia can contain structured linking which is called _________.

4.3 Websites with rich media require large amounts of _________.

4.4 _________ determines the accuracy with which a sound can be digitized.

4.5 MIDI is device _________.

4.6 The _________ format was introduced by Microsoft and IBM with introduction of windows.

4.7 _________ is the wait period before streaming sound or video file begins to play.

4.8 _________ is the standard for video recording and playback.

4.9 Animation that occurs at the flat cartesian x and y axes is called _________.

4.10 Drawing the series of frames in between the first and last frames in an action is called _________.

Answers to Objective Type Questions

1.	1.1	c	1.2	a	1.3	a	1.4	a	1.5	b
	1.6	c	1.7	a	1.8	d	1.9	d	1.10	c
2.	2.1	T	2.2	T	2.3	F	2.4	T	2.5	T
	2.6	T	2.7	T	2.8	T	2.9	T	2.10	T
3.	3.1	b	3.2	a	3.3	d	3.4	c	3.5	f
	3.6	e	3.7	h	3.8	g	3.9	j	3.10	i
4.	4.1	b	4.2	f	4.3	a	4.4	e	4.5	j
	4.6	d	4.7	i	4.8	h	4.9	g	4.10	c

PART – TWO

(Answer any four questions)

5. (a) Discuss the importance of text in a multimedia.
   (b) How many types of tape formats in video recording?
6. Explain different audio file formats.
7. What is cel animation?
8. Discuss different hardware requirement for multimedia.
9. What are different types of authoring tools. Discuss.

APPENDIX A

Flash

A.1 INTRODUCTION

Adobe(r) Flash(r) Professional CS5 provides a complete interactive authoring environment for creating digital animation and interactive Websites. It is basically used to create rich interactive applications using video, sound, graphics and animation. With Adobe(r) Flash(r) Professional CS5, you can:

- Design expressive contents, write code precisely and efficiently, and deliver superior-quality video to audiences practically everywhere.
- Import images from other Adobe(r) applications, such as Photoshop or Illustrator.
- Quickly design simple animations.
- Use Adobe ActionScript 3.0 to develop interactive projects.

In addition to Flash Professional, Adobe offers Flash Catalyst and Flash Builder. Flash Catalyst is a design tool for rapidly creating expressive interfaces and interactive contents without writing code. Flash Builder (formerly known as Flex Builder) is a code-centric environment geared toward developers rather than animators or designers to create interactive content.

A Flash SWF (Shock Wave Flash) file runs in the Flash Player on your browser, in AIR (Adobe Integrated Runtime) on your desktop outside of your browser, or on your mobile phone.

A 2 NEW FEATURES OF FLASH(R) PROFESSIONAL CS5

New features of Flash(r) Professional CS5 are the following:

- **Text Layout Framework Text Engine** : The new TLF text engine provides significantly improved control over text properties and flow. The new text engine in Flash Professional CS5 also maintains layout and text formatting with greater fidelity when importing content from Adobe(r) InDesign software and other Adobe products.
- **Font Embedding Dialog** : Font embedding is now FLA (Flash) file-based instead of text object based. The new Font Embedding dialog box provides quick access to all font embedding functions.
- **FLVPlayback Live Preview on Stage** : The ActionScript 3.0 versions of the FLVPlayback components now allow you to preview Live video for externally loaded video on the Stage.
- **Video Cue Points Usability** : Video cue points are now much easier to add to videos in Flash Professional CS5.
- **New skins for FLVPlayback Component** :New skins have been provided for the FLVPlayback components to enable a wider variety of design styles in Flash Professional CS5 projects.
- **Editing with Photoshop CS5** : Now you can perform round-trip editing of bitmap graphics in Photoshop CS5.
- **New Deco Drawing Tool Effects** : Several new effects have been added to the Deco Drawing tool to help you create complex patterns and decorations easily and automatically.
- **Spring properties for IK (Inverse Kinematics) bones** : New properties of Spring (a physics simulation option for animation with inverse kinematics) have been added to IK bones that enable realistic physics effects in bone animation.
- **Code Snippets panel** : The new Code Snippets panel provides ready-to-go ActionScript code to non-programmers for common interactions like timeline navigation, actions, animation, audio and video, and event handlers without learning ActionScript 3.0. By injecting prebuilt code into projects, you can work faster, share code with others and freeing up more time for creativity.
- **Code Hinting for Custom Classes** : Code completion, or code hinting, is now enabled for custom ActionScript 3.0 classes in addition to the built-in classes. Novice developers can start projects and code hinting assist them as they try to grasp the fundamentals of the ActionScript language.
- **Auto Close-bracket Insertion** : Now when you type an open bracket { in the Actions panel or Script window, Flash Professional CS5 automatically adds the corresponding close bracket }. This saves time in writing code and debugging.
- **Motion Object JavaScript APIs** : Several new JavaScript APIs (Application Programming Intrfaces) have been added for manipulating motion, tweens in the Flash Professional CS5 authoring environment.
- **XFL File Format** : Flash FLA files now contain a new internal format called XFL (eXtensible Form Language). This new format is based on XML (eXtensible Markup Language). This compact and efficient file format both accurately maintains data in a Flash document and makes the individual elements easier to manage and use.
  i. **Uncompressed XFL file format**-The uncompressed XFL file format allows you to see each separate parts, or sub-files, that make up a Flash file. This enables working in team environments with source control systems.
  ii. **FXG file format**-The FXG (Flash XML Graphic) file format allows Flash to exchange graphics with other Adobe applications with full fidelity.

SWF Size History

Document Property inspector now displays the size of all SWF files generated during Test Movie, Publish, and Debug Movie operations.

New Templates

Flash Professional CS5 includes a range of new templates that make it easier to create common types of projects in Flash. The templates appear in the Welcome screen and in the New Document dialog box. AIR for iOS (support for iPhone and iPad Operating System) Flash Professional CS5 includes support for AIR

(Adobe Integrated Runtime) for iOS. This allows Flash files to be deployed as iOS applications that run on the Apple iPhone or iPad.

Community Help

Community Help is an integrated environment on adobe.com that gives you access to community-generated content moderated by Adobe and industry experts.

CS Live Services

In Flash Professional CS5, you can connect to CS Live services from within the Flash authoring environment. CS Live includes Web services, such as Acrobat.com, BrowserLab, Live Review, and more.

A.3 STARTING FLASH PROFESSIONAL CS5

To start Flash Professional CS5, do this:

- Click Start menu, highlight All Programs, again highlight Adobe Master Collection CS5 and then choose Adobe Flash Professional CS5 (See Figure A.1).

Figure A.1 Getting started with Flash Professional CS5

- When the first time you start Flash Professional CS5 you will see a Welcome screen with links to standard file templates, quick access to tutorials, and other help features (See Figure A.2). After you have opened or created a new file, the Start page automatically closes to make room on your desktop.
  a. **Create from Template:** Displays the list of templates which are used to create Flash files.
  b. **Open a Recent Item:** Displays a list of recently opened Flash files.
  c. **Create New:** Displays a list of different types of Flash Files, such as ActionScript 3.0, ActionScript 2.0, Adobe AIR 2 and so on.
  d. **Extend:** It contains Flash Exchange option that gives a link to the Flash Exchange Website to download helper applications and information related to Flash Professional CS5.
  e. **Learn:** It provides tutorials related to Flash Professional CS5.

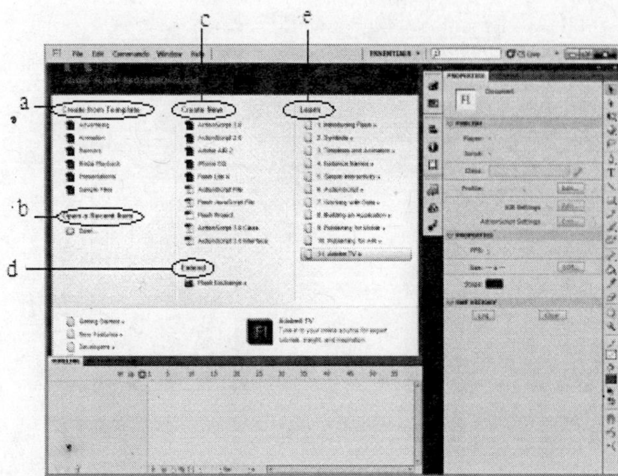

Figure A.2 Welcome Screen of Flash Professional CS5

A.4 CREATING NEW FLASH FILE

To create a simple animation, we have to add the photos and a title. For that firstly, we have to create new Flash file. The extension of the Flash file or movie file is .fla.

To create new Flash file, do this:

1. Click the **File** menu and choose **New....** A New Document dialog box appears as shown in Figure A.3.
2. Select the Flash file (ActionScript 3.0) option under the **General** tab (ActionScript 3.0 is the latest version of Flash's scripting language, which you use to add interactivity).
3. Then click **OK** button.

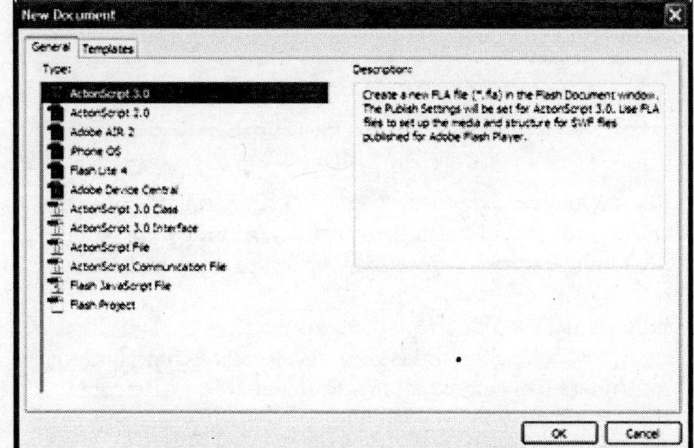

Figure A.3 New Document Dialog box

A.5 EXPLORING THE FLASH PROFESSIONAL CS5 WORKSPACE

Workspace of Adobe Flash Professional CS5 includes the command menus at the top of the screen and a variety of tools and panels for editing. By default, it displays the menu bar, Timeline, Stage, Tools panel, Property inspector, and a few other panels. As you work in Flash, you can open, close, dock, undock, and move panels around the screen to fit your work style or your screen resolution.

You create and manipulate your documents and files using various elements, such as panels, bars, and windows. Any arrangement of these elements is called a workspace.

Let us explore the various components of Flash Professional CS5 workspace. (See Figure A.4).

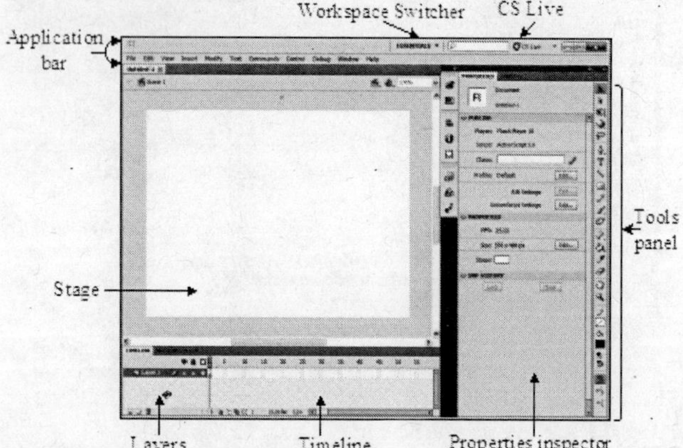

Figure A.4 · Elements of Flash Professional CS5 Workspace

A.5.1 The Application Bar

The Application bar is present at the top of the workspace. This bar contains Application Icon, Menu bar, Search Text box, and the Workspace Switcher. (See Figure A.4)

The elements that are present on the Application bar are·as follows:

Application Icon: It displays Minimizes, Maximizes/Restore or Close buttons in Flash Professional CS5 and has its own menu called *system icon.*

Menu bar: It contains various options to perform specific actions (See Figure A.5).

Figure A.5 Menu bar

- **File menu:** The File menu contains commands for opening, closing, saving, importing, exporting, printing and publishing movies, revert to previous version of a file and quitting from Flash Professional CS5.
- **Edit menu:** The Edit menu contains the Cut, Copy and Paste command, along with the Find and Replace command and the Preferences command. In addition to this, it also contains commands related to Timeline, symbols Tools panel and much more.
- **View menu:** It changes the view settings, such as the Zoom level and ruler, grids and guides. It also specifies snapping preferences for objects.
- **Insert menu:** It enables you to insert symbols, frames, keyframe, layers and scenes.
- **Modify menu:** It enables you to modify symbols, bitmaps, shapes, frame, timeline features. It also provides tools to change the properties of the currently selected object, such as transforming, aligning, grouping and ungrouping, etc.
- **Text menu:** It provides various options to format the text.
- **Commands menu:** This menu is useful to automate tasks and reuse previously performed commands in Flash Professional CS5.
- **Control menu:** It provides various control options for movies, scenes, sound and buttons.
- **Debug menu:** It provides tools for debugging ActionScript code.
- **Window menu:** It enables you to open duplicate windows, panels and workspaces.
- **Help menu:** This menu contains the command to launch the Extension Manager. There are numerous links to Adobe resources, including the Flash Support Center on the Adobe's Web site.Workspace Switcher: It toggles between the different workspace layout options.
- **Workspace Switcher**: It toggles between the different workspace layout options.
- **Search text box:** It allows user to search topics in Flash Professional CS5 application.

A.5.2 Stage

The Stage is a big white rectangular area in the middle of your computer screen (See Figure A.4). Like a theater Stage, the Stage in a Flash is the area where viewers can see a movie during playback. It contains the text, images, and video that appears on the screen.

Pasteboard is the grey area off the Stage where you can place elements that won't be visible to your audience.

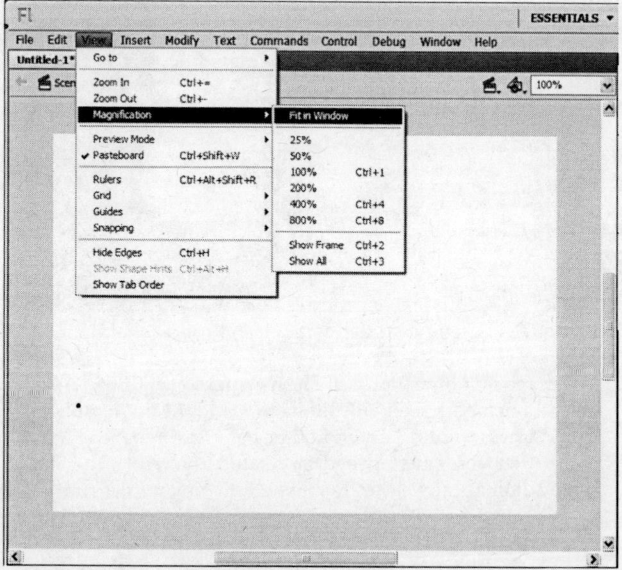

Figure A.6 Scale the Stage

To just see the Stage, do this:

1. Click the **View** menu and click on **Pasteboard** to deselect the option.

To scale the Stage, do this:

1. Click the **View** menu and then click **Magnification**.
2. Then choose **Fit in Window** option (See Figure A.6).
3. You can also choose different magnification view options from the pop-up menu just above the Stage (See Figure A.7).

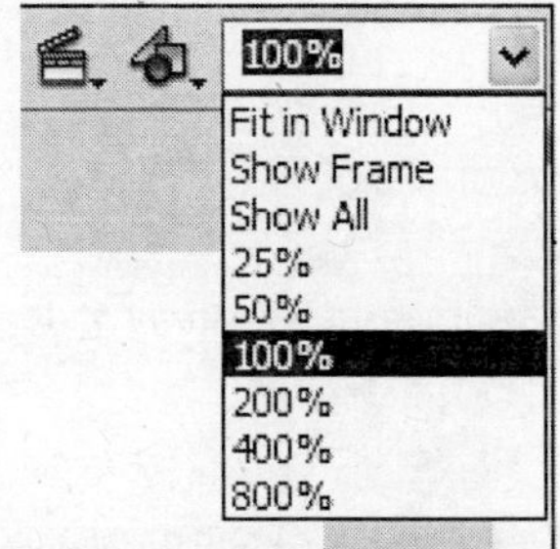

Figure A.7 Change magnification options

To change the Stage properties, do this:

1. At the bottom of the **Property inspector** (See Figure A.4), Click the **Edit** button. A **Document Settings** dialog box appears as shown in Figure A.8.

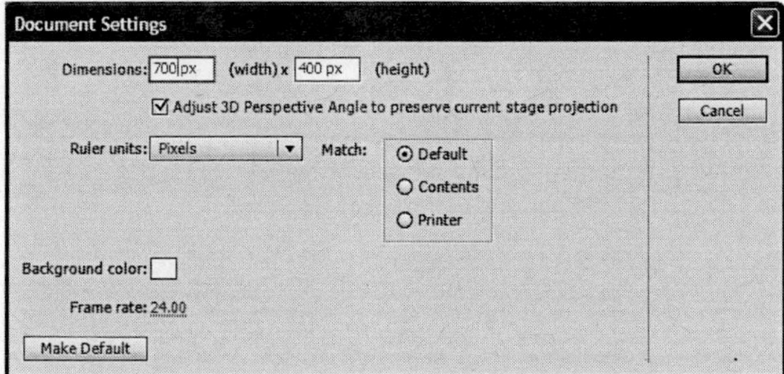

Figure A.8 Document Setting dialog box

2. In the **Dimensions:** group, in Width and Height boxes, enter new pixel dimensions.
3. Click the **Background color:** button and choose a new color for the Stage.
4. Then click **OK** button.

You can also change the Stage color by clicking on the Stage button directly in the Property inspector. You can change the Stage properties at any time.

A.5.3 Panels

Panels are small floating windows that let you see and change attributes or properties of objects. It provides an easy access to controls that helps to work with the contents in your document. These can be moved around the screen or closed as and when needed. Each Panel has tabs that let you add actions or add the effects. By default, the Property inspector, Library panel, and Tools panel appear together at the right of the screen; the Timeline and Motion Editor are at the bottom; and the Stage is on the top (See Figure A.4). However, you can move a panel to any position that is convenient for you. For example,

- To undock a panel from the right side of the screen, drag it by its tab to a new location.
- To dock a panel, drag it by its tab into the dock at a new position on the screen. You can drag it to the top, bottom, or in between other panels. A blue highlight indicates where you can dock a panel.
- To group a panel with another, drag its tab onto the other panel's tab.
- To move a panel group, drag the group by its dark gray top bar.

A.6 USING TOOLS PANEL

The Tools panel is a long, narrow panel on the far right side of the work area. It contains tools for creating and editing images, artwork, page elements, and so on. Related tools are grouped (See Figure A.9). The Tools panel contains selection tools, drawing and painting tools, retouching tools and navigation tools. The Options area in the Tools panel displays modifiers to let you modify the selected tool, if nothing is selected, the option section is blank. The expanded menu on the right shows the hidden tools. The single capital letters in parentheses indicate the keyboard shortcuts to select those tools. To use a particular tool, just click on that tool. The mouse pointer will change its shape according to the tool you have selected. Then you can click the tool pointer on your canvas and start your work. The following tools are available in the Tools panel of Flash Professional CS5.

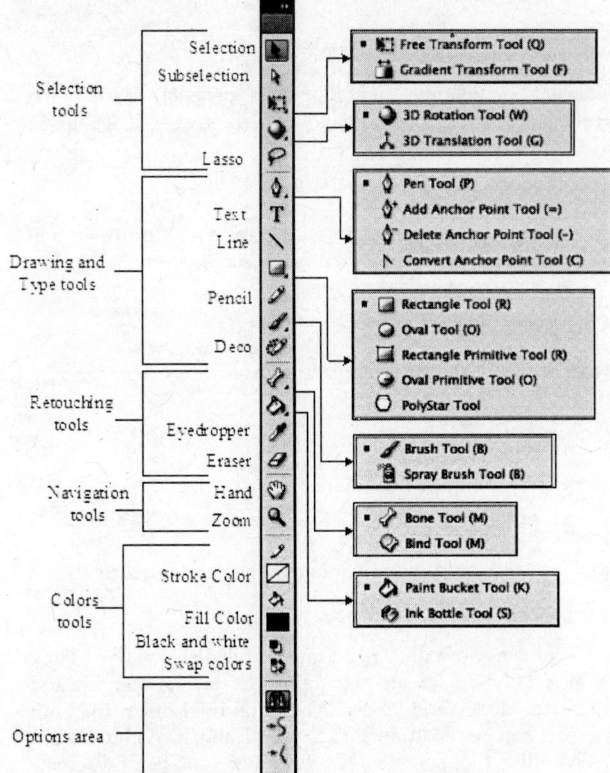

Figure A.9 Tools panel with expanded Flyouts

A.6.1 Selection Tool

The Selection tool lets you select entire object or a section of an object by clicking an object or by dragging to enclose the object within a rectangular selection called *marquee*.

A.6.2 Subselection Tool

The Subselection tool lets you select a specific point or line in an object. Subselection tools select objects by dragging a rectangular selection called marquee around the object.

A.6.3 Free Transform Tool

Free Transform tool is used to change an object's scale, rotation, or skew or distort an object by dragging control points around a bounding box.

A.6.4 Gradient Transform Tool

The Gradient Transform tool allows you to scale, rotate, or skew an image and its bitmap fill. It can also be used to squeeze the gradient in the front surface and reverse the gradient in the back surface.

A.6.5 3D Rotation Tool

3D Rotation tool rotate movie clip instances in 3D space. A 3D rotation control appears on the top of selected objects on the Stage. The X control is red, the Y control is green, and the Z control is blue.

A.6.6 3D Translation Tool

3D Translation tool move movie clip instances in 3D space. When you select a movie clip with this tool, its three axes, X, Y, and Z, appear on the top of the object.

A.6.7 Lasso Tool

Lasso tool lets you select objects by dragging a free-form selection marquee around the object. When an object is selected, a rectangular box appears around the object.

A.6.8 Pen Tool

Pen tool is used to create straight or curved lines. You can also create Bezier curves with Pen tool.

A.6.9 Text Tool

Text tool is used to create or edit text and text fields.

A.6.10 Line Tool

Line tool is used to draw straight lines between two points.

A.6.11 Shape Tool

Shape Tool can draw both filled and unfilled shapes, including rectangles, PolyStar (create either polygon or star shapes) and oval (creates circles and ovals). When you hold down the Shift key, shapes can be constrained to 45° or 90° angles. With the Rectangle Primitive tool and the Oval Primitive tool, you can create primitive shapes (individual objects that can be edited in the Property inspector).

A.6.12 Pencil Tool

Pencil tool is used to create lines in three modes-straighten, smooth, or ink.

A.6.13 Brush Tool

Brush tool is used to create shapes with fills only. It can also apply color to the image with different types of brushes.

A.6.14 Spray Brush Tool

The Spray Brush lets you "brush" a pattern of shapes onto the Stage at one time. Spray Brush emits a spray of dot particles using the currently selected fill color.

A.6.15 Deco Tool

Deco tool lets you create complex, geometric shapes and patterns to give the banner ad more punch, and floral decorations to adorn the edges. It is used to apply an effect to a selected object.

A.6.16 Bone Tool

Bone tool provides a method for animating an object or set of objects in relation to each other using an articulated structure of bones.

A.6.17 Bind Tool

Bind tool allows you to click a control point or a bone and display the connections between the bones and control points. You can then change the connections in a variety of ways.

A.6.18 Paint Bucket Tool

Paint Bucket tool is used to fill inside closed objects or change the fill color.

A.6.19 Ink Bottle Tool

This tool is used to modify the color of the strokes of lines or shape.

A.6.20 Eyedropper Tool

This tool is used to select color from an object or swatches or anywhere on the screen and apply the same to another object.

A.6.21 Eraser Tool

Eraser tool is used to erase parts of an image, i.e., fills or stroke.

A.6.22 Hand Tool

Hand tool is used to move the view of the Stage. When the Stage is magnified, you may not be able to see all of it. To change the view without having to change the magnification, use the Hand tool to move the Stage. In the Tools panel, select the Hand tool and drag the Stage. To temporarily switch between another tool and the Hand tool, hold down the Spacebar and click the tool in the Tools panel.

A.6.23 Zoom Tool

Zoom tool is used to see enlarged or reduced view of graphic or object. To zoom out, hold down the Alt key.

A.6.24 Stroke Color

Stroke Color is used to choose a color for stroking purpose.

A.6.25 Fill Color

Fill Color is used to choose a color to be filled in selected objects, drawings and graphics.

A.7 PROPERTY INSPECTOR OR PROPERTIES PANEL

The Property inspector provides an easy access to the most commonly used attributes of the currently selected object, either on the Stage or in the Timeline (See Figure A.10). You can make changes to the object's attributes in the Property inspector without accessing the menus or panels.

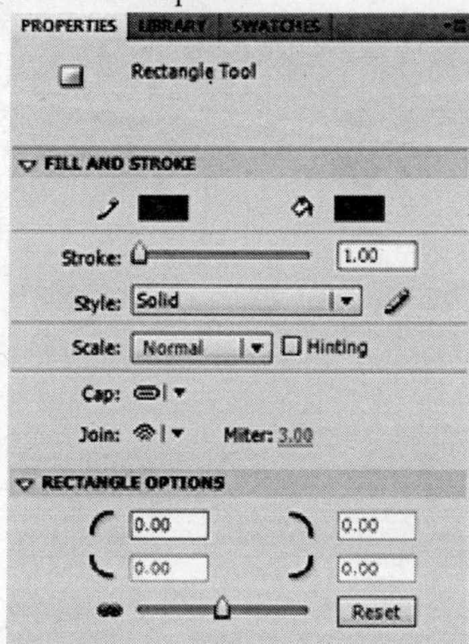

Figure A.10 Property Inspector for Rectangle tool

Depending on what you have selected, appears on the Property inspector. The Property inspector displays information and settings about the current document, text, symbol, shape, bitmap, video, group, frame, or tool. When two or more different types of objects are selected, the Property inspector displays information about the objects you have selected. For example, if nothing is selected, the Property inspector includes options for the general Flash document including changing the Stage color or dimensions. If an object on the Stage is selected, the Property inspector shows its X and Y coordinates, and its width and height, among other information (See Figure A.10). By default, the Property inspector is visible. You can also hide or show it.

To hide or show Property inspector, do this:

1. Click the Windows menu and click on Properties. Or alternatively, press Ctrl + F3 keys together.

A.7.1 Library Panel

The Library panel is accessible from a tab just to the right of the Property inspector. The Library panel is a place to store and organize symbols created in Flash Professional CS5, as well as imported files, including bitmaps, graphics, sound files, and video clips (See Figure A.11). Symbols are often used graphics used for animation and for interactivity.

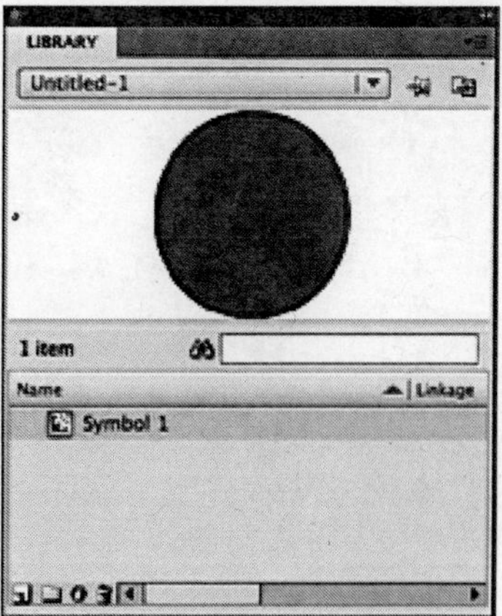

Figure A.11 Library Panel

The Library panel lets you organize library items in folders, see how often an item is used in a document, and sort items by type. When you import items into Flash Professional CS5, you can import them directly onto the Stage or into the library. However, any item you import onto the Stage is also added to the library. You can then easily access the items to add them to the Stage again, edit them, or see their properties.

A.7 2 Info Panel

The Info panel lets you see and manipulate visual properties of objects like height and width, the location of its registration point; its Red (R), Green (G), Blue (B), and Alpha (A) values and the location of the pointer. See the change in the X: and Y: coordinates in Info panel, as you move the cursor on the Stage. Also attributes for stroke and fill properties of objects can be set or modified from here (See Figure A.12).

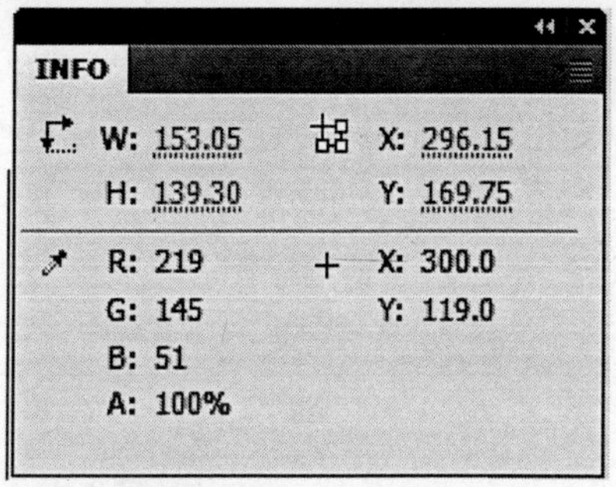

Figure A.12 Info Panel

A.7 3 Align Panel

The Align panel enables you to control the alignment of objects on the Stage. It provides you with tools to line up two or more objects vertically and horizontally and equally space among three or more objects (See Figure A.13).

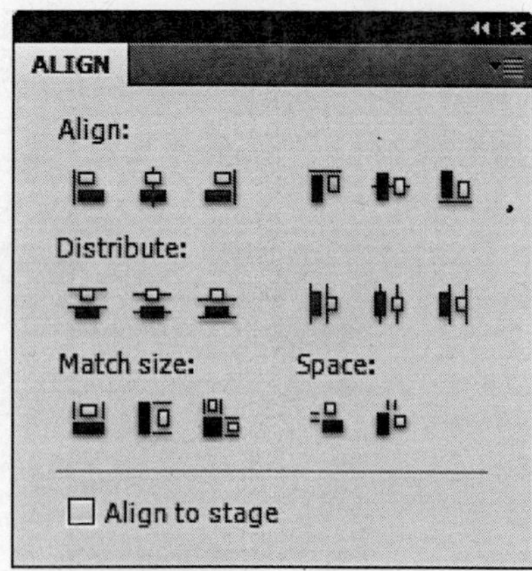

Figure A.13 Align Panel

A.7 4 Transform Panel

Transform panel enables you to scale, rotate and skew the objects and symbols that you create on Stage. This panel also lets you remove the transformations you applied and restore the original values (See Figure A.14).

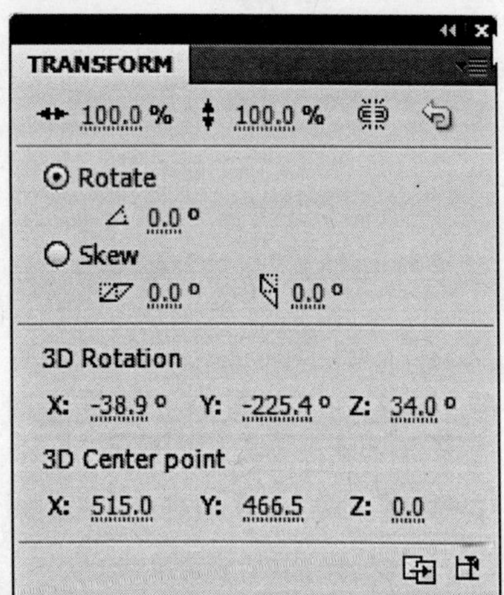

Figure A.14 Transform Panel

A.7 5 Swatches Panel

It is used for selecting and managing the colors. You can import, export, delete and modify the color palettes for a file using the Swatches panel. The Color palette displayed on clicking the Fill color and Stroke color buttons for all drawing tools. (See Figure A.15).

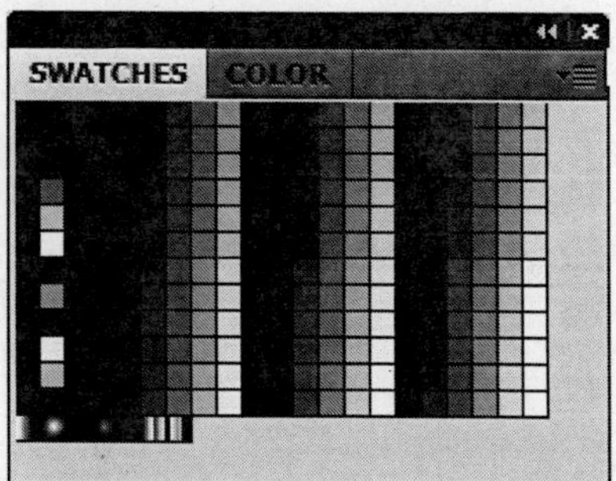

Figure A.15 Swatches Panel

A.7 6 Color Panel

It is used to create and edit solid colors and gradient fills, using the Color Mixer. If an object is selected on the Stage, the color modifications you make in the Color Mixer are applied to the selection. You can choose between the RGB (Red, Green, Blue) and HSB (Hue, Saturation, Brightness) mode of color specification or simply type in the hexadecimal value of the color. You have the control over the opacity/transparency of color using Alpha slider. The slider controls the lightness/darkness of the color (See Figure A.16).

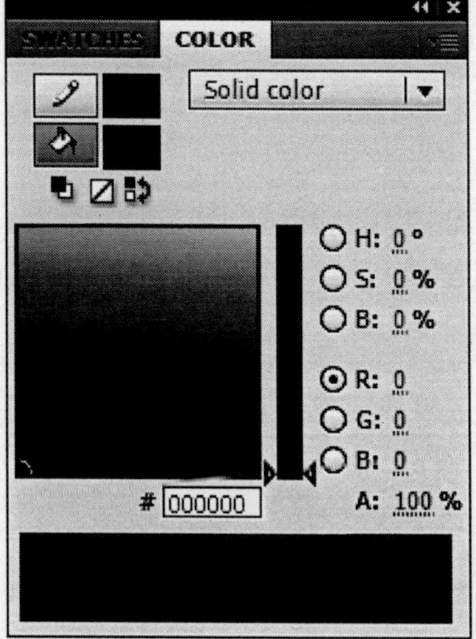

Figure A.16 Color Panel

A.7 7 Scene Panel

It displays a list of all the scenes you use to create a movie (See Figure A.17). The Scene panel is also used to create, delete and arrange the order of scenes in your movie. You can display the Scene panel by clicking on the Window menu and choose the Other panels option, and then select Scene option from the sub-menu. Or press Shift + F2 keys together.

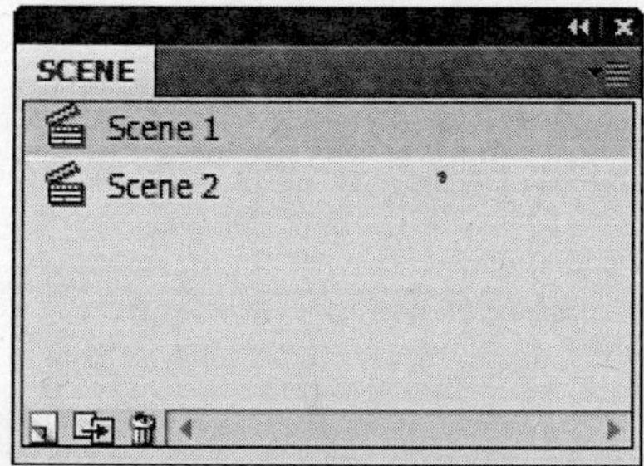

Figure A.17 Scene Panel

A.7 8 Movie Explorer Panel

You can use the Movie Explorer panel to view and organize the contents of a document containing screens. It also helps to interact with and perform a number of functions on the movie components like layers, frames, actions, sound, video, etc. Some of the functions you can perform from the Movie Explorer panel are:

1. Filter categories of items in the document.
2. Display the selected categories as scenes, symbol definitions, or both.
3. Expand and collapse the navigation tree.
4. Find an element in a document by name.
5. Find all the instances of a particular symbol or action.
6. Print the navigable display list that appears in the Movie Explorer. Elements in the Movie Explorer are arranged in folder like hierarchy with scenes, layers, symbol definitions, and other titles acting as containers to organize elements in the movie (See Figure A.18).

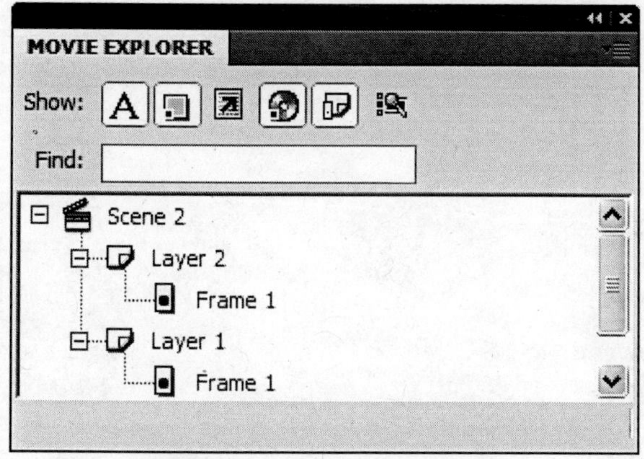

Figure A.18 Movie Explorer Panel

A.7 9 Actions Panel

The Actions Panel is used to create ActionScript for buttons and keyframe. It is divided into three parts one is Script pane, second is Script navigator, and third is Actions toolbox. The Actions toolbox provides a list of ActionScript language elements (functions, classes, operators and types, etc.). To add an element from the Actions toolbox into the Script pane, either double click the element or drag it from the toolbox. The Script navigator displays a hierarchical list of Flash elements that contain scripts. The Action panel provides a feature called Script Assist, which provides a visual interface for editing scripts. You can add or edit the parameters of a given ActionScript function in the boxes provided in the Script Assist section. To use the Script Assist feature, click the Script Assist button in the Actions panel (See Figure A.19). To display the actions panel, click Window menu and choose Actions or press F9 key.

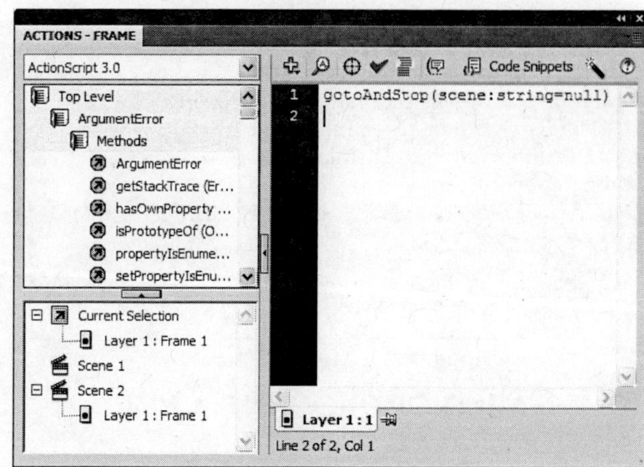

Figure A.19 Actions Panel

A.8 UNDERSTANDING TIMELINE AND LAYERS

Timeline is located below the Stage. Like films, a Flash movie consists of multiple images. These images are contained in frames. A user watching an animation sees images in frame 1 followed by frame 2 and so on. The timeline contains these image sequences one after the other starting with frame 1 on the left and last frame on the right. In other words, the Timeline covers a span of time divided into frames, with each frame corresponding to an action. Timeline appears like a ruler with numbers incremented at regular intervals. The images in these frames are displayed in sequence as time passes. When these frames are viewed in quick succession, our brain interprets it as if an action is taking place continuously. The Timeline status displayed at the bottom of the Timeline indicates the selected frame number, the current frame rate (how many frames play per second), and the time that has elapsed so far in the movie (See Figure A.20).

The Timeline also contains layers, which helps to organize the movie components. Layers can be defined as multiple film strips stacked on top of each other. Each layer contains a different image that appears on the Stage. Modifications or effects applied on graphics or images stored in a layer do not affect the components of other layers. The Layer area present at the left of Timeline lists the different layers of the current movie. The selected layer with the pencil icon is the active layer. Whatever effects you apply on it will affect only this selected layer. You can hide, show, lock, or unlock layers. Each layer's frames are unique, but you can drag them to a new location on the same layer or copy or move them to another layer.

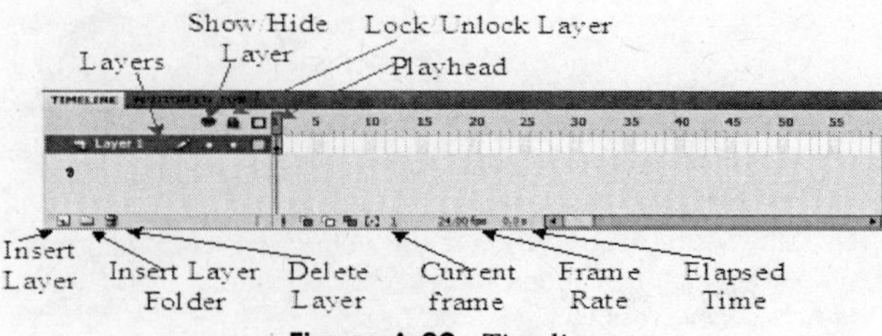

Figure A.20 Timeline

A.9 MOTION EDITOR

The Motion Editor is a special panel that is used to control the properties of fine tweening of individual properties (See Figure A.21). The Motion Editor is helpful when multiple properties are changing at different times. Therefore, it is also show the animation property-by-property.

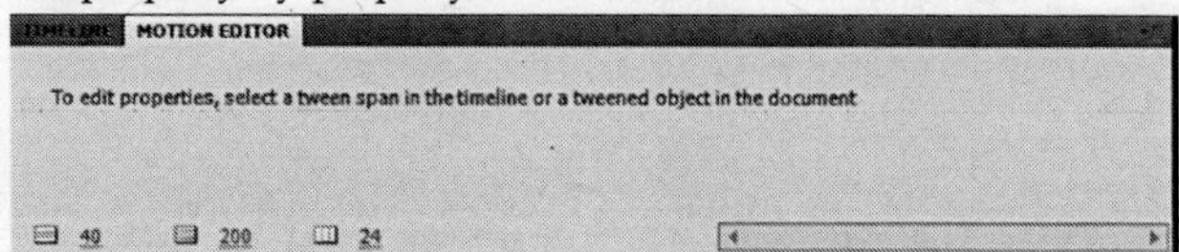

Figure A.21 Motion Editor

A.10 CREATING OR CHOOSING A NEW WORKSPACE

Flash Professional CS5 provides a few preset workspaces, arranged for particular tasks or types of users. These workspace are listed in a pull-down menu at the top right of the Flash Professional CS5 workspace as shown in Figure A.22 or you can access it from Window menu.

To switch between workspace, do this:

1. Click on the Workspace switcher button at the top right of the Flash Professional CS5 workspace (See Figure A.22).

Figure A.22 Switching between workspace

2. Choose a new workspace. The various panels are rearranged and resized according to the workspace you choose. For example, the Animator and Designer workspaces put the Timeline at the top for easy and frequent access. You can create a custom workspace by moving and manipulating panels, such as adding, removing, docking, grouping, or collapsing them. You can also save these custom workspaces.

To create a custom workspace, do this:

1. Make changes to an existing workspace, such as by moving panels, opening new panels or closing opened panels.
2. Click on the **Window** menu, highlight **Workspace** and then choose **New Workspace...** (or choose New Workspace... From Workspace switcher (See Figure A.22)).
3. The New Workspace dialog box appears as seen in Figure A.23.
4. In this dialog box, enter a name for the new workspace.
5. Then click OK.

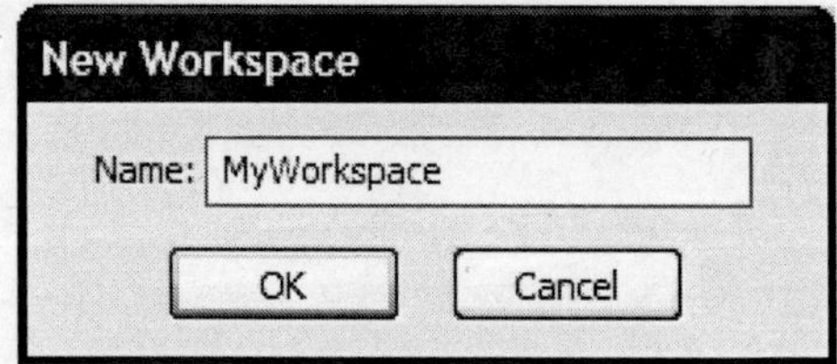

Figure A.23 New Workspace dialog box

The current arrangement of panels is saved. Your workspace is added in the options of the Workspace switcher pull-down menu, which you can access at any time.

A.11 SAVING FLASH FILES

After you have created a file or made changes to an existing file, you need to save the file. You can save a file with its current filename, location, or with a different filename, location and options. You can also save a copy of a file while leaving the current file open on your desktop. Flash file is saved with .fla extension. When a flash file contains unsaved changes, an asterisk (*) appears after the filename in the document tab. When you save the document, the asterisk is removed.

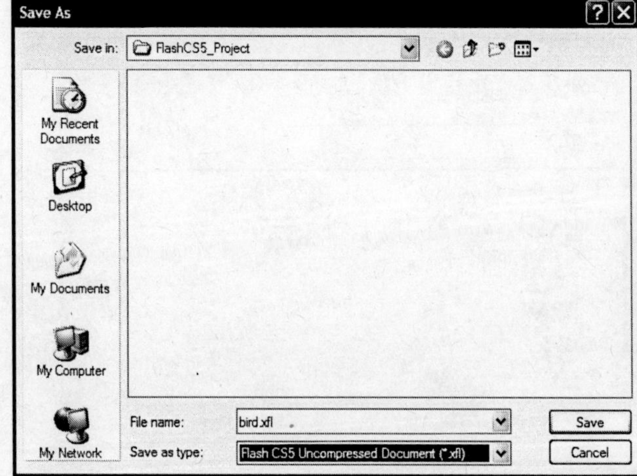

Figure A.24 Save As dialog box

To save a Flash file in the default FLA format, do this:

1. Click the **File** menu and choose **Save...** . Alternatively press Ctrl + S keys together. In **Save As** dialog box, provide the name of the file and then choose **Save** button.
2. Flash Professional CS5 saves your file and leaves it open for use.

To save a file with a different name and location, do this:

1. Click the **File** menu and choose **Save As...** . Alternatively, press Shift + Ctrl + S keys together. The Save As dialog box appears as shown in Figure A.24.
2. In this dialog box, navigate to the file location where you want to save the file.
3. Double-click on the File name: text box, then type a new name for your file.
4. From the Save as type: drop-down list, choose Flash Professional CS5 Uncompressed Document (*xfl).
5. Click on **Save** button. The Save As dialog box will close. Flash Professional CS5 saves the file and leaves it open for use.

The XFL format is actually a folder of files rather than a single document. This format exposes the contents of Flash movie so that other developers or animators can easily edit your file without having to open the movie in the Flash application. For example, all the imported photos in your Library panel appear in a Library folder within the XFL format. You can edit the library photos or swap them with new photos. Flash will make the substitutions in the movie automatically.

To revert to the last saved version of a document, do this:

1. Click the **File** menu and choose **Revert**.
2. Reverting is undoable. Therefore, a confirmation dialog box will display to confirm whether you want to revert a file or not. If you want to revert then click on **Revert** button otherwise click Cancel button (See Figure A.25).

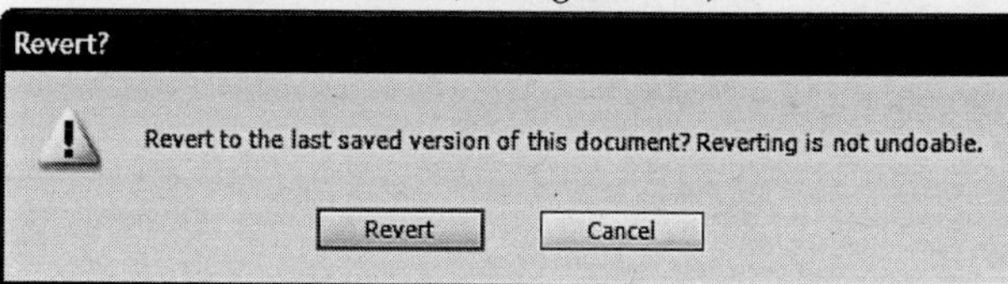

Figure A.25 Revert Confirmation dialog box

To Save a document as a template, do this:

1. Click the **File** menu and choose **Save As Template....** The **Save As** Template dialog box appears as shown in Figure A.26.

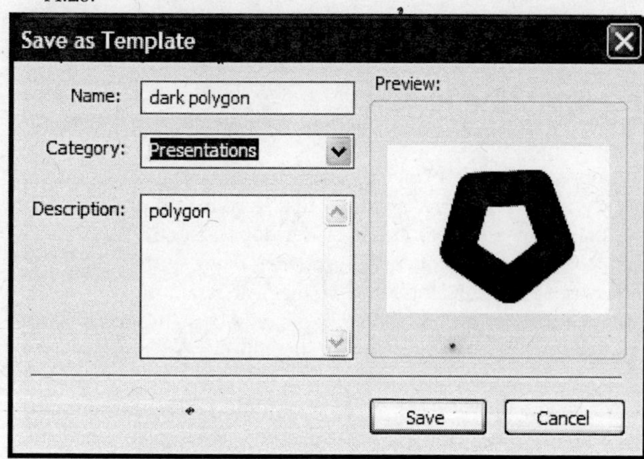

Figure A.26 Save As Template dialog box

2. In the Save As Template dialog box, enter a name for the template in the Name: box.
3. In the Category: drop-down list, select a category.
4. Enter a description of the template in the **Description**: box (up to 255 characters).
5. Then click **OK** button.

The written description about the template will appear in the New from Template dialog box, when the template is selected.

To close the Flash file, do this:

1. Click the **File menu** and choose **Close**. The Flash file is closed and the Welcome screen gets visible.

APPENDIX B

PowerPoint

B.1 INTRODUCTION

PowerPoint 2010 is a presentation software that allows you to create dynamic slide presentations that may include animation, narration, images, videos,etc. It is developed for the Windows and Mac OS computer operating systems. Being widely used by business people, educators, and trainers, it is among the most prevalent forms of persuasion technology. According to its vendor, Microsoft Corporation, some 30 million presentations are made with PowerPoint every day.

In Microsoft PowerPoint, as in most other presentation software, text, graphics, movies, and other objects are positioned on individual pages or "slides". The "slide" is a reference to the slide projector, a device which has become somewhat obsolete due to the use of PowerPoint and other presentation software. Slides can be printed, or displayed on-screen and navigated through at the command of the presenter. Transitions between slides can be animated in a variety of ways, as can the emergence of elements on a slide itself. The overall design of a presentation can be controlled with a master slide. The overall structure, extending to the text on each slide, can be edited using an outliner. Presentations can be saved and run in many types of file formats.

B.2 BASICS OF POWERPOINT

PowerPoint is a system in the Microsoft Office Suite that enables you to present information in office meetings, lectures and seminars to create maximum impact in a minimal amount of time. PowerPoint presentations can amplify your message, accelerate the information being absorbed and assist with comprehension enabling faster decision making.

PowerPoint is the largest selling presentation graphics software package by Microsoft Corporation of USA and since its introduction in 1987, PowerPoint has set new standards for the working of presentation graphics.

PowerPoint 2010 helps you bringing *ideas* and *information* that you want to convey to your audience with no difficulty. With PowerPoint 2010, you can:

- Quickly create *paper for Overhead Projector (OHP), 35mm slide,* or *on-screen* presentations.
- Supplement your presentations with *speaker's notes.*
- Use material you have created in other application packages, such as Word 2010 and Excel 2010.

B.2.1 Using PowerPoint

Presentations

You can make presentation in the form of *slides, handouts* or *speaker's notes.*

Slides

Slides are individual *"pages"* of a presentation. It may contain *text, graphs, clipart,* etc. Clipart includes pictures, sounds and videos. You can even print slides for overhead projector transparencies.

Handouts

Handouts consist of printed versions of your slides – either two, three, or six slides per page. If you would like to print slides that also include lines for audience notes you need to select Handouts (3 Slides Per Page).

B.2.2 Opening PowerPoint 2010 for Presentation

➡ **To start PowerPoint 2010, do this:**

1. Click the **Start** button on the Taskbar.
2. Highlight **All Programs** menu item and click **MS Office** and choose **MS Office PowerPoint 2010** (Figure B.1).

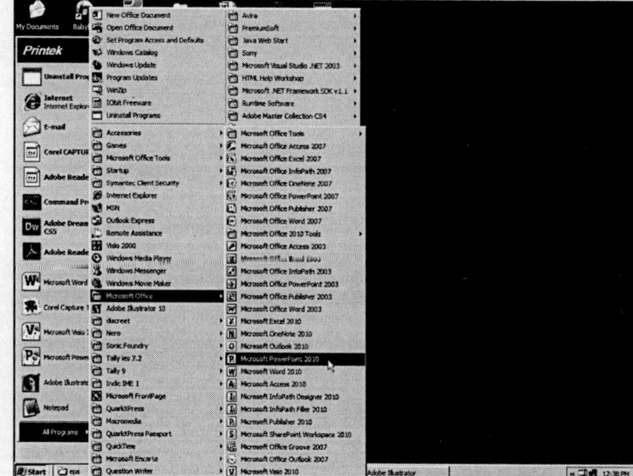

Figure B.1 Starting Powerpoint with the Start Button

When you first start PowerPoint 2010, it displays a blank presentation with a single slide showing. The layout is simple, with a title at the top and a subtitle below (See Figure B.2).

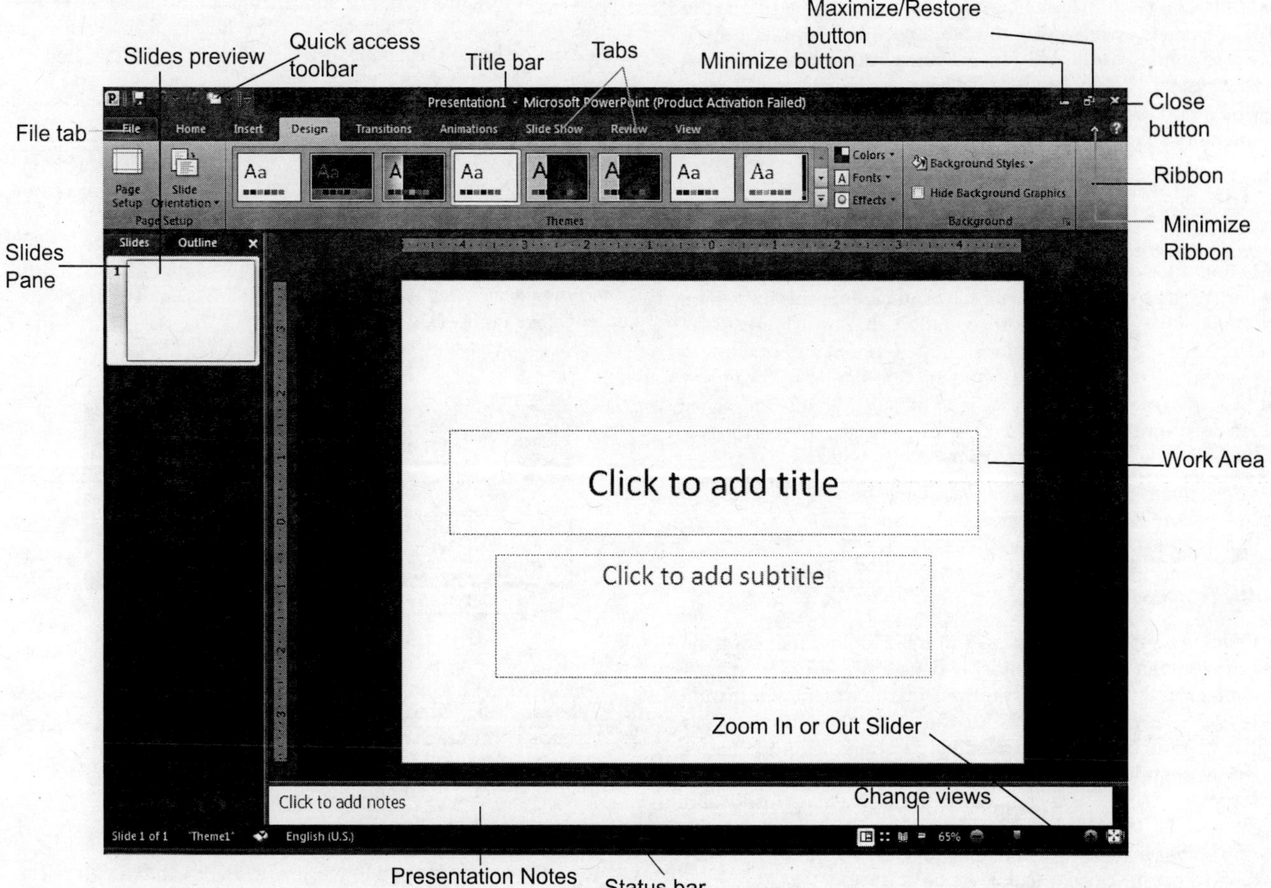

Figure B.2 A blank presentation displayed by PowerPoint

Understanding the Screen Elements

You will notice a close resemblance of the PowerPoint 2010 opening screen with the opening screens of Word 2007 and Excel 2007. The main elements of the PowerPoint window are as seen in Figure B.2.

Title bar: The *Title bar* is at the top of the screen (See Figure B.2). It shows the title PowerPoint and the name of presentation. If you have not yet saved any presentation then it displays the default name for the presentation which is *Presentation1*.

Ribbon: Ribbon is displayed just below the title bar. The Ribbon contains multiple tabs, each with several groups of commands. In Ribbon, Commands are organized in logical groups, which are collected together under tabs (Figure B.2). Some tabs, like "Drawing Tools" or "Table Tools", may appear only when you are working with certain items like images or tables. In addition, you can add your own customized tabs that contain your favorite commands.

Quick Access Toolbar: This toolbar is located by default at the top of PowerPoint 2010 window. By default, this toolbar displays the Save, Undo and Repeat buttons. You can add other commands to make it more convenient for you.

Minimize button: Shrinks the application window to a bar on the taskbar, you can click its button on the taskbar to reopen it.

Restore button: A double box at the right of a title bar that restores an application or document into a sizable window.

Close button: A box at the right of a title bar (X) that closes the window or dialog box.

Work area: Where active PowerPoint slide(s) appear. Figure B.2 shows it in Normal view, but other views are available that make the work area appear differently.

Status bar: It gives the information about the presentation and provides shortcuts for changing the view and the zoom.

Exploring PowerPoint 2010 Interface

There is a new look for PowerPoint 2010. There is also a new user interface that replaces menus, toolbars, and most of the task panes from previous versions of PowerPoint. The new user interface is designed to help you to be more productive in PowerPoint; more easily find the right features for various tasks and also be more efficient.

The PowerPoint 2010 interface consists of various components, which are as follows:

Minimize/Maximize/Restore and Close buttons

The Minimize, Maximize and Close buttons are located on the top right corner of the MS PowerPoint window. The Minimize button is used to minimize the MS PowerPoint window over the Task bar whereas the Maximize button is helps to restore or maximize the MS PowerPoint window. The Close button is used to close the document (See Figure B.2).

File Tab

File tab is the colored tab which is located in the upper-left corner of Microsoft Office 2010 programs and below the Quick Access Toolbar. When you click the File tab, you can see the Backstage view. File tab replaces the office button in PowerPoint 2010. Backstage view gives you various options for saving, opening a file, printing, or sharing your document. It is similar to the Office Button Menu from PowerPoint 2007 or the File Menu from earlier versions of PowerPoint. However, instead of just a menu it is a full-page view, which makes it easier to work with.

☞ *File tab incorporates many of the features in the 2003 and 2007 versions of PowerPoint but makes them much more user friendly.*

Quick Access Toolbar

The Quick Access Toolbar is a customizable toolbar that contains a set of commands that are independent of the tab that is currently displayed. You can add buttons that represent commands to the Quick Access Toolbar. You can move the Quick Access Toolbar from one of the two possible locations. This toolbar is located by default at the top of PowerPoint 2010 window. It provides tools that you use frequently, such as Save, Undo and Repeat buttons (See Figure B.2). You can customize the Quick Access Toolbar by adding commands to it.

➡ **To add command to Quick Access Toolbar, do this:**

1. Right click the appropriate command that you want to add to the Quick Access Toolbar (See Figure B.3).
2. Then click **Add to Quick Access Toolbar** from the context menu as shown in Figure B.3.

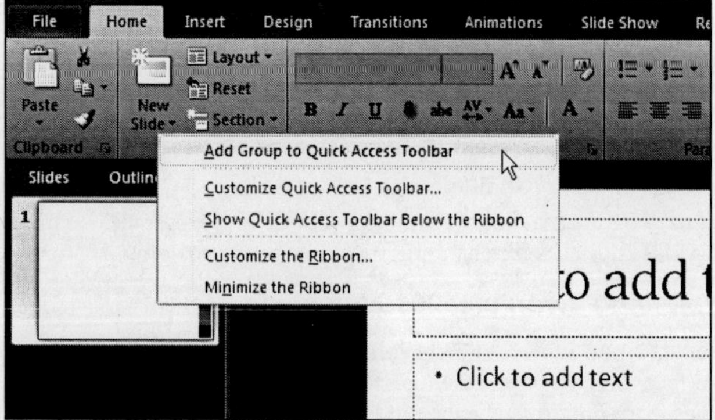

Figure B.3 Add command to Quick Access toolbar

Dialog Box Launchers

The dialog box launchers are small icons that appear in some groups on the Ribbon. Clicking a Dialog Box Launcher opens a related dialog box or task pane, providing more options related to that group.

Ribbon

The primary replacement for menus and toolbars in PowerPoint 2010 is the Ribbon. Designed for easy browsing, the Ribbon consists of tabs that are organized around specific scenarios or objects. The controls on each tab are further organized into several groups. The Ribbon can host richer content than menus and toolbars can, including buttons, galleries, and dialog box contents (See Figure B.4).

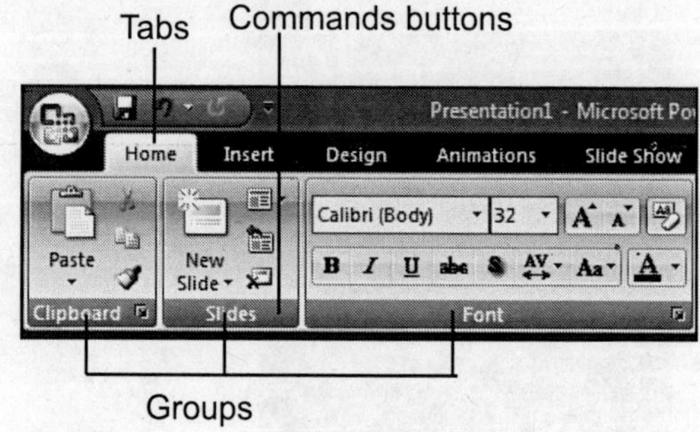

Figure B.4

1. Tabs are designed to be task-oriented.
2. Groups within each tab break a task into subtasks.
3. Command buttons in each group carry out a command or display a menu of commands.

Contextual Tools

Contextual tools enable you to work with an object that you select on the page, such as table, picture, or drawing. When you click the object, the pertinent set of contextual tabs appear in color next to the standard tabs (See Figure B.5).

Scroll Bar

The Scroll bar appears at the right side of the PowerPoint. You can also scroll between different slides by using the up and down arrow buttons present in the scroll bar.

Work Area

Where active PowerPoint slide(s) appears. It shows it in Normal view, but other views are available that make the work area different.

Status Bar

It gives the information about the presentation and provides about the current slide, such as slide number and theme name. The slide number displays the currently selected slide with the total number of the slides present in the presentations; whereas, the theme name represents the name of the theme applied to the presentation.

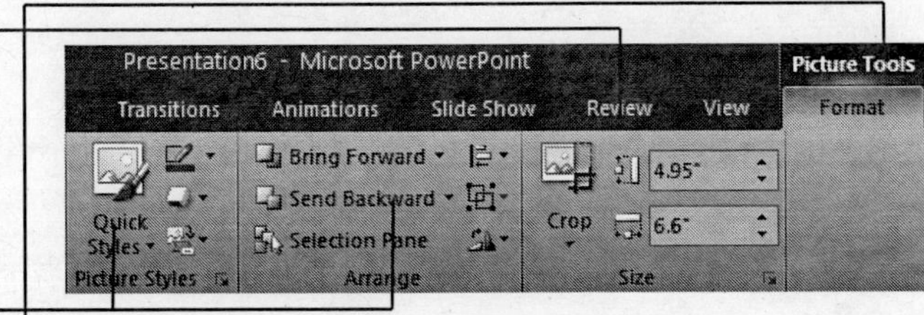

1. Select an object in your presentation.
2. The name of the applicable contextual tools appears in an accent color, and the contextual tabs appear next to the standard set of tabs.
3. The contextual tabs provide controls for working with the selected item.
4. A standard tab available on the Ribbon.

Figure B.5 Contextual Tools

Slides Pane

In the upper-right section of the PowerPoint window, the Slide pane displays a large view of the current slide. With the current slide shown in this view, you can add text and insert pictures (picture: A file (such as a metafile) that you can ungroup and manipulate as two or more objects, or a file that stays as a single object (such as bitmaps).), tables, SmartArt graphics, charts, drawing objects, text boxes, movies, sounds, hyperlinks, and animations.

Notes Pane

In the Notes pane below the Slide pane, you can type notes that apply to the current slide. Later, you can print your notes and refer to them when you give your presentation. You can also print notes to hand out to your audience or include the notes in a presentation that you send to the audience or post on a Web page.

Zoom Control

You can use Zoom controls to get a larger or smaller view of your presentation by drag the Zoom slider right to left. You can click the Zoom In (+ plus) button to get a larger view of the presentation and the Out (- minus) button to get a smaller view of the presentation.

Exploring the Tabs

Ribbon in PowerPoint 2010 is a group of tabs. This tab consists of two types, command tabs and contextual tabs. A command tab is a collection of commands of a specific category. Commands in a command tab are placed into different group. Each command set representing a subcategory of commands. Contextual tabs appear on the Ribbon when you add or select some object, such as image, a table, or a chart on a PowerPoint slide. An example of a contextual tab is the Format tab Some of the tabs are discuss in the following sections.

Home Tab: When you click it, this tab is active. Buttons related to working with document contents are organized in this tab. It has six groups: Clipboard, Slides, Font, Paragraph, Drawing and Editing. Only the button representing commands that can be performed on the currently selected document element are active (See Figure B.6).

The groups for the Home Tab are:

(a) ***Clipboard:*** This contains the Cut, Copy, and Paste commands.

(b) ***Slides:*** This section allows you to insert new slides (clicking on the 'New Slide' button allows you to select the slide type you wish), as well as adjust the layout of your individual slides, reset slides to default, and delete slides.

(c) ***Font:*** Select the font here. Adjust the font type and size. Make it bold, italic, or underline. Change the colour or highlighting. Using the tab, you can also change case of selected text to uppercase or lowercase.

(d) ***Paragraph:*** Bullets or numbered lists. It also changes the alignment of text and change the spacing between lines.

(e) ***Drawing:*** Insert shapes. Arrange objects on a given slide. It also applies fill colour in the selected shape and add effect to the shapes.

(f) ***Editing:*** Find, edit, select, and replace text.

Insert Tab: Click this button for related items you can insert. These are organizing on this tab. It has seven groups: *Tables*, *Images*, *Illustrations*, *links*, *Text*, *Symbols* and *Media* (See Figure B.7).

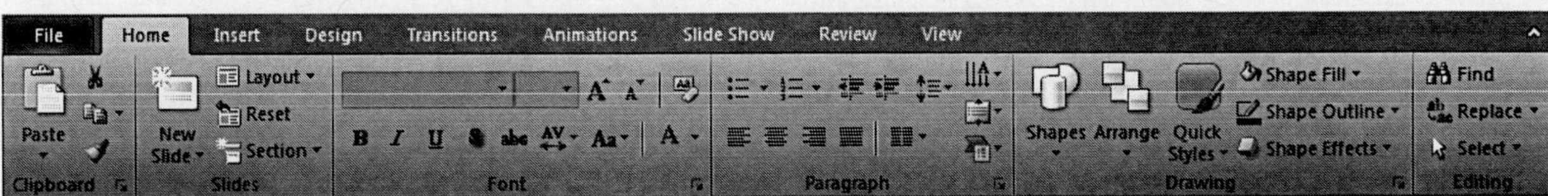

Figure B.6 Home tab

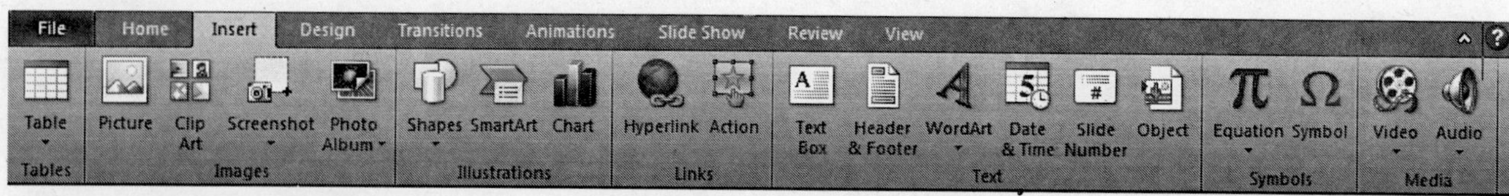

Figure B.7 Insert

When you need to insert anything into your slide show, this is where you come to do it. The groups available to you are:

(a) *Tables:* Insert tables into the slide. These can be pre-made, or you can make them as you like.

(b) *Images:* It allows you to insert pictures from a file as well as from the Clip Art in a slide. You can also create photo album and apply visual effects to pictures. Screenshot which allows you take screenshot of all currently opened windows on the computer.

(c) *Illustrations:* It allows you to insert pre-defined shapes, Smart Arts and charts in the presentation.

(d) *Links:* Add a hyperlink, to take you out of your slideshow to a Web resource. Add an action to cause something to happen in the slide show if you point to an object with the mouse. Hyperlinks are used to allow a presenter a way to access a website during the presentation by pressing a link inserted into the slide.

(e) *Text:* It is not just about typing text into a slide: Insert text boxes, which allow you to play with the location and orientation of words. Insert headers and footers. Turn your text into "*Word Art*". Insert date, times, slide numbers and other embedded objects.

(f) *Symbols:* It allows you to insert and edit equations and insert symbols in the presentation.

(g) *Media:* Insert video and sound into your slide, to create a truly vibrant presentation.

Design tab: Click this tab which will show buttons that are related to items. You can give design to your slides. They are organized on this tab. It has three groups: *Page Setup, Themes, Background* (See Figure B.8).

Adjust the look of individual slides with the contents of the design tab. Change just one slide, or apply your changes to the whole presentation:

(a) *Page Setup:* Adjust margins, page size, and orientation (portrait or landscape).

(b) *Themes:* A theme includes a background design, color scheme, font types, font sizes, and placeholder positions in one package. Every new presentation starts out with the default theme, called Office theme, which is a white background and black text. However you can change the theme to a wide variety of options.

(c) *Background:* It adjust the background look of your slides by changing the color, or adding special images like watermarks.

Transitions: The transitions tab let you preview the presentation after applying effects, add transitions to a slide, and set the timing for the slide show of the presentation. It has three groups: *Preview, Transition to this slide, timing* (See Figure B.9).

(a) *Preview:* It helps to view the slide after the transition effect is applied.

(b) *Transition to this slide:* It allows you to apply transition to a slide and set the effect option specific to a transition.

(c) *Timing:* It allows you to add transition sound and set the time to move to the next slide.

Animations tab: Click this tab which will show buttons that are related to items. You can give animations to your slides. For example, you can animate individual objects on the slide. They are organized on this tab. It has three groups: *Preview, Animation, Advance Animation* and *Timing* (See Figure B.10).

(a) *Preview:* To preview the animation applied in the slide, include transition effect and animation applied on objects and text.

(b) *Animation:* Slide animations create animated effects to text and graphics during a slide show. There are a variety of animations that can be applied to text or graphics in multiple ways from a single word to all of the text on a slide. It allows you to apply animation to a slide and the effect based on the animation type.

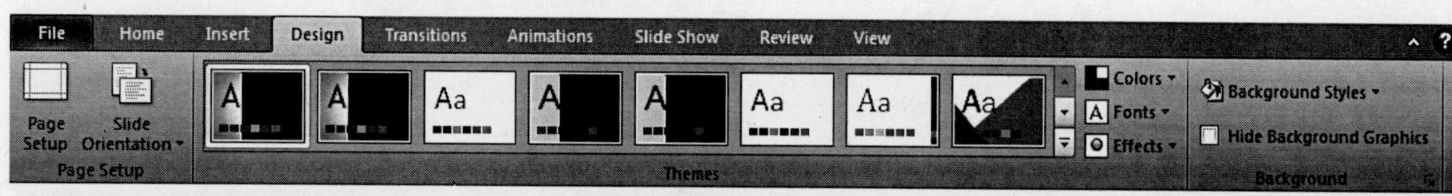

Figure B.8 Design tab

Figure B.9 Transitions

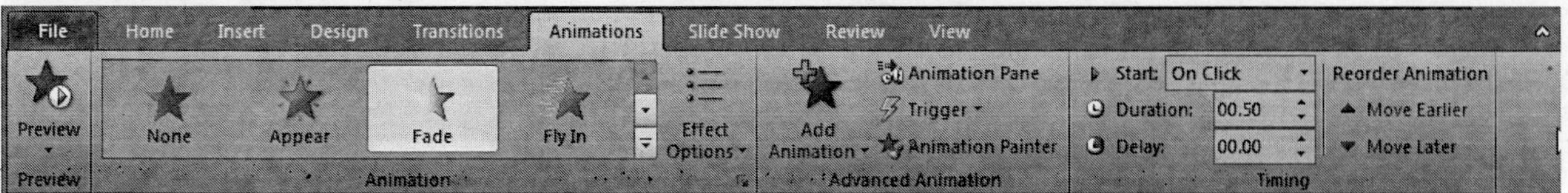

Figure B.10 Animations tab

(c) ***Advanced Animation:*** It allows you to apply advanced features to the applied animation and apply trigger effect.

(d) ***Timings:*** To set the duration of the slides and delay between the slides. You can reorder the animation.

Slide Show: Click this tab which will show buttons that are related to items. In this tab, you can view; take up the full computer screen, like an actual presentation. For example, you can see how your graphics animated effects will look during the presentation. It has three groups: *Start slide show*, *Set Up* and *Monitors* (See Figure B.11).

(a) ***Start Slide Show:*** Run it from the beginning or from a selected slide. Or, create a second slide show using only those slides in the presentation you want to use.

(b) ***Set Up:*** Record narration for your slide show. Practice your timing as you speak while the show's slides transition automatically.

(c) ***Monitors:*** It allows you to select a screen resolution or a presenter view.

Review tab: Click this tab which will show buttons that are related to items. In this tab, you can view and add comments to your presentation and you might prefer to check spelling all at once when you finish your document. It has three groups: *Proofing*, *Language*, *Comments* and *Compare* (See Figure B.12).

(a) ***Proofing:*** Check the spelling, open research task pane to references for more information; find synonyms so you do not use the same word repeatedly, check the grammar etc.

(b) ***Language:*** It allows you to translate the text in other language.

(c) ***Comments:*** Add or edit comments about a given slide, or about a specific bit of content on a slide. Helpful when planning narration.

(d) ***Compare:*** To compare different presentations, accept or reject the changes, and show the review pane.

View tab: Click this tab which will show buttons that are related to changing the view during presentation. It has six groups: *Presentation views*, *Master Views*, *Show/Hide*, *Zoom*, *Color/Grayscale*, *Window* and *Macros* (See Figure B.13).

(a) ***Presentation View:*** Choose from normal, slide sorter, notes view, handout view, and other options, either for on screen viewing, or printouts.

(b) ***Master Views:*** To view the presentation in slide master view, handout master view and notes master view.

(c) ***Show/Hide:*** It display, gridlines, rulers and other tools to help you place objects into the slides exactly where you want them.

(d) ***Zoom:*** Zoom In or Out to change the size of the slide window.

(e) ***Color/Grayscale:*** View the presentation in color, grayscale or even black and white.

(f) ***Window:*** Arrange the windows in which you are working to help you be more productive.

(g) ***Macros:*** Create and use custom macros to do complex tasks with just a click or two.

B.2.3 Opening an Existing Presentation

PowerPoint 2010 opens files in any of the several format, such as (.pptx, .pptm, .potx, .ppt, .pot, etc.)

➡ **To open an existing presentation, do this:**

1. Open the **File** tab on the Ribbon. The Backstage view appears. Alternatively, press Ctrl+O (See Figure B.14).

Figure B.11 Slide Show

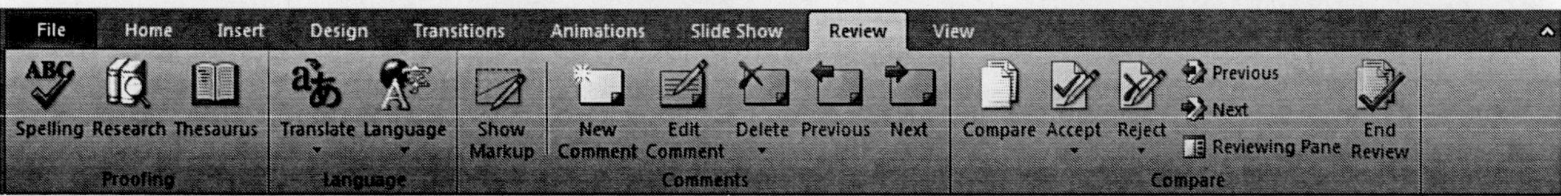

Figure B.12 Review tab

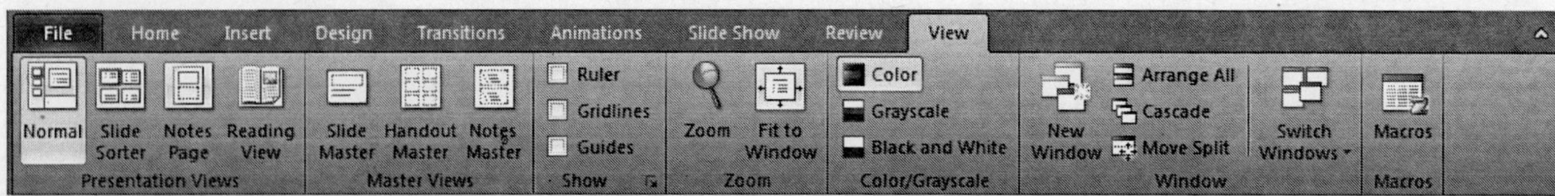

Figure B.13 View tab

Figure B.14 Selecting Open option from the File tab

2. Click the **Open** option from the Backstage view (See Figure B.15).
3. The **Open** dialog box appears as seen in Figure B.15.
4. Choose the files and folders in the **Look in:** drop-down list.
5. Select the name of the file you want to open from the list.
4. Click Open button to open the presentation.

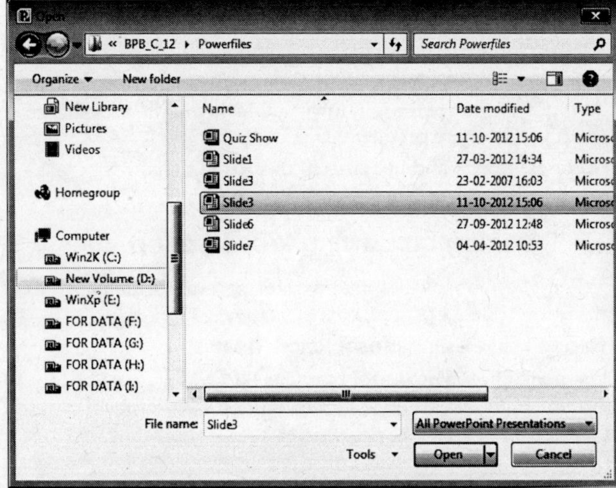

Figure B.15 PowerPoint's Open dialog box

B.2.4 Saving the Presentation

When working on a presentation, it is very important that you save it at regular intervals so that in case there is system failure you do not loose much of your work.

PowerPoint has two commands to save your file – Save and Save As command.

- The Save command is used to save the presentation.
- The Save As command is used when you want to save an existing presentation under a new name or you are saving your presentation for the first time.

➡ **To save a presentation, do this:**

1. Click the **File** tab and on the Ribbon. The Backstage view will appear. Select the **Save** option from the **File** tab. Or click the **Save** button on the Quick Access toolbar or from the keyboard press Ctrl+S.
2. If you have already saved the file then PowerPoint updates the earlier saved file. If you have not saved the file before, the **Save As** dialog box as in Figure B.16 appears.

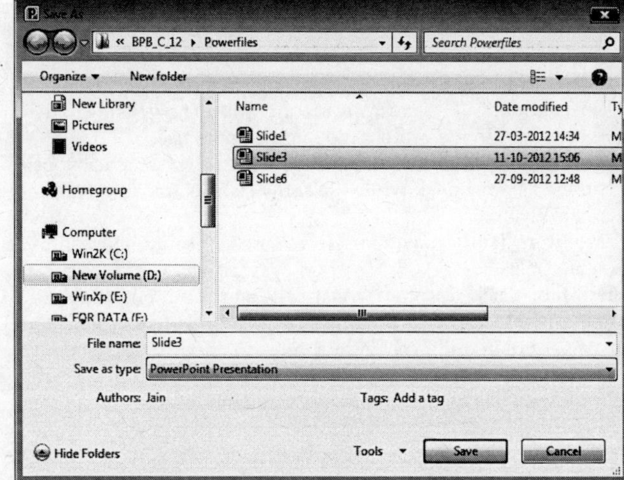

Figure B.16 PowerPoint's Save As dialog box

3. In the **Save As** list box specify the location where you want to save the file in the **Save in:** drop-down list. (Choose PowerPoint Template). It adds the template to your list of available templates.
4. Type the desired file name which you want to save the presentation in the **File Name:** list box.
5. Click **Save** button.

➡ **To save a presentation using Save As command, do this:**

1. Click the **File** tab and choose **Save As...** . The **Save As** dialog box in Figure B.16 appears. Now follow Step 1 through 5 in the save procedure.

B.3 CREATION OF PRESENTATION

PowerPoint is designed to give your slide presentations a consistent look. There are four ways that PowerPoint helps you control the look of your slides – with design related elements, Visual elements, colour schemes, and layouts of slides.

B.3.1 Creating a Presentation using an Installed Template

A template is a file that contains many types of documents, including resumes, cover letters, business plans, business cards, etc. Microsoft provided templates and presentations that come pre-installed with PowerPoint. These templates offer various layouts, visual elements, and other design-related elements to create presentations.

➡ **To create a presentation by using an installed template, do this:**

1. Click the **File** tab. The Backstage view appears as seen in Figure B.17.

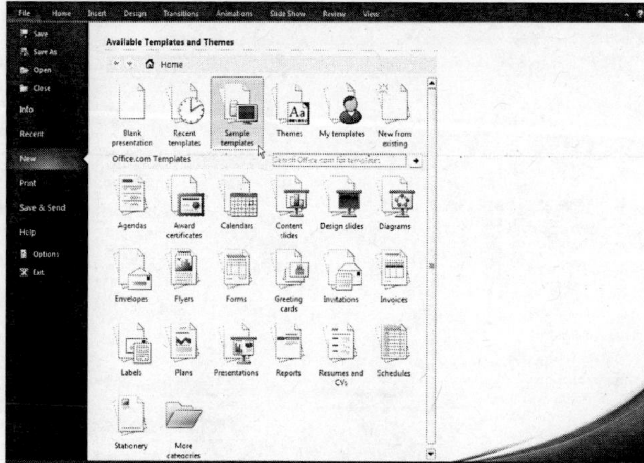

Figure B.17 Select Sample templates under the available templates themes

2. Select the **New** option from the Backstage view. It displays the list of all available templates appears in the middle pane as seen in Figure B.17.
3. Under the **Available Templates and Themes** category, select the **Sample templates** option.
4. In the Sample templates, you can see a different types of templates, with all formatting, such as background, themes colors, font, etc. (See Figure B.18).

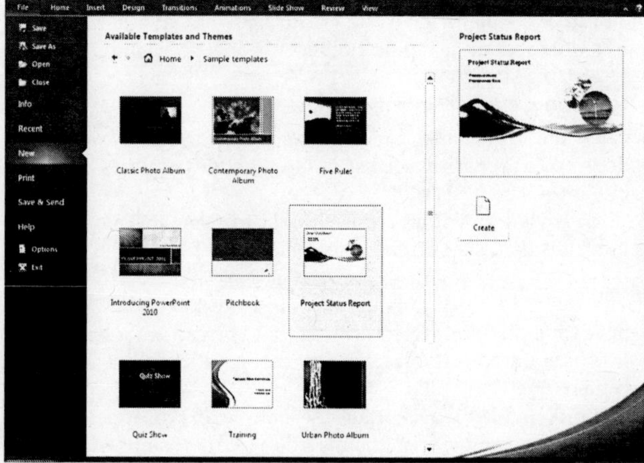

Figure B.18 Select desired template from the sample templates

5. Select the desired template you want to apply. For example, we have selected, **Project Status Report** (See Figure B.18).
6. In the **preview** box, you see a sample presentation for which the template is designed.
7. Click **Create** button.

B. You can see the selected template as default presentation title name (See Figure B.19).

B.3.2 Creating a Blank Presentation

When you start PowerPoint 2010, the program displays a blank title slide by default. You can begin to add text and pictures on that slide choose a different slide layout, apply a design, etc.

If you want to create a PowerPoint presentation on your own, you can use the blank template in PowerPoint 2010. The blank template offers only the basic visual elements of a presentation, such as placeholder to add a title to a slide.

☞ *When inserting a graphic using the icon in a placeholder causes the graphic to be automatically sized and positioned within the placeholder preventing you from entering text in the same placeholder.*

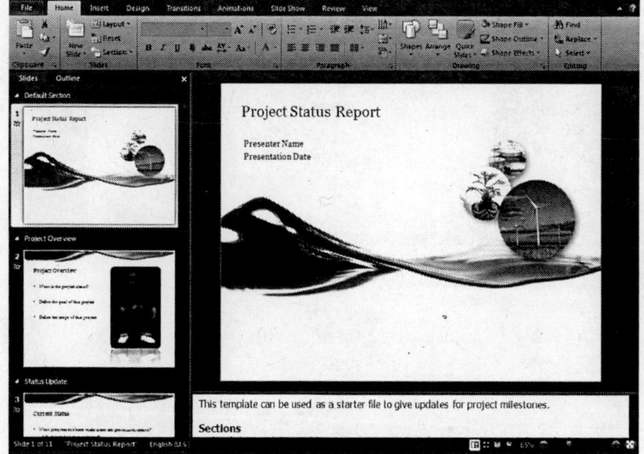

Figure B.19 PowerPoint opens the selected template

➡ **To create a presentation by using the blank template, do this:**

1. Click the **File** tab. The Backstage view appears, displaying various options as seen in Figure B.20.
2. Select the **New** option from the Backstage view.
3. The list of all available templates appears in the middle pane.
4. Under the **Available Templates and Themes** category, select the **Blank presentation** option.
5. Click the **Create** button.
6. The new presentation is created with the name Presentation2 as seen in Figure B.21.

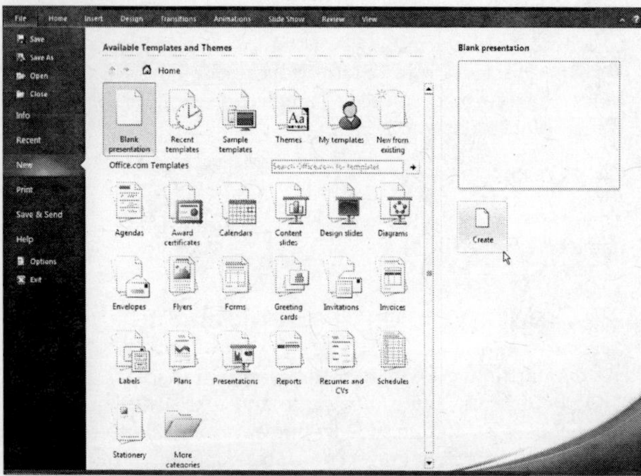

Figure B.20 File Backstage view

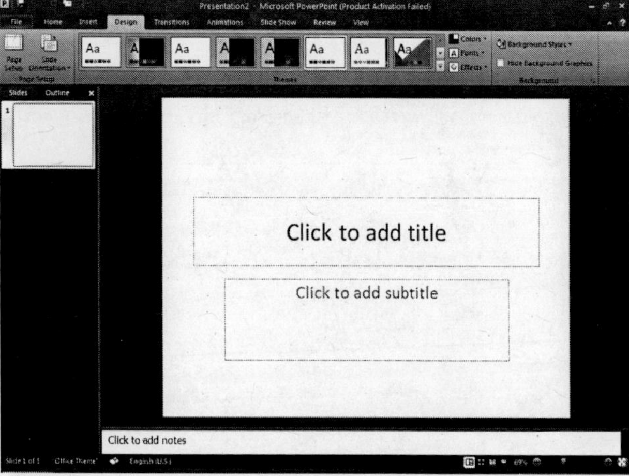

Figure B.21 Blank presentation with the default name presentation2

You can see that a blank presentation contains a single slide with text boxes (placeholders) to enter a title and a subtitle. You can also apply different styles and background to it.

Creating a New Template based on an Existing Presentation

You can create a template in almost the same way as you create a presentation. If you have a template that already has most of the features you want, you will save time by creating a new presentation based on that existing template.

1. Click the **File** tab on the ribbon. The Backstage view appears. A list of options appears as seen in B.20.
2. Click the **New** option from the list.
3. Under **Available Template and Themes** click **New from existing** icon (See Figure B.17).
4. The **New from Existing Presentation** dialog box appears as shown in Figure B.22.
5. Select the template that is similar to the one that you want to create.
6. Then click **Create New**. Make the changes you want to apply, such as themes colours, fonts and other formats.
7. Click the **Save As** button to save the template.
8. The **Save As** dialog box appears. Give the new name to template file in the **File name:** drop-down list.
9. Select the PowerPoint template in the **Save as type:** drop-down list, and then click **Save** button (See Figure B.16).

B.3.3 Entering and Editing Text

PowerPoint slide always contains text of some kind, even if it is just a title. Entering and editing text in PowerPoint is similar to entering and editing text in Word or Excel.

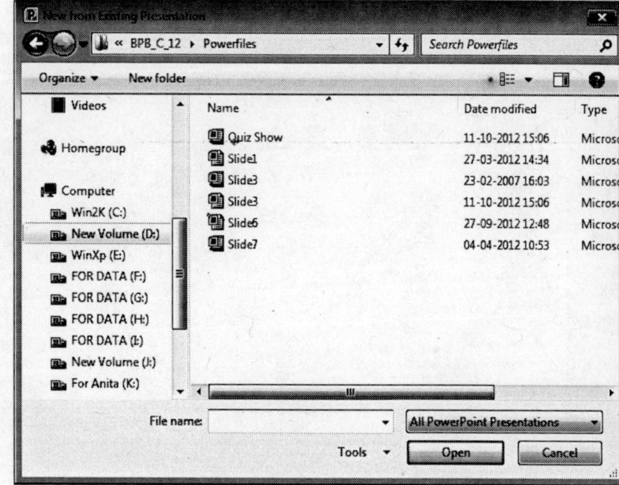

Figure B.22 New from existing presentation

Entering Text to Slides

You can enter text in a presentation in two ways:

- Inserting a new slide with text place holder.
- Inserting text in an existing slide.

Adding Text in a Placeholder

PowerPoint 2010 comes with predefined layouts you want to use, or you can add a blank slide and create a custom layout. Many of these layouts contain text placeholders for title, body and bulleted list.

➡ **To insert a new slide with text, do this:**

1. Click the **Home** tab. In the **Slides** group click New slide down pointing arrow. A list of layout slides appears as seen in Figure B.23.
2. Click anywhere within a placeholder to select it. This border indicates that the current placeholder is selected (See Figure B.24).
3. The sample text disappears and an insertion point appears inside the placeholder, indicating that you can enter text.
4. In a title or subtitle placeholder, the insertion point may be centered.
5. In a bulleted-list placeholder, the sample text disappears and the bullet remains, with the insertion point positioned where the text will begin.

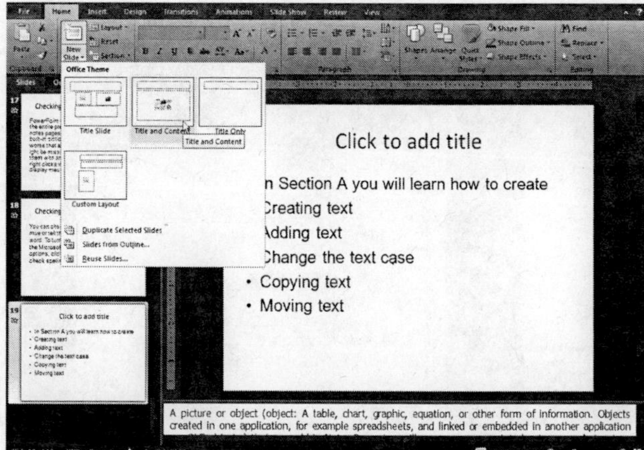

Figure B.23 Selecting slide layout with title and contents

6. Type the text for the slide inside the selected placeholder and press Enter key.
7. In the case of bullets, press Enter key when you want to begin a new bulleted item. If the bulleted text is too long to fit on one line, PowerPoint automatically wraps the text to the next line and aligns the text.
8. When you finish entering text, deselect the object by clicking a blank area of the slide of the gray border around the slide.

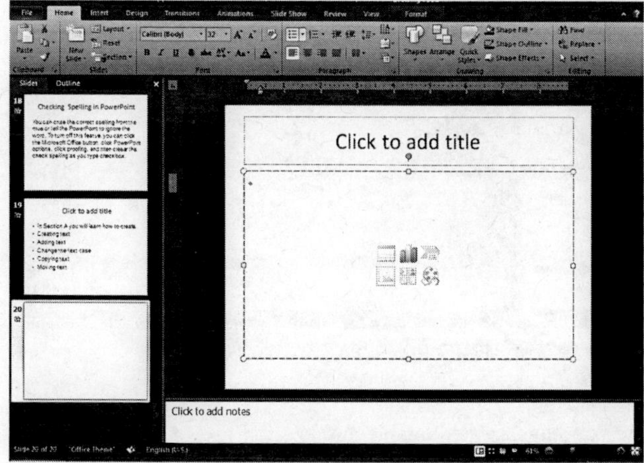

Figure B.24 The Slide Layout with Placeholder

Editing Text on a Slide

You can make changes to the text in any text object simply by clicking the object. An insertion point appears, indicating that the text is ready for editing. Then you can start making changes to the text. Before you can change existing text, you have to select it by using the following techniques:

- Select an individual word by double-clicking it. The word and the space following it are selected.
- *Alternatively,* position the insertion point at the beginning of the text you want to select, hold down the Shift key, and either press an arrow key to select characters one at a time or click the end of the text you want to select.
- Select an entire slide title by clicking its slide icon on the Outline tab.
- Select all the text in a placeholder by clicking inside the placeholder and then clicking select and then **Select All** in the **Editing** group on the **Home** tab.

Copying Text

You can copy text that appears in one place to another place. Copying of text occurs with the assistance of the Windows Clipboard. The *Clipboard* is an area of your computer's memory that is used for holding data. As long as the data is on the Clipboard, you can place it anywhere in any Windows software application. The data stays on the Clipboard until you replace it with new data, or until you exit Windows.

➡ **To copy text using ribbon command, do this:**

1. Select the text you want to copy.
2. In the **Home** tab, click copy icon on the **Clipboard** group or (press Ctrl+C keys together).
3. Move to the place in your presentation where you want to insert this text.
4. Click Paste down pointing arrow and choose Paste command on the **Clipboard** group (or press Ctrl+V keys together.

Moving Text

The move operation is similar to the copy operation except that text is moved, i.e., it is deleted from the original location and copied to a new place.

➡ **To move the text using Ribbon command, do this:**

1. Click the text to put the text box in edit mode.
2. Select the text you want to move.

☞ *Using Cut and Paste is the way to move text around between slides. Just select and cut the text, move to the appropriate slide, and paste it where you want it.*

3. Right-click and choose Cut from the shortcut menu or click the Cut button on the **Home** tab (or press Ctrl+X keys together). Move to the new location, right-click, and choose Paste or click the **Paste** button on the **Home** tab (or press Ctrl+V keys together) .

Deleting Text

You can delete characters, words, or all the text in a text box. Using one of these methods:

- The Delete key erases the character to the right of the cursor.
- The Backspace key erases the character to the left of the cursor.

If you delete text accidentally, you can undo your action by clicking the Undo button on the Quick Access toolbar. (You can also press Ctrl+Z keys together).

B.3.4 Inserting and Deleting Slides in a Presentation

➡ **To insert slide, do this:**

1. In the slide view, display the slide after which you want to insert the slide.

2. In the **Home** tab click **New Slide** drop-down arrow and then choose New slide with layout. The **New** slide is inserted.

B.3.5 Deleting Slides

➡ **To delete slide, do this:**

1. In the Slides pane select the slide you want to delete.
2. Press (Delete) key. The selected slide gets deleted.

B.4 PREPARATION OF SLIDES

B.4.1 Inserting Word Table or an Excel Worksheet

To add some tabulated data, you can do with many ways such as inserting table from word file or can choose layout options of Powerpoint. You can insert data from Excel worksheet as well. You can also create a table in your presentation without using Word 2010.

ß **To create a new slide with table, do this:**

1. Click the **Insert** tab. Click **New Slide** down pointing arrow in the **Slides** group. A list of slides appears.
2. Click the **Title and Content** Slide. A new slide appears as seen in Figure B.25.

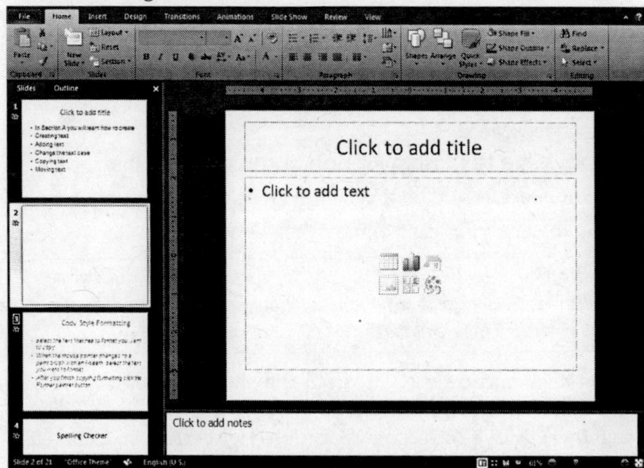

Figure B.25 A new slide with table placeholder

3. Click the **Insert table** place holder. **Insert Table** dialog box appears as seen in Figure B.26.
4. In the **Insert Table** dialog box, enter the number of *columns* and the number of *rows* you want to insert in the table. You can type the number of rows and the number of columns or click the up or down arrow on the right of the edit boxes to specify these numbers.
5. After you specify the number of rows and columns, click OK to create the table.
6. A table appears on the slide as seen in Figure B.27.

Entering Text in a Table

When you create a new table, an empty table appears within a gray frame on the slide as seen in Figure B.27. When you insert a table, the insertion point flashes in the first cell in the upper left corner of the table. The text you type appears at the insertion point. After entering the text in the table and to exit the editing mode, click anywhere outside the table.

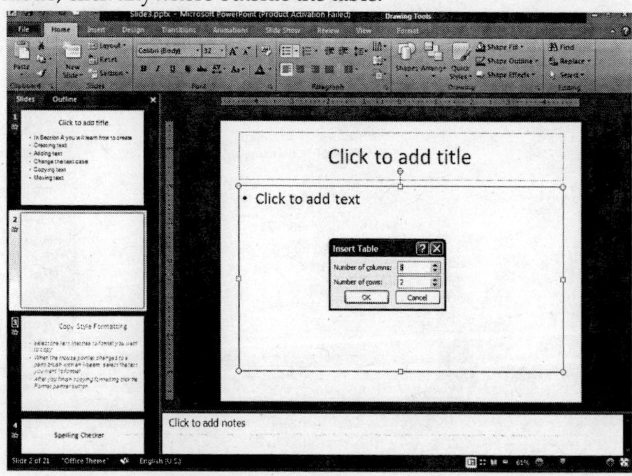

Figure B.26 Insert Table dialog box

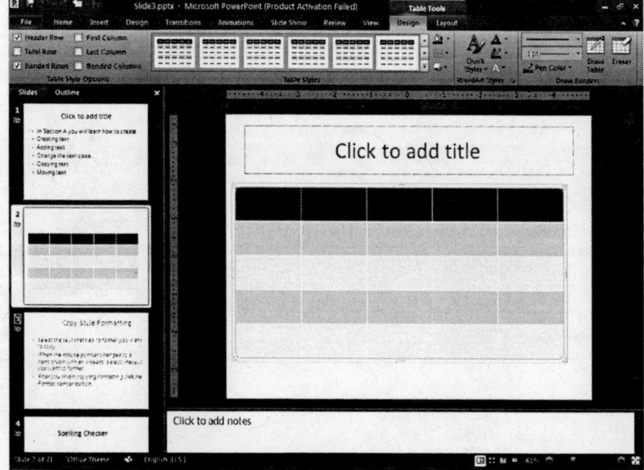

Figure B.27 Slide with a Table

Editing a Table

Once you have created a table and entered text or numbers, you can modify its structure by *adding, deleting, moving* and *copying* cells, columns and rows. You can also change the width of columns, height of rows and merge or split cells to accommodate typed text in the cells.

Selecting Cells, Columns and Rows

➡ **To select cells, do this:**

1. For selecting a single cell, position the mouse pointer near the left inside edge of the cell. Once the pointer changes to a right arrow, click the cell.
2. To select adjacent cells in the same column, click any where in the first cell and drag the mouse pointer down the column.
3. To select adjacent cells in the same row, click anywhere in the first cell, and drag the mouse pointer across the row.

4. To select multiple cells click the first cell, press and hold down the (Shift) key, and click the other cell. Both the cells and any cell in between these two cells are selected.

➡ **To select a row of cells, do this:**

1. Position the mouse pointer near the left ledge of the table. Once the pointer changes to a right arrow, click the row as seen in Figure B.2B. *Alternatively*, in **Table Tools** contextual tab, click **Layout** tab. In **Table** group, click Select down pointing arrow and choose Select Row.

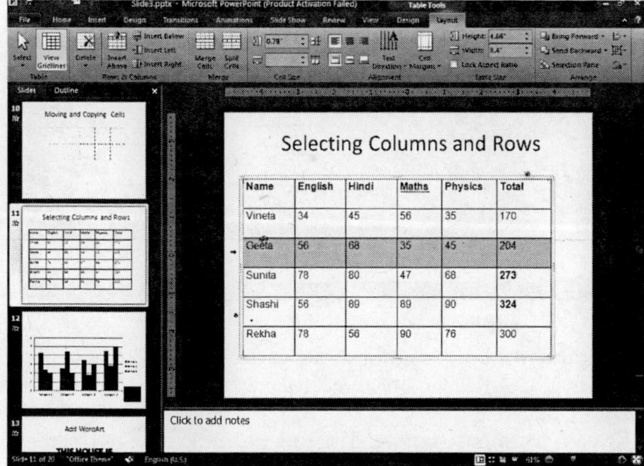

Figure B.28 Selecting the entire row in a table

➡ **To select column or columns of cells, do this:**

1. Position the mouse pointer on the top border of the column or columns. The pointer changes to a down arrow. Click the left mouse button to select the entire column or columns (See Figure B.29). *Alternatively*, in **Table Tools** contextual tab, click **Layout** tab. In **Table** group, click Select down pointing arrow and choose Select Column.

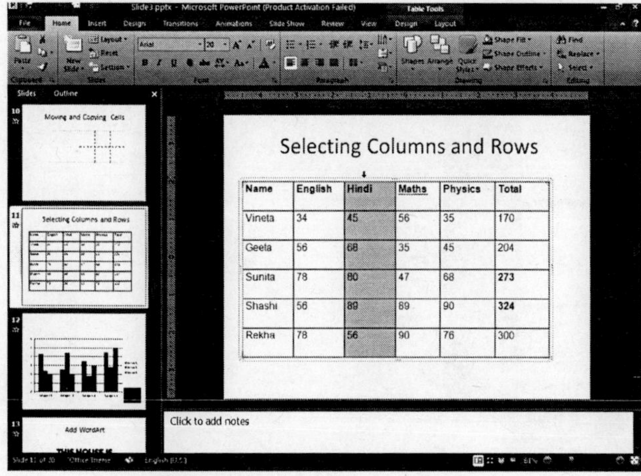

Figure B.29 Selecting a Column

Adding Columns and Rows

➡ **To insert a column, do this:**

1. Click anywhere in the column next to where you want the new column to appear.
2. In **Table Tools** contextual tab, click **Layout** tab. In **Rows & Columns** group choose **Insert Columns to the Left** or **Right**. A column is inserted to the left or right of the selected column. Or

   Right click the mouse, choose Insert, a sub menu appears, choose Insert Columns to the Left or Right.

➡ **To insert a row, do this:**

1. Click anywhere in the row next to where you want the new row to appear.
2. In **Table Tools** contextual tab, click **Layout** tab. In **Rows & Columns** group choose **Insert Rows to the Above** or **Below**. A row is inserted to the above or below of the selected row. Or

   Right click the mouse, choose Insert Rows Above or Insert Rows Below. A row is inserted above or below of the selected row.

Deleting Columns and Rows

➡ **To delete columns/rows, do this:**

1. Select the columns/rows you want to delete.
2. In **Table Tools** contextual tab, click **Layout** tab. In **Rows & Columns** group choose Delete Columns or Rows. Or right click the mouse, choose Delete Rows or Columns.

Copying and Moving Cells

Once you select the contents of a cell, you can *copy* or *move* these to another location using drag and drop. *Alternatively*, use the Cut, Copy and Paste commands from the **Home** tab or from the shortcut menu that appears when you select a cell and click the right mouse button.

➡ **To move or copy cell contents using *drag* and *drop*, do this:**

1. Select the text you want to move or copy.
2. From the **Home** tab of **Clipboard** group or from the shortcut menu, choose **Cut** (to move) or **Copy**.
3. Click in the table, to position the insertion point where you want to insert the cut or copied text.
4. From the **Home** tab **Clipboard** group or from the Shortcut menu, choose **Paste**. Cut or copied selected text is moved or copied at the insertion point.
5. *To move the selected text* – Position the mouse pointer over the selected text, press and hold down the left mouse button and drag the text to the destination cell.
6. *To copy the selected text* – Position the mouse pointer over the selected text, press and hold the (Ctrl) key, press and hold down the left mouse button and drag the text to the destination cell.

   A *plus* sign appears next to the pointer to indicate that you are copying instead of moving (See Figure B.30).

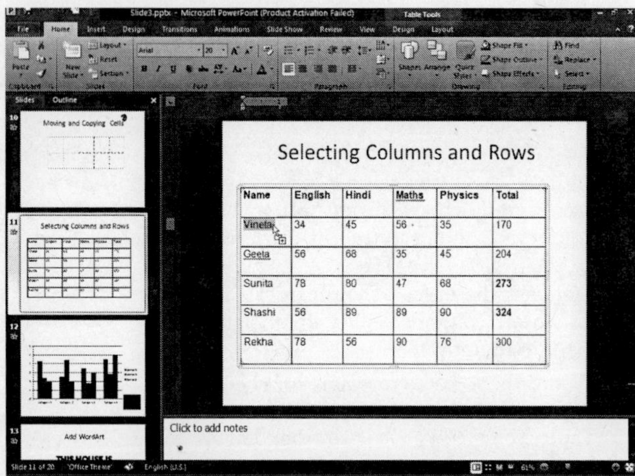

Figure B.30 Copying a cell with contents

Changing Column Width and Rows Height

You can change the size of *rows* of a table by adjusting the height of the rows. Similarly, you can also change the size of the *columns* by adjusting the width of the columns.

Changing Column Width

➡ **To change the width of a column in a table, do this:**

1. Position the pointer anywhere on the column's right border until the pointer changes to a double line and arrow (See Figure B.31).

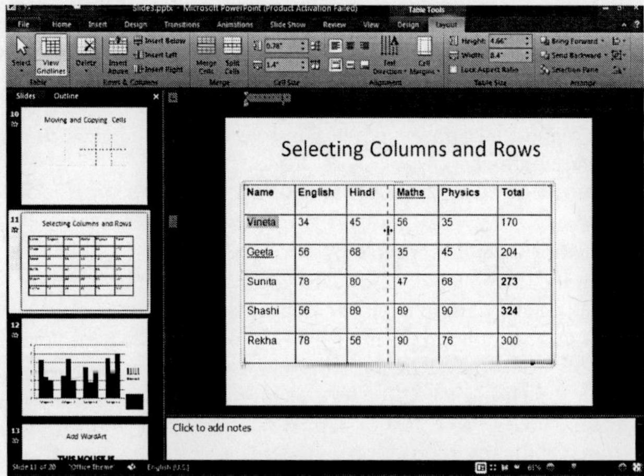

Figure B.31 Changing column width

2. Drag the column border to the left or right to decrease or increase the column width. A dashed line indicates the target column width.
3. Release the mouse button. The column width is changed to the new size you specified by dragging.
4. In **Table Tools** contextual tab, click **Layout** tab. In the **Cell Size** group, click the **Table Column Width** up and down arrow, to set the width of the selected cells.

Changing Row Height

➡ **To change the height of a row in a table, do this:**

1. Position the pointer anywhere on the row's right border until the pointer changes to a double line and arrow.

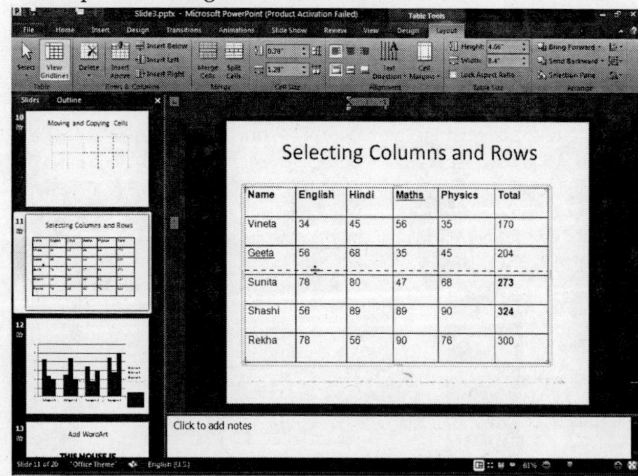

Figure B.32 Changing row height

2. Drag the row border up or down to decrease or increase the row height. A dashed line indicates the target row height (See Figure B.32).
3. Release the mouse button. The row height is changed to the new size you specified by dragging.
4. In **Table Tools** contextual tab, click **Layout** tab. In the **Cell Size** group, click the **Row height up** and **down** arrow, to set the height of the selected cells.

Merging and Splitting Cells

To create one cell that spans two or more cells, you can merge adjacent cells. In Figure B.33, merging cells allows you to enter a column heading in one large cell that occupies the same width as several smaller cells below.

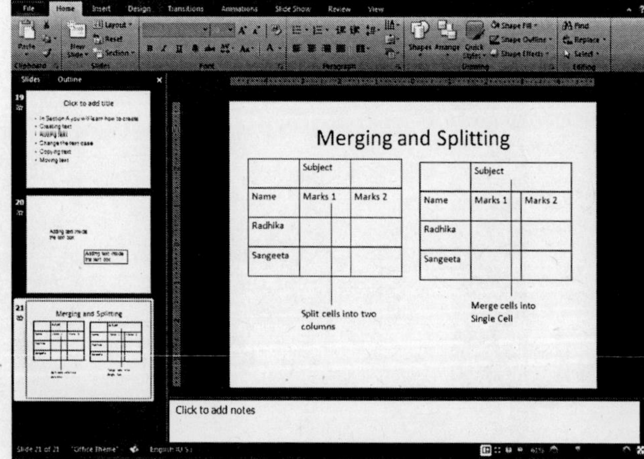

Figure B.33 Merging in cell in first row and split it in two cells in row 2

➡ **To merge two or more cells, do this:**

1. Select the cells you want to merge.
2. Click the **Table Tools** contextual tab, click the **Layout** tab. Click **Merge** cells in the **Merge** group.
   Or right click the mouse and choose Merge Cells.

➡ **To split a cell, do this:**

1. Select the cell that you want to split. You can only split one cell at a time.
2. Click the **Table Tools** contextual tab, click the **Layout** tab. Click **Split** cells in the **Merge** group.
3. The cell is split into two cells of equal width, with any text appearing in the cell on the left. Or right click the mouse and choose Split Cells... .

☞ *After splitting a cell, you might want to adjust the cell width to make it look right in your current cell structure and layout.*

Adding Borders and Fills

PowerPoint establishes default borders around cells and the table itself, on the current presentation template. You can change borders separating cells, columns and rows or around the entire table.

Changing Table Borders

You may specify a variety of ways for border formatting in a table. You can choose:

1. The border format (*Top border, bottom border, Left border, Right border, All border*, etc.)
2. The border style (solid line, dashed line, dotted line, etc.)
3. The border width (1/4 point to 6 points)
4. The border colour.

➡ **To select the table cells that you want to add or change the table border, do this:**

1. Select the entire table, or the cells, columns, or rows around which you want to specify the border.
2. Under **Table Tools**, on the **Design** tab, click **Border** down arrow in the **Table Styles** group. The actual name of this button changes depending on what was last selected. Borders option shows all the different border types (See Figure B.34).
3. Click the border you want. The selected portion of the table changes to reflect the new border type.
4. If you want to change the border line style, click Draw borders down arrow, and choose Pen Style. Pen Style palette drop-down menu appears as in Figure B.35.
5. Click the border style you want. The mouse pointer changes to pen style. Click the table row or column line. You can see the selected portion of your table changes to the new border style.
6. If you want to change the border width or border colour, repeat steps 2 to 4 with the border width and border colour button. After making a change, click the Border button if necessary to redraw the table with the new formatting.

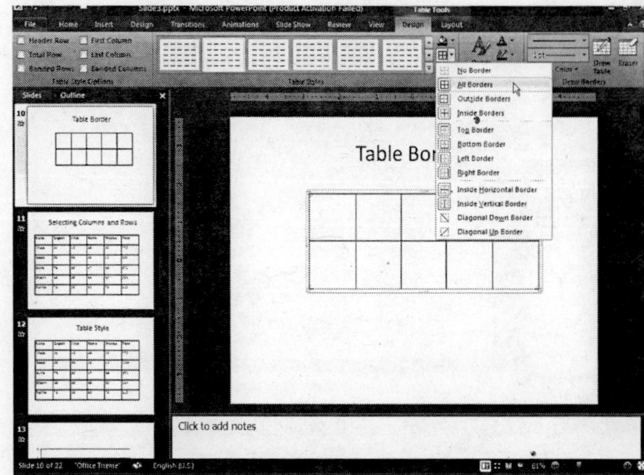

Figure B.34 Borders palette

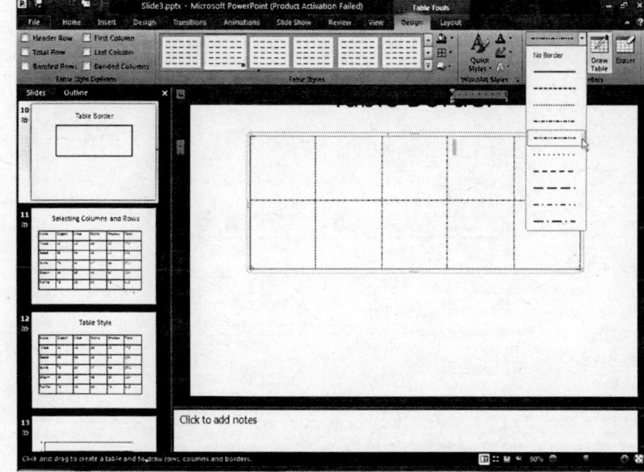

Figure B.35 Borders Style drop down list appears

7. If you want to delete borders between table cells, click Eraser, or press and hold (Shift) key while the pointer is a pencil, and then click the borders that you want to delete.

Creating a Chart Slide

PowerPoint creates or modifies a chart using MS-Graph. MS-Graph is a graphing program shared by all components like *Word, Excel, PowerPoint.* So if you know how to create graphics in one of the components, you can use the same technique in other components also.

Charts that you create will be embedded in PowerPoint 2010, and the chart data is stored in an Excel 2010 worksheet that is incorporated in the PowerPoint file.

➡ **To create a chart slide, do this:**

1. Click the **New slide** in the **Slides** group. It display, the slides after which you want to add the chart slide. Or click the **Insert** tab, on the **Illustrations** group, click the **Chart** icon.
2. The new slide appears. In the center of the slide contains *table, chart, Media clips, SmartArt*, etc., as seen in Figure B.36.
3. Click the Insert Chart in the new slide. The Insert Chart dialog box appears as seen in Figure B.37.

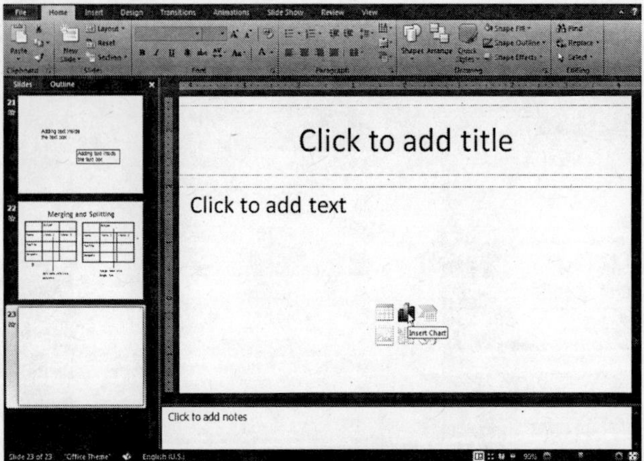

Figure B.36 A new slide contains chart

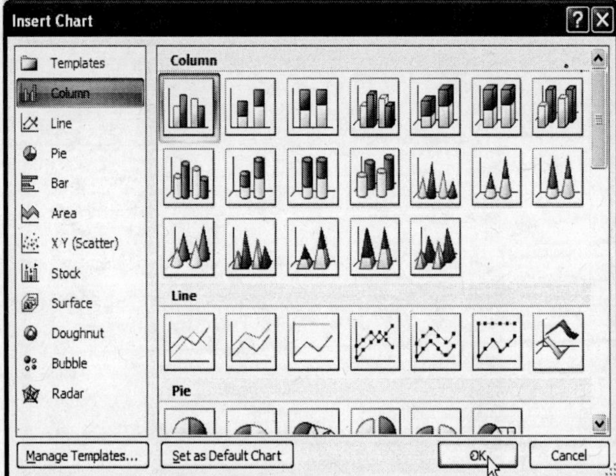

Figure B.37 Insert Chart dialog box

4. Select the chart type under **Templates**. For example, if you click the Column chart type, there are different types of columns in the column section. Select the desired chart type. Click OK.
5. A sample chart appears in the Excel worksheet and the data sheet window containing the sample data for the chart overlays as seen in Figure B.38.
6. In Excel to replace the sample data, click a cell on the worksheet, and then type the data that you want. When you enter data in Excel you can see the PowerPoint the data as well chart also simultaneously appearing in the PowerPoint (Figure B.39).
7. In Excel, click the Office Button and then click **Save As**.
8. In the **Save As** dialog box in the **save in:** list, select the folder or drive that you want to save the worksheet.
9. In the **File name:** box, type a new name for the file.
10. Click **Save**.

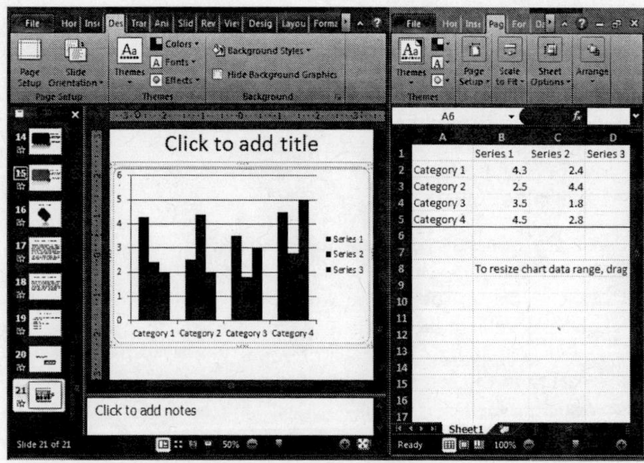

Figure B.38 Sample Data graphically displayed

11. In Excel, Click the Office button and then click Close.

Entering Data in the Datasheet

Entering data in the Datasheet consists of two steps. These are:

- Entering the labels in the left most column and top most row.
- Entering the data to be graphed in the remaining cells.

➡ **To enter data in a datasheet, do this:**

1. Click the top cell in column A and enter the category labels across the top row. (The categories along the rows appear along the *x-axis* in the graph).
2. Enter the name of the data series along the column, starting from the first cell labeled. Each row represents the data series for each category.
3. Enter the values for each category in the cell (See Figure B.40).

Now type the numbers for each cell along the column and press (Enter). For practice, enter the numbers given below.

20.4	27.4	29.4
30.6	38.6	31.6
45.9	46.9	43.9
32.1	31.6	45

B.4.2 Adding Clip Art Pictures

Clip Art gallery is a collection of graphic files in PowerPoint that you can insert in presentations. It has built a gallery of Clip Art images into the Clip Art gallery. But you also have your own collection of artwork available.

PowerPoint can help you select an appropriate piece of art for your slides by looking at keywords in your presentation and trying to find pictures to match.

Inserting a picture from the Clip Art Gallery

1. Select the slide that contain a Clip Art slide.
2. Click the Clip Art icon in the slide. A Clip Art task pane appears (Figure B.41).

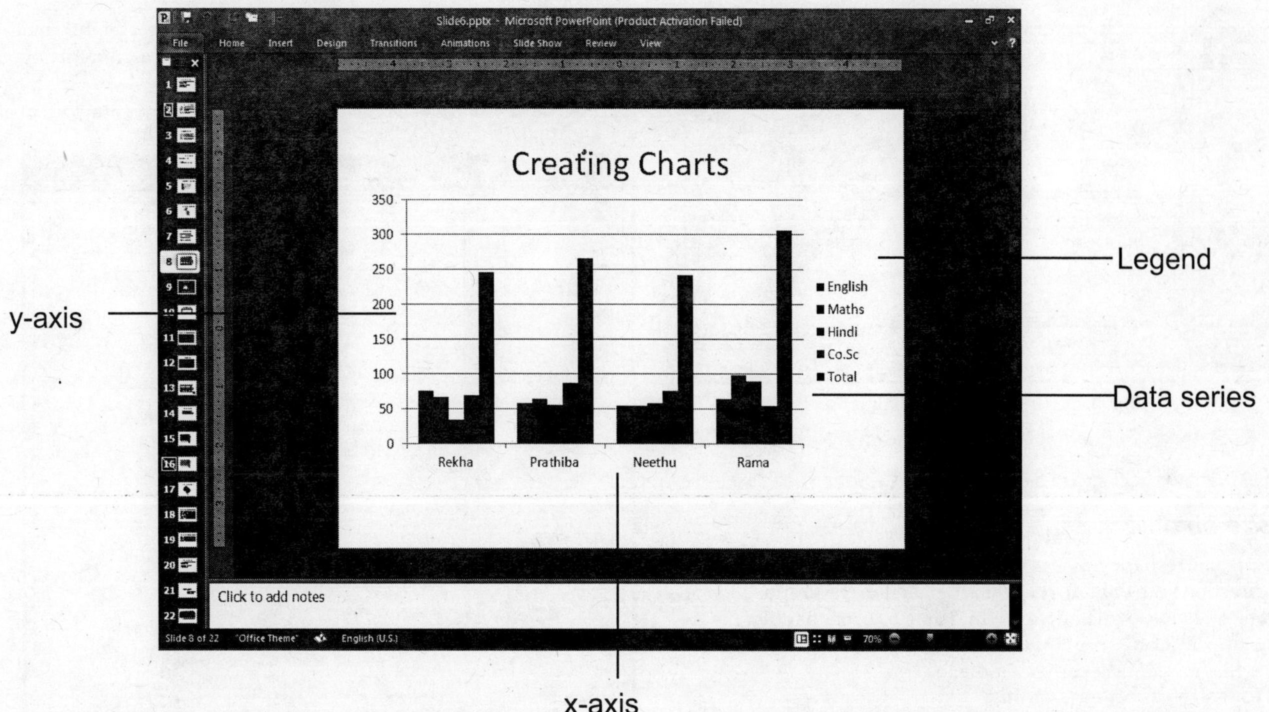

Figure B.39 A Sample Chart appearing in PowerPoint

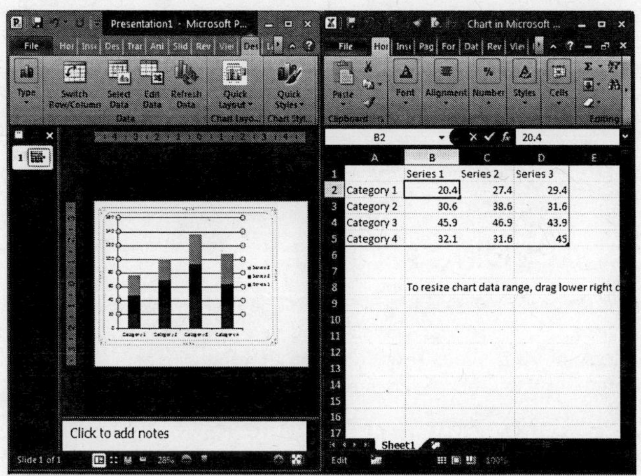

Figure B.40 Entering Data in the cell B2 of the datasheet

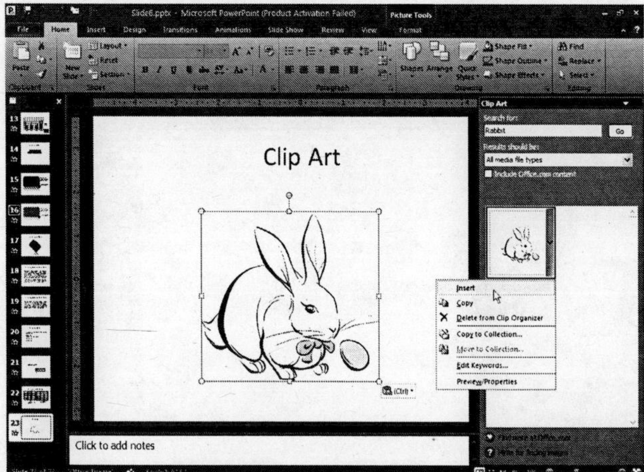

Figure B.41 Clip Art task pane

3. Select the current entry in the Search for: box or click in the box if there is no entry, type animals, and then click Go. The task pane displays animals list.
4. Click the selected picture, once it appears at the center of the slide or select the picture, it appears a small arrow at the right of the side of the picture. Click the arrow and then Insert (See Figure B.41).
5. When you are finished using the Clip Gallery, click the Close button on the Clip Gallery title bar.

B.4.3 Inserting Other Objects

You may want to add a particular graphic to a presentation but not maintain it in the Clip Gallery. You can insert picture from another application.

➡ **To insert a picture from a file, do this:**

1. Click where you want to insert the picture.
2. On the **Insert** tab, in the **Images** group, click **Picture**.
3. The **Insert Picture** dialog box appears as shown in Figure B.42.
3. Search a file in the **Look in:** drop-down list.

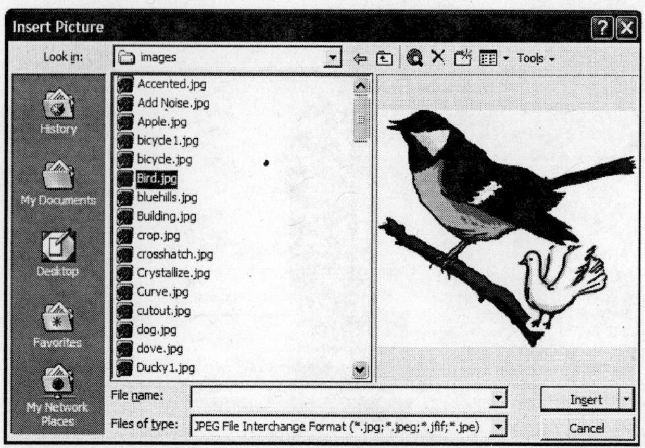

Figure B.42 Insert Picture dialog box

4. Click **Insert** button to place the graphic on the current slide.

B.4.4 Resizing and Scaling an Object

Resize an object

To resize or reshape an object, drag one of the object's handles in the direction you want. If you want to maintain the proportions of the object, hold down Shift key while drag a corner handle. If you want the object to grow out from its current center, hold down Ctrl while you drag a corner handle.

➡ **To resize an object, do this:**

1. Select the object you want to resize.
2. Drag a size handle until the object gets desired shape and size as you want (See Figure B.43). Or

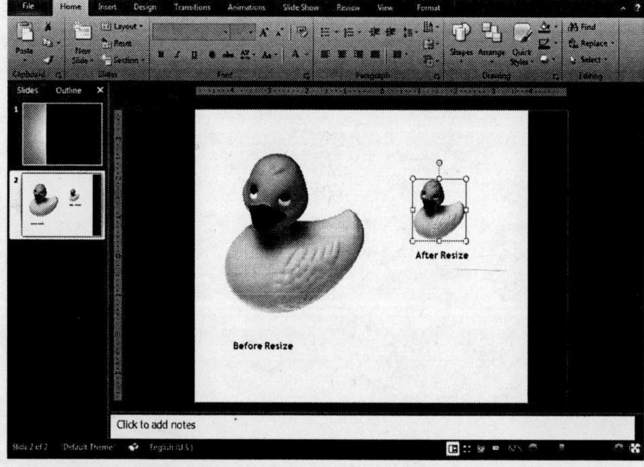

Figure B.43 Object has to be resized

Scaling an object

Rather than drag objects into position, you can set object placements and sizing on the size and position tabs of the Format Picture.

➡ **To scale an object, do this:**

1. Select the object you want to scale.
2. Click the **Picture Tools** contextual **Format** tab in the **Size** group.
4. Enter the percentage you want change in the **Height:** and **Width:** boxes. *Alternatively*, click the **Size and Position** dialog box launcher dialog box.
5. The **Format Picture** dialog box appears as shown in Figure B.44.

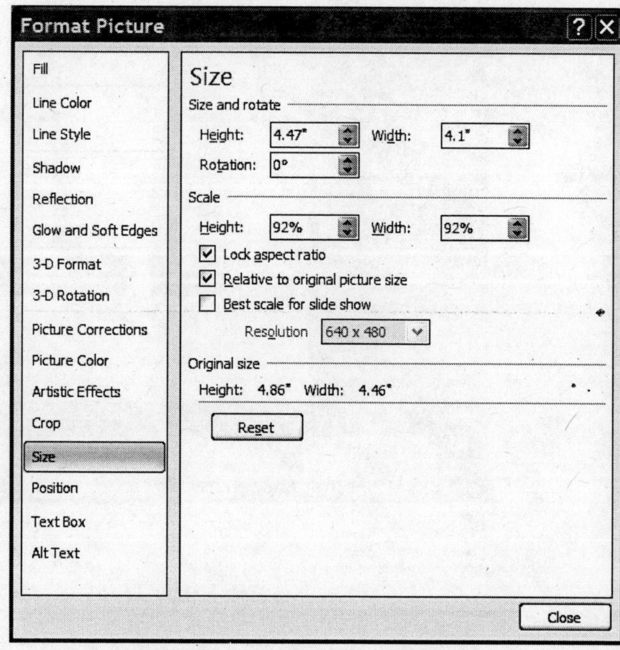

Figure B.44 Format Picture dialog box

6. Click the Size tab, under the Scale, enter the percentage you want change in the **Height:** and **Width:** box.

☞ *To maintain the ratio between the object's height and width whenever to resize it, select the Lock aspect ratio check box on the size tab.*

B.5 PROVIDING AESTHETICS

PowerPoint is designed to give your slide presentations a consistent look. There are four ways that PowerPoint helps you control the look of your slides – with design templates, masters, colour schemes, and layouts of slides.

B.5.1 Enhancing Text Presentation

Enhancing the text presentation makes your presentation in a more presentable manner by formatting features, such as bold, italic, underline, alignment of text, font size, font style, colours, etc.

Aligning Text in a Slide

Alignment is the way text is placed between the margins of a page or a text box on a slide. The alignment choices are summarized in Table B.1.

Table B.1 Aligning Text in a Slide

Alignment	Effect
Left Align	The left margin of each line is at the same place on the left, while the right edge of each line ends wherever appropriate (called a *ragged right edge*).
Right Align	The right margin of each line is at the same place on the right. The left edge of each line falls in a different place, depending on the contents of the line (called a *ragged left edge*).
Center	Each line is centered. The left and right edges of each line will differ, depending upon the number and size of characters in the line.
Justified	Each line starts at the left margin and ends at the right margin. There are no ragged edges.

➡ **To align the text, do this:**

1. Select the text, then click the Left, Center, or Right alignment button on the Formatting toolbar. *Alternatively*, click the **Paragraph Launcher** dialog box and select the desired option in the alignment section.

Changing Fonts

Fonts are also called *typefaces* in computer programs. There are groups of characters that share the same style or look.
Fonts are divided into two groups.

- On the basis of the way, characters are spaced – *monospaced* or *proportionately* spaced (See Figure B.45). In *monospaced* font, all the characters have the same width. In *proportionately* spaced font the widths are different, i.e., w has more width than i.
- On the basis of the finishing strokes. That is Serif and Sans serif. In Sans Serif the finishing strokes are not there (See Figure B.45). In Serif fonts the finishing strokes are there.

While choosing fonts for your presentation, keep in mind the following points:

- Using too many fonts on the same slide looks unprofessional. It is advisable to use one font for the headline and another for the rest of the text or a third font for bulleted items. But do not use too many fonts.
- Fancy fonts, do not work well on slides, especially for headlines.
- Sans - Serif fonts tend to have a more authoritative and bold look.
- Proportional fonts work extremely well in body text.

➡ **To change the font of any text in a slide, do this:**

1. Select the text you want to change.
2. Click the **Home** tab and choose **Font** group. Or select the text, a mini toolbar appears. Select the font themes appears choose the desired font you want to apply. Or
3. Click the right mouse button and choose Font... from shortcut menu. The Font dialog box appears as in Figure B.46. Click the Font drop-down list and select the required font. *Alternatively*, click the down arrow to the right of the Font box on the Ribbon command. A drop-down list of available fonts appears.

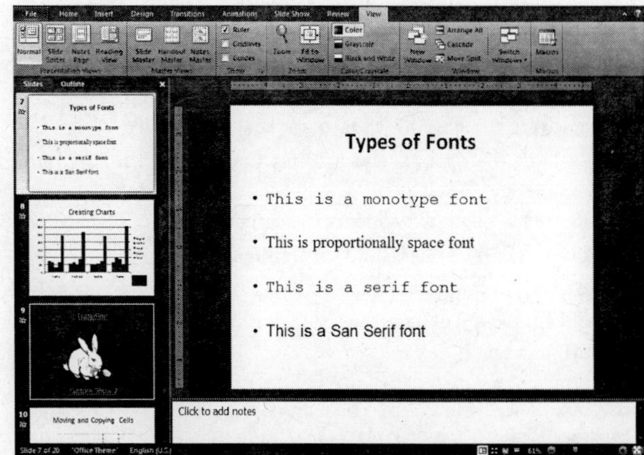

Figure B.45 Display of various kind of fonts

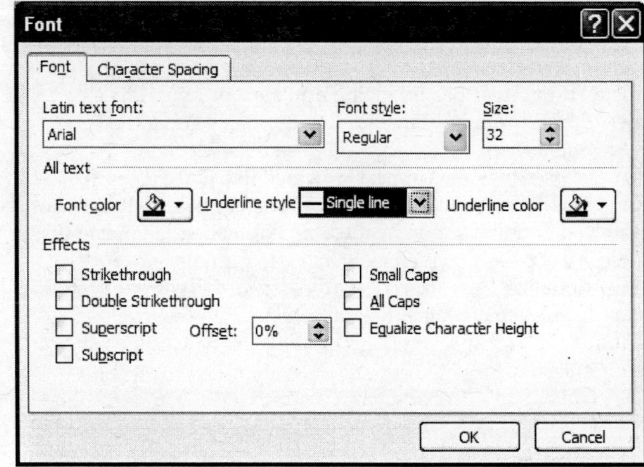

Figure B.46 Selecting font using dialog box

☞ *Right type and size of font creates good impression on your audience.*

4. Click the font you want to use. The selected text changes to the selected font.

Changing the Text Size

Font size is measured in *points*, which is a height measurement, each point is 1/72 of an inch.

➡ **To change the size of text, do this:**

1. Select the text you want to change.
2. Click the **Home** tab and choose **Font** group. Or select the text. A mini toolbar appears. Choose the desired font size you want to apply. Or click the right mouse button and choose Font... . In the Font dialog box that appears, click the size drop-down list and choose the desired size or type the size. *Alternatively*, click the arrow to the right of the Font Size box on the Ribbon command to see the list of available sizes.
3. Select the new size. Or
4. Click the Increase and decrease font size on the Ribbon command.

Adding Special Effects to Text

One of the easiest ways to make text stands out is to add special formatting effects to *characters*, *sentences*, or *paragraphs*. PowerPoint makes these tasks very easy.

➡ **To add special effect, do this:**

1. Select text to which you want to apply special effect.
2. In the Font dialog box, the options Font style: box has the following:
   - Regular—The text appears in regular way.
   - Bold—Text appears bold or highlighted.
   - Italic—Text appears italic.
   - Bold Italic—Text appears bold and italic.

   The All text has this option:
   - Font color— Specifies the colour of the selected text. In the box, select the color. You can see the colour under the bucket.
   - Underline style— Specifies whether selected text is in underlined. Click None to remove underlining.
   - Underline color— Specifies the color of the underlined text. This option remains unavailable until you apply an underline style.

   The Effect Areas has following options:
   - Strikethrough—Draws a line through selected text.
   - Superscript—Text appears raised like x^2y
   - Subscript—Text appears lowered like H_20
   - Small caps—Selected text appears reduce size. It does not affect on numbers, punctuation, non-alphabetic characters.
   - All caps—It converts lowercase to capitals.
   - Equalize Character Height—It reformats text effects to apply an even character height to text.

The font style and special effects of above explanation as shown in Figure B.47.

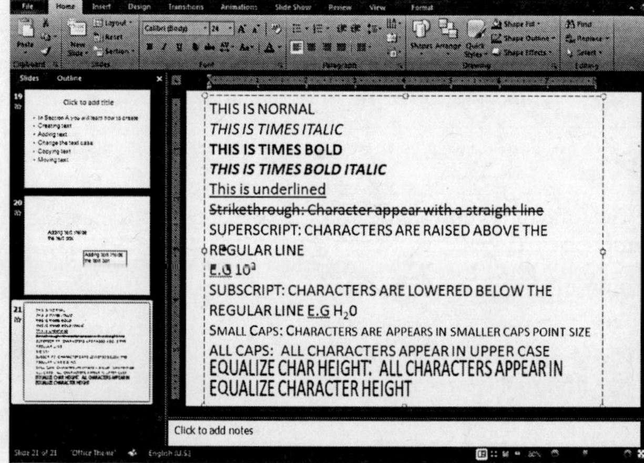

Figure B.47 The font style effect

Changing Text Colour

➡ **To change the text colour, do this:**

1. Select the text you want to change.
2. In the **Home** tab, click the **Font** group. Click the font colour by pointing arrow. The font colors theme palette appears.
3. Move the mouse pointer over the colour, you can see the effect changes in the text. Choose the desired colour you want to apply to the text.

Applying Character Formatting using the Keyboard

Most of the character formatting can also be applied using the keyboard shortcut as discussed in the following sections.

➡ **To format using shortcut keys, do this:**

1. Select the text you want to format and use the shortcut key combinations for the desired formatting effects.

Format	Shortcut
Bold	Ctrl+B
Italic	Ctrl+I
Underline	Ctrl+U
Superscript	Ctrl+Shift++
Subscript	Ctrl+=
Copy formatting	Ctrl+Shift+C
Paste formatting	Ctrl+Shift+V
Remove formatting	Ctrl+Spacebar
Change case of letters	Shift+F3
Change the font	Ctrl+Shift+F
Change the font size	Ctrl+Shift+P
Increase the font size	Ctrl+Shift+>
Decrease the font size	Ctrl+Shift+<

Bullets and Numbering

PowerPoint 2010 provides the ability to create bulleted, numbered lists. A bulleted list is a list with a graphic character, very small picture or bullet at the beginning of each paragraph in the list. You might also consider using SmartArt for many bulleted or numbered lists. The style of each list type can be changed and different bullets can be used.

➡ **To create a bulleted list, do this:**

1. Select the text you want to add bullet.
2. Click the down arrow of the bullets command icon, in the Paragraph group.

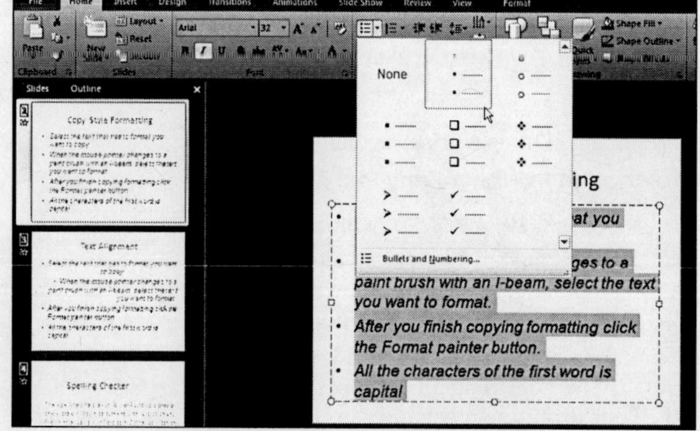

Figure B.48 Selecting Bullets in the paragraph group

3. A drop-down list shows with the pre-defined bullet list.

4. Select the desired bullet type from the drop-down list. For example, we have selected the circled bulleted List (See Figure B.48).
5. The selected bullet type is applied to the text as seen in Figure B.49.

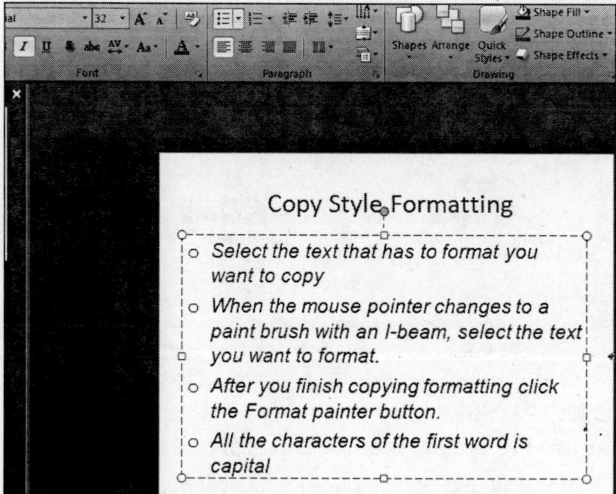

Figure B.49 Bullet applied in selected paragraph

Adding Symbols

PowerPoint provides a full range of special symbol characters like the copyright or trademarks, registration symbol, etc.

➡ **To add symbol, do this:**

1. Click the **Insert** tab. In the **Symbols** group, click Symbol icon. The **Symbol** dialog box appears as shown in Figure B.50.

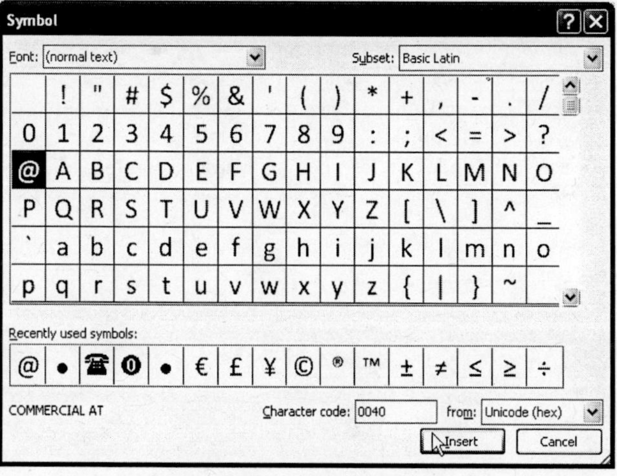

Figure B.50 Symbol dialog Box

2. By default, the **Font:** box is set to Symbol. Click the down arrow to see the choices for fonts, each of which provides a different set of symbols.
3. Select the font with the symbols you want to use. Select the symbols to insert by clicking it once. Or click the Insert button to insert the symbol.
4. In the **Subset:** name box, specify a subset of special characters for the selected font, if available. A font subset can include an extended list of language characters, such as Greek or Russian (Cryillic), or a category of characters, such as Currency Symbols.
5. In Symbol list represents the full list of symbols that can be inserted from the selected Font and Subset.
6. In **Recently used symbols:** box, lists the most frequently used symbols that have been inserted.
7. **Description:** Provides a meaningful description of the selected symbol. For example, if the ® symbol is selected, the description will appear as Registered sign.
8. **Character code:** list box displays a unique code representing a symbol.
9. **From:** drop-down list, specifies the character set on which the character code is based on. ASCII is a character-encoding standard based on the English alphabet. Unicode is a character-encoding standard that enables almost all of the written languages in the world to be represented by using a single character set.
10. Click Close to leave the Symbol dialog box and return to your slide.

Removing Bullets and Numbering

➡ **To remove bullets and numbering, do this:**

1. Select the text or placeholders you want to remove bullets and number form.
2. In the **Paragraph** group of **Home** tab, choose the bulleted down pointing arrow, a bullet palette list appears, choose None. Or
   You can press Backspace to remove bullet or numbering from an item in a list. PowerPoint automatically adjusts the number sequence of a numbered list.
3. If you want to reorganize the elements of the list after removing bullets and numbering, use the promote and demote bullet on the Quick Access toolbar.

B.5.2 Working with Themes Color and Line Style

In earlier version colour and line styles, contains a colour scheme that provides the various parts of a presentation with a coordinated set of eight default colours. The most distinctive design element of the presentation is the background, so the first colour in colour scheme is background colour. Other seven colours effectively complement the background colour and are applied to text, charts, and other objects that appear against the background.

A layout determines where text, graphics, charts and other elements appear on an individual slide. A theme determines the look of an entire presentations' colours, fonts, and overall format. A layout is to a slide what a theme is to an entire presentation. Both specify the way a slide or overall presentation looks.

In Latest version of PowerPoint 2010, Themes refer a set of unified design element that provides a look for your document by using *colors, fonts* and *graphics*. You can use predefined themes that come with PowerPoint, or you can define your own.

ß **To select a New slide and apply themes effect, do this:**

1. Click the **Home** tab, in the **slides** group. Click the **New Slide** down pointing arrow. PowerPoint opens a layout list from which you can select (See Figure B.51).
2. When you click to select a layout, PowerPoint inserts a new slide at that location in your presentation with that layout.
3. Click the **Design** tab, in the **Themes** group. In the Themes group click the **More** button at the lower right corner. A list of themes appears as seen in Figure B.52.
4. Select a desired style you want to apply your presentation.
5. If you want to modify the theme, select from the *Font*, *Colors*, and *Effect* buttons to the right of the Themes group.
6. After you have modified a theme to your liking, click down arrow next to the Ribbon's themes and select Save Current Theme.
7. The **Save Current Theme** dialog box appears as seen in Figure B.53.

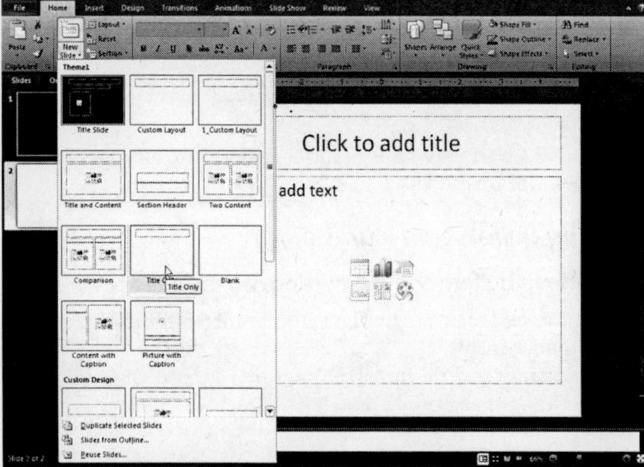

Figure B.51 Selecting a New Slide from Home tab

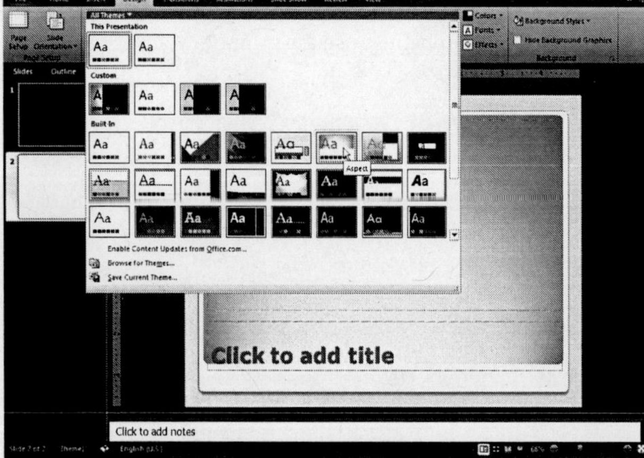

Figure B.52 Selecting a Themes from Design tab

B. In the **Save in:** drop-down list contains a default folder (Document Themes).

9. Give the name in the **File name:** in the drop-down list.
10. Click the **Save** button.

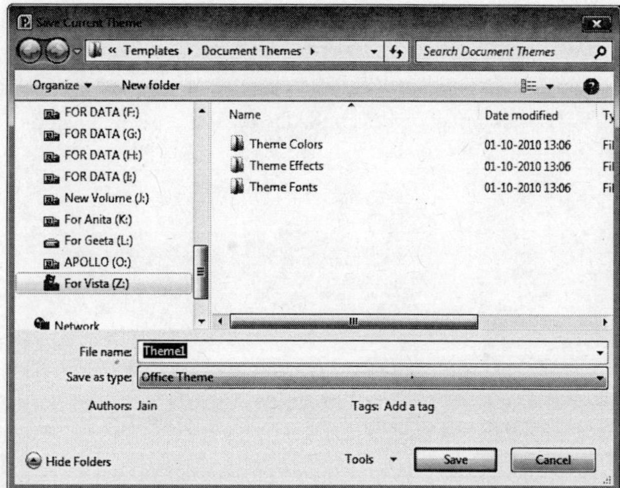

Figure B.53 Save Current Theme dialog box

11. After giving a name to the theme, PowerPoint makes that theme available in the Themes list.

Change the Color, Style and Weight of a Line

You can change the look of a line shape by changing its colour, line style, or weight.

- Add a Quick Style to a line
- Change the color of a line
- Make a line dashed
- Change the weight of a line

Add a Quick Style to a line

Quick Styles for lines include theme colours from the document theme, shadow, line styles and three-dimensional perspectives.

1. Select the line that you want to change.

   If you want to change multiple lines, select first line, and then press and hold Ctrl key while you select other lines.
2. Under **Drawing Tools** on the **Format** tab, in the **Shape Styles** group, click the Quick style that you want.
3. To see more Quick Styles, click the **More** button (See Figure B.54).

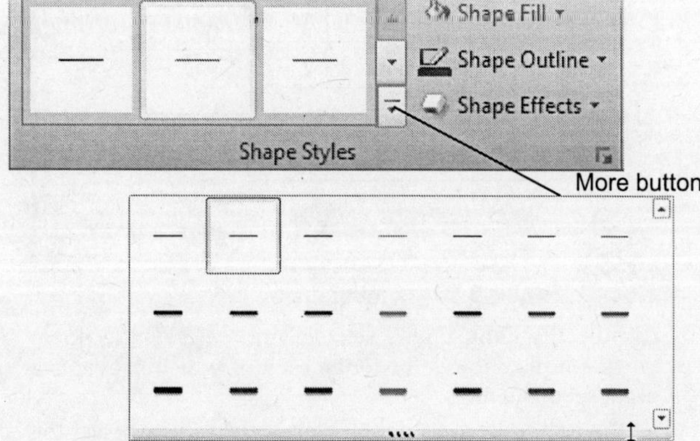

Figure B.54 Select the line style from the More button

Change the Color of a Line

1. Select the line that you want to change.
2. Under the **Drawing Tools**, on the **Format** tab, in the **Shape Styles** group, click the arrow next to **Shape Outline**, and then click the colour that you want (See Figure B.55).

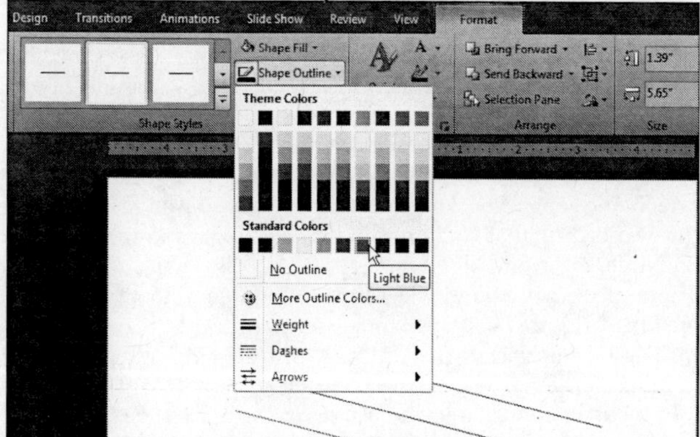

Figure B.55 Select the color of a line from the Shape Outline drop-down list

3. To change to a colour that is not in the theme colours, click **More Outline Colors**, and then either click the colour that you want on the **Standard tab**, or mix your own colour on the **Custom tab**. Custom colours and colours on the Standard tab are not updated if you later change the document theme.

Make a Line Dashed

You can change *thickness, style* and *color*. To format a line first select it by clicking it. For selecting multiple lines press and hold the (Shift) key while you click the lines. The selected lines appear dimmed and dashed.

1. Select the line that you want to change.
2. Under **Drawing Tools**, on the **Format** tab, in the **Shape Styles** group, click the arrow next to **Shape Outline**.
3. Point to **Dashes**, and then click the line style that you want (See Figure B.56).

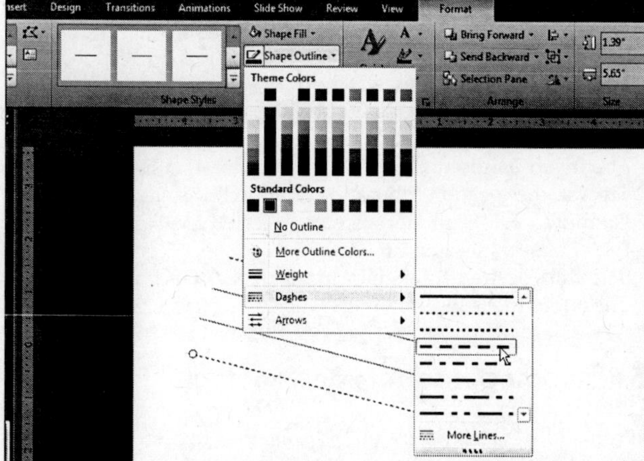

Figure B.56 Select the line Dashes from the Shape Outline drop-down list

4. To create a custom style, click **More Lines**, and then choose the options that you want.

Change the weight of a line

1. Select the line that you want to change. If you want to change multiple lines, select the first line, and then press and hold Ctrl while you select the other lines.
2. Under **Drawing Tools**, on the **Format** tab, in the **Shape Styles** group, click the arrow next to **Shape Outline**.
3. Point to **Weight**, and then click the line weight that you want (See Figure B.57).

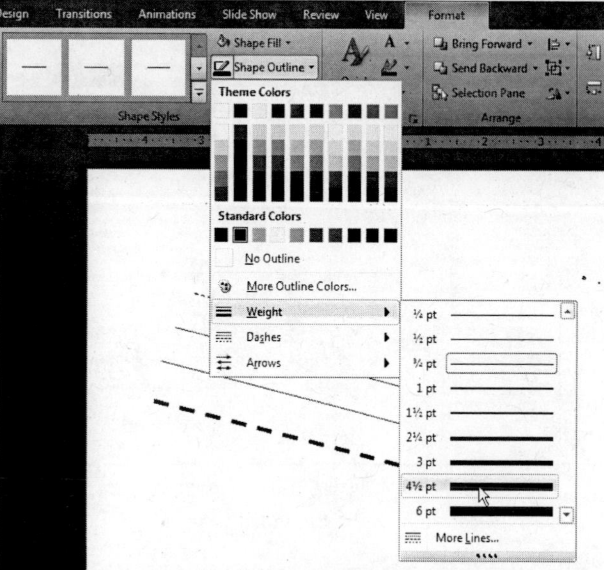

Figure B.57 Select the line weight from the Shape Outline drop-down list

4. To create a custom style, click **More Lines**, and then choose the options that you want.

B.5.3 Adding Movie or (Video) and Sound

You insert a music, sound, or video clip on a slide where you want it to play during a slide show. You can choose either to have the sound or video start automatically when you move to the slide, or to have the sound or video start only when you click its icon during a slide show.

One of the exciting new features in PowerPoint 2010 is that you now have the ability to edit and style the video clips you add to your slides. You can insert video files from your computer, download them from the Web, or insert video clips from Microsoft Office Clip Art. This enables you to add life to your slides and share compelling stories in a way that is sure to hold your audience's attention.

PowerPoint supports videos in various formats, such as Audio Video Interchange (.avi), Motion Pictures Group (.mpg) and Movie (.mov).

➡ **To insert a video from a Clip Art video, do this:**

1. Insert the new slide or display the slide that will contain **Media Clip Art**.
2. Click the **Insert** tab.

3. Click **Video** button under the **Media** Group. A drop-down list appears as seen in Figure B.58.

Figure B.58 Selecting Video from file from the Insert tab

4. Select the Video from File option from the list.
5. The **Insert Video** dialog box appears as seen in Figure B.59.

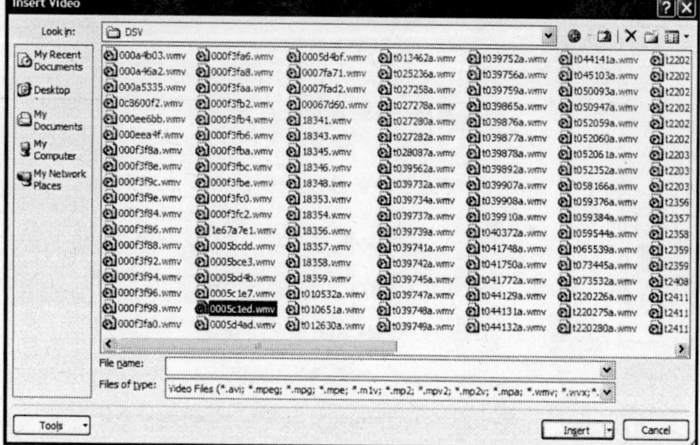

Figure B.59 Insert video dialog box

6. Browse the location where the video is saved on your computer.
7. Select the desired video file. Then click **Insert** button.
8. The desired video is inserted in the slide as seen in Figure B.60.

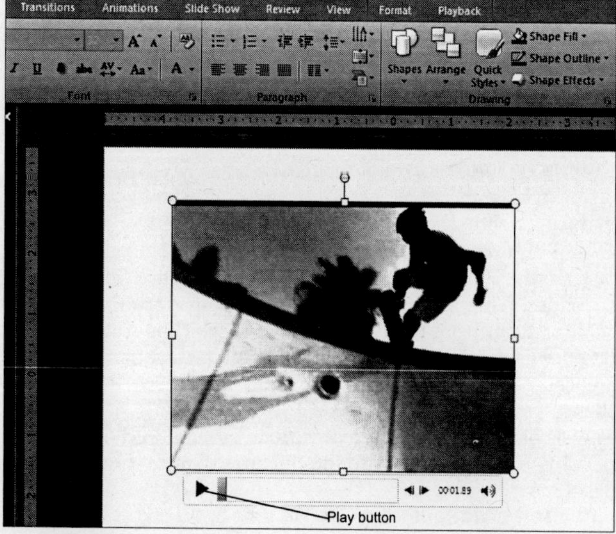

Figure B.60 The video file is inserted in the presentation

9. Drag the sizing handles of the image to set the size of your video, and then drag it to the location you want.
10. Play the video by clicking the Play button.

Adding Sound file

In PowerPoint 2010, you can easily add sound effects, voiceovers and music to individual slides. You can add a soundtrack and narration to the presentation as well. Sound effects, such as music and voice recordings, can add another level of professionalism to slide presentations. Music is an effective way to introduce or end a presentation and it gives your audience something to listen to as they enter and leave the presentation room. You could play a movie theme song as background music for several slides, or play a voice recording that contains advertising slogans to insert on a single slide, for example.

There are many sound file formats. Two common types are wave files (with the .wav filename extension) and Musical Instrument Digital Interface (MIDI) files (with the .mid, .midi, or .rmi filename extension).

➡ **To insert a sound, into the slide, do this:**

1. Select the slide in which you want to insert the desired sound.
2. Click the **Insert** tab.
3. Click the **Audio** button under the **Media** group as seen in Figure B.61.

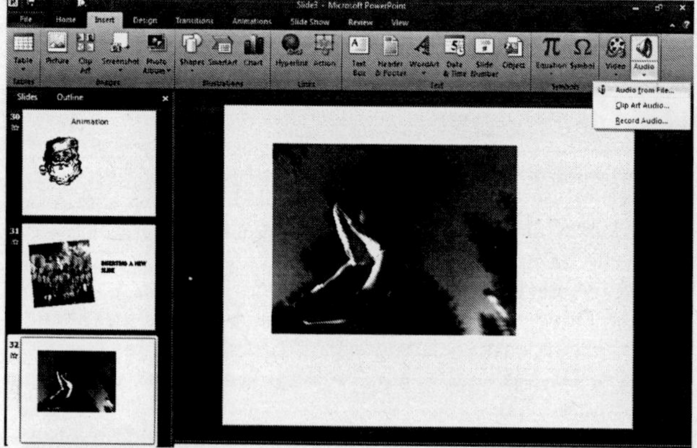

Figure B.61 Slecting Audio from file from the insert tab

4. A drop-down list appears.
5. Select the **Audio from file** option from the drop-down list as seen in Figure B.61.
6. The **Insert Audio** dialog box appears as seen in Figure B.62.
7. Browse the location where the sound clip is saved on your computer. For example, we have selected the Sample Music folder as seen in Figure B.62.
8. Select the desired sound clip and then click OK button.
9. The audio file is inserted in the slide as seen in Figure B.63.

B.5.4 Adding Headers and Footers

You can add *headers, footers* and *page numbers* to each of the slide or the Note Pages.

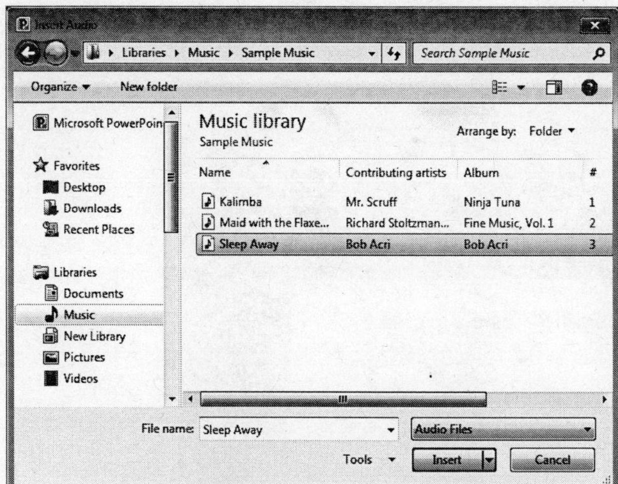

Figure B.62 Insert Sound dialog box

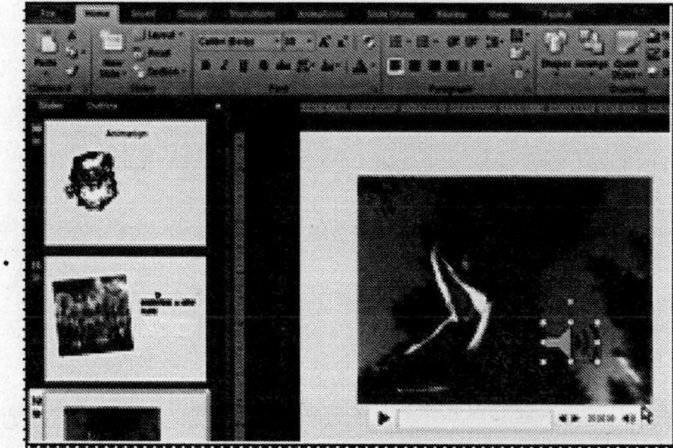

Figure B.63 The audio file is inserted in the presentation

➡ **To insert header and footer to the slide, do this:**

1. In the **Insert** tab, click **Header & Footer** in the **Text** group. Or In the **Print** Backstage view click **Edit Header & Footer** link option.
2. The **Header and Footer** dialog box appears. Now click the **Notes and Handouts** tab property sheet as in Figure B.64.

The Notes tab property sheet of Header and Footer dialog box offers the following options.

Date and time – If you select this option, the date and time appear in the upper-right corner of the page.

- Update automatically – select this option to print the actual date and time when printouts are made. Use the list box to select the format you would like the date and time to appear in.
- Fixed – Choose this option if you want to specify the specific date to be printed in text box.

Header – The header appears on the top left corner of the page. Enter the text for the header in the box below the option.

Page Number – The page numbers are shown as numerals only and appear in the lower-right corner of the page. Numbering is automatic increased once this option is on.

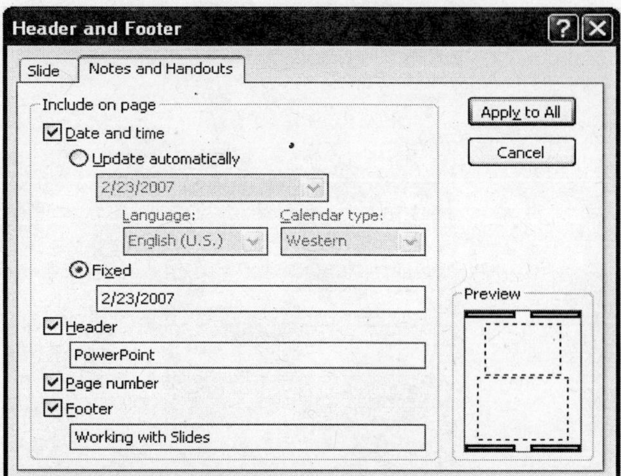

Figure B.64 Header and Footer dialog box with Notes and Handouts Tab

Footer – The footer appears in the lower-left corner of the page. Enter the text for the footer in the box below the option.

3. Click Apply to All to use the selected settings.

B.6 PRESENTATION OF SLIDES

B.6.1 Viewing a Presentation

PowerPoint offers five ways (*views*) to look at your presentation. Each view enables you to work on a different aspect of the presentation. The changes made in one view are also reflected in all other views.

To understand the function of views, consider that you are looking at a house. Now assume you are standing in front of a house. You see one view. Now you move to one of the sides and you see a different view of the same house. PowerPoint views also allow you to see a presentation in various ways.

The buttons located at the lower left corner of the PowerPoint window just above the status bar as shown in Figure B.65 help you to switch to different views.

In the following section, you will conceptually learn about the view.

Normal View

Normal view is the main editing view, where you write and design your presentation. The view has four working areas:

- Outline tab
- Slides tab
- Slide pane
- Notes pane

These panes let you work on all aspects of your presentation in one place. You can adjust the size of different panes by dragging the pane borders.

- **Outline tab:** Use the Outline tab to organize and develop the contents of your presentation. You can type all of the text of your presentation and rearrange bullet points, paragraphs and slides. The Outline tab shows your slide text in outline form.

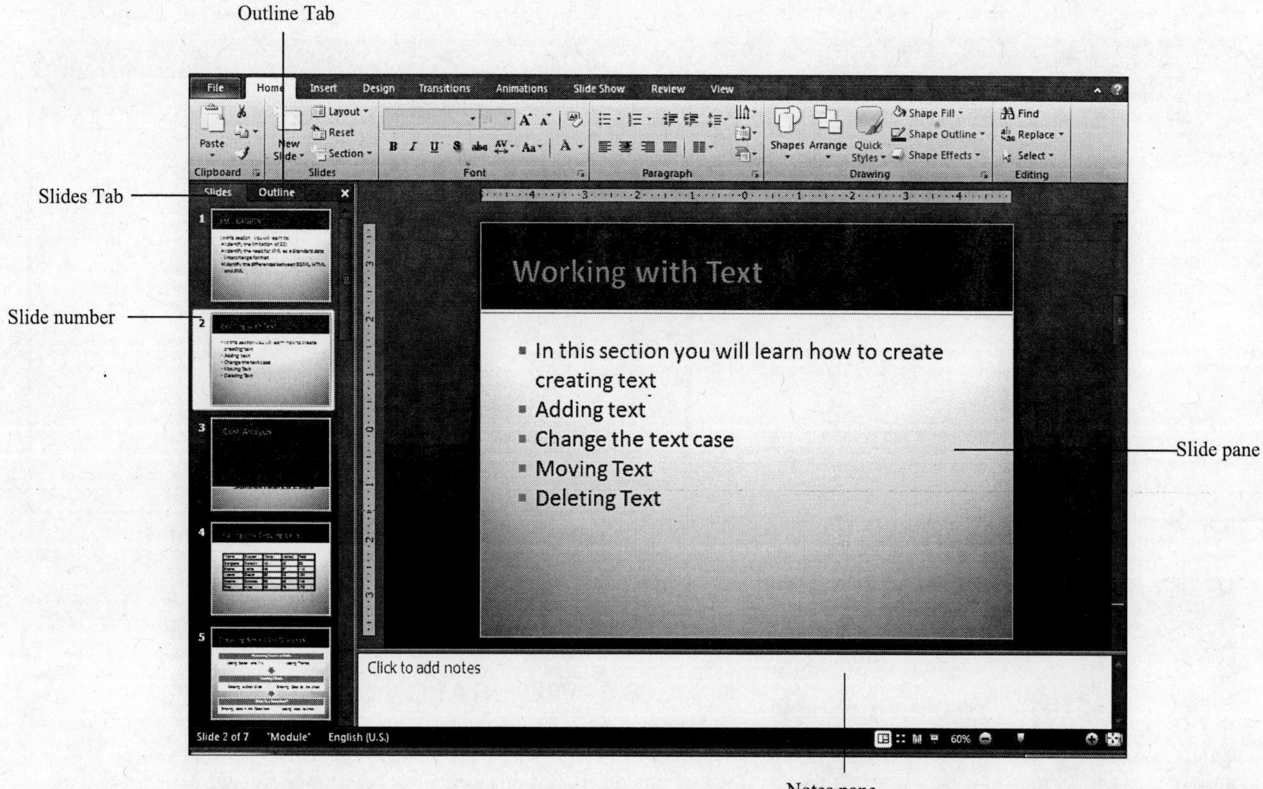

Figure B.65 Normal View

- **Slides tab:** This is a great place to view the slides in your presentation as thumbnail-sized images while you edit. The thumbnails make it easy for you to navigate through your presentation and to see the effect of any design changes. You can also easily rearrange, add or delete slides.
- **Slide pane***:* In the slide pane, you can see how your text looks on each slide. You can add SmartArt graphics, movies and sounds, create hyperlink and add animations to individual slides.
- **Notes pane:** The Notes pane lets you add speaker notes or information you want to share with the audience. If you want to have graphic in your notes, you must add the notes in Notes page view.

  These pane are also shown when you save a presentation as a Web page. The only difference is that the outline pane displays a table of contents so that you can navigate through the complete presentation.

Slide Sorter View

The slide sorter view is a view of your slides in thumbnail form. (See Figure B.66). Working in this view is like laying out the pages of your presentation or report on the table so that you can see them all at once. In this view, you can see the design consistency and the flow of your presentation. If need be, you can easily reorder the slides, copy or delete the slides.

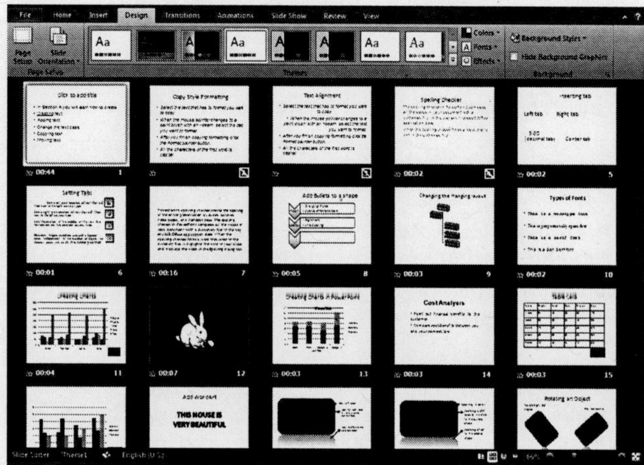

Figure B.66 PowerPoint's Slide Sorter View

Notes Page View

This view helps you to prepare the speaker notes used while making the presentation to your audience. Notes pages view produces a smaller version of the slide on the top part of a page and leaves the lower part free for notes or keypoints (See Figure B.67).

Slide Show View

This view of PowerPoint shows the progress of the presentation form slide to slide just like a real slide show. In this view, all *menus, toolbars, rulers, status bar, scrollbars,* and the Windows *taskbar* are removed from the screen (See Figure B.68).

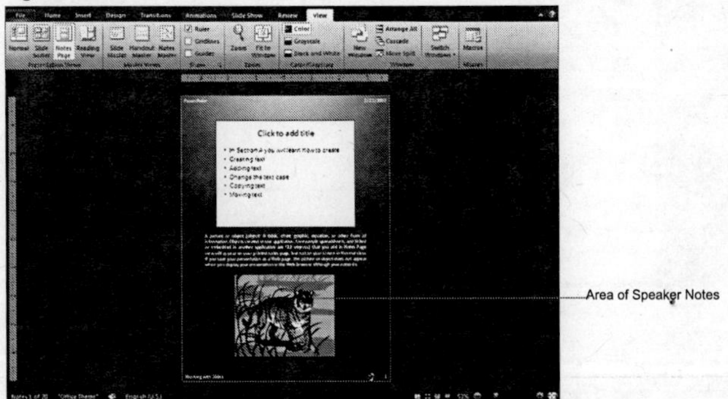

Figure B.67 PowerPoint's Notes Pages View

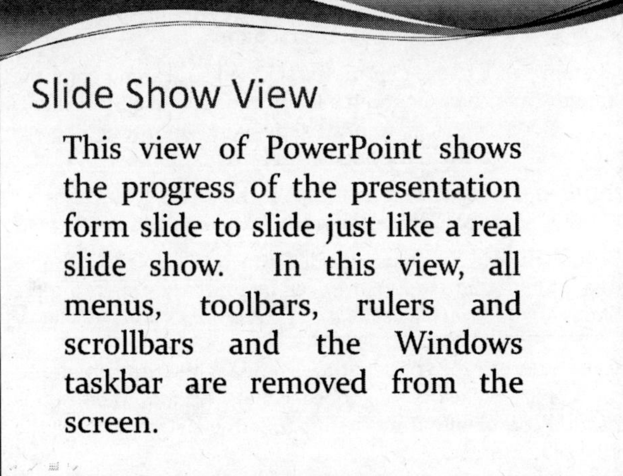

Figure B.68 Slide Show View

B.6.2 Choosing a Set Up for Presentation

With the options in the Set up dialog box, you can choose the type of show to run and how the show should proceed.

Starting the Slide Show

When you view a slide show, you have following options:

1. Click **Slide Show** tab in the **Start Slide Show group**, choose Slide Show from beginning or press (Shift)+(F5) keys together.
2. In the Slide show, you go to next slide, press (N) or click the (Backspace) key to go to the previous slide.

ß **To set a slide show option, do this:**

1. Click **Slide Show** tab in the **Set Up** group, choose Set Up Show icon. The Set Up Show dialog box appears as shown in Figure B.69.
2. To Show all slides in your presentation, Click All in the Show slides section.
3. To show a specific group of slides from your presentation, enter a starting and ending slide in From: and To: edit boxes.
4. To start a custom slide presentation that derives from another presentation, click Custom Show: drop-down list and then click the presentation that you want to view as a custom show.

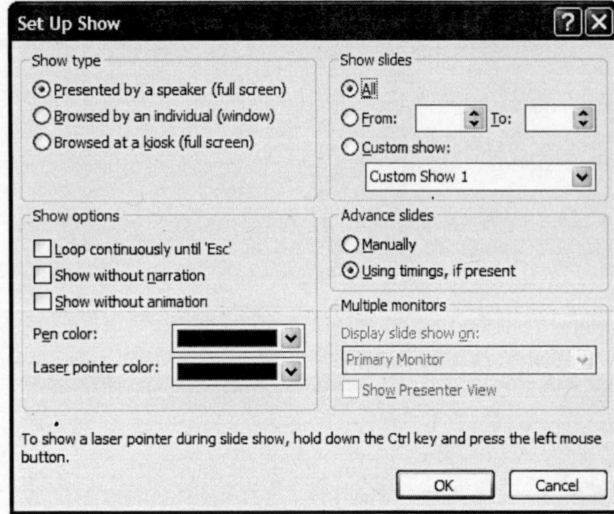

Figure B.69 The Set Up Show dialog box

Giving Special Show

PowerPoint offers three special slide show types. These are available on the Set Up Show dialog box (See Figure B.69).

1. *Click Presented by a Speaker (full screen)*: Is the traditional, full-screen slide show.
2. *Click Browsed by an Individual (window)*: Runs the slide show in a standard window.
3. *Click Browsed at a Kiosk (full screen)*: It displays a full screen as a self running show which restarts after 5 minutes.

B.6.3 Printing Slides and Handouts

Handout lets you include two, three, or six small images of the slides in your presentation. You can select the format when you print them.

Handouts can be created in the following two ways:

- Print the Handouts using the standard PowerPoint format, i.e., two, three or six slide on a page format.
- The Handout format can be customized to your requirement using the handout master.

If you make Handouts, PowerPoint shrinks the slides you have created and fits them on a page, according to the option you choose in the print Backstage view. To use standard Handout formats, you only have to select the number of slides you want to print on a page when you take the printouts for Handouts.

☞ *The header, footers, page numbers and the date on each handout will be printed if you have selected any of these items on your Notes Pages. The same is automatically applied to your Handouts.*

In case you want to have different headers, footers, page numbers or dates on your Handouts as compared to the Notes Pages then you are required to change these in the Headers and Footer dialog box.

☞ *The golden rule in presentations is "Say more than you show and handout more than you say". Therefore the material that you hand out (either before or after your presentation) should be more than just pictures of your slides.*

Printing Handouts

You can print your entire presentation – slides, outline, notes and audience handouts. You can also print specific slides, handouts, notes pages, or outline pages.

➡ **To print handouts, do this:**

1. Open the presentation you want to print.
2. Click the **File** tab, the Backstage view appears.
3. To click one or multiple slides per page in handout format, under **Handouts**, click the number of slides you want per page, and whether you want them to appear in order vertically or horizontally (See Figure B.70).
4. After applying the desired option, click OK.

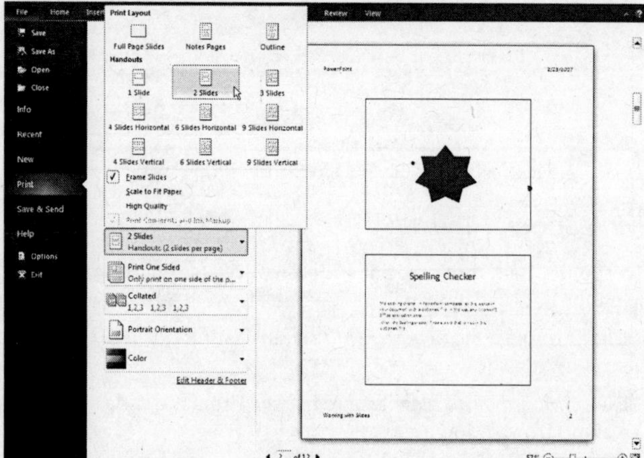

Figure B.70 Selecting slides per page in handout format in the File tab

Printing Slides

In PowerPoint 2010, you can either print all the slides or the current slide of a presentation. In addition, you can decide how many slides you want to print on a single page.

➡ **To print a slides, do this:**

1. Open the presentation that you want to print.
2. Click the **File** tab on the ribbon, click **Print** tab. The **Print** Backstage view appears as shown in Figure B.71.
3. The name of the currently selected printer is shown at the under **Printer** drop-down arrow. To print the presentation on a different printer, select the desired printer from the **Printer** drop-down list.
4. Specify the number of copies you want to print, for each slide in the **Copies:** spinner box.
5. The **Setting** drop-down list has the option which allows you to select the pages you want to print.

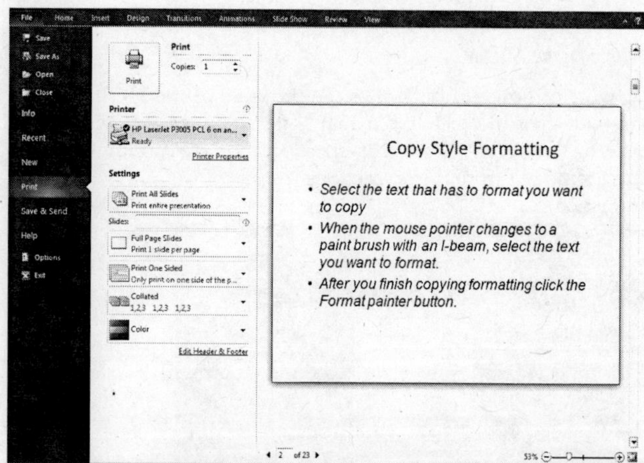

Figure B.71 Print Backstage view

Option	Description
Print All Slides	Choose Print All Slides option to print the entire presentation at one time.
Current slide	Choose the Current slide option to print the slide shown on the monitor.
Custom Range	Choose to print the selected slides, and enter the corresponding slide numbers in the **Slides:** edit box, e.g., to print slide 3 and 6 through 8, enter 3,6-8 in the Slides edit box.
Custom Show	Prints a certain custom show which has been set up. Each custom shows appears on the list.
Print Hidden Slides	If slides are hidden (do not display during a slide show), they can be printed by checking the *Print Hidden Slides* check box.

6. **Collate:** Specify if you want to arrange while printing multiple copies. When you choose collate option, each set is printed completely from first page to the last page. Then the next set is printed.
7. Click the Color button, and select the colour setting for the printouts:
   - **Color**–This is default. When you use this settings with a black-and-white printer, it results in slides with grayscale or black backgrounds.
   - **Grayscale**–To print in grayscale, select the grayscale check box.
   - **Pure black & white option**–converts all colours in the presentation to either black or white. Prefer this option if you need to print on a printer that cannot print gray shades.

B.7 SLIDE SHOW

B.7.1 Running a Slide Show

When you develop a slide show in Slide Sorter view, you can get a preview of transition effects for all slides. But to see the transitions full-screen and to see animated or bulleted text slides, you must select the presentation as a slide show.

Assigning Slide Transitions

Slides transitions are the animation-like effects that occur in the slide show view, when you move from one slide to the next. There are a variety of transitions that can be applied to each or all slides including sounds.

➡ **To assign the transitions, do this:**

1. Select the slide(s) you want to add a transition effect.
2. Click the **Transitions** tab. In the **Transition to This slide** group, click down arrow and then select the effect that will be applied during the slide show. For example here we select *Flash* under **subtle** (See Figure B.72).

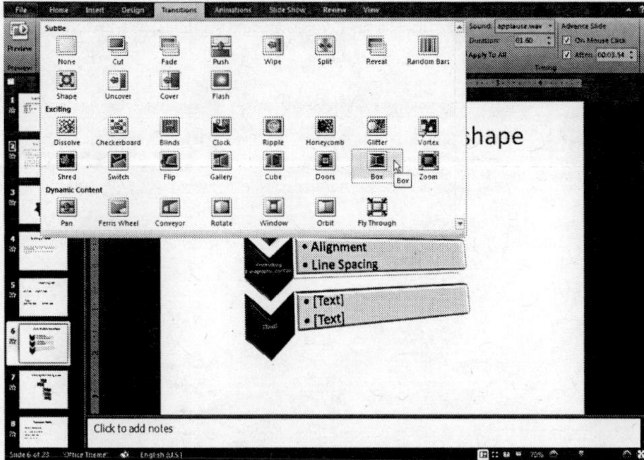

Figure B.72 Selecting Transition effect to Slide

3. If you Apply to all slides, click **Apply To All** in the **Timings** group.
4. Select the Sound option to give sound transitions to your slide show from the **Sound:** drop-down list in the **Timings** group.
5. The Advance section has two options for transition:
   - On mouse click check box – if you want the transition to take place on clicking the mouse.
   - Automatically after – in this case the transition takes place automatically after the time you specify in the *seconds* box.
6. After apply all options, you can see the effect in the Slide show. Click the **Slide Show** tab, in the **Start Slide Show** group, click **From Beginning** icon. Click the next button (i.e. →) to go to the next slide.
7. Click preview command to preview the current transitions effect in the **Preview** group

Controlling the Slide Show with a Mouse

During a slide Show, you can use the pop-up menu button. A pop-up menu appears as shown in Figure B.73. As mentioned earlier, the button appears in the lower left corner of the current slide as soon as you move the mouse pointer. You can then click the button to display slide show pop-up menu.

The Next and Previous commands on the pop-up menu let you move forward or backward through the slides in your slide show.

To move to a specific slide, click Go to Slide and then choose slide from the menu (See Figure B.73).

To stop a slide show at any time during a presentation, simply choose End Show from the pop-up menu.

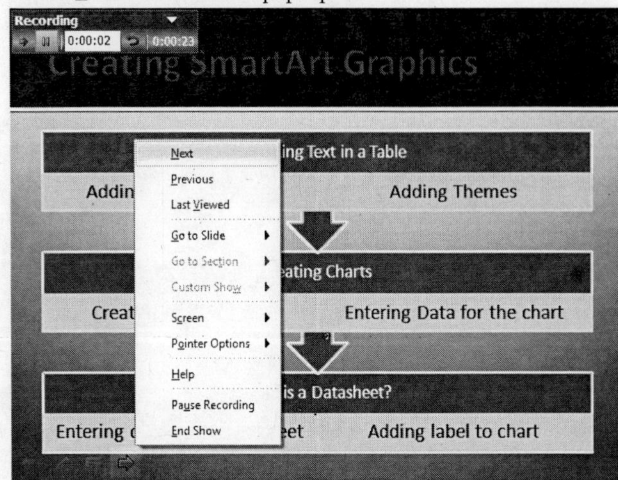

Figure B.73 Pop-up menu during Slide show

Controlling the Slide Show with a Keyboard

In addition to the slide show pop-up menu, you can use the keys listed in Table B.2 to control various aspects of the show.

Table B.2 Slide Show keyboard controls

Press This	To Perform This Action
Spacebar, →, ↓, PgDn, N	Advance to next slide.
Backspace, ←, ↑, PgUp, or P	Return to previous slide
Slide number + Enter	Go to slide number
B or period	Blacks/Unblacks the screen
W or comma	Whites/Unwhite the screen
Ctrl+A	Show mouse pointer as arrow
Ctrl+P	Show mouse pointer as pen
S or + (numeric keypad)	Stop/Restart automatic show
H	Go to next slide if hidden.
T	Rehearse – use new time
O	Rehearse – use original time
Esc, Ctrl+break or (-)	End Show

B.7.2 Transitions and Slide Timings

If you do not want to move through a slide show manually, there are two ways you can set the length of time a slide appears on the screen. One way is to set a time manually for each slide, and then run the slide show and view the timings you set. The other way is to use rehearsal feature, where you can record timings automatically as you rehearse. You can also ajdust the timings you have already set and then rehearse the new ones.

Setting Slide Show Timings Manually

1. On the **Slide Show** tab, in the **Set Up** group, click **Rehearse Timings** to start the show in rehearsal mode.
2. It starts a full-screen slide show in which you can rehearse your presentation.
3. The Rehearsal dialog box appears in the slide show as seen in Figure B.74. It starts slide timings in the first slide.
4. Click Next button in the Rehearsal dialog box, and fix the time in the second slide.
5. When you reach the end of the slide show, the PowerPoint dialog appears. It asks *The Total time for the slide show was 0:00:42. Do you want to keep the new slide timings to use when you view the slid show?* Yes or No. Click Yes to accept the timings or No to try again.
6. The amount of time you spend on each slide is recorded and you can save those timings to run the show automatically in the future.

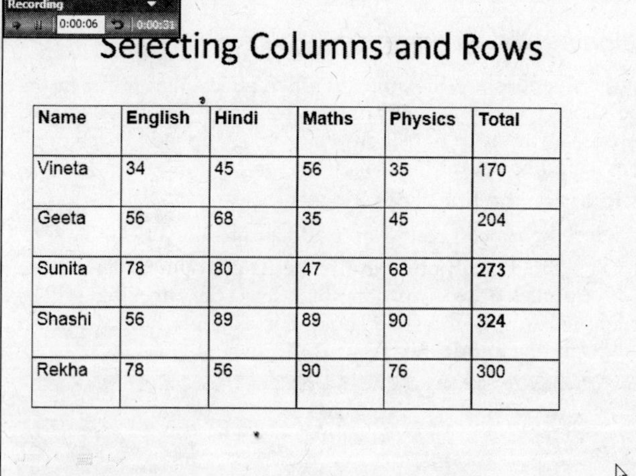

Figure B.74 Rehearsal Timings dialog box appears in the slide show

APPENDIX C

HTML

C.1 INTRODUCTION

HyperText Markup Language (HTML) is the main markup language for web pages. HTML was originally developed by Tim Berners-Lee while at CERN. HTML elements are the basic building-blocks of webpages. HTML standard were and are created by World Wide Web consortium (W3C). HTML5 is markup language for structuring and presenting content for the World Wide Web, and is a core technology of the Internet originally proposed by Opera Software. It is the fifth revision of the HTML standard (created in 1990 and standardized as HTML4 as of 1997) and, as of August 2012, is still under development. Its core aims have been to improve the language with support for the latest multimedia while keeping it easily readable by humans and consistently understood by computers and devices (web browsers, parsers, etc.)

HTML5 is a cooperation between the World Wide Web Consortium (W3C) and the Web Hypertext Application Technology Working Group (WHATWG). The new standard incorporates features like video playback and drag-and-drop that have been previously dependent on third-party browser plug-ins such as Adobe Flash, Microsoft Silverlight, and Google Gears. The latest versions of Apple Safari, Google Chrome, Mozilla Firefox, and Opera all support many HTML5 features and Internet Explorer 9.0 will also have support for some HTML5 functionality. The mobile web browsers that come pre-installed on iPhones, iPads, and Android phones all have excellent support for HTML5.

Some rules for HTML5 were established:

- New features should be based on HTML, CSS, DOM, and JavaScript.
- Reduce the need for external plugins (like Flash).
- Better error handling.
- More markup to replace scripting.
- HTML5 should be device independent.
- The development process should be visible to the public.
- HTML5 is a potential candidate for cross-platform mobile applications.
- HTML5 contains much better support for media, such as, audio and video tags.
- HTML5 defines an HTML syntax that is compatible with HTML4 and XHTML1 documents published on the Web.
- HTML5 can use the XML syntax.
- HTML5 has better support for local offline storage.
- HTML5 has new content specific elements, like article, footer, header, NAV, section.
- HTML5 has new form controls, like calendar, date, time, email, URL, search.
- HTML5 has new parsing rules. HTML5 is oriented towards flexible parsing and compatibility.
- HTML5 is not based on SGML.

C.1.1 Features of HTML5

HTML5 introduces a number of new elements and attributes that helps in building a modern websites. Following are great features introduced in HTML5. New features of HTML5 are:

- **New Semantic Elements**: These are like <header>, <footer>, and <section>.
- **Forms 2.0**: Improvements to HTML web forms where new attributes have been introduced for <input> tag.
- **Persistent Local Storage**: To achieve without resorting to third-party plugins.
- **WebSocket** : A a next-generation bidirectional communication technology for web applications.
- **Server-Sent Events**: HTML5 introduces events which flow from web server to the web browsers and they are called Server-Sent Events (SSE).
- **Canvas**: This supports a two-dimensional drawing surface that you can program with JavaScript. The canvas element creates a rectangular drawing surface on a web page with a height and width given by the value of the height and width attributes. The canvas element is a block element.
- **Audio & Video**: You can embed audio or video on your web pages without resorting to third-party plugins.
- **Geolocation**: Now visitors can choose to share their physical location with your web application.
- **Microdata**: This lets you create your own vocabularies beyond HTML5 and extend your web pages with custom semantics.
- **Drag and drop**: Drag and drop the items from one location to another location on a the same webpage.
- HTML5 is coming with lots of flexibility and would support Uppercase tag names, quotes are optional for attributes, attribute values are optional, closing empty elements are optional

C.1.2 Difference between HTML4 and HTML5

- **<!DOCTYPE html>** : In HTML 4.01, there are three different <!DOCTYPE> declarations but In HTML 5 there is only one
- **<a >**: In HTML 4.01, the <a> tag could be either a hyperlink or an anchor. In HTML5, the <a> tag is always a hyperlink, but if it has no href attribute, it is only a placeholder for a hyperlink.
- **<acronym>** : The <acronym> tag is not supported in HTML5. Use the <abbr> tag instead. The <acronym> tag was used to define acronyms in HTML 4.01.
- **<applet>**: The <applet> tag is not supported in HTML5. Use the <object> tag instead.
- **<strong>**: In HTML 4.01, the <strong> tag defines strong emphasized text, but in HTML5 it defines important text.
- **<body>** : In HTML5, all <body> specific attributes are removed, while in HTML 4.01 they were deprecated.

- **<hr>**: In HTML 4.01, the <hr> tag represented a horizontal rule. In HTML5, the <hr> tag defines a thematic break. The <hr> element is used to separate content (or define a change) in an HTML page.
- **<small>** : In HTML 4.01 the small element is displayed as smaller text. In HTML5 the small element defines small text and other side comments, and is displayed as smaller text.

C.1.3 HTML Design Patterns

The elements in HTML can be loosely grouped together in the following sets:

- **Root element**: The html element rightly stands alone, because it is the only element that contains all the other elements in a document.
- **Document metadata and scripting elements**: The head element contains metadata for the document, as well as CSS styles and JavaScript in many cases.
- **Document sectioning elements**: The body element encloses the content of the page, and new semantic sectioning elements define the header, footer, articles, and other sections on the page.
- **Content grouping elements**: The content in a specific section of the web page may be organized into paragraphs, lists, block quotes, figures, and so on.
- **Text-level semantics elements**: Individual runs of text may have words or sentences marked up to provide fine-grained control over the content's meaning, such as separating time, abbreviations, and superscripts from adjacent content or providing emphasis, importance, or other differences to the normal prose.
- **Tabular data elements**: Data that would be appropriate to display in a spreadsheet would likely be marked up using the rows and columns of the table and related elements.
- **Form elements**: These include the text fields, drop-down menus, check boxes, and other elements for gathering user input in web forms.
- **Embedded content elements**: These include external media embedded into a web page such as video, audio, a bitmap drawing surface
- **Interactive elements**: These include inherently interactive elements that require no further scripting.

C.1.4 Basic Structure of a Web Page

A web page is structured as follows.

The Doctype

The first item to appear in the source code of a web page is the doctype declaration. This provides the web browser with information about the type of markup language in which the page is written, which may or may not affect the way the browser renders the content. It refers to a known Document Type Definition, or DTD for short. The DTD sets out the rules and grammar for that flavor of markup, enabling the browser to render the content accordingly. The doctype begins with the string <!DOCTYPE>, which should be written in uppercase. DOCTYPEs in older versions of HTML were longer because the HTML language was SGML based and therefore required a reference to a DTD. HTML 5 authors would use simple syntax to specify DOCTYPE as follows:

<!DOCTYPE html>

All the above syntax is case-insensitive.

Html

Immediately after the doctype comes the html element-this is the root element of the document tree and everything that follows is a descendant of that root element.

Head

The head element contains meta data-information that describes the document itself, or associates it with related resources, such as scripts and style sheets.

body

This is where the bulk of the page is contained. Everything that you can see in the browser window (or viewport) is contained inside this element, including paragraphs, lists, links, images, tables, and more.

C.1.5 New Elements of HTML5

HTML5 offers new elements for better structure:

Tag	Description
<article>	Defines an article
<aside>	Defines content aside from the page content
<bdi>	Isolates a part of text that might be formatted in a different direction from other text outside it
<command>	Defines a command button that a user can invoke
<details>	Defines additional details that the user can view or hide
<summary>	Defines a visible heading for a <details> element
<figure>	Specifies self-contained content, like illustrations, diagrams, photos, code listings, etc.
<figcaption>	Defines a caption for a <figure> element
<footer>	Defines a footer for a document or section
<header>	Defines a header for a document or section
<hgroup>	Groups a set of <h1> to <h6> elements when a heading has multiple levels
<mark>	Defines marked/highlighted text
<meter>	Defines a scalar measurement within a known range (a gauge)
<nav>	Defines navigation links
<progress>	Represents the progress of a task
<ruby>	Defines a ruby annotation
<rt>	Defines an explanation/pronunciation of characters
<rp>	Defines what to show in browsers that do not support ruby annotations
<section>	Defines a section in a document
<time>	Defines a date/time
<wbr>	Defines a possible line-break

APPENDIX D

Dreamweaver

D.1 INTRODUCTION

Dreamweaver is the most popular professional Web creation tool. It is also a popular tool for independent Web developers who work on Websites for their clients. As a cross-platform tool, Dreamweaver works virtually identically on Macintosh and Windows-based computers and is popular on both platforms. The foundation of Dreamweaver, and Web development, is the HyperText Markup Language (HTML). A language used to describe the structure of content so that it can be viewed over the Web in a Web browser. The modern version of HTML called XHTML (Extensible HyperText Markup Language). Dreamweaver writes the XHTML for you, so you do not need to know how to write XHTML to get started using Dreamweaver. This Appendix describes an overview of Dreamweaver CS5 and helps you get started with the Dreamweaver application. It describes the Dreamweaver workspace and its various components, such as the Application bar, Document bar, Document window and the Properties Inspector. You will how to create a new Web page in Dreamweaver. You will also learn about working with the Dreamweaver workspace. Finally at the end of the chapter, you will learn how to save a Web page and quite the Dreamweaver application. Let us start with a brief an overview of Dreamweaver.

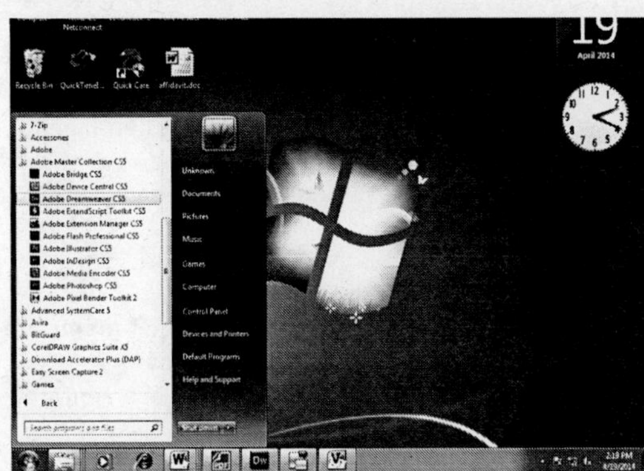

Figure D.1 Getting started with Dreamweaver

D.2 OVERVIEW OF DREAMWEAVER CS5

Dreamweaver is a part of Adobe Creative Suite that provides various Web application development and designing tools. It uses HyperText Markup Language (HTML), a language used to format content to view over the World Wide Web (WWW) using a Web browser. Dreamweaver is a full-featured Web application development tool. Its features not only help in creating and editing Web pages, but also managing and maintaining the Web site. It provides a What You See Is What You Get (WYSIWYG) interface, which you can use to add, view and edit contents in a Web page. You can write Hypertext Markup Language (HTML) code directly in the workspace. This workspace offers many tools to help you in building Website. Using the Dreamweaver editor, you can write code in HTML, Cascading Style Sheets (CSS), JavaScript, and other languages as needed by the browser to display on the Web page. Alternatively, you can also use the Code view to edit the source code directly.

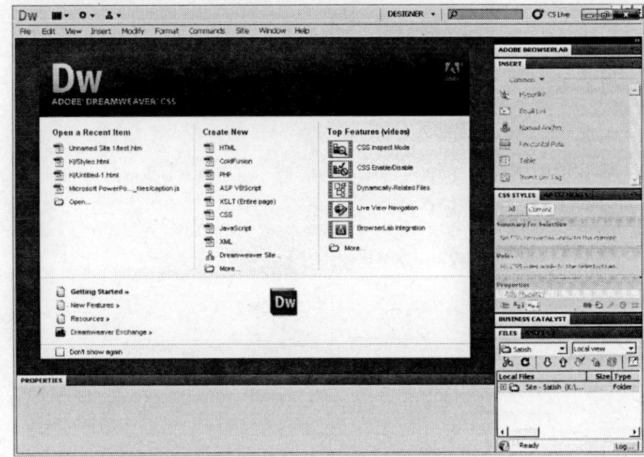

Figure D.2 Welcome Screen of Dreamweaver

D.3 GETTING STARTED WITH ADOBE DREAMWEAVER

To start Dreamweaver CS5, do this:

1. Click Start menu, highlight Programs, again highlight Adobe Master Collection CS5 and then choose Adobe Dreamweaver CS5 as shown in Figure D.1.
2. The Welcome screen of the Dreamweaver application appears as shown in Figure D.2.
   Dreamweaver displays a box with a green bar across the top. The Welcome screen lists common tasks, such as Open a Recent Item, Create New and Top Features. At the bottom of the screen displays Getting Started, New Features, Resources. Dreamweaver Exchange are links to Website. Whenever you do not have any Web pages open in Dreamweaver, it displays the Welcome screen. Welcome screen later looks different because a list of files recently opened in the Open a Recent Item column. It offers a quick way to open the files easily.

D.3.1 Exploring Dreamweaver Interface

Dreamweaver interface, such as Application bar, Document toolbar, Document window, Properties Inspector, the Standard toolbar, the coding toolbar, the Browse navigation toolbar and Panels group. Let us explore the various components of Dreamweaver CS5 workspace as shown in Figure D.3.

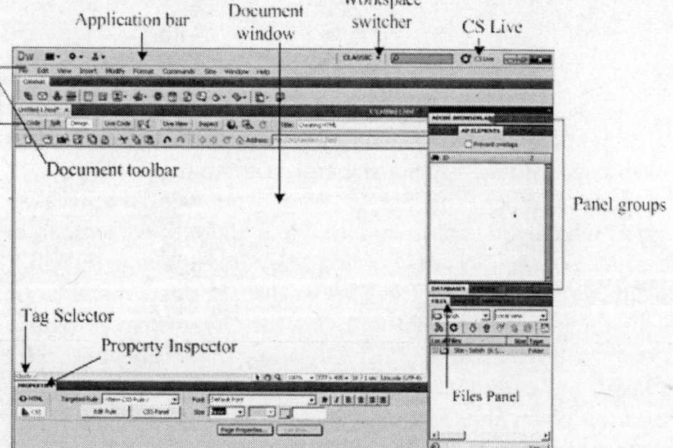

Figure D.3 Dreamweaver Elements

Let us describe the various components of Dreamweaver CS5 workspace.

D.3.2 Application Bar

The Application bar is present at the top of the workspace. This bar contains Dreamweaver logo, Layout drop-down list, Extended Dreamweaver drop-down list, Site button, Menu bar and Workspace Switcher (See Figure D.4).

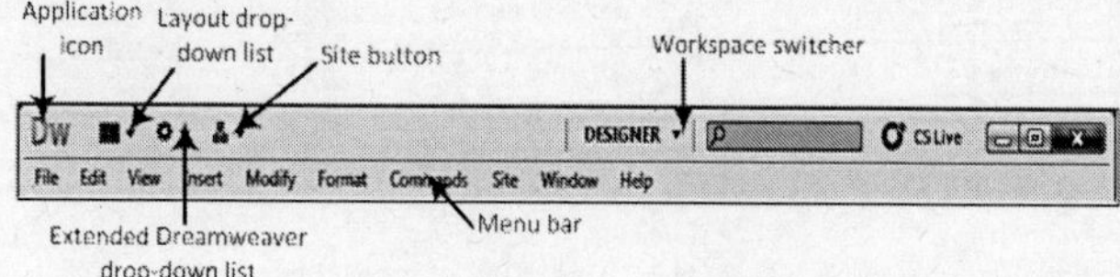

Figure D.4 Application bar

The elements that are present on the Application bar are as follows:

- **Dreamweaver logo**: It displays Minimizes, Maximizes/Restore or Closes a document in Dreamweaver.
- **Layout drop-down list**: It displays the Code and Design view.
- **Extended Dreamweaver drop-down list**: It accesses the Dreamweaver Exchange.
- **Site button**: It displays new Dreamweaver sites and manages existing ones.
- **Workspace Switcher**: It toggles between the different workspace layout options.
- **Menu bar**: It contains various menus to perform specific tasks. The menus in the Menu bar are as follows:
    - **File menu**: The File menu contains commands for opening, closing, saving, importing, exporting and printing files.
    - **Edit menu**: The Edit menu contains the Cut, Copy and Paste command, along with the Find and Replace command and the Preferences command. It configures many elements of the Dreamweaver user interface and its operation with the Preferences command.
    - **View menu**: It changes the view settings, such as the Zoom level and ruler guides of a document. It also displays head content and tracing image.
    - **Insert menu**: Inserts images and tables into a Web page.
    - **Modify menu**: It enables you to modify properties of the currently selected object.
    - **Format menu**: Formats the text and objects present on a Web page.
    - **Commands menu**: This command is useful to Clean Up Word HTML. It also formats and sorts a table, creates a photo album, and optimizes an image for the Web.
    - **Site menu**: It creates new sits and manages existing ones.
    - **Window menu**: This menu is important because it opens and closes all the Dreamweaver panels and inspectors.
    - **Help menu**: This menu contains the command to launch the Extension Manager. There are numerous links to Adobe resources, including the Dreamweaver Support Center on the Adobe's Website.

D.3.3 Document Toolbar

The Document toolbar contains buttons that let you toggle between different views of the document quickly. The toolbar also contains some common commands and options related to viewing the document and transferring it between the local and remote site. The options in the Document toolbar are the following (See Figure D.3).

- **Show Code View**: It displays only the Code view in the Document window.
- **Show Code and Design Views**: It splits the Document window between the Code and the Design views.
- **Show Design View**: It displays only the Design view in the Document window.
- **Live View**: It displays a non-editable, interactive, browser based view of the document.
- **Live Code View**: It displays the actual code used by the browser to execute the page.
- **Document Title**: It allows you to enter a title for your document, to be displayed in the browser's title bar.
- **File Management**: It displays the File Management pop-up menu.
- **Preview/Debug in Browser**: It allows you to preview or debug your document in a browser. Select a browser from the pop-up menu.
- **Refresh Design View**: It refreshes the document's Design view after you make changes in Code view. Changes you make in Code view do not automatically appear in Design view until you perform certain actions, such as saving the file or clicking this button.
- **Visual Aids**: It lets you use different visual aids to design your pages.

- **Validate Markup**: It lets you validate the current document or a selected tag.
- **Check Browser Compatibility**: It lets you check if your Cascading Style Sheet (CSS) is compatible across different browsers.

D.3.4 Document Window

Dreamweaver's work area is the Document window. The Document window shows the current document. You can select any of the following views described below.

- **Design view**: In this view, it displays a fully editable, visual representation of the document, similar to what you would see when viewing the page in a browser.
- **Code view**: A code for writing and editing HTML, JavaScript, server-language code, such as PHP or ColdFusion Markup Language (CFML) etc.
- **Split Code view**: A split version of Code view that lets you scroll to work on different sections of the document at the same time.
- **Code and Design view**: It lets you see both Code view and Design view for the same document in a single window.
- **Live view**: It lets you interact with the document exactly as you would in a browser. Live view is not editable. However, you can edit in Code view and refresh Live view to see your changes.

When a Document window is maximized (the default), tabs appear at the top of the Document window showing the filenames of open documents. Dreamweaver displays an asterisk after the filename if you have made changes that you have not saved yet.

D.3.5 Properties Inspector

The Property inspector is at the bottom of the workspace by default. You can undock it and make it a floating panel in the workspace (See Figure D.5).

The Property inspector displays the properties of the selected object, such as an image, text or table in the Document window. The content of the Properties inspector varies and depends on the selected element. For example, if you want to change the size of an image, you can select the image and enter a new size in the Properties inspector. Similarly, buttons, boxes and text boxes in Dreamweaver have their own properties, which are, displayed in the Properties inspector, when the object has been selected.

Figure D.5 Properties Inspector panel

D.3.6 Panel Groups

Panels groups are displayed vertically on the right side of the Dreamweaver workspace. The Panel group can be collapsed, expanded, docked or undocked along with other panel groups. The panel group contains various panels, such as Insert, CSS styles, AP Elements Files and Assets.

D.3.7 Status bar

The Status bar at the bottom of the Document window provides additional information about the document (See Figure D.6).

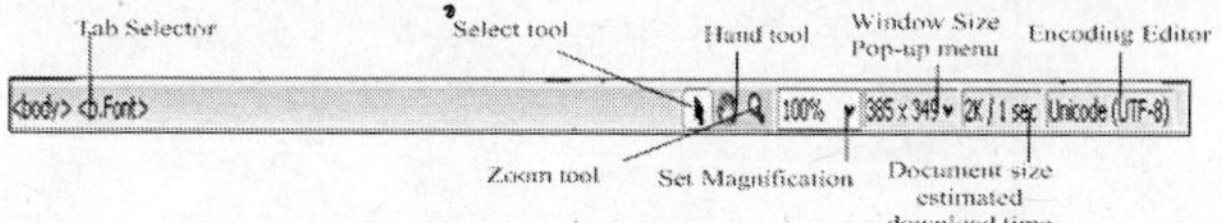

Figure D.6 Status bar

Tag selector: It shows the hierarchy of tags surrounding the current selection. Click any tag in the hierarchy to select that tag and all its contents. Click <body> to select the entire body of the document. To set the class or ID attributes for a tag in the tag selector, right-click the tag and select a class or ID from the context menu.

Select tool: It enables and disables the Hand tool.

Hand tool: Click the document and drag it in the Document window.

Zoom tool and Set Magnification pop-up menu: To set a magnification level for the document.

Window size pop-up menu: To resize the Document window to predetermined. (Not available in Code view).

Document size and download time: It shows the estimated document size and estimated download time for the page, including all dependent files, such as images and other media files.

Encoding indicator: It shows the text encoding for the current document. After learning about the various components of Dreamweaver CS5 workspace, now let us learn about to creating a new Web page in Dreamweaver.

D.3.8 Creating a New Web Page

The New Document dialog box enables you to select the type of document you want to create. This dialog box is organized into several categories. These are Blank Page, Blank Template, Page from Template, Page from Sample and other. To start with a blank HTML document, each category lists different types of documents and layouts.

To create a new Web page, do this:

1. Click File menu and choose New from the Menu bar as shown in Figure D.7. The New dialog box appears as shown in Figure D.7.
2. Select the Blank Page category in the New Document dialog box.
3. Select the desired page you want to create from the Page Type column. In this case, we select the HTML option to create a HTML page as shown in Figure D.8.
4. Based on you selection, a preview and description of the selected layout appears on the right side of the New document. Select a predesigned CSS layout or choose <None> option to create your own custom layout. In our case, we have selected the <None> option as shown in Figure D.8.
5. Click the drop-down arrow beside the DocType option and select a document type from the drop-down list. In our case, we have selected XHTML 1.0 Transitional as shown in Figure D.8.

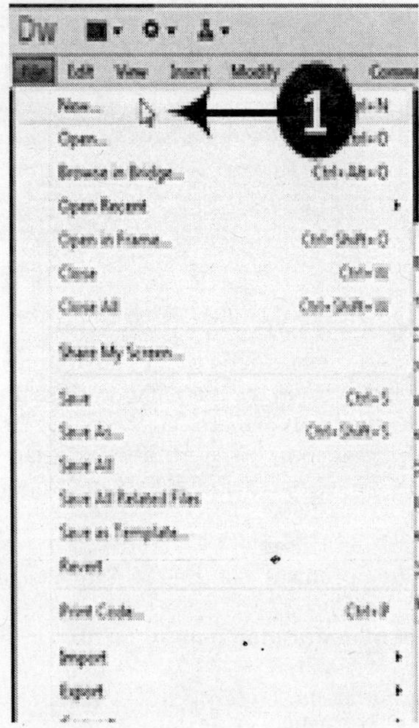

Figure D.7 Selecting New command

6. To set default document preferences for all new documents (such as document type, file extension, and encoding), click the Preferences button at the bottom of the New Document window.

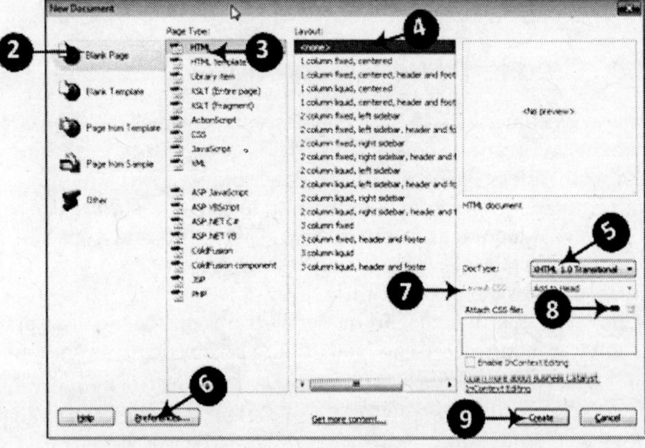

Figure D.8 Welcome Screen of Dreamweaver

In this case, the Layout CSS combo box is unenabled, as we have selected the <None> option in the page layout option as shown in Figure D.8.

7. If you select a CSS layout from the one of the Page Types with a Layout column, choose a location for the page's CSS files from the **Layout CSS**: drop-down menu.
   The Layout CSS combo box provides the following options:
   - Add to Head: It adds CSS layout in the head section of the Web page you are creating.
   - Create New File: It adds a CSS layout in a new external CSS file and makes a link in the Web page to the external CSS file.
   - Link To the Existing File: It specifies an existing CSS file needed for the layout. You can select an existing CSS file by clicking the Attach Style Sheet icon.
8. Click the Attach Style sheet icon at the left hand side of the Attach CSS file, to attach a CSS file with the new Web page as shown in Figure D.8.
   Note that While creating a new Web page, you can also attach a CSS file to it. This CSS file is not related to the CSS layout.
9. Click the Create button to create the new Web page, as shown in Figure D.8.

Now, let us learn how to work with the Dreamweaver workspace.

D.3.9 Working with the Workspace

To perform various tasks on the workspace according to the requirements of the users, such as opening the existing workspaces, creating a customized workspace and managing the workspace. Let us discuss these tasks one-by-one.

Opening the Predefined Workspaces

The default layout option is Designer Workspace. In the most design-oriented Dreamweaver interface many panels are organized into groups and docked on the right side of the window, with the panel names. However, you can open another workspace or create a workspace of your own.

To open a different workspace, do this:

1. Select the Workspace switcher on the Application bar. A drop-down list appears as shown in Figure D.9.
2. Select the Coder command from the drop-down list, as shown in Figure D.9.
3. The Coder workspace appears, as shown in Figure D.10.

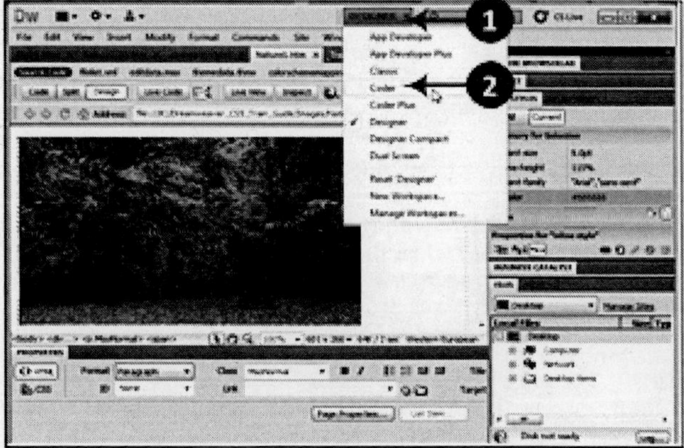

Figure D.9 Selecting different workspace

You can see the coder layout options, displays the panels on the left such CSS Styles, AP Elements, Files, Assets and Snippets. Similarly, you can navigate to any other workspace available in the drop-down list.

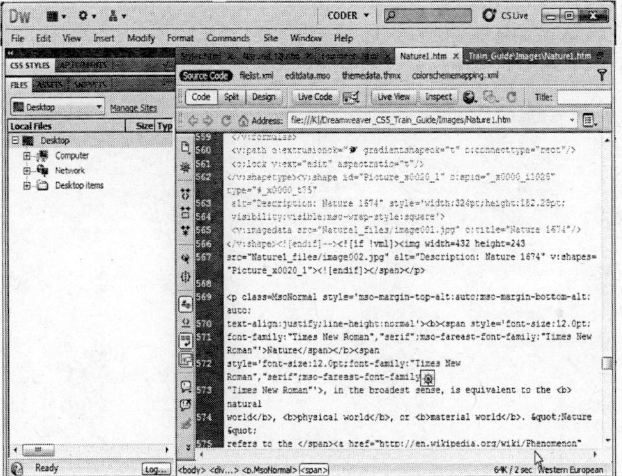

Figure D.10 Coder workspace window

Creating a Customized Workspace

You can create your own workspace by rearranging the position of the panels. After repositioning the panels, you can save that workspace as your default workspace.

1. Arrange the panels in the Dreamweaver workspace as per the requirement. In our case, we have expand the Files panel and Insert panel as shown in Figure D.11.
2. Click the Workspace switcher on the Application bar. A drop-down list appears as shown in Figure D.11.
3. Select the New Workspace command from the drop-down list as shown in Figure D.11. The New Workspace... dialog box appears as shown in Figure D.11.

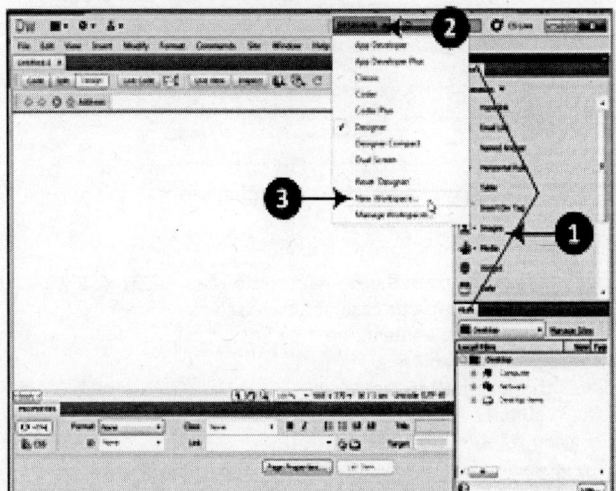

Figure D.11 Selecting New workspace

4. Type a name in the Name: text box for the new workspace. For example, here we type My_WebPage.
5. Click the OK button.
6. The workspace is saved with the name My_WebPage that appears in the Workspace switcher in the Application bar as shown in Figure D.12.

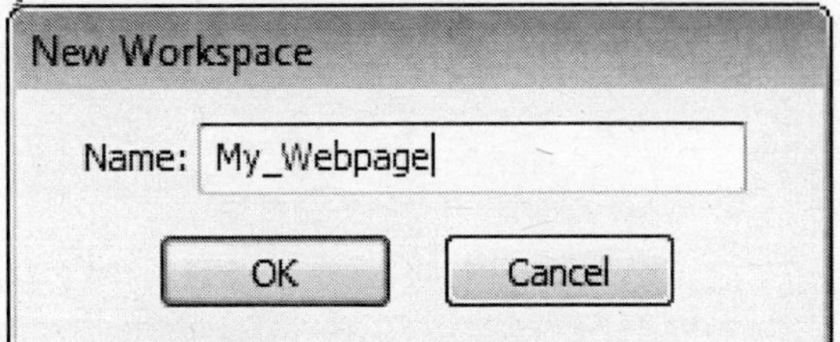

Figure D.12 New Workspace dialog box

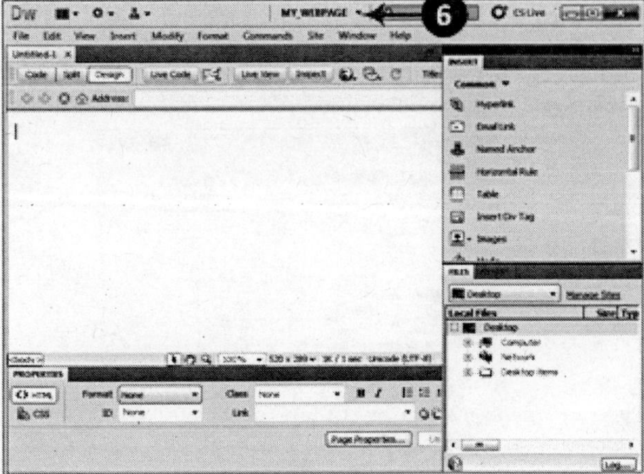

Figure D.13 Workspace name appear in the Application bar

Let us now learn about managing a workspace.

Managing a Workspace

Once you have saved a workspace, you can manage the workspace by either making changes or renaming it, or deleting the workspace.To manage a workspace by renaming it, do this:

1. Click the Workspace switcher in the Application bar. A drop-down list appears.
2. Select Manage Workspaces from the drop-down list as shown in Figure D.14. The Manage Workspaces... dialog box appears as shown in Figure D.15.

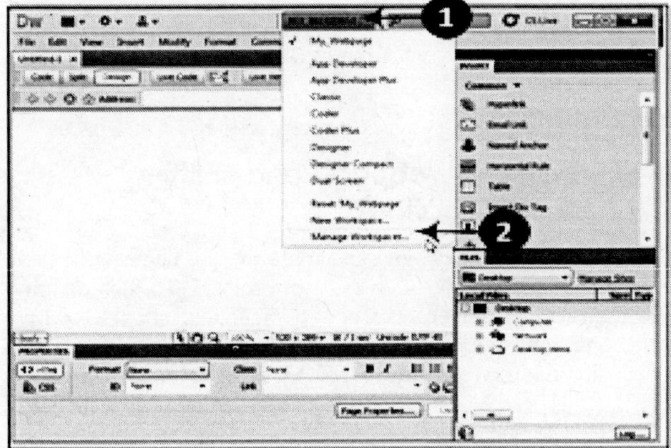

Figure D.14 Selecting Manage Workspaces

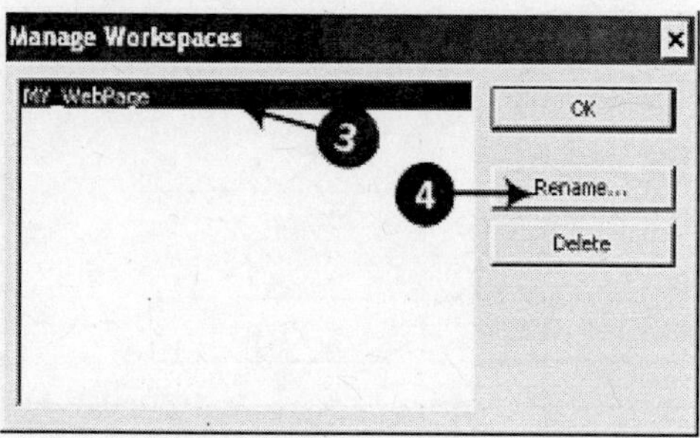

Figure D.15 Manage Workspaces dialog box

3. Select the name of the workspace from the right pane of the Manage Workspaces dialog box.
4. Click the Rename... button. The Rename Workspace dialog box appears as shown in Figure D.16.

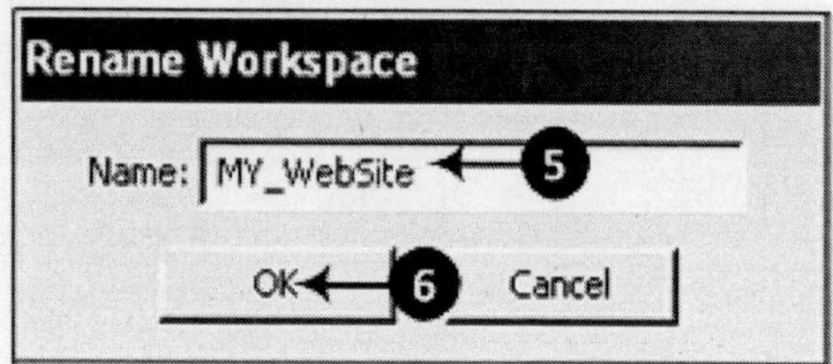

Figure D.16 Rename Workspace

5. Type a name in the Name: text box for the workspace in the Rename Workspace dialog box. In our case, we typed My_WebSite.
6. Click the OK button. The Rename Workspace dialog box is closed.
7. Click the OK button in the Manage Workspaces dialog box.
8. The Manage Workspaces dialog box closes and the changes made in the workspace appear on the Workspace switcher drop-down list.

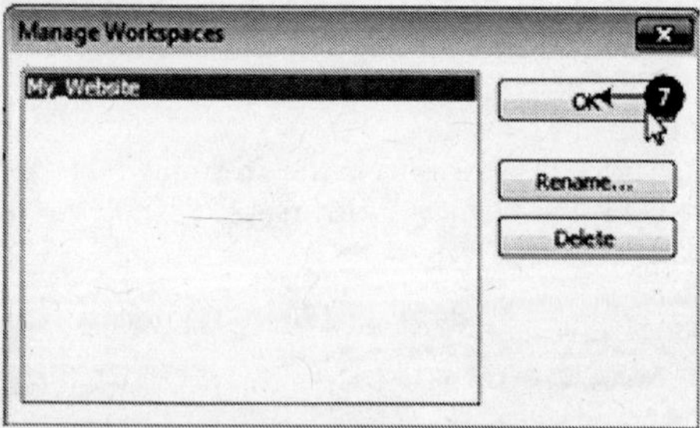

Figure D.17 Selecting OK option from Manage Workspaces

D.3.10 Saving a Webpage and Quitting the Application

When saving a document, give the file a unique name with the appropriate file extension such as, .html for HTML files or .gif images and save it to the root level of the managed site folder. By default, Dreamweaver assigns a default file extension to your untitled document, which for HTML files can be either .html or .htm. Before you to exit or quit before saving that last file you were working on, Dreamweaver prompts you to save or ignore any changes.

To save a Web page and then quit the Dreamweaver application, do this:

1. Click the File menu and choose Save from the menu as shown in Figure D.18. A Save As dialog box appears as shown in Figure D.19.

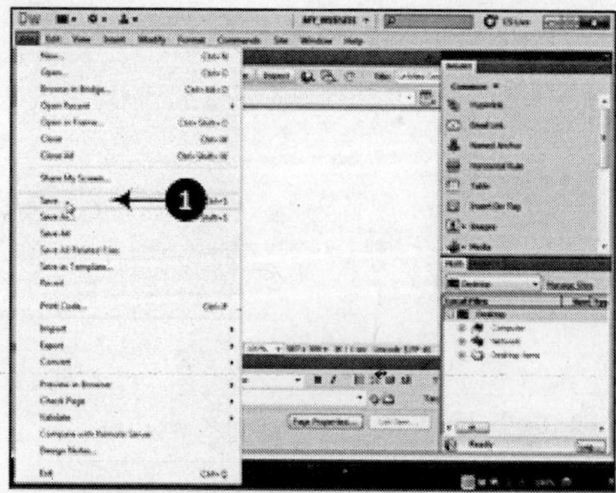

Figure D.18 Selecting Save command

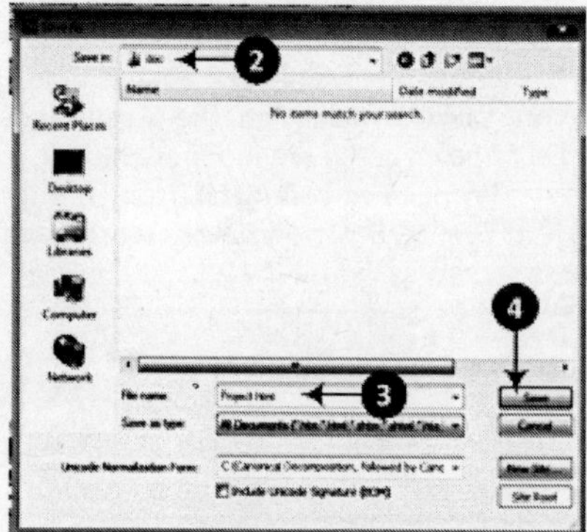

Figure D.19 Save As dialog box

2. Select a location from the Save in: combo box where you want to save your file. In our case, we have selected the doc folder.
3. Type a name of the File name: text box. In our case, we typed project.html as shown in Figure D.19.
4. Click the Save button.
   The Web page is saved with the specific name at the specified location, as shown in Figure D.20.
5. Now, select File menu and Close from the File menu, as shown in Figure D.20. The Project.html file closes and the Welcome screen of the Dreamweaver application appears.
6. Again, select File menu and choose Exit from the File menu to exit from the Dreamweaver application, as shown in Figure D.21.

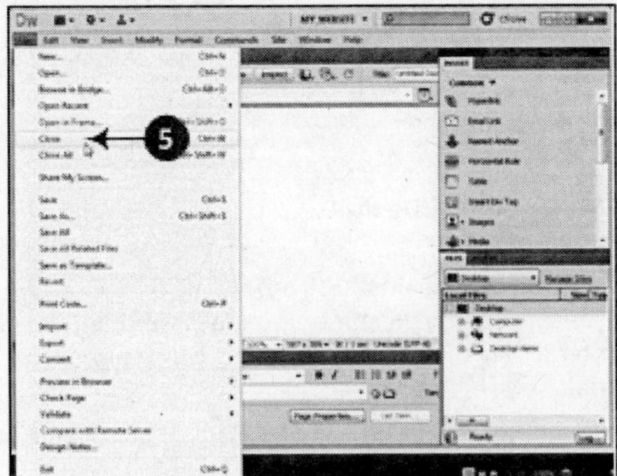

Figure D.20 Selecting close command

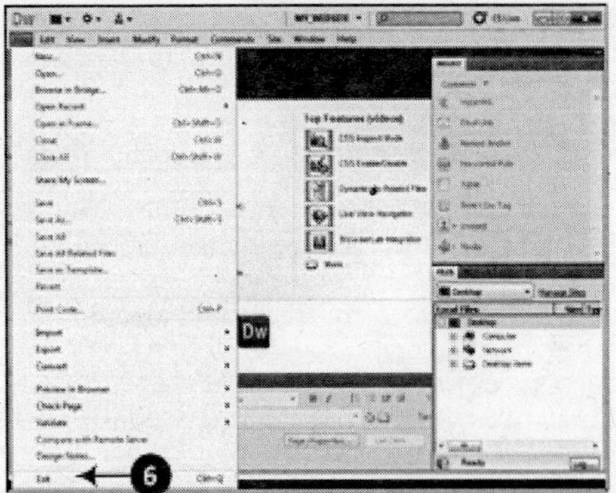

Figure D.21 Selecting Exit command

Glossary

Active Desktop A feature of Microsoft Internet Explorer, which allows the user to add HTML content to the desktop, along with some other features.

Active window The currently focused window in the current Window manager or Explorer.

Additive primary colours Red, green, and blue, which are used to create all other colours when direct, or transmitted light is used.

Adjustment layer Special type layer when you need to display a colour correction or effect, or hide it when not needed.

AIFF Audio Interchange File Format; an audio file format standard used for storing sound data.

Alpha channel A channel which is used to store a selection or mask for the image.

Anchor A named point on a Web page. HTML tag is used to create Hypertext links and anchors.

Anchor point When you create a curved path, each anchor point represents the transition between curved segments.

Anti-aliasing A correction that sharpens the jagged edges of a selection, preserving as much detail as possible. Without anti-alias, an image would look stair-stepped, without smooth transitions between colours.

ASP It is a Microsoft Technology and ASP stands for Active Server Pages. It is a program that runs inside IIS, that respond to user queries or data submitted from HTML forms and returns the results to the browser.

Attributes (HTML) Special code words used inside an HTML tag to control exactly what the tag does.

AU An audio file format for UNIX systems. AU is SUN Microsystem's proprietary format. Probably the most commonly used sound format on the Web.

Audio response An output medium that produces verbal responses from the computer system.

AVI (Audio/Video Interleaved) A video file format. Video quality is good, but files tend to be large. Windows format for saving video with sound.

Background processing The automatic execution of lower-priority (background) computer programs when higher-priority (foreground) programs are not using the system resources.

Backup Alternate facilities of programs, data files, hardware equipments etc., that are used in case the original one is destroyed, lost, or fails to operate.

Bandwidth A measure of the amount of data that can be sent through an electronic connection.

Bitmap Graphics Images in pixels, a patterned series of dots. One of the most commonly compatible types of graphic formats.

BMP file Graphics file in bitmap format (a Windows standard format for graphics files) with the file extension `.bmp`.

Browser A software program for viewing HTML pages.

CAD (Computer-Aided Design) Use of computers to automate design operations.

CAI (Computer Aided Instruction) Computer Assisted Instruction; a self-learning technique usually offline and online, involving interaction of the student with programmed instructional materials.

Canvas In Photoshop, the surface on which your image resides.

Cascading style sheets A style sheet language used for describing the look and formatting of a document written in a markup language.

Channel Photoshop divides the colours in a colour image into separate channels that you manage via the Channels palette. The default color mode, RGB color, uses four channels-one each for the red, green, and blue channels, plus a composite channel that shows the individual channels combined.
In the field of telecommunications and computer networking, it refers either to a physical transmission medium, such as a wire or to a logical connection over a multiplexed medium such as a radio channel.

Chip A thin wafer of silicon on which integrated electronic components are deposited.

CMYK Cyan, Magenta, Yellow, Key (Black); a color model which is used in color printing. The colours used in process printing. Each colour plate contains tiny dots of cyan, magenta, yellow or black. The densities of the coloured dots on each plate influence the surrounding colours when the eye mixes them together.

CMYK color mode A color mode that produces a full range of colour by printing tiny dots of cyan, magenta, yellow, and black ink. Because the coloured dots are so small, the eye mixes them together. The relative densities of groups of coloured dots produce variations in colour and tonality. CMYK is referred to as a subtractive colour system.

Color mode A system of displaying or printing in colour. Photoshop supports the HSB color model and RGB, CMYK, Lab, Indexed, Duotone, Grayscale, Multichannel, and Bitmap color modes.

COM (Computer Output Microfilm) An output device that records computer output on microfilm.

Comment This is the text in an HTML document (or computer program) that will be seen only by the people who edit the source for that page. Comments are normally invisible when a page is viewed with a Web browser.

Compile The process of taking a project's code components and making an EXE or OCX file out of them.

Component Object Model (COM) A specification for reusable software components. ActiveX controls fall under the DCOM, or Distributed Component Object Model specification, which in turn falls under the COM specification.

Computer graphics The area of computer science which is concerned with the generation, manipulation and display of pictures with the aid of a computer.

Content Model In the DTD, a description of what might occur within instances of a given element type.

Control Panel A program to change settings and customize the functionality of your computer basic system settings and controls via applets, such as adding hardware, adding and removing software, controlling user accounts, and changing accessibility options.

Control Unit The part of the central processor which directs the sequence of operations, interprets the coded instruction, and sees to the execution of program instructions.

CPU (Central Processing Unit) A central processing unit is the hardware within a computer that carries out the instructions of a computer program by performing the basic arithmetical, logical, and input/output operations of the system. The control unit and the arithmetic logic unit of a computer system are jointly known as the CPU. All calculations and comparisons are made inside the CPU and the CPU is also responsible for activating and controlling the operations of the other units of a computer system.

Crop A command used in computer graphics, to cut off the sides of an image to make it the proper size or to remove unwanted parts.

DCR A Shockwave audio format used in Shockwave movies. Requires the Shockwave plug-in.

Desktop Publishing Packages (DTP) Software that combines text and graphics manipulating capabilities to allow users to format charts and pictures with text and headlines.

DIB (Device Independent Bitmap) A Windows graphics file format.

Digitizer An input device used to convert graphic and pictorial data into binary, numeric inputs for a digital computer.

Distributed Component Object Model (DCOM) A protocol that permits software objects to interact over networks (including the Internet).

Document Type Declaration A set of markup declarations that define a document type for an SGML-family markup language like SGML, XML, and HTML. A declaration at the start of an XML document that specifies where the external DTD subset can be found and includes the internal DTD subset. A set of rules governing the element types that are allowed within an XML document and specifying the allowed content and attributes of each element type.

Download The process of transferring information from a remote computer to your computer. On the Internet, you can use a file transfer utility (such as FTP) to download or upload files.

Drag To drag an object means to position the *mouse pointer* on the object, then press and hold the active mouse button, then move the mouse to a new position, and release the mouse button.

Drag-and-drop Method of moving or copying information from one file to anther, or to another location in the same file.

Element A logical unit of information within an XML document.

Embedded An object that resides in another object. ActiveX controls and Java applets, for example, are said to be embedded in HTML pages through the use of the <OBJECT> tag.

Embedded object A technique in which information (the object) inserted into a file (the destination file). Once embedded, the object becomes part of the destination file. When you double-click an embedded object, it opens in the program (source program) it was created in. Any changes, you make to the embedded object are reflected in the destination file.

Empty Element An element containing no sub-elements or character data.

End tag A tag that marks the end of an element, such as </head>.

Entity Any data that can be treated as an object, such as an external file containing an image.

EPS (Encapsulated PostScript) Graphics file format used in desktop publishing applications including PageMaker.

Error A procedure that arrives at an incorrect result.

Error-handler A procedure that deals with an error condition in a procedure. In Visual Basic, error-handlers are declared with some form of On Error statement.

Executable file Any "runnable" application program with a file extension of . COM, .EXE, or .BAT.

External image A Web page image that the browser cannot handle, so it passes the buck to graphics program that displays the image in a separate window.

Fade-out rate The rate at which the Photoshop Paintbrush and airbrush tools fade out as you paint with them to simulate an actual brush stroke.

Feather edge The area along the border of a selection that is partially affected by changes you make to the selection.

Feathering A correction that blurs the edges of a selection by adding a shift zone of a pixel width that you specify.

Field In a record, it is a meaningful collection of one or more related characters treated as a unit.

File Management System (FMS) A software package that allows users to define data items, place these items into specified records, combine these records into designated files, and then manipulate and retrieve stored data in various ways to achieve user's goals.

Firmware A sequence of instruction (software) that is substituted for hardware and stored in read-only memory (ROM). Another example of Firmware is PROM, i.e. programmable read only memory.

FLC Pronounced as flick; a file name extension containing video created by Autodesk Animator Pro.

Font One complete collection of letters, punctuation marks, numbers, and special characters with a consistent and identifiable typeface, weight, posture, and size.

Footer A line of text package prints beyond the bottom margin of each page.

Form A page that includes areas to be filled out by the reader. HTML forms allow information to be sent back to the company or individuals, who made (or maintains) the page.

Format The way you arrange text on your screen, using commands for setting margins, centering text, etc.

Frame A rectangular region within the browser window that displays a Web page alongside other pages in other frames.

Frame Rate The rate, at which each frame in an animation is played back for the user.

Front-end processor A CPU designed specifically to handle the communications processing task. Its main purpose is to off-load communications processing task from the host computer, so that the host computer can be dedicated for applications and data processing jobs.

Function A user-defined or built-in set of statements that perform a task. It can also return a value when used with the return statement.

Gamut The gamut represents the range of colors that your system can actually display. You can set up Photoshop to display a warning if an image includes colours outside the gamut.

General software package A software package, such as payroll and word processing, developed for a general market comprising many users.

Graphic Interchange Format (GIF) A compressed format for storing graphics. An common web image format. Compression file format for graphics requiring a specific decoder to view.

Graphics Digitized pictures and computer-generated images.

Grayscale mode A Photoshop color mode that displays black-and-white images.

Grid In Photoshop, a series of equally spaced horizontal and vertical lines that create a visual matrix. A grid helps you to see the global relations between aligned elements on a page. Grids do not get printed.

Guide layer Layer that does not export when you export a Flash file. This layer can be used to help registration of various elements of a Flash file.

Hacker A programmer who hacks computer systems to steal, change or destroy information as a form of cyber-terrorism.

Header A line of text package that prints below the top margin of each page.

Hierarchy Navigator objects exist in a set relation to each other that reflects the structure of an HTML page. This is referred to as instance hierarchy because it only works with specific instances of objects, rather than general classes.

High-level language A programming language whose structure is application-oriented and is independent of the structure of the computer.

History list A list of uniform resource locators stored by a Web browser which store a list of all the Web pages the user has previously visited.

History palette The Photoshop palette that records all of the changes that you make to an image during a session, as a series of individual states.

Host computer The main control computer in a network of distributed processors and terminals.

HTML (HyperText Markup Language) The document formatting language used to create pages on the World Wide Web (WWW).

HTML editor A program that makes it easier to markup a document by using menu commands and toolbar buttons to insert tags.

HTTP (HyperText Transfer Protocol) The standard method for exchanging information between HTTP servers and clients on the Web.

Hypermedia Media with links to text, sound, graphics, movies and/or animations.

Hypertext Text that allows readers to jump spontaneously among onscreen documents and other resources by selecting highlighted keywords that appear on each screen of Web pages.

IIS IIS stands for Internet Information Services and comes as a free component with Windows 2000.

Image compression The mathematical manipulation that images are put through to squeeze out repetitive patterns. It makes them load and display much faster.

Image size The physical size and resolution of an image. The size of an image specifies the exact number of pixels that compose a picture.

ImageReady A companion program to Photoshop, used to create Web graphics.

Info palette The Photoshop palette that shows information about the current image.

Information The result of data manipulation or processing which can be used to help people make decisions.

Information technology (IT) Information Technology; the study or use of system in which applications of computer and telecommunications equipments are used to store, retrieve, transmit and manipulate data.

Input/Output Input refers to any information coming into the computer. Output refers to processed information going out of a computer.

Input device A device used to enter information into a computer or other data processing devices; for example, the keyboard.

Instance A copy of a symbol used in a movie.

Interpreter A language processor that translates a statement of a high-level language and immediately executes it before translating the next source language statement.

Inverse In Photoshop, feature is used to change the selected area to the portion that has not been selected with a selection tool.

JPEG Joint Photographic Experts Group; a lossy compression technique for color images. A file format that stores images in a compressed format.

Kbps (kilobits per second) A rate of transfer of information across a connection, such as the Internet.

Keyframe A frame in which you establish exactly what should appear on stage at that particular time.

Layer A software feature that allows you to isolate image elements so that you can work on each one individually. You can also rearrange the positions of layers, allowing parts of as image to appear in front of other parts. Earlier versions of Photoshop supported 99 layers; new versions of Photoshop support an unlimited number.

Layer set A layer management tool. Layer sets let you consolidate contiguous layers into a folder on the Layers palette. By highlighting the folder, you can apply certain operations to the layers as a group. For example, the layers in the layer set can be simultaneously hidden, displayed, moved or repositioned.

Layers palette The Photoshop palette that contains controls for working with layers, including creating and deleting layers, merging layers, and many other layer-related functions.

Light pen A pen shaped device that is used as an input device to computers by writing or sketching on the screen of a cathode ray tube.

Line printer A printer that prints one line at a time.

Linear A category in Multimedia which uses active content progressing often without any navigational control for the viewer, such as a cinema presentation. When users are not given navigational control, such case project is linear, starting at the beginning and running through to the end.

Link An icon, a picture, or a highlighted string of text that connects the current Web page to other Web pages, Internet sites, graphics, movies, or sounds. On the Web, you skip from page to page by clicking on links.

Linux Linux is an operating system kernal that behaves and performs similar to the famous UNIX operating system from AT & T Bells Labs but it is available free. It has all the features of a modern operating system: true multitasking, threads, virtual memory, shared libraries, demand loading, shared, copy-on-write executables, proper memory management, loadable device driver modules, video frame buffering, and TCP/IP networking.

Magnetic Ink Character Recognition (MICR) An input device that can read cards and paper documents printed with a special magnetic ink.

Magnetic tape A secondary storage device that uses a long plastic strip coated with a magnetic material as a recording medium.

Magneto-optical Drives An erasable or semi-erasable storage disk, similar to a CD-ROM disk and of very high capacity, in which a laser beam is used to heat the recording surface to point at which tiny region on the surface can be magnetically aligned to store bits of data.

Markup Information that is intermingled with the text of an XML document to indicate its logical and physical structure.

Mask A special type of select you use to hide part of layer, so you can manipulate only the visible portions of the layer.

Masking A kind of layer property with at least two layers. One for mask and one that is masked. The graphical contents of the mask layer will determine which parts of the masked layer will show through.

Master file A file containing relatively permanent data which is often updated by records in a transaction file.

Menu A screen display that list options or commands from which you can choose.

Method A function assigned to an object. For example, bigString.toUpperCase() returns an uppercase version of the string contained in bigString.

MID File extension used for MIDI-format music files `.mid`.

MIDI Musical Instrument Digital Interface, a standard for digital musical instruments and the computer hardware and software that works with them. An electronic music audio file format. A global software and hardware standard that allows musical instruments and synthesizers to be controlled from a computer program. Older browsers may require a plug-in.

Morph A kind of information that transitions one shape to another.

MP3 A CD-quality audio file format.

MPEG (Motion Picture Experts Group) The public domain, non-proprietary movie format, a quality video file format with relatively small file size.

Multimedia A file in which the use of computers to present text, graphics, video, animation, and sound in an integrated way.

Navigator palette The Photoshop palette that shows a map of the current image displayed as a thumbnail. It indicates the exact location of what appears in the image window relative to the entire image and provides features for scrolling and zooming.

Nibble 4 bits, that is half a byte.

Non-Linear A category in Multimedia which uses interactivity to control progress as with a video game or self-paced computer-based training like hypermedia is an example of non-linear content.

Object A location in memory having a value and referenced by an identifier. An object can be a variable, function, or data which is used in programming languages.
A construct with properties that are JavaScript variables or other objects. Functions associated with an object are known as the object's methods.

Optical Character Reader (OCR) An input device which can read characters directly from an ordinary piece of paper by using a scanning mechanism. These characters are written in special type fonts.

Optical Mark Reader (OMR) An input device that can interpret pencil marks on paper media.

Optimize palette The ImageReady palette that contains controls for optimizing images for Web applications.

Options bar When you select a toolbox tool, the options bar below the Photoshop menu bar presents choices you can use to adjust how the tool will operate.

Page Break A place in text where one page ends and another begins.

Palette A special collection of tools or settings. Photoshop organizes its palettes on tabs in special palette windows that appear at the right side of the Photoshop window by default.

Panel Special tools that allows seeing and changing almost any setting while editing a file. Example Character Panel, Info Panel, Mixer Panel, etc.

Panning An effect that makes a sound seem to move from left to right or right to left.

Paradigm A paradigm, pronounced "para-dime", means model, example or pattern. The term is gaining popularity in general and is being used more frequently within the computer industry.

Paragraph palette The Photoshop palette that contains settings that apply to entire text paragraphs, such as alignment and hyphenation.

Parser A parser is a program, usually part of a compiler, that receives input in the form of sequential source program instructions, interactive online commands or markup tags, and breaks them up into parts that can then be managed by other components in a compiler.

Parsing The process of analysing a string of symbols in computer languages, according to the rules of a formal grammar. To parse is to analyze something in an orderly way. In parsing, a statement is divided into parts that can be made useful for the computer, for developing further actions or for creating the instructions that form an executable program.

Password A secret code, known only to the user, that allows that user to access a computer that is protected by a security system.

PC Card PC cards offer large data storage and I/O capability, networking, modem and other functions with lower power consumption and fast data access speed in a compact size measuring the length and width of a credit card.

Photoshop A very popular photo manipulation and graphics software package created by Adobe.

PICT A graphic file format that can be viewed on Macintosh and PC. Most graphic programs can view a PICT file.

Pixel An individual square of coloured light, which is the smallest editable unit in a digital image. The pixels in digital image are usually so small that, when seen, the colours blend into what appears to be a continuous-tone image.

Pixel Depth (Also called "bit resolution"). A measurement of the number of bits of information stored with each pixel. Pixel depth will generally be expressed as either 8-bit, 16 bit or 24-bit. The greater the number of bits, the more different colours a pixel can create. 8 bit pixel depth can create 256 different colour (2^8), 16-bit pixel can create over 65,000 different colours (2^{16}) and 24-bit pixel depth can create more than 16 million different colours (2^{24}).

Pixels per inch (ppi) The number of pixels that can be displayed per inch, usually used to refer to pixel resolution from scanned image or on a monitor.

Plotter An output device that converts computer output into a graphic, hardcopy form.

Plug-ins Programs to view multimedia files that your web browser cannot display/play. Plug-ins allows you to view the file without downloading first.

Plug-and-Play Type of device that can communicate with Windows to provide its own configuration information.

Program A set of sequenced instructions used to direct and control the operations of the computer in order to solve a problem or to perform a particular task. Also called as routine.

QuickTime A video file format created by Apple Computer.

RPM RealAudio file format used for sound and video. Requires the RealAudio or RealPlayer plug-in.

Raster Graphic An image file format that contains the color information for each pixel.

Record A collection of information, in one or more fields, about a specific item or person.

RGB color mode A color mode that represents the three colors-red, green, and blue-used by devices such as scanners or monitors to display color.

RGB image A three-channel image that contains a red, green, and blue channel.

RIFF (Resource Interchange File Format) File format for storing sound and graphics so they can be played on different computer platforms.

Runtime The point at which the user is watching movie.

Saturation The intensity of a colour. Saturation, or chroma, is determined by the percentage of the hue in proportion to gray, from 0 to 100 percent.

Scale Resize. Flash movie retains aspect ratio when it scales.

Scene A component part of a Timeline in a Flash file.

Secondary storage Devices like hard disk to store data permanently.

SGML Standard Generalized Markup Language. It is a meta-language, i.e., a language for describing markup languages.

Shockwave An add-in to MacroMedia Director, creates highly-compressed interactive animations and movies.

Smart Clip A movie clip with parameters unique to each instance.

Smudge A tool you use to drag one color into another on a layer.

Source The actual text and commands stored in an HTML file, including tags, comments, and scripts that may not be visible when the page is viewed with a Web browser.

Speech recognition The ability to input data directly into a computer system by speaking to it.

Speech synthesis The artificial production of human speech. Computer output in the form of spoken word. No cassette tapes are involved, rather a small LSI microchip is used which has the capability of reproducing the human voice via a small loud-speaker amplifier. Presently multimedia is using this concept.

Stage The large white rectangle in the middle of the Flash workspace where a file is created.

Start tag A tag that marks the start of an element, such as <head>.

Static Graphics Graphics with no animation or interactivity.

Symbol Special characters that are not your keyboard, such as copyright and trademark symbols, paragraph marks, Unicode characters.

Table Text and/or images arranged into orderly rows and columns. HTML provides several tags specifically for creating tables.

Tag HTML code, enclosed in angle brackets (<) and (>).

Tagged Image File (TIF) The TIF Format (sometimes known as TIFF) is a graphics format used by most scanner and page layout applications.

Tele-conferencing A system in which persons sitting at CRT screens see and talk to each other via a computer-communications network, and web camera.

TIFF (Tagged Image File Format) A graphic image file format. Suitable for 24-bit color pictures, Good compression.

Timeline An object on the Flash workspace that contains the sequence of frames, layers and scenes composing an animation.

Uniform Resource Locator (URL) Server and path information that locates a document or other file on the Internet; for example, http://www.domain_name.com.

Vector Graphics The use of geometrical primitives, such as points, lines, curves, and shapes or polygons, based on mathematical expressions and vectors to represent images in computer graphics. Vector graphic file formats include: AutoCAD DXF, CBM, EPS, HGL, PIC, DRW, WMF and WPG.

Voice response unit An output device that uses words or messages recorded on a magnetic medium to produce audio response.

W3C World Wide Web Consortium. A group of vendor companies that acts as a sort of standards body for the web.

WAV Waveform Audio File Format (WAVE) is an audio file format standard used to store an audio bitstream on computer. Windows audio file format.

Web Camera A simple web camera consists of a digital camera attached to the computer through USB or parallel port. In digital camera, light strikes an array of photosensitive diodes instead of film. Software associated with web cam grabs a still image from the camera at a regular interval (say every 30 seconds). The software then turns that image into a normal JPG file and uploads it to the web server.

Windows A graphical partition of screen for user interface.

Windows 2000 Windows 2000 is a network operating system (NOS) which is designed by Microsoft Corp. of USA. This NOS has all the features and applications necessary for a complete network operating environment.

Windows API Microsoft's core set of application programming interfaces available in the Microsoft Windows operating systems.

MAT.O2.R0 : Introduction to Multimedia Question Paper Sept 2014

Total Time : 3 Hours

Total Marks 100
(Part One - 40 Part Two - 60)

PART – ONE

1. Multiple Choice

1.1 The process of planning a multimedia presentation is known as
   a. Design b. Storyboard
   c. Layout d. Development

1.2 Which one of these has audio?
   a. Cycle.jpg b. Bus.bmp
   c. Frogs.avi d. All of these

1.3 'Zipping' a file means
   a. Encrypting it b. Decrypting it
   c. Compressing it d. Transmitting it

1.4 Authoring tools help us to
   a. Write a storyboard b. Search the internet
   c. Control the presentation of multimedia elements d. All of the above

1.5 The elements of multimedia are
   a. Video, Animation, Interactivity
   b. Sound, Video, Animation, Interactivity
   c. Graphics, Sound, Video, Animation, Interactivity
   d. Text, Graphics, Sound, video, Animation, Interactivity

1.6 Which one of the following is not a video file extension?
   a. MP4 b. AVI
   c. QT d. JPG

1.7 Which img file format can be animated?
   a. GIF b. JPEG
   c. CDR d. TIFF

1.8 Power Point presentation is an example of
   a. Book metaphor b. Icon metaphor
   c. Timeline metaphor d. Slide show metaphor

1.9 When something is displaying at the same time as it is created, accessed or imported, it is known as
   a. Digital Time b. Online Time
   c. Batch Time d. Real Time

1.10 What does MPEG stand for?
   a. Motion Picture Experts Gang b. Modern Picture Experts Group
   c. Motion Picture Experts Group d. Modern Picture Experts Gang

2. State whether the following statements are TRUE or FALSE.

2.1 The word 'multimedia' comes from the Greek words 'multus' which means numerous and 'media' which means middle or center.

2.2 PNG is a standard used for compression of audio in multimedia.

2.3 Adobe Premier and Apple iMovie are examples of video editing software.

2.4 Simulation means a virtual platform of any real event.

2.5 A Flash file can be imported in a html page.

2.6 Sound can travel without a medium.

2.7 In lossy compression some data are discarded.

2.8 RGB stands for red, green and black.

2.9 CMY(K) is an example of subtractive color model.

2.10 The process of copying files to a CD is known as burning.

3. MATCH words and phrases in Column X with the nearest in meaning in Column Y.

	X		Y
3.1	A Video standard	A	Subtractive Color Model
3.2	RGB	B	Animation
3.3	Process used to remove jagged edges in computerized graphics	C	Changing and merging one computer image into another
3.4	Raster graphics	D	Pixels
3.5	CMYK	E	Additive Color Model
3.6	GIF	F	Compression
3.7	The tiny dots comprising a picture	G	Continuous
3.8	Analog	H	AVI
3.9	Process of reducing file size	I	Bitmap
3.10	Morphing	J	Anti-aliasing

4. FILL IN THE BLANKS in the following questions by choosing the most appropriate word or phrase from the following list.

a	Dithering	**b**	CAM
c	Joint Photographers Experts Group	**d**	Browser

e	CAD	f	Dots per inch
g	Tweening	h	HSV
i	Joint Picture Expert Gang	j	Gray-scale
k	AVI	l	Resolution

4.1 ______ creates in-between frames when we create the start and end points of the animation.

4.2 The clarity of a monitor is known as ________.

4.3 _________ stands for Hue Saturation Value.

4.4 ______ graphics allow each pixel to be shown on the monitor as black, white, or a shade of gray.

4.5 _______ is a software technique for diminishing jaggies.

4.6 A _______ is a software program that interprets mark document (such a HTML) and renders them visually on computer screens.

4.7 _________ software is used by engineers to design products.

4.8 _____ is a sound and video file format developed for Microsoft Windows platform.

4.9 DPI stands for ______

4.10 JPEG stands for ________.

PART – TWO

(Answer any four questions. Each question carries 15 marks)

5. (a) Why is compression required? State the difference between lossy and lossless compression?
   (b) What is the difference between jpeg and jpeg 2000? What is H.264 standard?
   (c) Explain the different types of hyperlink.

6. What is difference between HSB and HSV color models? How do they differ from HIS color model? Discuss in detail with illustrations.

7. (a) Define raster graphics and state its disadvantage. State the advantage and disadvantage of BMP.
   (b) State the difference between Serif and Sans-Serif fonts. Define aliasing.
   (c) State and explain any three characteristics of sound. Explain masking with reference to sound.

8. Write short notes on :
   (a) CIE Color Model
   (b) Masking in Animation
   (c) Pixel Addressability and resolution of monitor

9. Differentiate between any three of the following:
   (a) Hypermedia and Hypertext
   (b) Raster Graphics and Vector Graphics
   (c) Animation and Video

10. (a) Why is RGB called as device dependent model? Explain GAMUT.
    (b) State difference between RGB and CMYK models.
    (c) Why are RGB and CMYK called as complementary models?

11. (a) Define frequency and state its unit. Explain its relation with time period.
    (b) State and explain Nyquist sampling theorem.
    (c) State the properties of analog and digital signal.
    (d) Explain composite wave with appropriate diagrams.

OTHER TITLES OF INTEREST

Metaverse and **Web3**:
A Beginner's Guide
ISBN: 9789355511713

DTP, Web Page Development
And **Digital Photography**
ISBN: 9788183335836

Building Modern **Web Applications** With
Jakarta EE, NoSQL Databases & Microservices
ISBN: 9789389423341

Building Websites
with **Django**
ISBN: 9789389328288

Java
ISBN: 9789388176507

Java for **Web Development**
ISBN: 9789355511430

Let Us Java – 6th Edition
ISBN: 9789355513151

Java in Depth
ISBN: 9789386551573

Java Programming
Simplified
ISBN: 9789389845143

Java Professional
Interview Guide
ISBN: 9789391030056

100+ Solutions in **Java**
ISBN: 9789389845600

Java Projects
ISBN: 9788176569774

Java 9.0 to **17.0**
Cookbook
ISBN: 9789355512284

JAVA 9.0 to **13.0**
New Features
ISBN: 9789389328608

Getting Skilled with **Java**
ISBN: 9789391392499

Jakarta EE
for **Java Developers**
ISBN: 9789355510082

Selenium with **Java**
A Beginners Guide
ISBN: 9789391392680

Mastering Java
Persistence API (JPA)
ISBN: 9789355511263

Java in easy steps
ISBN: 9789387284210

Core Java Made Simple
ISBN: 9789386551979

OTHER TITLES OF INTEREST

Decoding JavaScript
ISBN: 9789390684816

JavaScript for Gurus
ISBN: 9789389423655

JavaScript for Modern
Web Development
ISBN: 9789389328721

JavaScript Study Guide
ISBN: 9789386551016

Beginner's Guide to
Instructional Design
ISBN: 9789355510778

Software Design Patterns for
Java Developers
ISBN: 9789391392475

Mastering **Game Design** with
Unity 2021
ISBN: 9789355512161

Hands-On **System Design**
ISBN: 9789355512369

Python In Easy Steps
ISBN: 9789388176361

Python Training Guide
ISBN: 9788183335416

Let Us **Python** -
5th Edition
ISBN: 9789355511867

Let Us **Python**
Solutions - 5th Ed.
ISBN: 9789355511843

Python for **Professionals**
ISBN: 9789389423754

Basics of
Python Programming
ISBN: 9789388511803

Basic **Core Python**
Programming
ISBN: 9789390684953

Advance **Core**
Python Programming
ISBN: 9789390684069

Learn AI with **Python**
ISBN: 9789391392611

Python
Interview Questions
ISBN: 9789389898460

Python Made Simple
ISBN: 9789388511025

Python Quick Interview Guide
ISBN: 9789389423303

Python for Developers
ISBN: 9788194401872

Python In-Depth
ISBN: 9789389328424